USB Complete

The Developer's Guide

Fourth Edition

Jan Axelson

Lakeview Research LLC
Madison, WI 53704

USB Complete: The Developer's Guide, Fourth Edition
by Jan Axelson

Published by Lakeview Research LLC, 5310 Chinook Ln., Madison WI 53704

www.Lvr.com

Distributed by Independent Publishers Group (ipgbook.com).

14 13 12 11 10 9 8 7 6 5 4 3 2 1

Mixed Sources
Product group from well-managed forests and other controlled sources
www.fsc.org Cert no. SW-COC-002283
© 1996 Forest Stewardship Council

FSC

Printed and bound in the United States of America

ISBN13 978-1-931448-08-6

Contents

3 A Transfer Type for Every Purpose

4 Enumeration:
How the Host Learns about Devices

5 Control Transfers:
Structured Requests for Critical Data

6 Chip Choices

7 Device Classes

8 How the Host Communicates

14 Using WinUSB for Vendor-Defined Functions

15 All About Hubs

16 Managing Power

17 Testing and Debugging

18 Packets on the Bus

19 The Electrical and Mechanical Interface

20 Hosts for Embedded Systems

Introduction

This book is for developers who are involved with designing or programming devices that use the Universal Serial Bus (USB) interface. If you are a hardware designer, if you write firmware that resides inside USB devices, or if you write applications that communicate with devices, this book is for you.

USB is versatile enough to serve a multitude of device functions. Familiar USB peripherals include mice, keyboards, drives, printers, speakers, and cameras. USB is also suitable for data-acquisition units, control systems, and other devices with specialized functions, including one-of-a-kind designs. The right choices of device hardware, software drivers and development tools and techniques can ease the path to designing devices that perform their functions without error or user aggravation. This book will guide you along the way.

What's Inside

The USB specifications are the ultimate authority on the USB interface, but by design they omit advice, example code, and other information that applies to specific device hardware, software, and other tools and products. This book bridges the gap between the specifications and real-world designs and will save you time and trouble when developing devices and the software to access them.

These are some of the questions this book answers:

- *How do USB devices communicate?* I don't attempt to restate everything in the USB specifications. Instead, my focus is on what you need to know to develop devices that communicate efficiently and reliably.

- *How can I decide if my device should use a USB interface?* Find out whether your device should use USB or another interface. If the choice is USB, you'll learn how to decide which of USB's four speeds—including USB 3.0's SuperSpeed—and which of USB's four transfer types are appropriate for your application.

- *What controller chip should my device use?* Every USB device contains an intelligent controller to manage USB communications. Dozens of silicon providers offer controller chips with different architectures and abilities. This book will help you select a controller based on your project's needs, your budget, and your preferences for chip architecture, programming languages, and tools.

- *How can applications communicate with my devices?* On a PC, an application accesses a USB device by communicating with a driver the operating system has assigned to the device. You'll learn if your device can use a class driver provided by the host's operating system. For devices that don't fit a supported class, you can explore options such as Microsoft's WinUSB driver, other generic drivers, and custom drivers. Example code shows how to detect and communicate with devices from Visual Basic and Visual C# applications.

- *What firmware does my device need to support USB communications?* Find out how to write firmware that enables your device to respond to USB requests and events and exchange data for any purpose.

- *Does my device need its own power supply?* The USB interface can provide power to devices, including charging current for battery-powered devices. Learn how to determine if a design can obtain all of its power from the bus, how to meet USB's requirements for conserving power, and how to charge battery-powered devices from the bus.

- *How can I implement wireless communications?* The Wireless USB specification defines a way for USB devices to communicate without wires. Other industry standards and vendor technologies offer additional options. Learn which technology is right for your device.

- *How can my device access other USB devices?* Find out how to develop a host for an embedded system or a USB On-The-Go device that can function as both a USB device and a limited-capability host that accesses other USB devices.

- *How can I ensure reliable communications?* All devices must respond to requests and other events on the USB port. The host computer must detect attached devices, locate appropriate drivers, and exchange data with the devices. This book provides tips, example code, and information about debugging software and hardware to help with these tasks.

To understand the material in the book, it's helpful to have some experience with digital logic, application programming for PCs and writing embedded code for peripherals. You don't have to know anything about USB.

What's New

The core of USB has remained much the same since the release of USB 1.0 in 1996. But the interface has expanded to support faster bus speeds, improved power management, more device classes, wireless communications, dual-role devices (device and host), and more. Plus, new and improved chips and development tools have eased the task of developing devices and software to access them.

This edition is revised and updated throughout. All new in the Fourth Edition is an introduction to USB 3.0 and the SuperSpeed bus. You'll also learn how to use Microsoft's WinUSB driver to access devices that perform vendor-specific functions. Topics with major updates include device-controller chips, technologies for wireless USB communications, protocols for conserving power, and USB device classes.

I provide example code for applications in both Visual Basic and Visual C#. For device firmware, I discuss using both microengineering Labs' PICBASIC PRO™ and Microchip Technology's MPLAB® C compiler.

Updates and More

To find out more about developing USB devices and the software that communicates with them, I invite you to visit my USB Central page at *www.Lvr.com*. You'll find code examples and links to articles, products, tools, and other information related to developing USB devices.

Corrections and updates to the book will also be available at *www.Lvr.com*. If you find an error, please let me know.

Example Code

At the start of each code example, a sidehead indicates the programming language:

Sidehead	Programming Language	Provider
VB	Visual Basic .NET	Microsoft
VC#	Visual C# .NET	Microsoft
PBP	PICBASIC PRO	microEngineering Labs, Inc.
C18	MPLAB C compiler for PIC18 CPUs	Microchip Technology Inc.

The .NET code is compatible with the .NET Framework Version 2.0 and later. Example applications are available for free download from *www.Lvr.com*.

Abbreviations

This book uses the abbreviations and symbols below to express quantities and units:

Multipliers

Symbol	Description	Multiplier
p	pico	10^{-12}
n	nano	10^{-9}
μ	micro	10^{-6}
m	milli	10^{-3}
k	kilo	10^{3}
K	kilo	2^{10} (1024)
M	mega	10^{6} or 2^{20} depending on context
G	giga	10^{9} or 2^{30} depending on context

Electrical

Symbol	Description
A	ampere
F	farad
Ω	ohm
V	volt

Time

Symbol	Description
s	second
Hz	Hertz (cycles per second)

Distance

Symbol	Description
in.	inch
ft	foot
m	meter

Data

Symbol	Description
b	bit
B	byte
bps	bits per second

Number Systems

Binary values have a trailing subscript "b". Example: 10100011_b. An exception is when it's clear from the context that the values are binary. Example: *Set bits 6..5 to 01*.

Hexadecimal values have a trailing "h". Example: *A3h*.

All other values are decimal. Example: *163*.

Acknowledgements

USB is much too big a topic to write about without help. I have many people to thank.

My technical reviewers provided feedback that helped make the book as complete and accurate as possible. With that said, every error in this book is mine and mine alone. A big thanks to Paul E. Berg, Greg Burk, Robert Dunstan, John Garney, Bill Jacobus, Kosta Koeman, and Matt Leptich.

Others I want to thank for their support are Phyllis Brown of J. Gordon Electronic Design, Michael DeVault of DeVaSys Embedded Systems, Traci Donnell of the USB-IF, David Flowers of Microchip Technology, Inc., Laurent Guinnard of Ellisys, Tim Harvey of CWAV, Inc., Blake Henry of Bitwise Systems, John Hyde of *usb-by-example.com*, Rahman Ismail and Jeff Ravencraft of Intel Corporation, Dr. Bob Miller of Trace Systems, Inc., and Jeff Schmoyer of microEngineering Labs, Inc.

For their help with the previous editions this edition builds on, thanks to Joshua Buergel, Gary Crowell, Fred Dart, Wendy Dee, Lucio DiJasio, Keith Dingwall, Dave Dowler, Mike Fahrion, David Goll, John M. Goodman, Lane Hauck, David James, Christer Johansson, Geert Knapen, Alan Lowne, Jon Lueker, Brad Markisohn, Rich Moran, Bob Nathan, Walter Oney, Amar Rajan, Marc Reinig, Rawin Rojvanit, Glenn M. Roberts, Robert Severson, Craig R. Smith, and Dave Wright.

I hope you find the book useful and welcome your comments at *jan@Lvr.com*.

1

USB Basics

At over two billion new installed units per year, USB is the most successful personal-computer interface ever. Every recent PC has USB ports that can connect to keyboards, mice, game controllers, scanners, cameras, printers, drives, and more. USB is reliable, fast, versatile, power-conserving, inexpensive, and supported by major operating systems. USB 3.0's new SuperSpeed bus means USB is likely to continue to dominate as the interface of choice for an ever-expanding selection of peripherals.

This chapter introduces USB, including its advantages and limits, some history about the interface and recent enhancements to it, and a look at what's involved in designing and programming a device with a USB interface.

Uses and Limits

USB is a likely solution any time you want to use a computer to communicate with an external device. Internal devices, such as fingerprint readers, can use USB as well. The interface is suitable for mass-produced, consumer devices as well as specialized, small-volume products and one-of-a-kind projects.

To be successful, an interface has to please two audiences: the users who want to use the devices and the developers who design the hardware and write the code that communicates with the devices. USB has features to please both groups.

Benefits for Users

From the user's perspective, the benefits of USB are ease of use, fast and reliable data transfers, low cost, and power conservation. Table 1-1 compares USB with other interfaces.

Easy to Use

Ease of use was a major design goal for USB, and the result is an interface that's a pleasure to use for many reasons:

One interface for many devices. USB is versatile enough for just about any standard PC peripheral function. Instead of having a different connector and cable type for each peripheral function, one interface serves many.

Automatic configuration. When a user connects a USB device to a PC, the operating system detects the device and loads the appropriate software driver. The first time the device connects, the operating system may prompt the user to insert a disc with driver software, but other than that, installation is automatic. Users don't need to reboot before using the device.

Easy to connect. A typical PC has multiple USB ports, and hubs make it easy to add ports without opening up the PC.

Convenient cables. USB connectors are small and compact compared to connectors used by other interfaces such as RS-232. To ensure reliable operation, the USB specification defines electrical requirements for cables. A cable segment can be as long as 5 m depending on bus speed. With hubs, again depending on bus speed, a device can be as far as 30 m from its host PC.

Wireless options. USB originated as a wired interface, but technologies are now available for wireless communications with USB devices.

Hot pluggable. Users can connect and disconnect a USB device whenever they want, whether or not the system and device are powered, without damaging the PC or device. The operating system detects when a device is attached and readies it for use.

No user settings. USB devices don't have user-selectable settings such as port addresses and interrupt-request (IRQ) lines, so users have no jumpers to set or configuration utilities to run.

Table 1-1: USB is more flexible than other interfaces, which often target a specific use.

Interface	Type	Number of Devices (including PC) (max.)	Distance (max. ft)	Speed (max. bps)	Typical Use
USB 3.0	dual simplex serial	127 (per bus)	9 (typical) (up to 49 with 5 hubs)	5 G	Mass storage, video
USB 2.0	half duplex serial	127 (per bus)	16 (98 ft. with 5 hubs)	1.5M, 12M, 480M	Keyboard, mouse, drive, speakers, printer, camera
eSATA	serial	2 (port multiplier supports 16)	6	3G	Drives
Ethernet	serial	1024	1600	10G	General network communications
IEEE-1394b (FireWire 800)	serial	64	300	3.2G	Video, mass storage
IEEE-488 (GPIB)	parallel	15	60	8M	Instrumentation
I^2C	synchronous serial	40	18	3.4M	Microcontroller communications
Microwire	synchronous serial	8	10	2M	Microcontroller communications
MIDI	serial current loop	2 (more with flow-through mode)	50	31.5k	Music, show control
Parallel Printer Port	parallel	2 (8 with daisy-chain support)	10–30	8M	Printers, scanners, disk drives
RS-232 (EIA/TIA-232)	asynchronous serial	2	50–100	20k (115k with some hardware)	Modem, mouse, instrumentation
RS-485 (TIA/EIA-485)	asynchronous serial	32 unit loads (some chips allow up to 256 devices)	4000	10M	Data acquisition and control systems
SPI	synchronous serial	8	10	2.1M	Microcontroller communications

3

No power supply required (sometimes). The USB interface includes power-supply and ground lines that provide a nominal +5V from the PC or a hub. A device that requires up to 500 mA (USB 2.0) or 900 mA (USB 3.0) can draw all of its power from the bus instead of using a dedicated power supply. In contrast, devices that use other interfaces may have to provide a power supply inside the device or an external supply.

Multiple Speeds

USB supports four bus speeds: SuperSpeed at 5 Gbps, high speed at 480 Mbps, full speed at 12 Mbps, and low speed at 1.5 Mbps. SuperSpeed requires a USB 3.0 host controller in the host PC. USB 2.0 host controllers support low, full, and high speeds.

The bus speeds describe the rate that information travels on the bus. In addition to application data, the bus must carry status, control, and error-checking information. Plus, multiple devices can share a bus. Thus, the data throughput for an individual device's data is less than the bus speed. The USB protocols support data transfers at around 400 MB/s for SuperSpeed, 53 MB/s for high speed, 1.2 MB/s for full speed, and 800 B/s for low speed. Hardware and software limitations can result in lower real-world rates, however.

The USB 1.0 specification defined low and full speeds. Full speed was intended for most peripherals that had been using RS-232 (serial) and parallel ports. Full-speed data-transfer rates are comparable to the speeds of these earlier interfaces. Mice tend to use low speed because the less stringent cable requirements allow flexible cables. Low-speed devices may have lower manufacturing cost due in part to cheaper cables. High speed became an option with the release of USB 2.0, and USB 3.0 defined SuperSpeed.

Reliable

USB's reliability is due to both the hardware and the protocols. The hardware specifications for USB drivers, receivers, and cables ensure an electrically quiet interface that eliminates most noise that could cause data errors. The USB protocols enable detecting errors in received data and notifying the sender so it can retransmit. Hardware performs the detecting, notifying, and retransmitting without software or user support.

Inexpensive

Because the host computer provides most of the intelligence to control the interface, components for USB devices are inexpensive. A device with a USB interface is likely to cost the same or less than an equivalent device with a different interface.

Power Saving

Power-saving circuits and protocols reduce a device's power consumption while keeping the device ready to communicate when needed. Reducing power consumption saves money, helps the environment, and for battery-powered devices, allows a longer time between recharges.

Benefits for Developers

Many of the user advantages described above also make things easier for developers. For example, USB's cable standards and error checking mean that developers don't have to worry about specifying cable characteristics or providing error checking in software.

Other advantages help the hardware designers who select components and design the circuits in devices and the programmers who write firmware embedded in the devices and software to communicate with devices.

The benefits result from the flexibility built into the USB protocol, the support in the controller chips and operating system, and the support available from the USB Implementers Forum.

Versatile

USB's four transfer types and four speeds make the interface feasible for many types of peripherals. USB has transfer types suited for exchanging large and small blocks of data, with and without time constraints. For data that can't tolerate delays, USB can guarantee bandwidth. These abilities are especially welcome under Windows where accessing peripherals in real time is often a challenge. Although the operating system, device drivers, and application software can introduce unavoidable delays, USB makes it as easy as possible to achieve transfers that are close to real time even on desktop systems.

Unlike other interfaces, USB doesn't assign specific functions to signal lines or make other assumptions about how the system will use the interface. For example, the status and control lines on the PC's parallel port were defined with the intention of communicating with line printers. USB makes no such assumptions and is suitable for just about any peripheral type.

For communicating with common peripherals such as printers, keyboards, and drives, USB classes specify device requirements and protocols. Developers can program a device to conform to a class specification instead of having to reinvent everything from the ground up.

Operating System Support

This book focuses on Windows programming for PCs, but other computers and operating systems also have USB support, including Linux and Apple Computer's Macintosh. Some real-time kernels also support USB.

At the most basic level, an operating system that supports USB must do three things:

- Detect when devices are attached to and removed from the system.
- Communicate with newly attached devices to find out how to exchange data with them.
- Provide a mechanism that enables software drivers to pass communications between the USB hardware and applications that want to access USB peripherals.

At a higher level, operating-system support may also mean the inclusion of class drivers that enable applications to access specific types of devices. If the operating system doesn't include a driver appropriate for a specific device, the device vendor must provide the driver.

Microsoft continues to improve and add to the class drivers included with Windows. Supported device types include human interface devices (keyboards, mice, game controllers), speakers and other audio devices, modems, drives, still-image and video cameras, scanners, printers, and smart-card readers. Filter drivers can support device-specific features and abilities within a class. Applications use Application Programming Interface (API) functions or other software components to access devices via their drivers.

Devices that have vendor-specific functions can sometimes use a supported class such as the communications-device or human-interface device class. Other options for vendor-specific functions include Microsoft's WinUSB driver and generic drivers from other sources. Some chip companies provide drivers that developers can use with the company's chips.

Writers of USB device drivers for Windows can use Microsoft's Windows Driver Foundation (WDF) model. The WDF provides a framework that simplifies the task of writing drivers.

Device Support

On the device side, the hardware must include a controller chip that manages USB communications. The device is responsible for responding to requests that identify and configure the device and for reading and writing other data on the bus. Some controllers perform some functions entirely in hardware.

Many USB controllers are based on popular microcontroller architectures such as Intel Corporation's 8051 or Microchip Technology's PIC® with added hardware support for USB communications. Other controllers don't contain a CPU but instead provide a serial or parallel interface to an external microcontroller. If you're already familiar with a chip architecture that has a USB-capable variant, you don't need to learn a new architecture. Most chip companies provide example code to help you get started.

USB Implementers Forum

The USB Implementers Forum, Inc., or USB-IF (*www.usb.org*), is the non-profit corporation founded by the companies that developed the USB specification.

The USB-IF's mission is to support the advancement and adoption of USB technology. To that end, the USB-IF offers information, tools, and testing support. The information includes the specification documents, white papers, FAQs, and a Web forum. The tools include software and hardware to help in developing and testing products. The support for testing includes compliance tests to verify proper operation and compliance workshops where developers can have their products tested and certified to display a USB logo.

What USB Can't Do

All of USB's advantages mean that it's a good candidate for many devices. But a single interface can't handle every task.

Interface Limits

Limits of USB include distance constraints, no support for peer-to-peer communications or broadcasting, and lack of support in older hardware and operating systems.

Distance. USB was designed as a desktop-expansion bus where devices are relatively close at hand. Other interfaces, including RS-232, RS-485, IEEE-1394b, and Ethernet, allow much longer cables. To extend the distance between a device and its host computer, an option is to use USB to connect to a nearby device that functions as a bridge to a long-distance interface to the end circuits.

Peer-to-Peer Communications. Every USB communication is between a host computer and a device (except for one option introduced with USB 3.0). The host is a PC or other computer with host-controller hardware. The device contains device-controller hardware. Hosts can't talk to each other directly, and devices can't talk to each other directly. Other interfaces, such as IEEE-1394, allow direct device-to-device communication.

USB provides a partial solution with the USB On-The-Go option. An On-The-Go device can function as both a device and a limited-capability host that communicates with other devices.

Two USB hosts can communicate with each other via a bridge cable that contains two USB devices with a shared buffer. USB 3.0 defines a new host-to-host cable for SuperSpeed. With driver support, this cable can support host-to-host communications.

Broadcasting. USB doesn't support sending data simultaneously to multiple devices (except for USB 3.0 timestamp packets). The host must send the data to each device individually. If you need broadcasting ability, use IEEE-1394 or Ethernet.

Legacy Hardware. Older "legacy" computers and peripherals don't have USB ports. The issue of supporting legacy equipment has faded, however, as older systems are retired.

If you need to connect a legacy peripheral to a USB port, a solution is an intelligent adapter that converts between USB and the older interface. Several sources have adapters for use with peripherals with RS-232, RS-485, and parallel ports. An adapter is useful only for devices that use protocols supported by the adapter's device driver. For example, most parallel-port adapters support communications only with printers, not with other parallel-port peripherals. RS-232 adapters work with most RS-232 devices.

If you want to use a USB device with a computer that doesn't support USB, a solution is to add USB capabilities to the computer. To do so, you need to add USB host-controller hardware and use an operating system that supports USB. The hardware is available on expansion cards that plug into a PCI slot or on a replacement motherboard. For Windows systems, the edition must be Windows 98 or later.

If upgrading the PC to support USB isn't feasible, you might think an adapter would be available to translate a peripheral's USB interface to the PC's RS-232, parallel, or other interface. An adapter is rarely an option when the computer has the legacy interface because an adapter that contains host-controller hardware and code is too expensive to design and manufacture for its limited market.

Even on new systems, users may occasionally run applications on older operating systems such as DOS. Without a driver, the operating system can't access a USB device. Although it's possible to write a USB driver for DOS, few device vendors provide one. An exception is mice and keyboards, which the system BIOS typically supports to ensure that the devices are usable any time, including from within DOS and from the BIOS screens that you can view on boot-up.

Developer Challenges

For developers, challenges to USB are the complexity of the protocols, operating-system support for some applications, and for small-scale developers, the need to obtain a Vendor ID.

Protocol Complexity. A USB device is an intelligent device that must respond to requests and other events on the bus. Controller chips vary in how much firmware support they require to perform USB communications. In most cases, to program a USB device, you need to be familiar with the USB protocols for exchanging data on the bus. On the host-computer side, device drivers insulate application programmers from having to know many of the low-level details about the protocols and hardware interface. Device-driver writers need to be familiar with USB protocols.

In contrast, some older interfaces can connect to very simple circuits that software addresses directly. For example, the PC's original parallel printer port is a series of digital inputs and outputs. You can connect to input and output circuits such as relays, switches, and analog-to-digital converters with no computer intelligence required on the device side. With a driver to enable port access, applications can monitor and control the individual bits on the ports.

USB is a shared bus with defined protocols, and the operating system prevents applications from directly accessing the hardware. To access a USB device, applications must communicate with a class or device driver that in turn communicates with the lower-level USB drivers that manage communications on the bus. Devices must support protocols that enable the PC to detect, identify, and communicate with the device.

Evolving Support in the Operating System. The class drivers included with Windows enable applications to communicate with many devices. Often, you can design a device to use one of the provided drivers. If not, you may be able to use or adapt a driver provided by a chip company or other source. If you need to provide your own driver, a third-party driver toolkit can help in developing the driver.

Fees. The USB-IF's website provides the USB specifications, related documents, software for compliance testing, and much more at no charge. Anyone can develop USB software without paying a licensing fee.

Every USB device contains a Vendor ID and a Product ID that identify the device to the operating system. At this writing, the USB-IF charges a $2000 administrative fee for the rights to a Vendor ID. The owner of the Vendor ID assigns Product IDs. Joining the USB-IF (at $4000/year) gets you a Vendor ID along with other benefits such as admittance to compliance workshops.

Devices that don't undergo compliance testing and don't display the USB-IF logo have lower-cost options. Some chip companies, including Future Technology Devices International Limited (FTDI) and Microchip Technology, will assign a range of Product IDs to a customer for use in products with the company's Vendor ID, typically at no charge. Chips that perform all of their USB communications in hardware can use a Vendor ID and Product ID embedded in the hardware. An example is FTDI's USB device controllers.

Companies that sell products that implement a USB specification must sign an adopters agreement. The agreement grants a royalty-free, non-exclusive patent license to implement the specification. You must submit a signed agreement within the later of one year after first sale of a product or one year after the specification's release. See the agreements (at *www.usb.org*) for the legal specifics.

USB versus Ethernet

For some devices, the choice is between USB and Ethernet. Ethernet's advantages include the ability to use very long cables, support for broadcasting, and familiar Internet protocols. Ethernet hardware is more complex and expensive than typical USB device hardware, however. USB is also more versatile, with four transfer types and defined classes for different device functions.

USB versus IEEE-1394

Another interface option for some devices is IEEE-1394. Apple Computer's implementation of the interface is called Firewire. Advantages to IEEE-1394 are support for peer-to-peer communications and broadcasting and more bus power available to devices (up to 1.5A at 30V).

Compared to USB, where a host computer manages the interface, IEEE-1394 devices have more responsibilities and thus tend to be more complex and expensive to implement. SuperSpeed USB exceeds IEEE-1394b's bus speed of 3.2 Gbps. While every new PC has USB ports, IEEE-1394 ports are less common and thus may require adding ports on expansion cards. For some devices, such as drives, either interface works well, and some devices support both interfaces.

Evolution of an Interface

The main reason why new interfaces don't appear very often is that existing interfaces have the advantage of all of the peripherals that users don't want to scrap. By choosing compatibility with the existing Centronics parallel interface and RS-232 serial-port interface, the developers of the original IBM PC sped up the design process and enabled users to connect to printers and modems already on the market. These interfaces proved serviceable for close to two decades. But as computers became more powerful and the number and kinds of peripherals increased, the older interfaces became a bottleneck of slow communications with limited options for expansion.

A break with tradition makes sense when the desire for enhancements is greater than the inconvenience and expense of change. This is the situation that prompted the development of USB.

USB 1.0

The *Universal Serial Bus Specification Revision 1.0* was released in January 1996. USB capability first became available on PCs with the release of Windows 95's OEM Service Release 2, available only to vendors installing Windows 95 on PCs they sold. The USB support in these versions was limited and buggy, and there weren't many USB peripherals available, so use of USB was limited in this era.

The situation improved with the release of Windows 98 in June 1998. By this time, many more vendors had USB peripherals available, and USB began to take hold as a popular interface. Windows 98 Second Edition (SE) fixed bugs and further enhanced the USB support. The original edition of Windows 98 is called Windows 98 Gold to distinguish it from Windows 98 SE.

This book concentrates on PCs running Windows XP and later. Much of the information also applies to Windows 98, Windows 2000, and Windows Me. Windows NT never supported USB except via third-party software. However, all of the editions mentioned above except Windows 95/98/Me are considered NT-based Windows editions because they build on the Windows NT kernel.

In this book, the term *PC* encompasses all of the various computers that share the common ancestor of the original IBM PC. A host computer is any computer that can communicate with USB devices.

USB 1.1

The *Universal Serial Bus Specification Revision 1.1* (September 1998) added one new transfer type (interrupt OUT). In this book, *USB 1.x* refers to USB 1.0 and 1.1.

USB 2.0

As USB gained in popularity and PCs became more powerful, demand grew for a faster bus speed. Investigation showed that a bus speed 40× faster than full speed could remain backwards-compatible with the low- and full-speed interfaces. April 2000 saw the release of the *Universal Serial Bus Specification Revision 2.0*, which added high speed at 480 Mbps. High speed made USB more attractive for peripherals such as printers, disk drives, and video cameras. Windows added support for USB 2.0 in Windows XP SP2. The USB 2.0 specification replaced USB 1.1.

Except for hubs, a USB 2.0 device can support low speed, full speed, or high speed, and a high-speed-capable device can support full speed when connected to a USB 1.x bus. A USB 2.0 hub must support all three USB 2.0 speeds. The ability to communicate at any speed increases the complexity of the hubs but conserves bus bandwidth and eliminates a need to use different hubs for different speeds.

USB 2.0 is backwards compatible with USB 1.x. In other words, USB 2.0 devices can use the same connectors and cables as 1.x devices, and a USB 2.0 device works when connected to a PC that supports USB 1.x or USB 2.0, except for a few devices that function only at high speed and thus require USB 2.0 support.

When USB 2.0 devices first became available, there was confusion among users about whether all USB 2.0 devices supported high speed. To reduce confusion, the USB-IF released naming and packaging recommendations that emphasize speed and compatibility rather than USB version numbers. A product that supports high speed should be labeled "Hi-Speed USB," and messages on the packaging might include *Fully compatible with Original USB* and *Compatible with the USB 2.0 Specification*. For products that support low or full speed only, the recommended messages on packaging are *Compatible with the USB 2.0 Specification* and *Works with USB and Hi-Speed USB systems, peripherals and cables*. The recommendations advise avoiding references to low or full speed on consumer packaging.

To use high speed, a high-speed-capable device must connect to a USB 2.0 or USB 3.0 host computer with only USB 2.0 or USB 3.0 hubs between the host and device. USB 2.0 and USB 3.0 hosts and hubs can also communicate with USB 1.x devices.

The USB-IF releases revisions and additions to the USB specification via Engineering Change Notices (ECNs). Table 1-2 lists ECNs to the USB 2.0 specification.

USB 3.0

The *Universal Serial Bus 3.0 Specification Revision 1.0* was released in November 2008, with the first USB 3.0 device-controller hardware expected to follow about a year later. Windows will likely support USB 3.0 sometime after the release of Windows 7, the successor to Windows Vista.

USB 3.0 defines a new dual-bus architecture with two physical buses that operate in parallel. USB 3.0 provides a pair of wires for USB 2.0 traffic and additional wires to support the new SuperSpeed bus at 5 Gbps. SuperSpeed offers a more than 10× increase over USB 2.0's high speed. Plus, unlike USB 2.0, SuperSpeed has a pair of wires for each direction and can transfer data in both directions at the same time. USB 3.0 also increases the amount of bus current devices can draw and defines protocols for more aggressive power saving and more efficient transfers.

USB 3.0 is backwards compatible with USB 2.0. USB 3.0 hosts and hubs support all four speeds. USB 2.0 cables fit USB 3.0 receptacles.

USB 3.0 supplements, but doesn't replace, USB 2.0. Low, full, and high-speed devices continue to comply with USB 2.0 and can't take advantage of USB 3.0's features such as higher bus-current limits and larger data packets.

Table 1-2: Engineering change notices (ECNs) correct, add to, and clarify the USB 2.0 specification.

Title	Date
Mini-B Connector	10/2000
Errata	12/2000
Pull-up/Pull-Down Resistors (loosened tolerances)	05/2002
Interface Association Descriptor	05/2003
Rounded Chamfer for the Mini-B Plug (recommendation)	10/2003
Unicode UTF-16LE for String Descriptors	02/2005
Inter-Chip USB Supplement (chip-to-chip interconnects without external cables)	03/2006
USB On-The-Go V1.3 (defines devices that can also function as hosts)	12/2006
Micro-USB connector	04/2007
Link Power Management (optional power saving capabilities)	07/2007
Hi-Speed Interchip Electrical Specification (chip-to-chip interconnects without external cables)	09/2007
Suspend Current Limit Changes	04/2008
USB 2.0 Phase-locked SOFs	12/2008
5V Short Circuit Withstand Requirement Change	12/2008
Device Capacitance	12/2008
Material Change	12/2008
MicroUSB Micro-B ID Pin Resistance and Tolerance stack-up between D+ and D-	12/2008

USB On-The-Go

As USB became the interface of choice for all kinds of peripherals, developers began to ask for a way for USB peripherals to access other USB devices. For example, a user might want to attach a printer to a camera or a keyboard to a PDA. The *On-The-Go (OTG) Supplement to the USB 2.0 Specification* defines a limited-capability host function that devices can implement to enable communicating with USB peripherals.

Wireless USB

Developers who want to design devices with wireless interfaces have several choices. The Wireless USB Promoter Group's *Wireless Universal Serial Bus Specification* defines the Certified Wireless USB (WUSB) interface for communicating at up to 480 Mbps. Cypress Semiconductor's WirelessUSB enables implementing wireless devices that function as low-speed USB devices. Another option is to use an adapter that converts between USB and a wireless interface such as Zigbee, Bluetooth, or WiFi.

Bus Components

USB communications require a host computer with USB support, one or more devices with USB ports, and hubs, connectors, and cables as needed to connect the devices to the host computer.

The host computer is a PC or other computer that contains a USB host controller and a root hub. The host controller formats data for transmitting on the bus and translates received data to a format that operating-system components understand. The host controller also helps manage communications on the bus. The root hub has one or more connectors for attaching devices. The root hub and host controller together detect attached and removed devices, carry out requests from the host controller, and pass data between devices and the host controller. In addition to the root hub, a bus may have one or more external hubs.

Each device has hardware and firmware as needed to communicate with the host computer. The USB specifications define the cables and connectors that connect devices to their hubs.

Topology

The topology, or arrangement of connections, on the bus is a tiered star (Figure 1-1). At the center of each star is a hub, and each connection to the hub is a point on the star. The root hub is in the host. An external hub has one upstream (host-side) connector for communicating with the host and one or more downstream (device-side) connectors or internal connections to embedded devices. A typical hub has two, four, or seven ports. When multiple hubs connect in series, you can think of the series as a tier, one above the next.

The tiered star describes only the physical connections. In programming, all that matters is the logical connection. Host applications and device firmware don't need to know or care whether the communication passes through one hub or five.

Up to five external hubs can connect in series with a limit of 127 peripherals and hubs including the root hub. However, bandwidth and scheduling limits can prevent a single host controller from communicating with this many

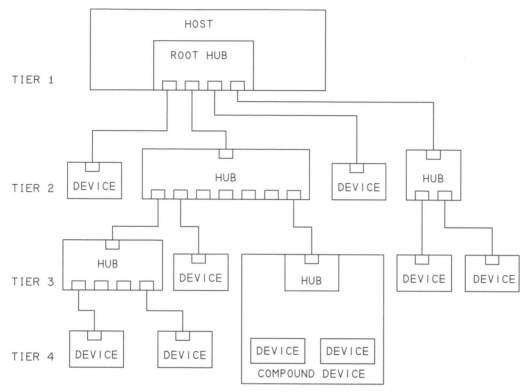

Figure 1-1. USB uses a tiered star topology. Each external hub has one upstream-facing port and one or more downstream-facing ports.

devices. To increase the available bandwidth for USB devices, many PCs have multiple host controllers, each controlling an independent bus.

Bus Speed Considerations

A USB 3.0 host supports all four speeds. A USB 2.0 host supports low, full, and high speed. A USB 1.x host supports low and full speeds only. Exceptions include On-The-Go devices and other special-purpose hosts in embedded systems, which may support only the speeds needed to access specific peripherals.

A USB 3.0 hub contains both a USB 2.0 hub and a SuperSpeed hub and handles traffic at any speed. SuperSpeed traffic uses the SuperSpeed hub's circuits and wires, and other traffic uses the USB 2.0 hub's circuits and wires.

A SuperSpeed-capable device communicates at SuperSpeed only if the host and all hubs between the host and device are USB 3.0 (Figure 1-2). Otherwise the device must use a slower speed. For compatibility with USB 2.0 hosts and hubs,

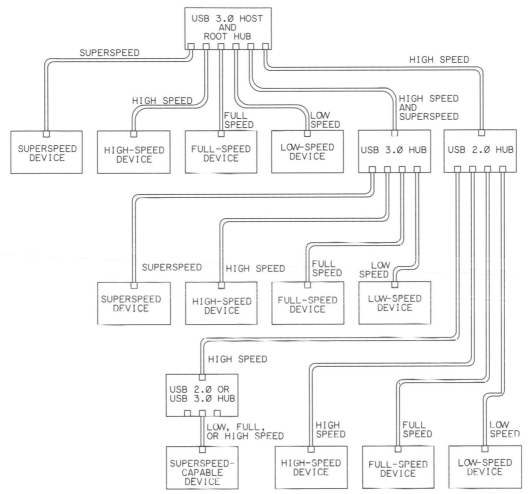

Figure 1-2. USB 3.0 hosts and hubs support all four speeds for downstream communications.

a SuperSpeed device that doesn't fully function at a lower speed must at least respond to bus resets and standard requests at another speed to inform the host that the device requires SuperSpeed to perform its function.

A non-SuperSpeed, high-speed-capable device communicates at high speed if the host and all hubs between are USB 2.0 or higher (Figure 1-3). For compatibility with USB 1.x hosts and hubs, a high-speed device that doesn't fully function at full speed must at least respond to bus resets and standard requests at full speed to inform the host that the device requires high speed to perform its function. Many high-speed devices function, if more slowly, at full speed because adding support for full speed is generally easy and is required to pass USB IF compliance tests.

A device that supports full or low speed communicates with its nearest hub at that speed. For any segments upstream from that hub, if all upstream hubs are USB 2.0 or higher, the device's traffic travels at high speed.

Terminology

In the world of USB, the words *function* and *device* have specific meanings. Also important is the concept of a USB port and how it differs from other ports such as RS-232.

Function

A USB function is a set of one or more related interfaces that expose a capability. Examples of functions are a mouse, a set of speakers, a data-acquisition unit, or a hub. A single physical device can contain multiple functions. For example,

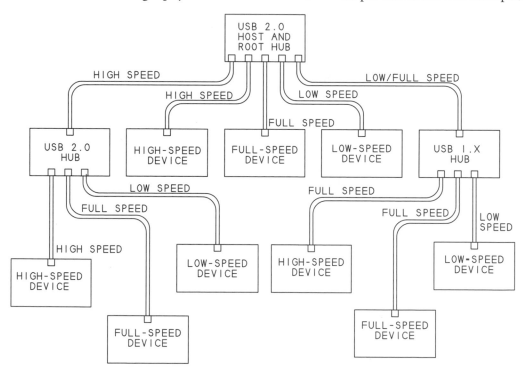

Figure 1-3. USB 2.0 hubs use high speed for upstream communications if the host and all hubs between are USB 2.0 or USB 3.0.

a device might provide both a printer and a scanner function. A host identifies a device's functions by requesting a device descriptor and one or more interface descriptors from the device. The descriptors are data structures that contain information about the device.

Device

A device is a logical or physical entity that performs one or more functions. Hubs and peripherals are devices. The host assigns a unique address to each device on the bus. A compound device contains a hub with one or more permanently attached devices. The host treats a compound device in much the same way as if the hub and its functions were separate physical devices. The hub and embedded devices each have a unique address. A USB 3.0 hub is a special case. The hub contains both a USB 2.0 hub function and a USB 3.0 hub function.

A composite device has one bus address but multiple, independent interfaces that each provide a function. Each interface can use a different driver on the host. For example, a composite device could have interfaces for mass storage and a keyboard.

Port

In general terms, a hardware computer port is an addressable location that can connect to peripheral circuits. A port's circuits can terminate at a cable connector or be hard-wired to peripheral circuits. For USB, each downstream-facing connector on a hub represents a USB port. Host applications can't access USB ports directly but instead communicate with drivers assigned to the devices attached to ports. A USB host controller may reside at a series of port addresses the system's CPU accesses, but these ports are distinct from the ports on the bus.

Division of Labor

The host and its devices each have defined responsibilities. The host bears most of the burden of managing communications, but a device must have the intelligence to respond to communications from the host and other events on the bus.

The Host's Duties

To communicate with USB devices, a computer needs hardware and software that support the USB host function. The hardware consists of a USB host controller and a root hub with one or more USB ports. The software support is typically an operating system that enables device drivers to communicate with lower-level drivers that access the USB hardware.

A typical PC has one or more hardware host controllers that each support multiple ports. The host is in charge of the bus. The host has to know what devices are on the bus and the capabilities of each device. The host must also do its best to ensure that all devices on the bus can send and receive data as needed. A bus may have many devices, each with different requirements, all wanting to transfer data at the same time. The host's job isn't trivial.

Fortunately, the host-controller hardware and drivers in Windows and other operating systems do much of the work of managing the bus. Each device attached to the host must have an assigned device driver that enables applications to communicate with the device. System-level software components manage communications between the device driver and the host controller and root hub.

Applications don't have to know the hardware-specific details of communicating with devices. All the application has to do is send and receive data using standard operating-system functions or other software components. Often the application doesn't have to know or care whether the device uses USB or another interface.

The host performs each of the tasks described below.

Detect Devices

On power-up, hubs make the host aware of all attached USB devices. In a process called enumeration, the host determines what bus speed to use, assigns an address, and requests additional information. After power-up, whenever a device is removed or attached, a hub informs the host of the event, and the host enumerates any newly attached device and removes any detached device from its list of devices available to applications.

Manage Data Flow

The host manages traffic on the bus. Multiple devices may want to transfer data at the same time. The host controller divides the available time into intervals and gives each transmission a portion of the available time. A USB 3.0 host can simultaneously transmit SuperSpeed data, receive SuperSpeeed data, and transmit or receive data at a USB 2.0 speed. A USB 2.0 bus carries data at one speed at a time and in one direction at a time.

During enumeration, a device's driver requests bandwidth for transfers that must have guaranteed timing. If the bandwidth isn't available, the driver can request a smaller portion of the bandwidth or wait until the requested bandwidth is available. Transfers that have no guaranteed timing use the remaining bandwidth and must wait if the bus is busy.

Error Checking

When transferring data, the host adds error-checking bits. On receiving data, the device performs calculations on the data and compares the result with received error-checking bits. If the results don't match, the device doesn't acknowledge receiving the data and the host knows it should retransmit. In a similar way, the host error-checks data received from devices. USB also supports a transfer type without acknowledgments for use with data such as real-time audio that tolerates errors to enable a constant transfer rate.

If a transmission attempt fails after multiple tries, the host can inform the device's driver of the problem, and the driver can notify the application so it can take action as needed.

Provide and Manage Power

In addition to data wires, a USB cable has wires for a +5V supply and ground. Some devices draw all of their power from the bus. The host provides power to all devices on power up or attachment and works with the devices to conserve power when possible. A high-power USB 2.0 device can draw up to 500 mA from the bus. A high-power SuperSpeed device can draw up to 900 mA from a USB 3.0 bus. Ports on some battery-powered hosts and hubs support only low-power devices, which are limited to 100 mA (USB 2.0) or 150 mA (SuperSpeed). To conserve power when the bus is idle, a host can require devices to enter a low-power state and reduce their use of bus current.

Exchange Data with Devices

All of the above tasks support the host's main job, which is to exchange data with devices. In some cases, a device driver requests the host to attempt to send or receive data at defined intervals, while in others the host communicates only when an application or other software component requests a transfer.

The Device's Duties

In many ways, a device's duties are a mirror image of the host's. When the host initiates communications, the device must respond. But devices also have duties that are unique. The device-controller hardware typically handles many responsibilities. The amount of firmware support varies with the chip architecture. Devices must perform all of the tasks described below.

Detect Communications Directed to the Chip

Devices must detect communications directed to the device's address on the bus. The device stores received data in a buffer and returns a status code or sends requested data from a buffer or a status code. In almost all chips, these functions are built into the hardware and require no support in code beyond preparing the buffers to send or receive data. The firmware doesn't have to take other action or make decisions until the chip has detected a communication intended for the device's address. SuperSpeed devices have less of a burden in detecting communications because the host routes SuperSpeed communications only to the target device.

Respond to Standard Requests

On power up or when a device attaches to a powered system, a device must respond to standard requests sent by the host computer during enumeration. The host may also send requests any time after enumeration completes.

All devices must respond to these requests, which query the capabilities and status of the device or request the device to take other action. On receiving a request, the device places data or status information in a buffer to send to the host. For some requests, such as selecting a configuration, the device takes other action in addition to responding to the host computer.

The USB specification defines requests, and a class or vendor may define additional requests. On receiving a request the device doesn't support, the device responds with a status code.

Error Check

Like the host, a device adds error-checking bits to the data it sends. On receiving data that includes error-checking bits, the device performs the error-checking calculations. The device's response or lack of response tells the host whether to re-transmit. The device also detects the acknowledgement the host returns on receiving data from the device. The device controller's hardware typically performs these functions.

Manage Power

A device may have its own power supply, obtain power from the bus, or use power from both sources. A host can request a device to enter the low-power Suspend state, which requires the device to draw no more than 2.5 mA of bus current. Some devices support remote wakeup, which can request to exit the Suspend state. USB 3.0 hosts can place individual functions within a USB 3.0 device in the Suspend state. With host support, devices can use additional, less restrictive low-power states to conserve power and extend battery life.

Exchange Data with the Host

All of the above tasks support the main job of a device's USB port, which is to exchange data with the host. For most transfers where the host sends data to the device, the device responds to each transfer attempt by sending a code that indicates whether the device accepted the data or was too busy to accept it. For most transfers where the device sends data to the host, the device must respond to each attempt by returning data or a code indicating the device has no data to send. Typically, the hardware responds according to firmware settings and the error-checking result. Some transfers don't use acknowledgements, and the sender receives no feedback about whether the receiver accepted transmitted data.

Devices send data only when the host requests data. SuperSpeed devices can send a packet that causes the host to request data from the device.

The controller chip's hardware handles the details of formatting the data for the bus. The formatting includes adding error-checking bits to data to transmit, checking for errors in received data, and sending and receiving the individual bits on the bus.

Of course, the device must also do whatever other tasks it's responsible for. For example, a mouse must be ready to detect movement and button clicks, a data-acquisition unit has to read the data from its sensors, and a printer must translate received data into images on paper.

Bus Speeds and Data Throughput

The data throughput, or rate of transfer of application data, between a device and host is less than the bus speed and isn't always predictable. Some of the transmitted bits identify, synchronize, and error-check the data, and the throughput also varies with the transfer type and how busy the bus is.

For time-sensitive data, USB supports transfer types that have a guaranteed rate or guaranteed maximum latency. Isochronous transfers have a guaranteed rate, where the host can request a specific number of bytes to transfer at defined intervals. The intervals can be as short as 1 ms at full speed or 125 µs at high speed and SuperSpeed. Isochronous transfers have no error correcting, however. Interrupt transfers have error correcting and guaranteed maximum latency. The device specifies a maximum interval, and when a driver has requested a data transfer, the host allows no more than the specified interval, or maximum latency, to elapse between transfer attempts. The requested maximum interval can have a range of 10–255 ms at low speed, 1–255 ms at full speed, and 125 µs to 4.096 s at high speed and SuperSpeed.

Because all devices share the bus, a device has no guarantee that a particular rate or maximum latency will be available on attachment. If the bus is too busy to allow a requested transfer rate or maximum latency, the host refuses to complete the configuration process that enables the host to schedule transfers. The device's driver can then request a configuration or interface that requires less bandwidth. To take full advantage of reserved bandwidth, the device driver and application software and device firmware must eliminate retries as much as possible. The device should have data ready to send when the host requests it and should be ready to accept data when the host sends it.

Of USB's four transfer types, the fastest on an otherwise idle bus are bulk transfers, with theoretical maximums of around 1.2 MB/s at full speed, 53 MB/s at high speed, and 400 MB/s at SuperSpeed. Isochronous transfers can request the most bandwidth (1.023 MB/s at full speed, 24.576 MB/s at high speed, and 393 MB/s at SuperSpeed). Low speed doesn't support bulk or isochronous transfers, and the maximum guaranteed bandwidth for a single low-speed transfer is 800 bytes per second.

Developing a Device

Designing a USB device for PCs involves both getting the device up and running and providing software to communicate with the device.

Components

A USB device needs the following:

- A device-controller chip with a USB interface and a CPU or other intelligent hardware that communicates with the controller. The CPU can be in the same chip as the controller or in a different chip.
- Program code, hardware, or a combination of these to carry out the USB communications in the device.
- Hardware and code to carry out the device's function (processing data, reading inputs, writing to outputs).

The host that communicates with the device needs the following:

- Host controller hardware and software (typically included with the operating system).
- Device-driver software on the host to enable applications to communicate with the device. The driver may be included with the operating system or provided by the vendor, the chip company, or another source.
- Application software to enable users to access the device. For standard device types such as a mouse, keyboard, or disk drive, you don't need custom application software, though you may want to write a test application.

Tools for Developing

To develop a USB device, you need the following tools:

- An assembler or compiler to create the device firmware (the code that runs inside the device's controller chip).
- Device-programmer hardware that enables storing the assembled or compiled code in the controller's program memory.
- A compiler for writing and debugging host software, which may include a combination of a device driver, filter driver, and application code.

Also recommended are a monitor program for debugging the device firmware and a protocol analyzer for viewing USB traffic.

Steps in Developing a Project

The steps in project development include initial decisions, enumerating, and exchanging data.

Initial Decisions

Before you can begin programming, you need to select device hardware and a host driver:

1. Specify the device's requirements. For the USB interface, define the required rate of data transfer and timing or bandwidth requirements. Consider what else your device needs to carry out its function. For example, a data logger might need an analog input. Chapter 3 has more about the capabilities of the different transfer types and how they relate to device requirements.

2. Decide whether the PC can access the device using a driver included with the operating system or a driver you provide. Chapter 7 has more about drivers.

3. Select a device controller chip. Chapter 6 has more about selecting chips.

Enumerating

To enable a host to enumerate your device, do the following:

1. Write or obtain device firmware to respond to standard USB requests from the host and other events on the bus. The requests ask for a series of descriptors, which are data structures that describe the device's USB capabilities. Chip companies generally provide example code that you can modify for a specific application. A few controllers can enumerate with no device firmware required.

2. For a Windows host, identify or create a device driver and INF (information) file to enable identifying the device and assigning a driver. The INF file is a text file that names the driver the device will use on the host computer. If your device fits a class supported by Windows, you may be able to use an INF file included with Windows. Other operating systems use different methods to match a driver to a device.

3.Build or obtain a development board or other circuit to test the chip and your firmware. Chip companies typically offer development boards for their chips.

4. Load the code into the device and attach the device to the bus. A Windows host will enumerate the device and add it to the Device Manager.

Exchanging Data

When the device enumerates successfully, you can begin to add components and code to carry out the device's function. If needed, write application code to communicate with and test the device. When the code is debugged, you're ready to test on your final hardware.

USB 3.0 Frequently Asked Questions

USB 3.0 is a major update to the USB specification. This section is for those who are familiar with USB 2.0 and want to know what's new.

Features

USB 3.0 incorporates many new features while continuing to support USB 2.0.

Does USB 3.0 replace USB 2.0?

No. USB 3.0 defines a new SuperSpeed bus that operates parallel to the USB 2.0 bus. Devices that don't support SuperSpeed should continue to comply with USB 2.0. SuperSpeed devices comply with USB 3.0 when operating at SuperSpeed and comply with USB 2.0 when operating at a lower speed. USB 3.0 also relies on USB 2.0 to define many aspects of the interface that apply to all speeds, including transfer types, descriptors, and bus topology.

The introduction of USB 3.0 thus differs from the change from USB 1.1 to USB 2.0. When USB 2.0 was released, USB 1.1 became obsolete, and USB 2.0 became the current specification for low, full, and high-speed devices. In contrast, USB 3.0 supplements, but doesn't replace, USB 2.0.

What devices will benefit from USB 3.0?

The first devices will likely be mass storage. A USB-IF device working group is developing a Mass Storage USB Attached SCSI Protocol (UASP) for efficient transfers at SuperSpeed (and improved efficiency at other speeds). Video and power-sensitive applications will also benefit from USB 3.0.

How fast is USB 3.0?

The SuperSpeed bus has a signaling rate (the speed of the bits on the wires) of 5 Gb/s, which is over 10x faster than high-speed USB. Unlike USB 2.0, Super Speed has a pair of wires for each direction, so data can travel in both directions at the same time. After encoding and other overhead, the bus can carry around 400 MB/s of application data in each direction.

Other features that can increase data throughput include these:

- Endpoints can asynchronously (without waiting for the host to request the information) notify the host when they have data to send. The host thus doesn't have to use up bandwidth polling endpoints that have nothing to send.
- Bulk transfers can use a streaming protocol for improved performance.

What stays the same?
These features remain essentially unchanged in USB 3.0:

- Tiered star topology.
- Four transfer types (control, bulk, interrupt, isochronous).
- Use of descriptors to provide device information. (USB 3.0 adds new descriptors and adds new information in some fields in descriptors defined in USB 2.0.)
- Device classes and many class drivers.
- Low, full, and high-speed protocols and cabling for these speeds.

What changes besides the new bus speed?
Besides the 5-Gbps bus speed, other changes with USB 3.0 include these:

- Direct routing. Hubs route downstream traffic only to the receiving device rather than to every SuperSpeed-capable port.
- No polling. When a host requests data from a SuperSpeed, non-isochronous endpoint that is busy or has no data, the endpoint returns Not Ready (NRDY). The host can then leave the endpoint alone until the device sends an Endpoint Ready (ERDY) notification indicating that the endpoint has data to send.
- New, aggressive power-saving modes and protocols.
- More bus current available to devices.
- Support for bursts, where a host or device sends multiple data packets without waiting for each previous packet's acknowledgement.
- Streaming on bulk endpoints. Multiple, independent data streams can use the same endpoint with a dedicated buffer for each stream.

Compatibility

USB 3.0 is backwards compatible with USB 2.0.

Will USB 1.x and USB 2.0 devices work with USB 3.0 hosts?
Yes. A USB 3.0 host has a USB 2.0 bus in parallel with a SuperSpeed bus.

Will USB 3.0 devices work with USB 2.0 or 1.x hosts?
Sometimes. Every SuperSpeed device must also support a USB 2.0 speed but doesn't have to fully function at that speed. A device that can't perform its function at the lower speed informs the host that the device requires USB 3.0 to function. A USB 3.0 device that supports only SuperSpeed and high speed won't work with a USB 1.x host or a USB 1.x upstream hub.

What will change in host software?

The operating system must provide a driver for the USB 3.0 host controller. Class and device drivers that support isochronous transfers are likely to require changes to support SuperSpeed.

What changes do I need to make to a USB 2.0 device to comply with USB 3.0?

The USB 3.0 specification doesn't apply to USB 2.0 devices. Devices that don't support SuperSpeed should continue to comply with USB 2.0.

Can a low-, full-, or high-speed device use USB 3.0's higher bus currents?

No. SuperSpeed devices should comply with USB 3.0 when operating at Super-Speed and comply with USB 2.0 when operating at a lower speed. A high-power device that can operate at both SuperSpeed and high speed can draw 900 mA at SuperSpeed but only 500 mA at high speed.

Must USB 3.0 hubs support all speeds?

Yes. A USB 3.0 hub contains a SuperSpeed hub and a USB 2.0 hub that share power and ground lines and logic to control power to the bus. The hub enumerates as two devices, a SuperSpeed hub on the SuperSpeed bus and a USB 2.0 hub on the USB 2.0 bus.

Can a USB 3.0 device communicate at multiple speeds at the same time?

No, except for hubs, each USB 3.0 device communicates at the highest speed supported by the device, the host, and the hubs between them.

Cables

USB 3.0 defines new cables and connectors.

Can I use USB 2.0 cables with a SuperSpeed host or device?

Yes, for traffic at USB 2.0 speeds. USB 2.0 cables fit USB 3.0 receptacles but don't have wires to carry SuperSpeed traffic.

Can I use a USB 3.0 cable with a USB 2.0 host?

Yes. The USB 3.0 Standard-A plug fits the USB 2.0 Standard-A receptacle, so you can use a USB 3.0 cable to attach a USB 3.0 device to a USB 2.0 host. The device will communicate at a USB 2.0 speed.

Can I use USB 3.0 cable with a USB 2.0 device?

No. A USB 3.0 cable has a USB 3.0 Standard-B or USB 3.0 Micro-B plug, and these plugs don't fit USB 2.0 receptacles.

What is the maximum cable length?

The USB 3.0 specification defines performance requirements but not maximum cable length. In practical terms the limit is 3 m using 26 AWG wires for data and 22 AWG wires for power.

Can two SuperSpeed hosts connect directly to each other?

USB 3.0 defines a new cable with a USB 3.0 Standard-A plug on each end. The cable is intended for debugging and other host-to-host applications with driver support. The SuperSpeed wires cross-connect, routing each output to its corresponding input. The cable doesn't contain wires for VBUS, D+, or D-. The cable won't hurt USB 2.0 hosts because the only line that connects on these hosts is GND.

Power

USB 3.0 provides both more power and more power-saving options to devices.

How much bus power can devices draw?

A USB 3.0 host or hub can provide up to 900 mA to high-power SuperSpeed devices and up to 150 mA to low-power SuperSpeed devices. When operating at low, full, or high speed, USB 2.0's limits apply: high power devices can draw up to 500 mA, and low power devices can draw up to 100 mA.

What other new power capabilities does USB 3.0 define?

A USB 3.0 device can have a Powered-B receptacle with two extra contacts that enable the device to provide up to 5V at 1A to a device such as a Wireless USB adapter. The adapter thus doesn't need its own power supply. In a wired connection to a host or hub, the extra contacts are unused.

2

Inside USB Transfers

This chapter looks at the elements that make up a USB transfer. You don't need to know every detail about USB transfers to get a project up and running, but understanding something about how the transfers work can help in deciding which transfer types a device should use, writing device firmware, and debugging.

Transfer Basics

To send or receive data, a host initiates a USB transfer. Each transfer uses a defined format to send data, addressing information, error-detecting bits, and status and control information. The format varies with the transfer type and direction.

The Essentials

Every USB communication (with one exception in USB 3.0) is between a host and a device. The host manages traffic on the bus, and the device responds to communications from the host. An endpoint is a device buffer that stores received data or data to transmit. Each endpoint has a number, a direction, and a maximum number of data bytes the endpoint can send or receive in a transaction.

Each USB transfer consists of one or more transactions that can carry data to or from an endpoint. A USB 2.0 transaction begins when the host sends a token packet on the bus. The token packet contains the target endpoint number and direction. An IN token packet requests a data packet from the endpoint. An OUT token packet precedes a data packet from the host. In addition to data, each data packet contains error-checking bits and a Packet ID (PID) with a data-sequencing value. Many transactions also have a handshake packet where the receiver of the data reports success or failure of the transaction. For USB 3.0 transactions, the packet types and protocols differ, but the transactions contain similar addressing, error-checking, and data-sequencing values along with the data.

USB supports four transfer types: control, bulk, interrupt, and isochronous. In a control transfer, the host sends a defined request to the device. On device attachment, the host uses control transfers to request a series of data structures called descriptors from the device. The descriptors provide information about the device's capabilities and help the host decide what driver to assign to the device. A class specification or vendor can also define requests.

Control transfers have up to three stages: Setup, Data (optional), and Status. The Setup stage contains the request. When present, the Data stage contains data from the host or device, depending on the request. The Status stage contains information about the success of the transfer. In a control read transfer, the device sends data in the Data stage. In a control write transfer, the host sends data in the Data stage, or the Data stage is absent.

The other transfer types don't have defined stages. Instead, higher-level software defines how to interpret the raw data. Bulk transfers are the fastest on an otherwise idle bus but have no guaranteed timing. Printers and USB virtual COM-port data use bulk transfers. Interrupt transfers have guaranteed maximum latency, or time between transaction attempts. Mice and keyboards use interrupt transfers. Isochronous transfers have guaranteed timing but no error correcting. Streaming audio and video use isochronous transfers.

Purposes for Communication

USB communications fall into two general categories: communications that help to identify and configure the device and communications that carry out the device's purpose. During enumeration, the host learns about the device and requests a configuration that prepares the device to perform its function. When enumeration is complete, the host can send and request data as needed to carry out the device's purpose.

During enumeration, the device's firmware responds to a series of standard requests from the host. The device must decode the requests, return requested information, and take other actions to carry out the requests.

On Windows PCs, the operating system performs enumeration with no application programming required. The first time a device attaches to a system, the Plug-and-Play (PnP) Manager must locate an INF file that identifies the name and location of one or more driver files to assign to the device. If the required files are available and the firmware functions correctly, the enumeration process is generally invisible to users. Chapter 9 has more about device drivers and INF files.

After the host has enumerated the device and a device driver has been assigned and loaded, application communications can begin. At the host, applications can use Windows API functions or other software components to read and write to the device. At the device, transferring data typically requires either placing data to send in an endpoint's transmit buffer or retrieving received data from an endpoint's receive buffer, and on completing a transaction, ensuring that the endpoint is ready for another transaction. Most devices also require firmware support for handling errors and other events.

Managing Data on the Bus

The host schedules the transfers on the bus. A USB 2.0 host controller manages traffic by dividing time into 1-ms frames at low and full speeds and 125-μs microframes at high speed. The host allocates a portion of each (micro)frame to each transfer. Each (micro)frame begins with a Start-of-Frame (SOF) timing reference. The SuperSpeed bus doesn't use SOFs, but a USB 3.0 host schedules SuperSpeed transfers within 125-μs bus intervals. A USB 3.0 host also sends timstamp packets once every bus interval to all SuperSpeed ports that aren't in a low-power state.

Each transfer consists of one or more transactions. Control transfers always have multiple transactions because they have multiple stages, each consisting of one or more transactions. Other transfer types use multiple transactions when they have more data than will fit in a single transaction. Depending on how the host schedules the transactions and the speed of a device's response, the transactions in a transfer may all be in a single (micro)frame or bus interval, or the transactions may be spread over multiple (micro)frames or bus intervals.

Every device has a unique address assigned by the host, and all data travels to or from the host. Except for remote wakeup signaling, everything a USB 2.0 device sends is in response to receiving a packet sent by the host. Because multiple devices can share a data path on the bus, each USB 2.0 transaction includes a device address that identifies the transaction's destination.

SuperSpeed devices can send status and control information to the host without waiting for the host to request the information. Every SuperSpeed Data Packet and Transaction Packet includes a device address. SuperSpeed also uses Link Management Packets packets that travel only between a device and the nearest hub and thus don't need addressing information.

Elements of a Transfer

Every USB transfer consists of one or more transactions, and each transaction in turn contains packets of information. To understand transactions, packets, and their contents, you also need to understand endpoints and pipes. So that's where we'll begin.

Endpoints: the Source and Sink of Data

All bus traffic travels to or from a device endpoint. The endpoint is a buffer that typically stores multiple bytes and consists of a block of data memory or a register in the device-controller chip. The data stored at an endpoint may be received data or data waiting to transmit. The host also has buffers that hold received data and data waiting to transmit, but the host doesn't have endpoints. Instead, the host serves as the source and destination for communications with device endpoints.

An endpoint address consists of an endpoint number and direction. The number is a value in the range 0–15. The direction is defined from the host's perspective: an IN endpoint provides data to send to the host and an OUT endpoint stores data received from the host. An endpoint configured for control transfers must transfer data in both directions, so a control endpoint consists of a pair of IN and OUT endpoint addresses that share an endpoint number.

Every device must have endpoint zero configured as a control endpoint. There's rarely if ever a need for additional control endpoints.

For other transfer types, data flows in one direction, though status and control information can travel in the opposite direction. A single endpoint number can support both IN and OUT endpoint addresses. For example, a device might have endpoint 1 IN for sending data to the host and endpoint 1 OUT for receiving data from the host.

In addition to endpoint zero, a full- or high-speed device can have up to 30 additional endpoint addresses (1–15 IN and OUT). A low-speed device can have at most two additional endpoint addresses which can be two IN, two OUT, or one in each direction.

Transaction Types

Every USB 2.0 transaction begins with a packet that contains an endpoint number and a code that indicates the direction of data flow and whether the transaction is initiating a control transfer:

Transaction Type	Source of Data	Types of Transfers that Use the Transaction Type	Contents
IN	device	all	data or status information
OUT	host	all	data or status information
Setup	host	control	a request

As with endpoint directions, the naming convention for IN and OUT transactions is from the perspective of the host. In an IN transaction, data travels from the device to the host. In an OUT transaction, data travels from the host to the device.

A Setup transaction is like an OUT transaction because data travels from the host to the device, but a Setup transaction is a special case because it initiates a control transfer. Devices need to identify Setup transactions because these are the only transactions that devices must always accept and because the device must identify and respond to the request contained in the received data. Any transfer type may use IN or OUT transactions.

In every USB 2.0 transaction, the host sends an *addressing triple* that consists of a device address, an endpoint number, and endpoint direction. On receiving an OUT or Setup packet, the endpoint stores the data that follows the packet, and the device hardware typically triggers an interrupt. Firmware can then process the received data and take any other required action. On receiving an IN packet, if the endpoint has data ready to send to the host, the hardware sends the data on the bus and typically triggers an interrupt. Firmware can then do whatever is needed to get ready to send data in the next IN transaction. An endpoint that isn't ready to send or receive data in response to an IN or OUT packet sends a status code.

For SuperSpeed transactions, the protocol differs as described later in this chapter.

Pipes: Connecting Endpoints to the Host

Before data can transfer, the host and device must establish a pipe. A pipe is an association between a device's endpoint and the host controller's software. Host software establishes a pipe with each endpoint address the host wants to communicate with.

The host establishes pipes during enumeration. If a user detaches a device from the bus, the host removes the no longer needed pipes. The host can also request new pipes or remove unneeded pipes by using control transfers to request an alternate configuration or interface for a device. Every device has a default control pipe that uses endpoint zero.

The configuration information received by the host includes an endpoint descriptor for each endpoint that the device wants to use. Each endpoint descriptor contains an endpoint address, the type of transfer the endpoint supports, the maximum size of data packets, and, when appropriate, the desired interval for transfers.

Types of Transfers

Devices with varied and differing requirements for transfer rate, response time, and error correcting can all use USB. Each of the four types of data transfers meets different needs. Each device can support the transfer types that are best suited for its purpose. Table 2-1 summarizes the features and uses of each type.

Control transfers are the only type with functions defined by the USB specification. Control transfers enable the host to read information about a device, set a device's address, and select configurations and other settings. With driver support, control transfers can also contain class- and vendor-specific requests that send and receive data for any purpose. All USB devices must support control transfers.

Table 2-1: Each of the USB's four transfer types is suited for different uses.

Transfer Type	Control	Bulk	Interrupt	Isochronous
Typical Use	Identification and configuration	Printer, scanner, drive	Mouse, keyboard	Streaming audio, video
Support required?	yes	no	no	no
Low speed allowed?	yes	no	yes	no
Maximum packet size; maximum guaranteed packets/interval (SuperSpeed).	512; none	1024; none	1024; 3 / 125 μs	1024; 48 / 125 μs
Maximum packet size; maximum guaranteed packets/interval (high speed).	64; none	512; none	1024; 3 / 125 μs	1024; 3 / 125 μs
Maximum packet size; maximum guaranteed packets/interval (full speed).	64; none	64; none	64; 1 / ms	1023; 1 / ms
Maximum packet size; maximum guaranteed packets/interval (low speed).	8; none	not allowed	8; 1 / 10 ms	not allowed
Direction of data flow	IN and OUT	IN or OUT	IN or OUT (IN only for USB 1.0)	IN or OUT
Reserved bandwidth for all transfers of the type	10% at low/full speed, 20% at high speed & SuperSpeed	none	90% at low/full speed, 80% at high speed and SuperSpeed (isochronous and interrupt combined, maximum)	
Message or Stream data?	message	stream	stream	stream
Error correction?	yes	yes	yes	no
Guaranteed delivery rate?	no	no	no	yes
Guaranteed latency (maximum time between transfers attempts)?	no	no	yes	yes

Bulk transfers are intended for applications where the rate of transfer isn't critical, such as sending a file to a printer, receiving data from a scanner, or accessing files on a drive. For these applications, quick transfers are nice, but the data can wait if necessary. On a busy bus, bulk transfers have to wait, but on a bus that is otherwise idle, bulk transfers are the fastest type. Low speed devices don't support bulk endpoints. Devices aren't required to support bulk transfers, but a specific device class can require them.

Interrupt transfers are for devices that must receive the host's or device's attention periodically, or with low latency, or delay. Other than control transfers, interrupt transfers are the only way low-speed devices can transfer data. Keyboards and mice use interrupt transfers to send keypress and mouse-movement data. Interrupt transfers can use any speed. Devices aren't required to support interrupt transfers, but a specific device class can require them.

Isochronous transfers have guaranteed delivery time but no error correcting. Data that uses isochronous transfers incudes streaming audio and video. Isochronous is the only transfer type that doesn't support automatic re-transmitting of data received with errors, so occasional errors must be acceptable. Low-speed devices don't support isochronous endpoints. Devices aren't required to support isochronous transfers, but a specific device class can require them.

Stream and Message Pipes

In addition to classifying a pipe by the type of transfer it carries, the USB specification defines pipes as either stream or message. Control transfers use bidirectional message pipes; all other transfer types use unidirectional stream pipes.

Control Transfers

In a control transfer's message pipe, a transfer begins with a transaction containing a request. Depending on the request, to complete the transfer, the host and device may exchange data and status information, or the device may just send status information. Each control transfer has at least one transaction that sends information in each direction.

If a device supports a received request, the device takes the requested action. If a device doesn't support the request, the device responds with a code to indicate that the request isn't supported.

Other Transfers

The data in a stream pipe has no structure defined by the USB specification. The receiver just accepts or rejects the data that arrives. The device firmware or host software can process the data in whatever way is appropriate for the application.

Of course, even with stream data, the sending and receiving devices must agree on a format of some type. For example, a host application may define a format for a received series of bytes that contain a temperature reading and the time of the reading.

Initiating a Transfer

The USB 2.0 specification defines a transfer as one or more bus transactions that move information between a software client and its function. A transfer may be very short, sending as little as a byte of application data, or very long, sending the contents of a large file.

Windows applications can access some USB devices by calling API functions to open a handle to the device and request data transfers. The operating system passes a request to transfer data to a device or class driver, which in turn passes the request to other system-level drivers and on to the host controller. The host controller initiates the transfer on the bus.

For devices in standard classes, a programming language can provide alternate ways to access a device. In many cases, the application doesn't have to know or care whether the device uses USB or another interface. For example, the .NET Framework includes Directory and File classes for accessing files on drives, which may use USB. A vendor-supplied driver can also define API functions. For example, chip company FTDI provides a driver that exposes functions for setting communications parameters and exchanging data with FTDI's controller chips.

For receiving data from a device, some drivers request the host controller to poll an endpoint at intervals, while other drivers don't initiate communications unless an application has requested data from the device.

USB 2.0 Transactions

Figure 2-1 shows the elements of a typical USB 2.0 transfer. A lot of the terminology here begins to sound the same. There are transfers and transactions, stages and phases, data transactions and data packets. There are Status stages and handshake phases. Data stages have handshake packets and Status stages have data packets. It can take a while to absorb it all. Table 2-2 lists the elements that make up each of the four transfer types.

Each transfer consists of one or more transactions, and each transaction in turn consists of two or three packets. (Start-of-Frame markers transmit in single packets.) The USB 2.0 specification defines a transaction as the delivery of service to an endpoint. *Service* in this case can mean either the host's sending information to the device or the host's requesting and receiving information from the device. Setup transactions send control-transfer requests to a device. OUT transactions send other data or status information to the device. IN transactions send data or status information to the host.

Each USB 2.0 transaction includes identifying, error-checking, status, and control information as well as any data to be exchanged. A transfer may take place over multiple frames or microframes, but each USB 2.0 transaction completes within a frame or microframe without interruption. No other packets on the bus can break into the middle of a transaction. Devices must respond quickly with requested data or status information. Device firmware typically arms (sets up, or configures) an endpoint's response to a received packet, and on receiving a packet, the hardware places the response on the bus.

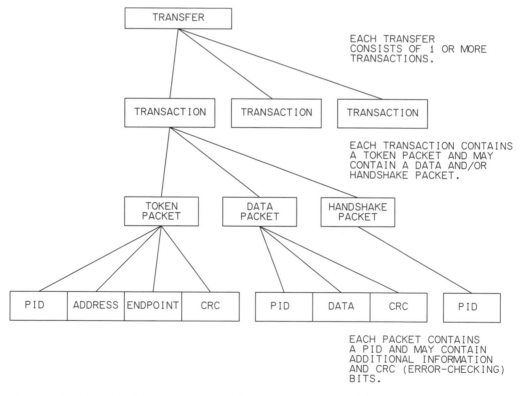

Figure 2-1. A USB 2.0 transfer consists of transactions. The transactions in turn contain packets, and the packets contain a packet identifier (PID) and sometimes additional information.

Table 2-2: Each USB 2.0 transaction has two or three phases. (Not shown are additional transactions required for split transactions, the PING protocol used in some transfers, and the PRE packet that precedes downstream, low-speed packets.)

Transfer Type	Number and Direction of Transactions		Phases (packets)
Control	Setup Stage	One (SETUP)	Token
			Data
			Handshake
	Data Stage	Zero or more (IN or OUT)	Token
			Data
			Handshake
	Status Stage	One (opposite direction of the transaction(s) in the Data stage or IN if there is no Data stage)	Token
			Data
			Handshake
Bulk	One or more (IN or OUT)		Token
			Data
			Handshake
Interrupt	One or more (IN or OUT)		Token
			Data
			Handshake
Isochronous	One or more (IN or OUT)		Token
			Data

A non-control transfer with a small amount of data may complete in a single transaction. Other transfers use multiple transactions with each carrying a portion of the data.

Transaction Phases

Each transaction has up to three phases, or parts that occur in sequence: token, data, and handshake. Each phase consists of one or two transmitted packets. Each packet is a block of information with a defined format. All packets begin with a Packet ID (PID) that contains identifying information (Table 2-3). Depending on the transaction, the PID may be followed by an endpoint address, data, status information, or a frame number, along with error-checking bits.

Table 2-3: The PID provides information about a transaction. (Part 1 of 2)

Packet Type	PID Name	Value (binary)	Transfer types used in	Source	Bus Speed	Description
Token (identifies transaction type)	OUT	0001	all	host	all	Device and endpoint address for OUT transaction.
	IN	1001	all	host	all	Device and endpoint address for IN transaction.
	SOF	0101	Start of Frame	host	all	Start-of-Frame marker and frame number.
	SETUP	1101	control	host	all	Device and endpoint address for Setup transaction.
Data (carries data or status code)	DATA0	0011	all	host, device	all	Data toggle or data PID sequencing
	DATA1	1011	all	host, device	all	Data toggle or data PID sequencing
	DATA2	0111	isochronous	host, device	high	Data PID sequencing
	MDATA	1111	isochronous, split transactions	host, device	high	Data PID sequencing
Handshake (carries status code)	ACK	0010	control, bulk, interrupt	host, device	all	Receiver accepts error-free data packet.
	NAK	1010	control, bulk, interrupt	device	all	Receiver can't accept data or sender can't send data or has no data to transmit.
	STALL	1110	control, bulk, interrupt	device	all	A control request isn't supported or the endpoint is halted.
	NYET	0110	control write, bulk OUT, split transactions	device	high	Device accepts an error-free data packet but isn't ready for another, or a hub doesn't yet have complete-split data.

Table 2-3: The PID provides information about a transaction. (Part 2 of 2)

Packet Type	PID Name	Value (binary)	Transfer types used in	Source	Bus Speed	Description
Special	PRE	1100	control, interrupt	host	full	Preamble issued by a host to indicate that the next packet is low speed (low/full-speed segment only).
	ERR	1100	all	hub	high	Returned by a hub to report a low- or full-speed error in a split transaction (high-speed segment only).
	SPLIT	1000	all	host	high	Precedes a token packet to indicate a split transaction.
	PING	0100	control write, bulk OUT	host	high	Busy check for bulk OUT and control write data transactions after NYET.
	EXT	0000	–	host	all	Protocol extension token

In the token phase of a transaction, the host initiates a communication by sending a token packet. The PID indicates the transaction type, such as Setup, IN, OUT, or SOF.

In the data phase, the host or device may transfer any kind of information in a data packet. The PID includes a data-toggle or data PID sequencing value that guards against lost or duplicated data when a transfer has multiple data packets.

In the handshake phase, the host or device sends status information in a handshake packet. The PID contains a status code (ACK, NAK, STALL, or NYET). The USB 2.0 specification sometimes uses the terms *status phase* and *status packet* to refer to the handshake phase and packet.

The token phase has one additional use. A token packet can carry a Start-of-Frame (SOF) marker, which is a timing reference that the host sends at 1-ms intervals at full speed and at 125-μs intervals at high speed. This packet also contains a frame number that increments, rolling over on exceeding the maximum value. The number indicates the frame count, so the eight microframes within a frame all have the same number. An endpoint can synchronize to the SOF packet or use the frame count as a timing reference. The SOF marker also keeps devices from entering the low-power Suspend state when the bus has no other USB traffic.

Low-speed devices don't see the SOF packet. Instead, the hub the device attaches to provides an End-of-Packet (EOP) signal, called the low-speed keep-alive signal, once per frame. As the SOF does for full- and high-speed devices, the low-speed keep-alive keeps low-speed devices from entering the Suspend state.

The PRE PID contains a preamble code that tells hubs that the next packet is low speed. On receiving a PRE PID, the hub enables communications with any attached low-speed devices. On a low- and full-speed bus, the PRE PID precedes all token, data, and handshake packets directed to low-speed devices. High-speed buses encode the PRE in the SPLIT packet, rather than sending the PRE separately. Low-speed packets sent by a device don't require a PRE PID.

In a high-speed bulk or control transfer with multiple data packets, before sending the second and any subsequent data packets, the host may send a PING PID to find out if the endpoint is ready to receive more data. The device responds with a status code.

The SPLIT PID identifies a token packet as part of a split transaction, as explained later in this chapter. The ERR PID is only for split transactions. A USB 2.0 hub uses this PID to report an error in a downstream low- or full-speed transaction. The ERR and PRE PIDs have the same value but don't cause confusion because a hub never sends a PRE to the host or an ERR to a device. Also, ERR is only for high-speed segments and PRE never transmits on high-speed segments.

The *Link Power Management* addendum to the USB 2.0 specification defines the EXT PID. The host follows an EXT token packet with an extended token packet for a specific function. Chapter 16 has more about an extended token packet for use in power management.

Packet Sequences

Every USB 2.0 transaction has a token packet. The host is always the source of this packet, which sets up the transaction by identifying the packet type, the receiving device and endpoint, and the direction of any data the transaction will transfer. For low-speed transactions on a full-speed bus, a PRE packet precedes the token packet. For split transactions, a SPLIT packet precedes the token packet.

Depending on the transfer type and whether the host or device has information to send, a data packet may follow the token packet. The direction specified in the token packet determines whether the host or device sends the data packet.

In all transfer types except isochronous, the receiver of the data packet (or the device if there is no data packet) returns a handshake packet containing a code that indicates the success or failure of the transaction. The absence of an expected handshake packet can indicate a more serious error or an unsupported Packet ID.

Timing Constraints and Guarantees

The allowed delays between the token, data, and handshake packets of a USB 2.0 transaction are very short, intended to allow only for cable delays and switching times plus a brief time to allow hardware (not firmware) to determine a response, such as data or a status code, in response to a received packet.

A common mistake in writing firmware is to assume that the firmware should wait for an interrupt before providing data to send to the host. Instead, before the host requests the data, the firmware must copy the data to send into the endpoint's buffer and arm the endpoint to send the data on receiving an IN token packet. The interrupt occurs when the transaction completes. After a successful transaction, the interrupt informs the firmware that the endpoint's buffer is ready to store data for the next transaction. If the firmware waits for an interrupt before providing the initial data, the interrupt never happens and data doesn't transfer.

A single transaction can carry data bytes up to the maximum packet size the device specifics for the endpoint. A data packet with fewer than the maximum packet size's number of bytes is a *short packet*. A transfer with multiple transactions can take place over multiple frames or microframes, which don't have to be contiguous. For example, in a full-speed bulk transfer of 512 bytes, the maximum number of bytes in a single transaction is 64, so transferring all of the data requires at least eight transactions, which may occur in one or more frames.

A data packet that contains a Data PID and error-checking bits but no data bytes is a *zero-length packet* (ZLP). A ZLP can indicate the end of a transfer or successful completion of a control transfer.

Split Transactions

A USB 2.0 hub communicates with a USB 2.0 host at high speed unless a USB 1.x hub is between the host and hub. When a low- or full-speed device is attached to a USB 2.0 hub, the hub converts between speeds as needed. But speed conversion isn't all a hub does to manage multiple speeds. High speed is 40× faster than full speed and 320× faster than low speed. It doesn't make sense for the entire bus to wait while a hub exchanges low- or full-speed data with a device.

The solution is split transactions. A USB 2.0 host uses split transactions when communicating with a low- or full-speed device on a high-speed bus. What would be a single transaction at low or full speed usually requires two types of split transactions: one or more start-split transactions to send information to the device and one or more complete-split transactions to receive information from the device. The exception is isochronous OUT transactions, which don't use complete-split transactions because the device has nothing to send.

Split transactions require more transactions to complete a transfer but make better use of bus time because they minimize the time spent waiting for a low- or full-speed device to transfer data. The components responsible for performing split transactions are the USB 2.0 host controller and a USB 2.0 hub that has an upstream connection to a high-speed bus segment and a downstream connection to a low/full-speed bus segment. The transactions at the device are identical whether the host is using split transactions or not. At the host, device drivers and application software don't have to know or care whether the host is using split transactions because the protocol is handled at a lower level. Chapter 15 has more about how the host and hubs manage split transactions.

Ensuring Successful Transfers

USB 2.0 transfers use status and control codes and error-checking to help ensure that data gets to its destination as quickly as possible and without errors.

Status and Control

The USB 2.0 specification defines handshake codes that indicate acceptance of received data, support or non-support of a control request, flow-control conditions, and an endpoint's HALT state.

A code indicates the success or failure of all transactions except those in isochronous transfers. In addition, in control transfers, the Status stage reports the success or failure of an entire transfer.

The handshake codes travel in the handshake or data packet of a transaction. The defined status codes are ACK, NAK, STALL, NYET, and ERR. The absence of an expected handshake code indicates an error. In all cases, the expected receiver of the handshake uses the information to help decide what to do next. Table 2-4 shows the status indicators and where they transmit in each transaction type.

ACK

ACK (acknowledge) indicates that a host or device has received data without error. Devices must return ACK in the handshake packets of Setup transactions if the token and data packets were received without error. Devices may also return ACK in the handshake packets of OUT transactions. The host returns ACK in the handshake packets of IN transactions if the token and data packets were received without error.

NAK

NAK (negative acknowledge) means the device is busy or has no data to return. If the host sends data when the device is too busy to accept data, the endpoint returns NAK in the handshake packet. If the host requests data when the device has nothing to send, the endpoint returns NAK in the data packet. In either case, NAK indicates a temporary condition, and the host normally retries later up to a driver-defined limit.

Hosts never send NAK. Isochronous transactions don't use NAK because they have no handshake packet for returning a NAK. If a device or the host doesn't receive transmitted isochronous data, it's lost.

STALL

The STALL handshake can mean an unsupported control request, control request failed, or endpoint failed.

On receiving an unsupported control-transfer request, the device returns STALL in the Data or Status stage. The device also returns STALL if the device supports the request but for some reason can't take the requested action. For example, if the host sends a Set Configuration request to set the device configuration to 2, and the device supports only configuration 1, the device returns

Table 2-4: The location, source, and contents of the handshake code depend on the type of transaction.

Transaction Type or PING Query	Data Packet		Handshake Packet	
	Source	Contents	Source	Contents
Setup	host	data	device	ACK
OUT	host	data	device	ACK, NAK, STALL, NYET (high speed only), ERR (from hub in complete split)
IN	device	data, NAK, STALL, ERR (from hub in complete split)	host	ACK
PING (high speed only)	no data packet	–	device	ACK, NAK, STALL

STALL. To clear this type of stall, the host sends another Setup packet to begin a new control transfer. The USB 2.0 specification calls this type of stall a protocol stall.

Another use of STALL is a response when the endpoint's Halt feature is set, which means that the endpoint is unable to send or receive data at all. The specification calls this type of stall a functional stall.

Bulk and interrupt endpoints must support the functional stall. USB 2.0 control endpoints may support the functional stall but have little reason to do so. A control endpoint in a functional stall must continue to respond normally to other requests that monitor and control the stall condition. An endpoint that is capable of responding to these requests is capable of communicating and thus shouldn't be stalled. Isochronous transactions don't use STALL because they have no handshake packet for returning the STALL. SuperSpeed control endpoints can't use the functional STALL.

On receiving a functional STALL, the host drops all pending requests to the device and doesn't resume communications until the host has sent a successful control request to clear the Halt feature on the device. Hosts never send STALL.

NYET

Only high-speed devices send NYET (*not yet*). High-speed bulk and control transfers support a protocol that enables the host to find out before sending data if a device is ready to receive the data. At low and full speeds, when the host wants to send data in a control, bulk, or interrupt transfer, the host sends the token and data packets and receives a reply from the device in the transaction's handshake packet. If not ready for the data, the device returns NAK and the host retries later. Retrying can waste a lot of bus time if the data packets are large and the device is often not ready.

High-speed bulk and control transfers with multiple data packets have a better way. After receiving a data packet, a device endpoint can return a NYET handshake, which says the endpoint accepted the data but is not yet ready to receive another data packet. When the host thinks the device might be ready, the host can send a PING token packet, and the endpoint returns either an ACK to indicate the device is ready for the next data packet or NAK or STALL if the device isn't ready. Sending a PING is more efficient than sending the entire data packet only to find out the device wasn't ready and having to resend later. Even after responding to a PING or OUT with ACK, an endpoint is allowed to return NAK on receiving the data packet that follows but should do so rarely. The host then tries again with another PING. The use of PING by the host is optional.

A USB 2.0 hub may return NYET in a complete-split transaction. Hosts and low- and full-speed devices never send NYET.

ERR

The ERR handshake is for use only by high-speed hubs in complete-split transactions. ERR indicates the device didn't return an expected handshake in the transaction the hub is completing with the host.

No Response

Another type of status indication occurs when the host or a device expects to receive a handshake but receives nothing. This lack of response can occur if the receiver's error-checking calculation detected an error. On receiving no response, the sender knows it should retry. After multiple failures, the sender can take other action.

Reporting the Status of Control Transfers

In control transfers, the data and handshake packets in the Status stage indicate the status of the transfer. Table 2-5 shows the status indicators for control transfers.

Table 2-5: The Status stage of a control transfer indicates the success or failure of the transaction. (A device may also return STALL in the Data stage.)

Control Transfer Type	Status Stage		
	Data Direction	Data Packet	Handshake Packet
Write (Host sends data to device or no Data stage)	IN	ZLP (success), NAK (busy), or STALL (failed)	ACK
Read (Device sends data to host)	OUT	ZLP	ACK (success), NAK (busy), or STALL (failed)

For control write transfers, the device returns the status of the transfer in the data packet of the Status stage. On accepting the request and receiving data in the Data stage (if present) without error, the device returns a ZLP. Or the device may return NAK (busy) or STALL (failure). The host returns ACK to complete the transfer. For an unsupported request, a device may return STALL in the Data stage to end the transfer.

For control read transfers, on receiving data in the Data stage without error, the host sends a ZLP in the data packet of the Status stage. The device responds with ACK (transaction complete), NAK (busy), or STALL (failure). A host may begin the Status stage before the device has sent all of the requested data packets, and if so, the device must abandon the Data stage and return a handshake code.

Error Checking

The USB specifications define hardware requirements that ensure that errors due to line noise are rare. Still, a noise glitch or unexpectedly disconnected cable could corrupt a transmission. USB packets include error-checking bits that enable a receiver to identify just about any received data that doesn't match what was sent. For transfers that use multiple transactions, a data-toggle value keeps the transmitter and receiver synchronized to ensure no transactions are missed.

Error-checking Bits

Token, data, and SOF packets include bits for use in error-checking. The bit values are calculated using the cyclic redundancy check (CRC) algorithm detailed in the USB 2.0 specification. Hardware performs the calculations, which must be fast to enable the device to meet the specification's timing requirements.

The CRC is applied to the data to be checked. The sender, whether host or device, performs the calculation and sends the result along with the data. The receiver performs the identical calculation on the received data. If the results match, the data has arrived without error and the receiver returns ACK. If the results don't match, the receiver sends no handshake. The absence of the expected handshake tells the sender to retry. Hosts typically try a total of three times. On giving up, the host can inform the driver that requested the transfer.

The PID field in token packets uses a simpler form of error checking. The lower four bits in the field are the PID, and the upper four bits are the complement. The receiver can check the integrity of the PID by complementing the upper four bits and ensuring that they match the PID. If not, the packet is corrupted and the receiver ignores the contents.

The Data Toggle

The data-toggle value enables detecting missed or duplicate data packets in control, bulk, and interrupt transfers. IN and OUT transactions have a data-toggle value in the data packet's PID field. DATA0 is a code of 0011, and DATA1 is 1011. In controller chips, a register bit often indicates the data-toggle state, so the data-toggle value is sometimes called the data-toggle bit. Each endpoint maintains its own data toggle.

Both the sender and receiver keep track of the data toggle. Host controllers handle data toggles at a low level that is invisible to applications and device drivers. Some device controller chips handle the data toggles completely in hardware, while others require some firmware control. If you're debugging a device where the correct data is transmitting on the bus but the receiver is ignoring or discarding the data, chances are good that the device isn't sending or expecting the correct data-toggle value.

When the host configures a device on power up or attachment, the host and device each set their data toggles to DATA0 for all except some high-speed isochronous endpoints. On detecting an incoming data packet, the host or device compares the state of its data toggle with the received data toggle. If the values match, the receiver toggles its value and returns an ACK handshake packet. The ACK causes the sender to toggle its value for the next transaction.

The next received packet in the transfer should contain a data toggle of DATA1, and again the receiver toggles its bit and returns ACK. The data toggle on each end continues to alternate in each transaction, except for control transfers as explained below.

If the receiver is busy and returns NAK, or if the receiver detects corrupted data and returns no response, the sender doesn't toggle its bit and instead tries again with the same data and data toggle.

If a receiver returns ACK but for some reason the sender doesn't see the ACK, the sender will think that the receiver didn't get the data and will try again using the same data and data-toggle bit. In this case, the receiver of the repeated data ignores the data, doesn't toggle the data toggle, and returns ACK. The ACK re-synchronizes the data toggles. If the sender mistakenly sends two packets in a row with the same data-toggle value, on receiving the second packet, the receiver ignores the data, doesn't toggle its value, and returns ACK.

Control transfers always use DATA0 in the Setup stage, use DATA1 in the first transaction of the Data stage, toggle the value in any additional Data-stage transactions, and use DATA1 in the Status stage. Bulk endpoints toggle the value in every transaction, resetting the data toggle only after completing a Set Configuration, Set Interface, or Clear Feature(ENDPOINT_HALT) request. Interrupt endpoints can behave the same as bulk endpoints. Or to simplify processing with the risk of losing some data, an interrupt IN endpoint can toggle its data toggle in each transaction without checking for the host's ACK. Full-speed isochronous transfers always use DATA0. Isochronous transfers can't use the data toggle to correct errors because there is no packet for returning ACK or NAK and no time to resend missed data.

Data PID Sequencing

Some high-speed isochronous transfers use DATA0, DATA1, and additional PIDs of DATA2 and MDATA. This use of the DATA and MDATA PIDs is called data PID sequencing. High-speed isochronous IN transfers with two or three transactions per microframe use DATA0, DATA1, and DATA2 encoding to indicate a transaction's position in the microframe:

Number of IN Transactions per Microframe	Data PID		
	First Transaction	Second Transaction	Third Transaction
1	DATA0	–	–
2	DATA1	DATA0	–
3	DATA2	DATA1	DATA0

High-speed isochronous OUT transfers that have two or three transactions per microframe use DATA0, DATA1, and MDATA encoding to indicate whether more data will follow in the microframe:

Number of OUT Transactions per Microframe	Data PID		
	First Transaction	Second Transaction	Third Transaction
1	DATA0	–	–
2	MDATA	DATA1	–
3	MDATA	MDATA	DATA2

SuperSpeed Transactions

Like USB 2.0, SuperSpeed buses carry data, addressing, and status and control information. But SuperSpeed has a dedicated data path for each direction, more support for power conservation, and other enhancements for greater efficiency. To support these differences, SuperSpeed transactions use different packet formats and protocols.

Packet Types

SuperSpeed communications use two packet types when transferring data:

A Transaction Packet (TP) carries status and control information.

A Data Packet (DP) carries data and status and control information.

Two additional packet types perform other functions:

An Isochronous Timestamp Packet (ITP) carries timing information that devices can use for synchronization. The host multicasts an ITP following each bus-interval boundary to all links that aren't in a low-power state. The timestamp holds a count from zero to 3FFFh and rolls over on overflow.

A Link Management Packet (LMP) travels only in the link between a device's port and the hub port the device connects to. The ports are called link partners. LMPs help manage the link.

SuperSpeed doesn't use token packets because packet headers contain the token packet's information. Instead of data toggles, SuperSpeed uses 5-bit sequence numbers that roll over from 31 to zero.

Table 2-6: Each SuperSpeed packet has Type value, a CRC, and a Link Control Word.

Bits	Length (bits)	Use	
0–4	5	Type	Packet header
5–95	91	Fields specific to the packet type	
96–111	16	CRC	
112–127	16	Link Control Word	

Format

Each SuperSpeed packet has a 14-byte header followed by a 2-byte Link Control Word (Table 2-6). The first five bits in the header are a Type field that identifies the packet as one of the four types above. Every header also contains type-specific information and a 16-bit CRC. The Link Control Word (Table 2-7) provides information used in managing the transmission.

A Data Packet consists of a Data Packet Header (DPH) followed immediately by a Data Packet Payload (DPP). The Data Packet Header (Table 2-8) consists of the 14-byte packet header and a Link Control Word. The Data Packet Payload contains the transaction's data and a 4-byte CRC. A Data Packet Payload with less than the endpoint's maximum packet size bytes is a short packet. A Data Packet Payload consisting of just the CRC and no data is a zero-length Data Payload.

The other three packet types are always 128 bytes. In a Transaction Packet, the Subtype field indicates the transaction's purpose (Table 2-9). All Transaction Packets have a device address that indicates the source or destination of the packet. All Transaction Packets sent by the host contain a Route String that hubs use in routing the packet to its destination.

Transferring Data

A SuperSpeed transaction has one or two phases that each contain a Data Packet or a Transaction Packet.

In a non-isochronous IN transaction, the host sends an ACK Transaction Packet to request data, and the device returns a Data Packet or a NRDY or STALL Transaction Packet.

In an isochronous IN transaction, the host sends an ACK Transaction Packet to request data, and the device returns a Data Packet.

Table 2-7: Each packet has a Link Control Word with information used in managing the transmission.

Bits	Name	Description
0–2	Header Sequence Number	Valid values are 0–7 in continuous sequence.
3–5	Reserved	–
6–8	Hub Depth	Valid only if Deferred is set. Identifies the hub that deferred the packet.
9	Delayed	Set to 1 if a hub resends or delays sending a Header Packet.
10	Deferred	Set to 1 if a hub can't send a packet because the downstream port is in a power-managed state.
11–15	CRC	Error checking bits

In a non-isochronous OUT transaction, the host sends a Data Packet and the device returns an ACK, NRDY, or STALL Transaction Packet.

In an isochronous OUT transaction, the host sends a Data Packet.

Sequence Numbers

Table 2-10 shows the contents of the ACK Transaction Packet. In an IN transaction, on receiving an ACK Transaction Packet with NumP = 1, the endpoint sends a Data Packet with the Data Packet Header containing the Sequence Number of the received ACK Transaction Packet. Except for isochronous transactions, on receiving the Data Packet, the host acknowledges receiving the data by incrementing the Sequence Number and sending another ACK Transaction Packet. If NumP > 0, the ACK Transaction Packet also serves as a request for more data. In other words, instead of requiring separate transactions to ACK received data and request more data, a single ACK Transaction Packet can perform both functions.

In an OUT transaction, the Data Packet from the host contains a Sequence Number. The ACK Transaction Packet the device sends in response contains the Sequence Number of the next expected Data Packet and serves as an implicit acknowledgement of receiving the previous Data Packet.

In a control transfer, the Setup transaction packet and the first Data Packet Header each use a Sequence Number of zero. (Note that this differs from USB 2.0, where the Data Stage begins with DATA1.) For any additional Data Packets, the Sequence Number increments, resetting to zero on rollover.

Table 2-8: The Data Packet Header provides the Data Packet's length and other information. (Reserved fields not shown.)

Field	Bits	Function
Type	5	Data Packet Header (01000_b)
Route String or reserved	20	In downstream communications, used by hubs to route a packet to the correct port. Otherwise reserved.
Device Address	7	The device that is the source or receiver of the Data Packet.
Sequence Number	5	Identifies the Data Packet.
End of Burst (EOB) (non-isochronous) or Last Packet Flag (LPF) (isochronous)	1	For non-isochronous IN endpoints, identifies the last packet in a burst. For non-isochronous OUT endpoints, zero. For isochronous endpoints, identifies the last packet in a service interval.
Direction	1	0 = host to device; 1 = device to host.
Endpoint Number	4	The endpoint that is the source or receiver of the Data Packet.
Setup	1	Set by the host when the Data Packet is a Setup packet.
Data Length	16	The number of data bytes in the Data Packet Payload.
Stream ID or reserved	16	For bulk endpoints, can identify a stream.
Packets Pending	1	Set by the host when it has another packet scheduled for the target endpoint.
CRC-16	16	For error checking.
Link Control Word	16	For link management.

Bulk and interrupt endpoints increment the Sequence Number for every transaction, resetting to zero on rollover or after completing a Set Configuration, Set Interface, or Clear Feature(ENDPOINT_HALT) request. In isochronous transfers, the Sequence Number resets to zero at the start of a service interval and increments on each additional Data Packet within the service interval. The endpoint descriptor specifies the length of a service interval and the maximum number of Data Packets per service interval.

On detecting an error in a received Data Packet, the host or device sends an ACK Transaction Packet with the Retry bit set and the Sequence Number of the packet that contained the error. The sender of the Data Packet must then resend all sent Data Packets beginning with that Sequence Number.

Table 2-9: Hosts and devices use Transaction Packets to send status and control information.

Subtype	Source	Description
ACK	Host	Requests data from an IN endpoint and acknowledges a previously received data packet.
	Device	Acknowledges data received on an OUT endpoint and specifies how many data packet buffers are available after receiving this packet.
NRDY	Device	On receiving a Data Packet on an OUT endpoint, informs the host that the device has no buffer space to accept the data. On receiving an ACK Transaction Packet on an IN endpoint, informs the host that the device can't return a data packet. Valid for non-isochronous endpoints.
ERDY	Device	An endpoint is ready to send or receive Data Packets. Valid for non-isochronous endpoints.
STATUS	Host	The host has initiated the Status stage of a control transfer. Valid for control endpoints.
STALL	Device	The endpoint is halted or a requested control transfer is invalid or unsupported.
DEV_NOTIFICATION	Device	A change in a device or interface state has occurred. The high nibble is the type of change: 0h reserved 1h function wake 2h latency tolerance message 3h bus interval adjustment message 4h–Fh reserved
PING	Host	Before initiating an isochronous transfer when a link is in a low-power state, requests all paths between the host and the isochronous endpoint to transition to the active state.
PING_RESPONSE	Device	Response to PING.

Burst Transactions

SuperSpeed bulk and interrupt endpoints can support burst transactions, where the host or device sends multiple Data Packets without waiting for ACK Transaction Packets to acknowledge previous received data. Every data payload in a burst except the last must equal the endpoint's maximum packet size.

The NumP field in an ACK Transaction Packet sets the number of Data Packets a device or host can receive in a burst. Valid values are zero or any value from one less than the value in the previous ACK packet to bMaxBurst + 1 in the endpoint companion descriptor. Note that bMaxBurst is zero-based, with zero

Table 2-10: An ACK Transaction Packet can acknowledge received data and request new data. (Reserved fields not shown.)

Number of Bits	Field Name	Description
20	Route String	Used by hubs in routing packets downstream.
7	Device Address	The address assigned during enumeration.
4	SubType	ACK
1	Retry Data Packet	If set, the host or device requests a resend due to not receiving a packet or receiving a corrupted packet.
1	Direction	The direction of the endpoint sending or receiving the data: 0 = host to device; 1 = device to host.
4	Endpoint Number	The endpoint sending or receiving the data.
1	Host Error	For host-to-device ACK Transaction Packets, indicates that host was unable to accept a valid data packet.
5	Number of Packets (NumP)	The number of Data Packets the receiver can accept in a burst.
5	Sequence Number (Seq Num)	The sequence number of the next expected Data Packet.
16	Stream ID	For bulk endpoints, can identify a stream.
1	Packets Pending	Indicates whether the host has another packet for the endpoint.

indicating a maximum burst of 1 packet, while NumP indicates the actual number of packets a receiver can accept (which may be zero).

A Set Configuration, Set Interface, or Clear Feature(ENDPOINT_HALT) request resets the burst size of the associated endpoint(s).

Isochronous endpoints can support isochronous burst transactions, which consist of multiple Data Packets transferred in a service interval with each packet except the last required to be the endpoint's maximum packet size. Isochronous transactions never use ACK.

Timing Constraints

Devices and hosts must respond quickly to received Data Packets and ACK Transaction Packets that request data. On receiving an ACK Transaction Packet with NumP > 0, a device must begin to return a Data Packet or NRDY Transaction Packet within 250 ns. On receiving a Data Packet, a device must begin to return an ACK or NRDY Transaction Packet within 250 ns. On receiving a Data Packet, a host must begin to return an ACK or NRDY Transaction Packet within 3 μs. The maximum interval between Data Packets in a burst is 100 ns. The device hardware thus handles responding to received packets.

Notifying the Host

To conserve bandwidth and to enable inactive links to transition to low-power states, USB 3.0 hosts stop requesting to send or receive data from SuperSpeed endpoints that are in the flow control condition. This condition indicates that the endpoint temporarily can't send or receive data. To request to resume communications, the endpoint sends an ERDY Transaction Packet. A device can send the ERDY at any time without waiting for the host to request a packet. On receiving the ERDY, the host resumes communications with the endpoint.

An IN endpoint is in the flow control condition after responding to an ACK Transaction Packet with either of the following:

A NRDY Transaction Packet.

A Data Packet with the End of Burst (EOB) field set to 1, indicating that the packet is the last in a burst. The device sets EOB if the data payload is equal to the endpoint's maximum packet size and the endpoint is returning fewer than the number of packets requested in the previous ACK Transaction Packet.

An OUT endpoint is in the flow control condition on responding to a Data Packet with either of the following:

A NRDY Transaction Packet.

An ACK Transaction Packet with the NumP field set to zero, indicating that the endpoint can't accept any Data Packets.

Hosts retain the option to attempt communications with bulk endpoints in the flow-control condition before receiving ERDY.

Link Management Packets

Link Management Packets have these subtypes:

- Set Link Function defines a bit for use in testing.
- U2 Inactivity Timeout specifies the timeout for transitioning between low-power states.
- Vendor Device Test provides a mechanism for vendor-specific tests.
- Port Capabilities indicates if the port can be configured as an upstream-fac-

ing port, a downstream-facing port, or both. The ports in a link exchange this packet after initializing the link. For situations where both ports in a link support both port types, a tiebreaker field and protocol determines which port is upstream-facing and which is downstream-facing.

- Port Configuration contains a bit to specify a speed of 5 Gbps. A downstream-facing port sends this packet to its link partner.
- Port Configuration Response accepts or rejects a received Port Configuration LMP.

3

A Transfer Type
for Every Purpose

This chapter takes a closer look at USB's four transfer types: control, bulk, interrupt, and isochronous. Each type has features that make it suitable for specific purposes.

Control Transfers

Control transfers have two uses. For all devices, control transfers carry the standard requests that the host uses to learn about and configure devices. Control transfers can also carry requests defined by a class or vendor for any purpose.

Availability

Every device must support control transfers over the default pipe at endpoint zero. A device may also have additional pipes for control transfers, but in reality there's no need for more than one. Even if a device needs to send a lot of control requests, hosts allocate bandwidth for control transfers according to the number and size of requests, not by the number of control endpoints, so additional control endpoints offer no advantage.

Structure

Chapter 2 introduced control transfers and their Setup, Data, and Status stages. Each stage consists of one or more transactions.

Every control transfer must have a Setup stage and a Status stage. Not all transfers have Data stages, though specific requests can require them. Because every control transfer requires transferring information in both directions, the control transfer's message pipe uses both the IN and OUT endpoint addresses.

In a control write transfer, the data in the Data stage travels from the host to the device. Control transfers that have no Data stage are also considered to be control write transfers. In a control read transfer, the data in the Data stage travels from the device to the host. Figure 3-1 and Figure 3-2 show the stages of control read and control write transfers at low and full speeds on a low/full-speed bus. There are differences, described later in this chapter, for some high-speed transfers, low- and full-speed transfers with USB 2.0 hubs on high-speed buses, and SuperSpeed transfers.

In the Setup stage, the host begins a Setup transaction by sending information about the request. The token packet's SETUP PID identifies the transaction as a Setup transaction that begins a control transfer. The data packet contains eight bytes of information about the request, including the request number, whether or not the transfer has a Data stage, and if so, in which direction the data will travel.

The USB 2.0 and USB 3.0 specifications define standard requests. Successful enumeration requires specific responses to some requests, such as the request that sets a device's address. For other requests, a device can return STALL to indicate that the request isn't supported. A STALL ends the transfer. A class may require a device to support class-specific requests, and devices can support requests defined by a vendor-specific driver.

When present, the Data stage consists of one or more transactions. Depending on the request, the host or peripheral may be the source of the data in these transactions, but all data packets in this stage are in the same direction.

The Status stage consists of one IN or OUT transaction where the device reports the success or failure of the transfer. The source of the Status stage's data packet is the receiver of the data in the Data stage. When there is no Data stage, the device sends the Status stage's data packet. On completing or abandoning the current transfer, the host can begin a new control transfer.

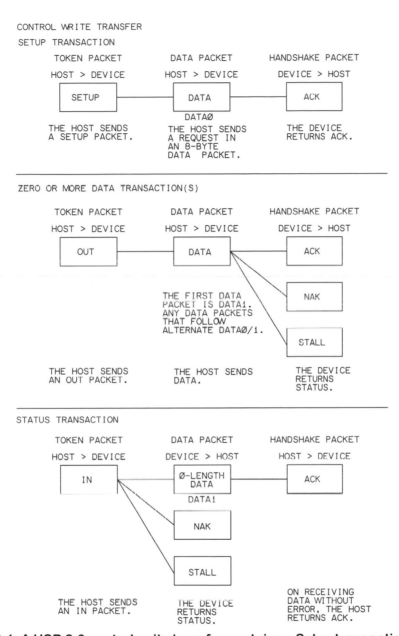

Figure 3-1. A USB 2.0 control write transfer contains a Setup transaction, zero or more Data transactions, and a Status transaction. Not shown are the PING protocol used in some high-speed transfers with multiple data packets and the split transactions used with low- and full-speed devices on a high-speed bus.

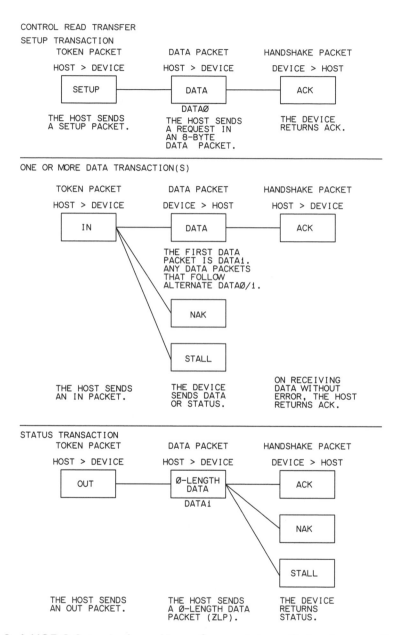

Figure 3-2. A USB 2.0 control read transfer contains a Setup transaction, one or more data transactions, and a status transaction. Not shown are the split transactions used with low- and full-speed devices on a high-speed bus.

High Speed Differences

As described in Chapter 2, if a high-speed control write transfer has more than one data packet in the Data stage and the device returns NYET after receiving a data packet, the host may use the PING protocol before sending the next data packet.

If a host is performing a control transfer with a low- or full-speed device on a high-speed bus, the host uses split transactions for all of the transfer's transactions. To the device, the transaction is no different than a transaction with a USB 1.x host. The USB 2.0 or USB 3.0 hub nearest the device initiates transactions with the device and returns data and status information to the host.

SuperSpeed Differences

On a SuperSpeed bus, the Setup stage's Setup Data Packet contains the eight bytes of Setup data. The Data Packet Header uses the following values:

Sequence Number = 0

Data Length = 8

Setup = 1

Figure 3-3 shows the structure of a SuperSpeed control write transfer. The host begins the transfer with a Setup Data Packet, and on receiving the packet without error, the device responds with an ACK Transaction Packet. If the transfer has a Data stage, the host sends one or more Data Packets, and the device responds to each with an ACK Transaction Packet. If the transfer has multiple Data packets, the Sequence Numbers in the Data and ACK packets increment for each Data packet. In the Status stage, the host sends a STATUS Transaction Packet, and the device returns ACK.

Figure 3-4 shows the structure of a SuperSpeed control read transfer., which is identical to a control write transfer except for the Data stage. In the Data stage, the host sends one or more ACK Transaction Packets, and the device responds to each with a Data Packet.

A device can control the flow of a control transfer by responding to the Setup Data Packet with an ACK Transaction Packet with NumP = 0 and Sequence Number = 0. The device then requests to start the Data and Status stages by sending an ERDY Transaction Packet.

In the Data or Status stage, an endpoint can return a STALL or NRDY Transaction Packet instead of ACK. A STALL ends the transfer. NRDY halts the transfer until the device returns ERDY.

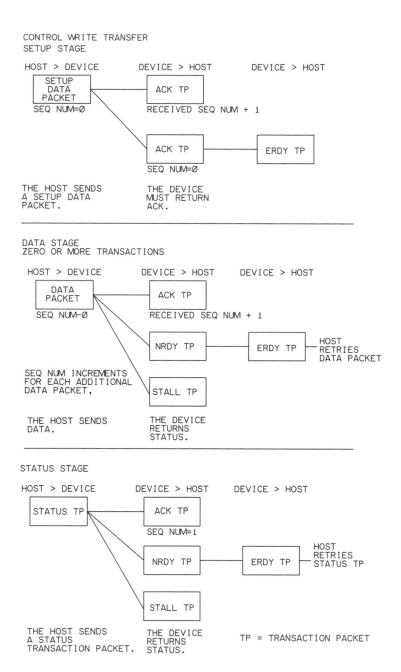

Figure 3-3. A Setup Data packet initiates a SuperSpeed control write transfer. A Status transaction packet initiates the Status stage.

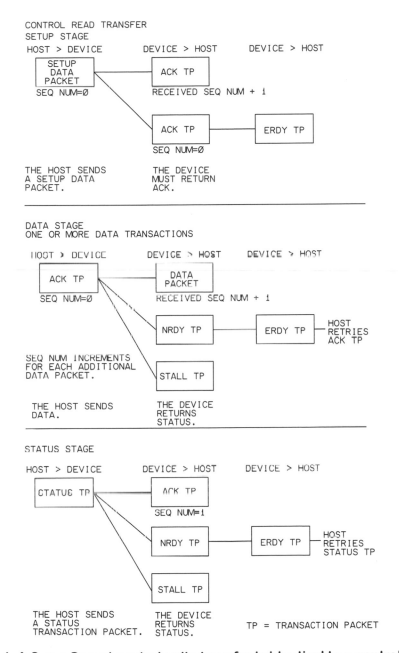

CONTROL READ TRANSFER
SETUP STAGE

Figure 3-4. A SuperSpeed control write transfer is identical to a control read transfer except for the direction of the Data stage.

Data Size

In a control transfer's Data stage, the allowed maximum data packet size varies with bus speed:

Bus Speed	Maximum Data Packet Size
Low	8
Full	8, 16, 32, or 64
High	64
SuperSpeed	512

These bytes include only the information transferred in the data packet (USB 2.0) or Data Packet Payload (SuperSpeed), excluding PID and CRC bits.

In the Data stage, all data packets except the last must be the maximum packet size for the endpoint. The maximum packet size for the default control pipe is in the device descriptor that the host retrieves during enumeration. If a transfer has more data than will fit in one data transaction, the host sends or receives the data in multiple transactions.

For some control read transfers, the amount of data returned by the device can vary. If the amount is less than the requested number of bytes and is an even multiple of the endpoint's maximum packet size, the device should indicate when it has no more data to send by returning a ZLP (USB 2.0) or a zero-length Data Payload (SuperSpeed) in response to a request for data after the device has sent all of its data.

Speed

The host must make its best effort to ensure that all control transfers complete as quickly as possible. The host controller reserves a portion of the bus bandwidth for control transfers: 10% for low- and full-speed buses and 20% for high-speed and SuperSpeed buses. If the control transfers don't need all of the reserved bandwidth, bulk transfers can use what remains. If the bus has other unused bandwidth, control transfers can use more than the reserved amount. The host attempts to parcel out the available time as fairly as possible to all devices. A single frame, microframe, or bus interval can contain multiple transactions for the same transfer, or a transfer's transactions can be spread among multiple (micro)frames or bus intervals.

There are two opinions on whether control transfers are appropriate for transferring data other than enumeration and configuration data. Some believe control transfers should be reserved as much as possible for servicing the standard USB requests and performing other infrequent configuration tasks. This approach helps ensure that the transfers complete quickly by keeping the reserved bandwidth as open as possible. But the USB specifications don't forbid other uses for control transfers, and some see no problem in using control transfers for any purpose. Low-speed devices have no other option except periodic interrupt transfers that can waste bandwidth if data transfers are infrequent.

Control transfers aren't the most efficient way to transfer data. Each transfer has significant overhead. At low speed, a single control transfer with 8 data bytes uses over 1/3 of a frame's bandwidth, though the transfer's individual transactions may travel in multiple frames. In a control transfer with multiple data packets in the Data stage, the data may travel in the same or different (micro)frames or bus intervals. On a busy bus, all control transfers may have to share the reserved portion of the bandwidth.

The USB specifications define timing limits that apply to control requests unless a class requires a faster response. Where stricter timing isn't specified, in a transfer where the host requests data from the device, a device may delay as long as 500 ms before making the data available to the host. To find out if data is available, a USB 2.0 host sends a token packet to request the data. If the data is ready, the device returns the data in that transaction's data packet. Otherwise the device returns NAK to advise the host to retry later. The host keeps trying at intervals for up to 500 ms. SuperSpeed devices can delay communications by setting NumP = 0 and Sequence Number = 0 in response to a Setup Data Packet or by sending NRDY in response to requested or received data. In a transfer where the host sends data to the device, if the host sends the data at the maximum rate the device can accept the data, a USB 2.0 device can take up to 5 seconds to accept all of the data and complete the Status stage (though once begun, the Status stage must complete within 50 ms). USB 3.0 devices must complete each transaction within 50 ms. Additional delays by the host extend the allowed time. In a transfer with no Data stage, the device must complete the request and the Status stage within 50 ms. The host and its drivers aren't required to enforce the limits, but all devices should comply with the limits to ensure proper operation with any host. For the hub class, USB 2.0 and USB 3.0 recommend average response times of under 5 ms.

Detecting and Handling Errors

If a USB 2.0 device doesn't return an expected handshake packet during a control transfer, the host retries. On receiving no response after a (typical) total of three tries, the host notifies the software that requested the transfer and stops communicating with the endpoint until the problem is resolved. The two retries include only those sent in response to no handshake at all. A NAK triggers a retry but doesn't increment the error count.

Control transfers use data toggles (USB 2.0) or Sequence Numbers (SuperSpeed) to protect against lost data. In the Data stage of a USB 2.0 Control read transfer, on receiving the data from the device, the host normally returns ACK and then sends an OUT token packet to begin the Status stage. If the device for any reason doesn't see the ACK returned after the transfer's final data packet, the device must interpret a received OUT token packet as evidence that the Status stage has begun.

Devices must accept all error-free Setup packets. If a new Setup packet arrives before a previous control transfer completes, the device must abandon the previous transfer and start the new one.

Device Responsibilities

A USB 2.0 device has these responsibilities for transfers on a control endpoint:

- Send ACK in response to every Setup packet received without error.
- For supported control write requests, send ACK in response to received data in the Data stage (if present) and return a ZLP in the Status stage.
- For supported control read requests, send data in response to IN token packets in the Data stage and ACK the received ZLP in the Status stage.
- For unsupported requests, return STALL in the Data or Status stage.

A SuperSpeed device has these responsibilities for transfers on a control endpoint:

- Send an ACK Transaction Packet in response to Setup data received without error in Data Packets.
- For supported control write requests, when there is a Data stage, send an ACK Transaction Packet in response to received data in Data Packets. In the Status stage, send an ACK Transaction Packet in response to a received STATUS Transaction Packet.
- For supported control read requests, receive acknowledgements and requests to send data in ACK Transaction Packets and send data in Data Packets. In the Status stage, send an ACK Transaction Packet in response to a received STATUS Transaction Packet.

- For unsupported requests, return a STALL Transaction packet in the Data or Status stage.

Bulk Transfers

Bulk transfers are useful for transferring data when time isn't critical. A bulk transfer can send large amounts of data without clogging the bus because the transfers defer to the other transfer types, waiting until time is available. Uses for bulk transfers include sending data to a printer, sending data from a scanner, and reading and writing to a drive. On an otherwise idle bus, bulk transfers are the fastest transfer type.

Availability

Low speed doesn't support bulk transfers. Devices aren't required to support bulk transfers, but a specific device class may require them. For example, a mass-storage device must have a bulk endpoint in each direction.

Structure

A USB 2.0 bulk transfer consists of one or more IN or OUT transactions (Figure 3-5). All data travels in one direction. Transferring data in both directions requires a separate pipe and transfer for each direction.

A bulk transfer ends successfully when the expected amount of data has transferred or when a transaction contains less than the endpoint's maximum packet size, including zero data bytes. The USB 2.0 specification doesn't define a protocol for indicating the number of data bytes in a bulk transfer. When needed, the device and host can use a class-specific or vendor-specific protocol to pass this information. For example, a transfer can begin with a header that specifies the number of bytes to be transferred, or the device or host can use a class-specific or vendor-specific protocol to request a quantity of data.

High Speed Differences

To conserve bus time, a host may use the PING protocol in some high-speed bulk transfers. If a high-speed bulk OUT transfer has more than one data packet and the device returns NYET after receiving a packet, the host may use PING to find out when it's OK to send more data. In a bulk transfer on a high-speed bus with a low- or full-speed device, the host uses split transactions for all of the transfer's transactions.

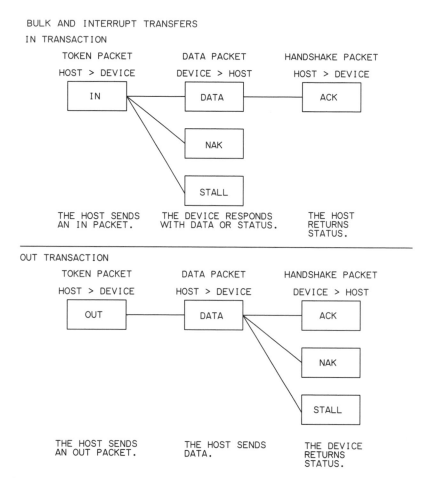

BULK AND INTERRUPT TRANSFERS

IN TRANSACTION

TOKEN PACKET   DATA PACKET   HANDSHAKE PACKET

HOST > DEVICE   DEVICE > HOST   HOST > DEVICE

IN   DATA   ACK

NAK

STALL

THE HOST SENDS   THE DEVICE RESPONDS   THE HOST
AN IN PACKET.   WITH DATA OR STATUS.   RETURNS
     STATUS.

OUT TRANSACTION

TOKEN PACKET   DATA PACKET   HANDSHAKE PACKET

HOST > DEVICE   HOST > DEVICE   DEVICE > HOST

OUT   DATA   ACK

NAK

STALL

THE HOST SENDS   THE HOST SENDS   THE DEVICE
AN OUT PACKET.   DATA.   RETURNS
     STATUS.

Figure 3-5. USB 2.0 bulk and interrupt transfers have identical structure, but different scheduling by the host. Not shown are the PING protocol used in some high-speed bulk OUT transfers with multiple data packets or the split transactions used with low- and full-speed devices on a high-speed bus.

SuperSpeed Differences

Figure 3-6 shows SuperSpeed bulk IN and OUT transactions. In an IN transaction, the host sends an ACK Transaction Packet to request one or more Data Packets and acknowledge previous data, if any, and the device sends Data Packet(s), NRDY, or STALL. On receiving a Data Packet, the host returns an ACK Transaction Packet. If the host requests multiple Data Packets by setting NumP > 1, the device doesn't have to wait for each ACK before sending the next packet. If NumP > 0 in an ACK Transaction Packet that the host sends in

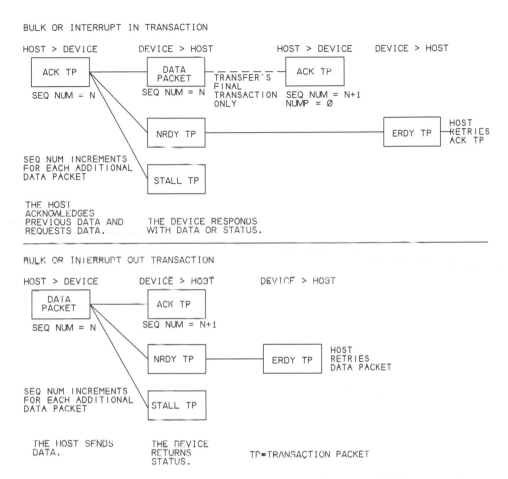

BULK OR INTERRUPT IN TRANSACTION

HOST > DEVICE DEVICE > HOST HOST > DEVICE DEVICE > HOST

ACK TP DATA PACKET TRANSFER'S FINAL TRANSACTION ONLY ACK TP

SEQ NUM = N SEQ NUM = N SEQ NUM = N+1 NUMP = 0

NRDY TP ERDY TP HOST RETRIES ACK TP

SEQ NUM INCREMENTS FOR EACH ADDITIONAL DATA PACKET STALL TP

THE HOST ACKNOWLEDGES PREVIOUS DATA AND REQUESTS DATA. THE DEVICE RESPONDS WITH DATA OR STATUS.

BULK OR INTERRUPT OUT TRANSACTION

HOST > DEVICE DEVICE > HOST DEVICE > HOST

DATA PACKET ACK TP

SEQ NUM = N SEQ NUM = N+1

NRDY TP ERDY TP HOST RETRIES DATA PACKET

SEQ NUM INCREMENTS FOR EACH ADDITIONAL DATA PACKET STALL TP

THE HOST SENDS DATA. THE DEVICE RETURNS STATUS. TP=TRANSACTION PACKET

Figure 3-6. SuperSpeed bulk and interrupt transfers use ACK transaction packets to request and acknowledge data.

response to received data, the packet also serves as a request for more data. In an OUT transaction, the host sends data in Data Packets, and the device acknowledges receiving data in ACK Transaction Packets or returns NRDY or STALL. After an endpoint has sent NRDY, a host can attempt to resume communications even if the endpoint hasn't sent ERDY.

SuperSpeed bulk transfers can use a Stream Protocol to transfer multiple, independent data streams using a single endpoint. A class or other host driver can define uses for the streams. Each stream has its own endpoint buffer. A CStream ID identifies the current stream in Data Packet Headers and in ACK, NRDY, and ERDY Transaction Packets.

Data Size

The allowed maximum data bytes in a bulk transaction's data packet vary with the bus speed:

Bus Speed	Maximum Data Packet Size
Full	8, 16, 32, or 64
High	512
SuperSpeed	1024

These bytes include only the information transferred in the data packet (USB 2.0) or Data Packet Payload (SuperSpeed), excluding PID and CRC bits.

During enumeration, the host reads the maximum packet size for each bulk endpoint from the device's descriptors. The amount of data in a transfer may be less than, equal to, or greater than the maximum packet size. If the data doesn't fit in a single packet, the host uses multiple transactions to complete the transfer.

Speed

The host controller guarantees that bulk transfers will complete eventually but doesn't reserve bandwidth for them. Control transfers are guaranteed to have 10% of the bandwidth at low and full speeds and 20% at high speed and Super-Speed. Interrupt and isochronous transfers may use the rest. So if a bus is very busy, a bulk transfer can take a very long time.

However, when the bus is otherwise idle, bulk transfers can use the most bandwidth of any type and have low overhead and thus are the fastest of all. When a full-speed bulk endpoint's maximum packet size is less than 64, some host controllers schedule no more than one packet per frame even if more bandwidth is available. Thus for best performance, a full-speed bulk endpoint should have a maximum packet size of 64.

At full speed on an otherwise idle bus, up to nineteen 64-byte bulk transfers can transfer up to 1,216 data bytes per frame, for a data rate of 1.216 MB/s. In theory, at high speed on an otherwise idle bus, up to thirteen 512-byte bulk transfers can transfer up to 6,656 data bytes per microframe, for a data rate of 53.248 MB/s. Real-world performance varies with the host-controller hardware and driver and the host architecture, including latencies when accessing system memory. Some high-speed hosts can transfer bulk data at around 35 MB/s. A SuperSpeed bus can transfer around 400 MB/s in bulk transfers.

Detecting and Handling Errors

If a USB 2.0 device doesn't return an expected handshake packet, the host tries up to twice more. A host also retries on receiving NAK. The class or device driver determines whether the host eventually gives up on receiving multiple NAKs. For SuperSpeed endpoints, a device uses NRDY and ERDY to cause the host to stop requesting to send or receive data when an endpoint isn't ready to receive data or has no data to send. Data toggles (USB 2.0) or Sequence Numbers (SuperSpeed) detect lost or repeated data.

Device Responsibilities

A USB 2.0 device has these responsibilities for transfers on a bulk endpoint:

- For OUT transfers, ACK data received in data packets.
- For IN transfers, return data in data packets in response to IN token packets.

A SuperSpeed device has these responsibilities for transfers on a bulk endpoint:

- For OUT transfers, send ACK Transaction Packets to acknowledge data received in Data Packets.
- For IN transfers, receive requests to send data and acknowledgements of received data in ACK Transaction Packets and send data in Data Packets.

Interrupt Transfers

Interrupt transfers are useful when data has to transfer without delay. Typical applications include keyboards, pointing devices, game controllers, and hub status reports. Users don't want a noticeable delay between pressing a key or moving a mouse and seeing the result on screen. A hub needs to report the attachment or removal of devices promptly. Low-speed devices, which support only control and interrupt transfers, are likely to use interrupt transfers.

At low and full speeds, the bandwidth available for an interrupt endpoint is limited, but high speed and SuperSpeed loosen the limits.

Interrupt transfers are interrupt-like because they guarantee fast response from the host. For both bulk and interrupt endpoints, firmware typically uses interrupts to detect new received data. On a USB 2.0 bus, both bulk and interrupt endpoints must wait for the host to request data before sending data. Super-Speed bulk and interrupt endpoints can notify the host that they have data to send by sending an ERDY Transaction Packet but still must wait for the host to request data packets.

Availability

All speeds allow interrupt transfers. Devices aren't required to support interrupt transfers, but a device class may require it. For example, a HID-class device must support interrupt IN transfers for sending data to the host.

Structure

A USB 2.0 interrupt transfer consists of one or more IN transactions or one or more OUT transactions. Transferring data in both directions requires a separate transfer and pipe for each direction.

On the bus, interrupt transactions are identical to bulk transactions (Figure 3-5 and Figure 3-6) with these differences:

- Interrupt transactions have guaranteed maximum latency and thus different scheduling by the host.
- The host doesn't use the PING protocol in high-speed interrupt transfers.
- SuperSpeed interrupt transfers don't support Streams.
- On a SuperSpeed bus, after receiving NRDY, a host must wait for ERDY before resuming communications with an interrupt endpoint. (Waiting is optional for bulk endpoints.)

An interrupt transfer ends successfully when the expected amount of data has transferred or when a transaction contains less than the endpoint's maximum packet size, including zero data bytes. The USB specification doesn't define a protocol for specifying the amount of data in an interrupt transfer. When needed, the device and host can use a class-specific or vendor-specific protocol to pass this information.

High Speed Differences

In an interrupt transfer on a high-speed bus with a low- or full-speed device, the host uses split transactions for all of the transfer's transactions. Unlike high-speed bulk OUT transfers, high-speed interrupt OUT transfers can't use the PING protocol when a transfer has multiple transactions.

SuperSpeed Differences

The host schedules ACK Transaction Packets to an IN endpoint until the device has sent all of the transfer's data, or the device returns a Data Packet Header with the End Of Burst bit set, or the device returns an ERDY or STALL Transaction Packet. The host sends Data Packets to an OUT endpoint until the host has no more data to send or the device returns a NRDY or STALL Transaction Packet. After receiving NRDY, the host must receive an ERDY Transaction Packet to resume communications with the endpoint. To ensure fast response when a device is ready to communicate, the host's delay between receiving an ERDY and sending an ACK Transaction Packet is at most 2× the service interval specified in the endpoint's descriptor.

The USB 3.0 specification advises that SuperSpeed interrupt transfers are intended only for small amounts of data that must transfer within defined service intervals. In other words, to transfer a large block of data, another transfer type such as bulk is a better choice.

Data Size

The allowed maximum data bytes in an interrupt transaction's data packet varies with bus speed and the number of packets per microframe (high speed) or the number of packets per bus interval and the bMaxBurst value (SuperSpeed):

Bus Speed	Maximum Data Packet Size	Maximum Guaranteed Packets / Interval
Low	1–8	1 / 10 frames
Full	1–64	1 / frame
High	1–1024	1 / microframe
	513–1024	2 / microframe
	683–1024	3 / microframe
SuperSpeed	1–1024 and bMaxBurst = 0	1 / bus interval
	1024 and bMaxBurst > 0	3 / bus interval

These bytes include only the information transferred in the data packet (USB 2.0) or Data Packet Payload (SuperSpeed), excluding PID and CRC bits.

USB 2.0 and USB 3.0 require interrupt endpoints in a default interface to have a maximum packet size of 64 bytes or less. If the data doesn't fit in a single transaction, the host uses multiple transactions to complete the transfer.

Speed

An interrupt transfer guarantees a maximum latency, or time between transaction attempts. In other words, there is no guaranteed transfer rate, just the guarantee that the host will make bandwidth available for a transaction attempt in each maximum latency period.

A SuperSpeed endpoint can request a burst of up to three 1024-byte packets per bus interval for a maximum data throughput of 24.576 MB/s. A high-speed endpoint can request up to three 1024-byte packets per microframe, which also results in a maximum throughput of 24.576 MB/s. A high-speed endpoint that requests more than 1024 bytes per microframe is called a high-bandwidth endpoint. For hosts that don't support high-bandwidth interrupt endpoints, the maximum is 8.192 MB/s. At this writing, the Windows drivers don't support high-speed, high-bandwidth interrupt endpoints. If the host's driver doesn't support alternate interfaces, the maximum is the 64 kB/s allowed for the default interface. A full-speed endpoint can request up to 64 bytes per frame, or 64 kB/s. A low-speed endpoint can request only up to 8 bytes every 10 ms. Devices with endpoints that need to transfer more than 800 bytes/sec. should not be low speed. On a USB 1.x bus, low-speed traffic uses much more bandwidth than full-speed traffic. Limiting the bandwidth available to low-speed endpoints helps keep the bus available for other devices

The endpoint descriptor stored in the device specifies the maximum latency period. For low-speed devices, the maximum latency can be any value from 10–255 ms. For full speed, the range is 1–255 ms. For high speed and SuperSpeed, the range is 125 μs to 4.096 s in increments of 125 μs. In addition, a high-speed or SuperSpeed interrupt endpoint with a maximum latency of 125 μs can request 1, 2, or 3 transactions per interval.

The host can begin each transaction at any time up to the specified maximum latency since the previous transaction began. So, for example, on a full-speed bus with a 10 ms maximum latency, five transfers could take as long as 50 ms or as little as 5 ms. OHCI host controllers for low and full speeds schedule transactions in periods of 1, 2, 4, 8, 16, or 32 ms. For a full-speed device that requests a maximum anywhere from 8 to 15 ms, an OHCI host will begin a transaction every 8 ms, while a maximum latency from 32 to 255 will cause a transaction attempt every 32 ms. However, devices shouldn't rely on behavior that is specific to a type of host controller and should assume only that the host complies with the specification. Chapter 8 has more about host-controller types.

Because the host is free to transfer data more quickly than the requested rate, interrupt transfers don't guarantee a precise rate of delivery. The only exceptions are when the maximum latency equals the fastest possible rate. For example, on a USB 1.x host, a full-speed interrupt pipe configured for 1 transaction per ms will have reserved bandwidth for one transaction per frame. A class driver or device driver for an interrupt IN endpoint can cause the host controller to schedule an IN transaction in each interval. The HID driver is an example. Or a driver can request the host controller to schedule an IN transaction only when an application has requested data. The WinUSB driver is an example of this behavior. For interrupt OUT data, the driver requests transactions only when an application or other software component has provided data to send.

High-speed interrupt and isochronous transfers combined can use no more than 80% of a microframe. SuperSpeed interrupt and isochronous transfers combined can use no more than 80% of a bus interval. Full-speed isochronous transfers and low- and full-speed interrupt transfers combined can use no more than 90% of a frame. The section *More about Time-critical Transfers* below has more about the capabilities and limits of interrupt transfers.

Detecting and Handling Errors

If a device doesn't return an expected handshake packet, host controllers retry up to twice more. On receiving NAK, a USB 2.0 host may retry without limit. For example, a keyboard might sit idle for days before someone presses a key. A host driver might increment an error count on every incomplete transaction (with no received handshake packet), resetting the count when the device returns data or ACK and stopping communications to the endpoint if the error count reaches a defined number. These errors should be rare, yet a device that is NAKing for a long time might accumulate enough errors to cause the host to stop communicating. If you can't change the driver to cause it to reset the error counter and retry in this situation, a solution is for the device to send data periodically, defining a "no operation" code if needed for this situation.

SuperSpeed endpoints use NRDY and ERDY as described in Chapter 2 to cause the host to stop requesting to send or receive data when an endpoint isn't ready to receive data or has no data to send and to enable an endpoint to request to resume communications.

Interrupt transfers can use data toggles (USB 2.0) or Sequence Numbers (SuperSpeed) to ensure that all data is received without errors. A receiving endpoint that cares only about getting the most recent data can ignore the data toggle or Sequence Number.

Device Responsibilities

Device responsibilities for interrupt endpoints are the same as for bulk endpoints.

Isochronous Transfers

Isochronous transfers are streaming, real-time transfers that are useful when data must arrive at a constant rate or within a specific time limit and occasional errors are tolerable. At full speed and SuperSpeed, isochronous transfers can transfer more data per frame or bus interval compared to interrupt transfers, but the transfer type doesn't support automatic resending of data received with errors.

Examples of uses for isochronous transfers include encoded voice and music to be played in real time. Data that will eventually be consumed at a constant rate doesn't always require an isochronous transfer. For example, a host can use a bulk transfer to send a music file to a device. After receiving the file, the device can stream the music on request.

Nor does the data in an isochronous transfer have to be real-time data such as audio and video. An isochronous transfer is a way to ensure that any block of data has reserved bandwidth on a busy bus. Unlike with bulk transfers, a host guarantees that a configuration's requested isochronous bandwidth will be available, so the completion time is predictable.

Availability

Low speed doesn't support isochronous transfers. Devices aren't required to support isochronous transfers but a device class may require them. For example, many audio- and video-class devices use isochronous endpoints.

Structure

Isochronous means that the data has a fixed transfer rate, with a defined number of bytes transferring in every frame, microframe, or bus interval.

A USB 2.0 isochronous transfer consists of one or more IN transactions or one or more OUT transactions at equal intervals. Transferring data in both directions requires a separate transfer and pipe for each direction. High-speed and

SuperSpeed isochronous transfers are more flexible. They can request as many as 3 transactions per microframe (USB 2.0) or 48 transactions per bus interval (SuperSpeed) or as little as 1 transaction every 32,768 microframes/bus intervals.

Figure 3-7 shows the packets in full-speed isochronous IN and OUT transactions. An isochronous transfer is one way. The transactions in a transfer must all be IN transactions or all OUT transactions. Transferring data in both directions requires a separate pipe and transfer for each direction.

The USB 2.0 specification doesn't define a protocol for specifying the amount of data in an isochronous transfer. When needed, the device and host can use a class-specific or vendor-specific protocol to pass this information.

Before requesting a device configuration that consumes isochronous bandwidth, the host controller determines whether the requested bandwidth is available by comparing the available unreserved bus bandwidth with the maximum packet size and requested transfer rate of the configuration's isochronous endpoint(s).

Every USB 2.0 or USB 3.0 device with isochronous endpoints must have an interface that requests no isochronous bandwidth so the host can configure the

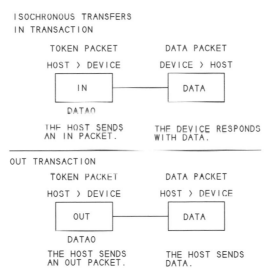

Figure 3-7. USB 2.0 isochronous transfers don't have handshake packets, so occasional errors must be acceptable. Not shown are the split transactions used with full-speed devices on a high-speed bus or the data PID sequencing in high-speed transfers with multiple data packets per microframe.

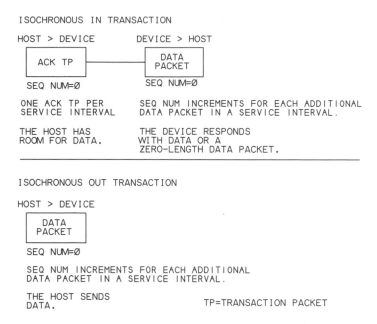

Figure 3-8. As with USB 2.0, SuperSpeed endpoints don't acknowledge isochronous data packets.

device even if the bus has no available reservable bandwidth. In addition to this interface and an alternate interface that requests the optimum bandwidth for a device, a device can support additional alternate interfaces that have smaller isochronous data packets or transfer fewer isochronous packets per microframe. The device driver can then request to use an interface that transfers data at a slower rate if needed. Or the driver can try again later in the hope that the bandwidth will be available. After the host configures the device and selects an interface, the transfers are guaranteed to have the time they need.

Each transaction has overhead and must share the bus with other devices. The host can schedule a transaction anywhere within a scheduled (micro)frame or bus interval. Isochronous transfers may also synchronize to another data source or recipient, SOF packets (USB 2.0), or Isochronous Timestamp Packets (SuperSpeed). For example, a microphone's input may synchronize to the output of speakers. The descriptor for a USB 2.0 or higher isochronous endpoint can specify a synchronization type and a usage value that indicates whether the endpoint contains data or feedback information used to maintain synchronization.

High Speed Differences

If a host is performing an isochronous transfer with a full-speed device on a high-speed bus, the host uses the split transactions introduced in Chapter 2 for all of the transfer's transactions. Isochronous OUT transactions use start-split transactions but don't use complete-splits because there is no status information to report back to the host. Isochronous transfers don't use the PING protocol.

SuperSpeed Differences

Figure 3-8 shows SuperSpeed isochronous IN and OUT transactions. The first Data Packet in a service interval has Sequence Number = 0. The Sequence Number increments with each Data Packet that follows in the service interval. In an IN transaction, the host sends a single ACK Transaction Packet to request one or more Data Packets in a service interval, and the device sends the packet(s). In an OUT transaction, the host sends data in Data Packets, and the device sends nothing. The endpoint descriptor specifies the length of a service interval and the number of Data Packets per service interval. For the last data packet in the service interval, the sender sets the last packet flag in the Data Packet Header.

Data Size

The allowed maximum data bytes in an isochronous transaction's data packet varies with bus speed and the number of packets per microframe (high speed) or the number of packets per bus interval and bMaxBurst (SuperSpeed):

Bus Speed	Maximum Data Packet Size	Maximum Number of Packets / Interval
Full	0–1023	1 / frame
High	0–1024	1 / microframe
	513–1024	2 / microframe
	683–1024	3 / microframe
SuperSpeed	0–1024 and bMaxBurst = 0	3 / bus interval
	1024 and bMaxBurst > 0	48 / bus interval

These bytes include only the information transferred in the data packet (USB 2.0) or Data Packet Payload (SuperSpeed), excluding PID and CRC bits.

If the data doesn't fit in a single packet, the host completes the transfer in multiple transactions. Within a USB 2.0 transfer, the amount of data in each transaction doesn't have to be the same and doesn't have to be the maximum packet size. For example, data at 44,100 samples per second could use a sequence of 9 packets containing 44 samples each, followed by 1 packet containing 45 samples.

SuperSpeed endpoints can support up to 3 burst transactions per service interval, with each burst consisting of up to 16 Data Packets. All but the last Data Packet in a burst must be the endpoint's maximum packet size. In addition, each burst except the last must have an equal number of Data Packets, and the number of Data Packets in each burst except the last must be 2, 4, 8, or 16.

For example, with endpoint support for 16 Data Packets per burst, the quickest way to send 48 maximum-size Data Packets is in 3 bursts of 16 Data Packets each. With endpoint support for 3 bursts per service interval, all of the data can transfer within one service interval. But the sender also has the option to send the data in 6 bursts of 8 Data Packets each, 12 bursts of 4 Data Packets each, 24 bursts of 2 Data Packets each, or 48 non-burst Data Packets.

In a similar way, transferring 47 Data Packets can use 2 bursts of 16 Data Packets each followed by one burst of 15 packets, 5 bursts of 8 Data Packets each followed by one burst of 7 packets, 11 bursts of 4 Data Packets each followed by one burst of 3 packets, 23 bursts of 2 Data Packets each followed by one burst of 1 packet, or 47 non-burst Data Packets.

Speed

A full-speed isochronous transaction can transfer up to 1023 bytes per frame, or up to 1.023 MB/s. A high-speed isochronous transaction can transfer up to 1024 bytes. A high-speed isochronous endpoint that requires more than 1024 bytes per microframe can request 2 or 3 transactions per microframe, for a maximum data throughput of 24.576 MB/s. A SuperSpeed isochronous transaction can transfer up to 1024 bytes. A SuperSpeed isochronous burst transaction consists of up to sixteen 1024-byte data packets in a service interval. An endpoint can request up to 3 burst transactions per service interval, for a maximum data throughput of over 393 MB/s.

A high-speed endpoint that requests multiple transactions per microframe is a high-bandwidth endpoint. Recent Windows editions support high-bandwidth isochronous endpoints. High-speed and SuperSpeed isochronous endpoints don't have to reserve bandwidth in every (micro)frame or service interval and thus can request less bandwidth than full-speed transfers. The minimum requested bandwidth is one byte every 4.096 seconds. However, any endpoint can transfer less data than the maximum reserved bandwidth by skipping available transactions or by transferring less than the maximum data per transfer. A SuperSpeed isochronous IN endpoint that has no data to transmit responds to a request for data with a zero-length Data Payload.

On a high-speed bus, interrupt and isochronous transfers combined can use no more than 80% of a microframe. On a SuperSpeed bus, interrupt and isochronous transfers combined can use no more than 80% of a bus interval. On a full-speed bus, isochronous transfers and low- and full-speed interrupt transfers combined can use no more than 90% of a frame.

The section *More about Time-critical Transfers* below has more about the capabilities of isochronous transfers.

Detecting and Handling Errors

The price for guaranteed on-time delivery of large blocks of data is no error correcting. Isochronous transfers are intended for uses where occasional errors are acceptable. For example, listeners may tolerate or not notice a short dropout in voice or music. In reality, under normal circumstances, a USB transfer should experience only infrequent errors due to line noise. Because isochronous transfers must keep to a schedule, the receiver can't request the sender to retransmit if the receiver is busy or detects an error. A receiver that suspects errors could ask the sender to resend the entire transfer, but this approach isn't very efficient.

A device or host that doesn't receive an expected data packet or receives a data packet with an error can define what to do. The options include using the data as is, skipping the data, or inserting a packet identical to the previous packet or other "dummy" data.

Device Responsibilities

A USB 2.0 device has these responsibilities for transfers on an isochronous endpoint:

- For OUT transfers, accept received data in data packets.
- For IN transfers, return data in data packets in response to IN tokens.

A SuperSpeed device has these responsibilities for transfers on a isochronous endpoint:

- For OUT transfers, accept data in Data Packets.
- For IN transfers, send data in Data Packets in response to requests in ACK Transaction Packets.

More about Time-critical Transfers

Just because an endpoint is capable of a rate of data transfer doesn't mean that a particular device and host will be able to achieve the rate. Several things can limit an application's ability to send or receive data at the rate that a device requests. The limiting factors include bus bandwidth, the capabilities of the device, the capabilities of the device driver and application software, and latencies in the host's hardware and software.

Bus Bandwidth

When a device requests more interrupt or isochronous bandwidth than is available, the host refuses to configure the device. A high-speed interrupt endpoint can request up to three 1024-byte data packets in each microframe, using as much as 40% of the bus bandwidth. To help ensure that devices can enumerate without problems, the interrupt endpoints in default interfaces must specify a maximum packet size of 64 bytes or less. The device driver is then free to try to increase the endpoint's reserved bandwidth by requesting alternate interface settings or configurations. Many drivers don't support requesting alternate interface settings or configurations, however.

Isochronous endpoints might also request more bandwidth than is available. In particular, full-speed endpoints on a 1.x bus and SuperSpeed endpoints can request over half of the bus bandwidth. To help ensure that devices will enumerate without problems, default interfaces in USB 2.0 and USB 3.0 devices must request no isochronous bandwidth. In other words, a default interface can transfer no isochronous data at all and typically includes no isochronous endpoints. After enumeration, the device driver can request isochronous bandwidth by requesting an alternate interface setting or a configuration with one or more isochronous endpoints. Note that even full-speed endpoints must meet this requirement to comply with USB 2.0.

A specific host might configure a device with non-compliant default interfaces, but future editions of the operating system might enforce this part of the specification and refuse to configure the device.

Device Capabilities

If the host has promised that the requested USB bandwidth will be available, there's still no guarantee that a device will be ready to send or receive data when needed.

To transfer data efficiently, a device should be ready to send and receive data on request. To send data, the device must write the data into the endpoint's buffer so the data is ready to send when requested by the host. Otherwise, in all but isochronous transfers, the endpoint returns NAK or NRDY and the host wastes time retrying. When receiving data, the device must read previously received data from the endpoint's buffer before new data arrives from the host. Otherwise the old data will be overwritten, or the endpoint will return NAK or NRDY and require the host to retry.

One way to help ensure that a device is always ready for a transfer is to use a device controller that supports multiple buffers as described in Chapter 6. Double or quadruple buffering gives the firmware extra time to load the next data to transfer or to retrieve received data.

Host Capabilities

The capabilities of the device driver and application software on the host can also affect whether transfers occur as efficiently as possible and without losing data.

A device driver requests a transfer by submitting an I/O request packet (IRP) to a lower-level driver. For interrupt and isochronous transfers, the host controller attempts a scheduled transaction only if the host has an outstanding IRP for the endpoint. To ensure that no transfer opportunities are missed, drivers with large amounts of data to send or request typically submit a new IRP immediately on completing the previous one.

The application software that uses the data also has to be able to keep up with the transfers. For example, the Windows driver for HID-class devices places report data received in interrupt transfers in a buffer, and applications use Read-File to retrieve reports from the buffer. If the buffer is full when a new report arrives, the driver discards the oldest report and replaces it with the newest one. If the application can't keep up with reading the buffer, some reports are lost. A solution is to increase the size of the buffer the driver uses to store received data or increase the size of the ReadFile buffer to enable reading multiple reports at once.

One way to help ensure that an application sends or receives data with minimal delay is to place the code that communicates with the device driver in its own program thread. The thread should have few responsibilities other than managing these communications.

Doing fewer, larger transfers rather than multiple, small transfers can also help. A host application can typically send or request a few large chunks of data more efficiently than sending or requesting many smaller chunks. Lower-level drivers manage the scheduling for transfers with multiple transactions.

Host Latencies

Another factor in the performance of time-critical USB transfers under Windows is latencies due to how the operating system handles multi-tasking. Windows was never designed as a real-time operating system that can guarantee a rate of data transfer with a peripheral.

With multi-tasking, multiple program threads run at the same time, and the operating system grants a portion of the available time to each thread. Different threads can have different priorities, but under Windows, no thread has guaranteed CPU time at a defined rate such as once per millisecond. Latencies under Windows are often well under 1 ms, but in some cases a thread can keep other code from executing for over 100 ms. Newer Windows editions tend to have improved performance over older editions.

A USB device and its software have no control over what other tasks the host CPU is performing and how fast the CPU performs them. If possible, the device should handle any critical, real-time processing so the timing of the host communications can be as non-critical as possible. For example, consider a full-speed device that reads a sensor once per millisecond. The device could attempt to send each reading to the host in a separate interrupt transfer, but if a transfer fails to occur for any reason, the data will never catch up. If the device instead collects a series of readings and transfers them using less frequent, larger transfers, the timing of the bus transfers is less critical. Data compression can also help by reducing the number of bytes that transfer.

4

Enumeration: How the Host Learns about Devices

Before applications can communicate with a device, the host needs to learn about the device and assign a driver. Enumeration is the exchange of information that accomplishes these tasks. The process includes assigning an address to the device, reading descriptors from the device, assigning and loading a driver, and selecting a configuration that specifies the device's power requirements and interfaces. The device is then ready to transfer data.

This chapter describes the enumeration process, including the structure of the descriptors that the host reads from the device during enumeration. Understanding enumeration is essential in creating the descriptors that will reside in the device and in writing firmware that responds to enumeration requests.

The Process

One of a hub's duties is to detect attachment and removal of devices on its downstream ports. Each hub has an interrupt IN endpoint for reporting these events to the host. On system boot-up, hubs inform the host if any devices are attached, including additional downstream hubs and any devices attached to those hubs. After boot-up, a host continues to poll periodically (USB 2.0) or receives ERDY Transaction Packets (SuperSpeed) that request communications to learn of any newly attached or removed devices.

On learning of a new device, the host sends requests to the device's hub to cause the hub to establish a communications path between the host and device. The host then attempts to enumerate the device by issuing control transfers containing standard USB requests to the device. All USB devices must support control transfers, the standard requests, and endpoint zero. For a successful enumeration, the device must respond to requests by returning requested information and taking other requested actions.

From the user's perspective, enumeration is invisible and automatic except for possibly a message that announces the new device and whether the attempt to configure it succeeded. Sometimes on first use, the user needs to assist in selecting a driver or telling the host where to look for driver files. Under Windows, when enumeration is complete, the new device appears in the Device Manager. (Right-click Computer, click Manage, and in the Computer Management pane, select Device Manager.) When a user removes a device from the bus, the device disappears from the Device Manager. In a typical device, firmware decodes and responds to requests for information. Some controllers can manage enumeration entirely in hardware except possibly for vendor-provided values in EEPROM. On the host side, the operating system handles enumeration.

Enumeration Steps

The USB 2.0 specification defines six device states. During enumeration, a device moves through the Powered, Default, Address, and Configured states. (The other states are Attached and Suspend.) In each state, the device has defined capabilities and behavior.

Typical USB 2.0 Sequence

The steps below are a typical sequence of events that occurs during enumeration of a USB 2.0 device under Windows. Device firmware shouldn't assume that enumeration requests and events will occur in a particular order. To func-

Item	Device	Payload
▽	▽	▽
⏚ Reset (2.3 s)		
⏚ Suspended (114.0 ms)		
⏚ Reset (10.0 ms)		
⏚ High speed Detection Handshake		
⊞ GetDescriptor (Device)	0 (5)	8 bytes (12 01 00 02 FF 00 00 08)
⏚ Reset (10.0 ms)		
⏚ High speed Detection Handshake		
⊞ SetAddress (5)	0 (5)	No data
⊞ GetDescriptor (Device)	5	18 bytes (12 01 00 02 FF 00 00 08 ...
⊞ GetDescriptor (Configuration)	5	9 bytes (09 02 2E 00 01 01 00 A0 32)
⊞ GetDescriptor (Configuration)	5	46 bytes (09 02 2E 00 01 01 00 A0 ...
⊞ GetDescriptor (String lang IDs)	5	4 bytes (04 03 09 04)
⊞ GetDescriptor (String iProduct)	5	24 bytes (18 03 57 00 69 00 6E 00 ...
⊞ GetDescriptor (String lang IDs)	5	4 bytes (04 03 09 04)
⊞ GetDescriptor (String iProduct)	5	24 bytes (18 03 57 00 69 00 6E 00 ...
⊞ GetDescriptor (Device)	5	18 bytes (12 01 00 02 FF 00 00 08 ...
⊞ GetDescriptor (Configuration)	5	9 bytes (09 02 2E 00 01 01 00 A0 32)
⊞ GetDescriptor (Configuration)	5	46 bytes (09 02 2E 00 01 01 00 A0 ...
⊞ GetStatus (Device)	5	2 bytes (00 00)
⊞ SetConfiguration (1)	5	No data

Figure 4-1. To enumerate a newly attached device, the host sends a series of requests to obtain descriptors and set the device's bus address and configuration. (Screen capture from Ellisys USB Explorer analyzer.)

tion successfully, a device must detect and respond to any control request or other bus event at any time. Figure 4-1 shows received requests and other events at a device during a device enumeration.

1. The system has a new device. A user attaches a device to a USB port, or the system powers up with a device attached. The port may be on the root hub at the host or on a hub that connects downstream from the host. The hub provides power to the port, and the device is in the Powered state. The device can draw up to 100 mA from the bus.

2. The hub detects the device. The hub monitors the voltages on the signal lines (D+ and D-) at each of its ports. The hub has a pull-down resistor of

14.25k–24.8kΩ on each line. A device has a pull-up resistor of 900–1575Ω on D+ for a full-speed device or D- for a low-speed device. High-speed-capable devices attach at full speed. On attaching to a port, the device's pull-up brings its line high, enabling the hub to detect that a device is attached. On detecting a device, the hub continues to provide power but doesn't yet transmit USB traffic to the device. Chapter 15 has more on how hubs detect devices.

3. The host learns of the new device. Each hub uses its interrupt endpoint to report events at the hub. The report indicates only whether the hub or a port (and if so, which port) has experienced an event. On learning of an event, the host sends the hub a Get Port Status request to find out more. Get Port Status and the other hub-class requests described are standard requests that all hubs support. The information returned tells the host when a device is newly attached.

4. The hub detects whether a device is low or full speed. Just before resetting the device, the hub determines whether the device is low or full speed by examining the voltages on the two signal lines. The hub detects the device's speed by determining which line has a higher voltage when idle. The hub sends the information to the host in response to the next Get Port Status request. A USB 1.x hub may instead detect the device's speed just after a bus reset. USB 2.0 requires speed detection before the reset so the hub knows whether to check for a high-speed-capable device during reset as described below.

5. The hub resets the device. When a host learns of a new device, the host sends the hub a Set Port Feature request that asks the hub to reset the port. The hub places the device's USB data lines in the Reset condition for at least 10 ms. Reset is a special condition where both D+ and D- are logic low. (Normally, the lines have opposite logic states.) The hub sends the reset only to the new device. Other hubs and devices on the bus don't see the reset.

6. The host learns if a full-speed device supports high speed. Detecting whether a device supports high speed uses two special signal states. In the Chirp J state, only the D+ line is driven and in the Chirp K state, only the D- line is driven.

During the reset, a device that supports high speed sends a Chirp K. A high-speed-capable hub detects the Chirp K and responds with a series of alternating Chirp K and Chirp J. On detecting the pattern KJKJKJ, the device removes its full-speed pull-up and performs all further communications at high speed. If the hub doesn't respond to the device's Chirp K, the device knows it must continue to communicate at full speed. All high-speed devices must be capable of responding to control requests at full speed.

7. The hub establishes a signal path between the device and the bus. The host verifies that the device has exited the reset state by sending a Get Port Status request. A bit in the returned data indicates whether the device is still in the reset state. If necessary, the host repeats the request until the device has exited the reset state.

When the hub removes the reset, the device is in the Default state. The device's USB registers are in their reset states, and the device is ready to respond to control transfers at endpoint zero. The device communicates with the host using the default address of 00h.

8. The host sends a Get Descriptor request to learn the maximum packet size of the default pipe. The host sends the request to device address 00h, endpoint zero. Because the host enumerates only one device at a time, only one device will respond to communications addressed to device address 00h even if several devices attach at once.

The eighth byte of the device descriptor contains the maximum packet size supported by endpoint zero. A Windows host requests 64 bytes but after receiving just one packet (whether or not it has 64 bytes), the host begins the Status stage of the transfer. On completing the Status stage, Windows requests the hub to reset the device as in step 5 above. The USB 2.0 specification doesn't require a reset here. The reset is a precaution that ensures that the device will be in a known state when the reset ends.

9. The host assigns an address. When the reset is complete, the host controller assigns a unique address to the device by sending a Set Address request. The device completes the Status stage of the request using the default address and then implements the new address. The device is now in the Address state. All communications from this point on use the new address. The address is valid until the device is detached, a hub resets the port, or the system reboots. On the next enumeration, the host may assign a different address to the device.

10. The host learns about the device's abilities. The host sends a Get Descriptor request to the new address to read the device descriptor. This time the host retrieves the entire descriptor. The descriptor contains the maximum packet size for endpoint zero, the number of configurations the device supports, and other basic information about the device.

The host continues to learn about the device by requesting the one or more configuration descriptors specified in the device descriptor. A request for a configuration descriptor is actually a request for the configuration descriptor followed by all of its subordinate descriptors up to the number of bytes requested. A Windows host begins by requesting just the configuration descriptor's nine bytes. Included in these bytes is the total length of the configuration descriptor and its subordinate descriptors.

Windows then requests the configuration descriptor again, this time requesting the number of bytes in the retrieved total length. The device responds by sending the configuration descriptor followed by all of the configuration's subordinate descriptors, including interface descriptor(s), with each interface descriptor followed by any endpoint descriptors for the interface. Some configurations also have class- or vendor-specific descriptors. This chapter has more on what the descriptors contain.

11. The host assigns and loads a device driver (except for composite devices). After learning about a device from its descriptors, the host looks for the best match in a driver to manage communications with the device. Windows hosts use INF files to identify the best match. The INF file may be a system file for a USB class or a vendor-provided file that contains the device's Vendor ID and Product ID. Chapter 9 has more about selecting a driver.

For devices that have been enumerated previously, Windows may use stored information instead of searching the INF files. After the operating system assigns and loads the driver, the driver may request the device to resend descriptors or send other class-specific descriptors.

An exception to this sequence is composite devices, which can have different drivers assigned to multiple interfaces in a configuration. The host can assign these drivers only after enabling the interfaces, so the host must first configure the device as described below.

12. The host's device driver selects a configuration. After learning about a device from the descriptors, the device driver requests a configuration by sending a Set Configuration request with the desired configuration number. Many devices support only one configuration. If a device supports multiple configurations, the driver can decide which configuration to request based on information the driver has about how the device will be used, or the driver can ask the user what to do or just select the first configuration. (Many drivers only select the first configuration.) On receiving the request, the device implements the requested configuration. The device is now in the Configured state and the device's interface(s) are enabled.

For composite devices, the host can now assign drivers. As with other devices, the host uses the information retrieved from the device to find a driver for each active interface in the configuration. The device is then ready for use.

Hubs are also USB devices, and the host enumerates a newly attached hub in the same way as other devices. If the hub has devices attached, the host enumerates these after the hub informs the host of their presence.

Attached state. If the hub isn't providing power to a device's VBUS line, the device is in the Attached state. The absence of power may occur if the hub has detected an over-current condition or if the host requests the hub to remove power from the port. With no power on VBUS, the host and device can't communicate, so from their perspective, the situation is the same as when the device isn't attached.

Suspend State. A device enters the Suspend state after detecting no bus activity, including SOF markers, for at least 3 ms. In the Suspend state, the device should limit its use of bus power. Both configured and unconfigured devices must support this state. Chapter 16 has more about the Suspend state.

SuperSpeed Differences

Enumerating SuperSpeed devices has some differences compared to USB 2.0:

- On detecting a downstream SuperSpeed termination at a port, a hub initializes and trains the port's link. Enumeration then proceeds at SuperSpeed with no need for further speed detecting.
- The host isn't required to reset the port after learning of a new device.
- The bus-current limits are 150 mA before configuration and 900 mA after configuration.
- The host sends a Set Isochronous Delay request to inform the device of the bus delay for isochronous packets.
- The host sends a Set SEL request to inform the device of the system exit latency (the amount of time required to transition out of a low-power state).
- Protocols for entering and exiting the Suspend state differ.
- For hubs, the host sends a Set Hub Depth request to set the hub-depth value.

Device Removal

When a user removes a device from the bus, the hub disables the device's port. The host knows that the removal occurred after the hub notifies the host that an event has occurred, and the host sends a Get Port Status request to learn what the event was. The device disappears from the Device Manager and the device's address becomes available to another newly attached device.

Tips for Successful Enumeration

Without successful enumeration, the device and host can't perform other communications. Most chip companies provide example code, which can serve as a model even if your application doesn't exactly match the example application. If your controller interfaces to an external CPU, you may have to adapt code written for another chip.

In general, a device should assume nothing about what requests or events the host will initiate and should concentrate on responding to requests and events as they occur. The following tips can help avoid problems.

Don't assume requests or events will occur in a specific order. Some requests, such as Set Configuration, require the device to be in the Address or Configured state, so the request is valid only after the device has accepted a Set Address request. But the host has some flexibility in what requests to issue and in what order during enumeration. A host might also reset or suspend the bus at any time, and the device must detect the event and respond appropriately.

Be ready to abandon a control transfer or end it early. On receiving a new Setup packet, a device must abandon any transfer in progress and begin the new one. On receiving an OUT token packet (USB 2.0) or STATUS Transaction Packet (SuperSpeed), the device must assume that the host is beginning the Status stage of the transfer even if the device hasn't sent all of the requested data in the Data stage.

Don't attempt to send more data than the host requests. In the Data stage of a control read transfer, a device should send no more than the amount of data the host has requested. If the host requests nine bytes, the device should send no more than nine bytes.

Send a zero-length data packet when required. In some cases, the device returns less than the requested amount of data, and the amount of data is an exact multiple of the endpoint's maximum packet size. On receiving a request for more data, the device should indicate that it has no more data by returning a ZLP (USB 2.0) or a zero-length Data Payload (SuperSpeed).

Stall unsupported requests. A device shouldn't assume it knows every request the host might send. The device should return a STALL in response to any request the device doesn't support.

Don't set the address too soon. In a Set Address request, the device should set its new address only after the Status stage of the request is complete.

Be ready to enter the Suspend state. A host can suspend the bus when the device is in any powered state, including before the device has been configured. When the bus is suspended, the device must reduce its use of bus power.

Test under different host-controller types. Some full-speed host controllers schedule multiple stages of a control transfer in a single frame, while others don't. Devices should be able to handle either way. Chapter 8 has more about host controllers.

Descriptors

USB descriptors are the data structures that enable the host to learn about a device. Each descriptor contains information about the device as a whole or an element in the device.

All USB devices must respond to requests for the standard USB descriptors. The device must store the contents of its descriptors and respond to requests for the descriptors.

Types

Table 4-1 lists the descriptors defined in the USB 2.0 and USB 3.0 specifications. Except for compound devices, each device has one and only one device descriptor that contains information about the device and specifies the number of configurations the device supports. For each configuration, each device has a configuration descriptor with information about the device's use of power and the number of interfaces the configuration supports. For each interface, the device has an interface descriptor that specifies the number of endpoints. Each endpoint has an endpoint descriptor that contains information needed to communicate with the endpoint. An interface with no endpoint descriptors uses the control endpoint for all communications.

On receiving a request for a configuration descriptor, a device should return the configuration descriptor and all of the configuration's interface, endpoint, and

Table 4-1: The bDescriptorType field in a descriptor contains a value that identifies the descriptor type.

bDescriptorType	Descriptor Type	Required?
01h	device	Yes.
02h	configuration	Yes.
03h	string	No, unless a driver requires it. Optional descriptive text.
04h	interface	Yes.
05h	endpoint	Yes, to use other than endpoint zero.
06h	device_qualifier	Yes for devices that support both full and high speeds. Not allowed for other devices.
07h	other_speed_configuration	Yes for devices that support both full and high speeds. Not allowed for other devices.
08h	interface_power	No (proposed but never approved or implemented).
09h	OTG	Yes for On-The-Go devices.
0Ah	debug	No.
0Bh	interface_association	Yes for some composite devices.
0Ch	security	For wireless devices.
0Dh	key	
0Eh	encryption type	
0Fh	binary device object store (BOS)	Yes for SuperSpeed devices, wireless devices, and devices that support link power management.
10h	device capability	
11h	wireless endpoint companion	For wireless devices.
30h	SuperSpeed_endpoint_companion	Yes for SuperSpeed devices. Not supported for other speeds.

other subordinate descriptors up to the requested number of bytes. A host can't request to retrieve, for example, only an endpoint descriptor. Devices that support both full and high speeds support two additional descriptor types: device_qualifier and other_speed_configuration. These and their subordinate descriptors contain information about the device when using the speed not currently in use.

SuperSpeed devices must provide a binary device object store (BOS) descriptor and at least two subordinate device capability descriptors: a SuperSpeed USB descriptor and a USB 2.0 Extension descriptor. Other devices may also use BOS and device capability descriptors. Every SuperSpeed endpoint descriptor has a subordinate SuperSpeed endpoint companion descriptor.

A string descriptor can store text such as the vendor's or device's name or a serial number. Another descriptor may contain an index value that points to the string descriptor. The host reads string descriptors using Get Descriptor requests.

Class- and vendor-specific descriptors offer a structured way for a device or interface to provide more detailed information about a function. For example, if an interface descriptor specifies that the interface belongs to the HID class, the interface also has a HID class descriptor.

Standard descriptors begin with a bLength byte that gives the descriptor's length in bytes followed by a bDescriptorType byte that identifies the descriptor's type. Table 4-1 shows values for standard descriptor types.

In a Get Descriptor request, the Setup stage's data packet passes wValue and wLength values to the device. The wValue field identifies the descriptor being requested. The wLength field is the number of bytes the host is requesting from the device. Chapter 5 has more about the Get Descriptor request.

Some class- or vendor-specific descriptors modify or extend other descriptors. In the descriptors returned in response to a request for a configuration and subordinate descriptors, a descriptor that extends or modifies a descriptor follows that descriptor. Like standard descriptors, these class- and vendor-specific descriptors begin with a bLength byte followed by a bDescriptorType byte.

For descriptors that don't modify or extend a standard descriptor, such as a request for a HID-class report descriptor, the host uses a Get Descriptor request that specifies the class- or vendor-specific descriptor type and the index of the request. The class or vendor defines the format for these descriptors.

Each descriptor below begins with bLength and bDescriptorType fields. The other fields vary with the descriptor type.

Device

The device descriptor is the first descriptor the host reads on device attachment. The descriptor contains information the host needs to retrieve additional information from the device. A host retrieves a device descriptor by sending a Get Descriptor request with the high byte of the Setup transaction's wValue field equal to 01h.

Table 4-2: The device descriptor identifies the product and its manufacturer, sets the maximum packet size for endpoint zero, and can specify a device class.

Offset (decimal)	Field	Size (bytes)	Description
0	bLength	1	Descriptor size in bytes (12h)
1	bDescriptorType	1	The constant DEVICE (01h)
2	bcdUSB	2	USB specification release number (BCD)
4	bDeviceClass	1	Class code
5	bDeviceSubclass	1	Subclass code
6	bDeviceProtocol	1	Protocol Code
7	bMaxPacketSize0	1	Maximum packet size for endpoint zero
8	idVendor	2	Vendor ID
10	idProduct	2	Product ID
12	bcdDevice	2	Device release number (BCD)
14	iManufacturer	1	Index of string descriptor for the manufacturer
15	iProduct	1	Index of string descriptor for the product
16	iSerialNumber	1	Index of string descriptor for the serial number
17	bNumConfigurations	1	Number of possible configurations

The descriptor (Table 4-2) provides information about the device, its configurations, and any classes the device belongs to.

bcdUSB is the USB specification version that the device and its descriptors comply with in BCD (binary-coded decimal) format. If you think of the version's value as a decimal number, the upper byte represents the integer, the next four bits are tenths, and the final four bits are hundredths. USB 1.1 is 0110h (*not* 0101h). USB 2.0 is 0200h. USB 3.0 is 0300h.

A device with bcdUSB = 0210h or higher must support the BOS descriptor. A device or device wire adapter that complies with Wireless USB V1.0 should set bcdUSB to 0250h.

bDeviceClass specifies the device's class for devices whose function is defined at the device level. Values from 01h to FEh are reserved for classes defined by USB specifications. Table 4-3 shows defined codes. Vendor-defined classes use FFh. Most devices specify their class or classes in interface descriptors. For these devices, bDeviceClass in the device descriptor equals 00h if the function doesn't use an interface association descriptor or EFh if the function uses an interface association descriptor.

Table 4-3: The bDeviceClass field in the device descriptor can name a class the device belongs to.

bDeviceClass	Description
00h	The interface descriptor specifies the class and the function doesn't use an interface association descriptor. (See EFh below.)
02h	Communications device (can instead be declared at the interface level)
09h	Hub
0Fh	Personal healthcare device (declaring at the interface level preferred)
DCh	Diagnostic device (can instead be declared at the interface level) bDeviceSubclass = 01h, bDeviceProtocol = 01h: USB2 Compliance Device
E0h	Wireless Controller (can instead be declared at the interface level) bDeviceSubclass = 01h: Bluetooth programming interface

EFh	Miscellaneous
	bDeviceSubclass = 01h
	   bDeviceProtocol = 01h: active sync
	   bDeviceProtocol = 02h: Palm sync
	bDeviceSubclass = 02h
	   bDeviceProtocol = 01h: interface association descriptor
	   bDeviceProtocol = 01h: wire adapter multifunction peripheral (Wireless USB).

FFh	Vendor-specific (can instead be declared at the interface level)

bDeviceSubclass can specify a subclass within a class. A subclass can add support for additional features and abilities shared by a group of functions in a class. If bDeviceClass is 00h, bDeviceSubclass must be 00h. If bDeviceClass is in the range 01h–FEh, bDeviceSubclass equals 00h or a code defined for the device's class. Vendor-defined subclasses in standard classes use FFh.

bDeviceProtocol can specify a protocol for the selected class and subclass. For example, a USB 2.0 hub uses this field to indicate whether the hub is currently supporting high speed and if so, if the hub supports one or multiple transaction translators. If bDeviceClass is in the range 01–FEh, the protocol equals 00h or a code defined by the device's class.

bMaxPacketSize0 specifies the maximum packet size for endpoint zero. The host uses this information in the requests that follow the request for the device descriptor. For USB 2.0, the maximum packet size equals the field's value and must be 8 for low speed; 8, 16, 32, or 64 for full speed; and 64 for high speed. For SuperSpeed, the maximum packet size equals $2^{bMaxPacketSize0}$ and bMaxPacketSize0 must equal 9 to specify a maximum packet size of 512.

idVendor is a Vendor ID assigned by the USB-IF to members of the USB-IF and others who pay an administrative fee. The host may have an INF file that contains this value, and if so, Windows may use the value to help select a driver for the device. Except for devices used only in house where the user is responsible for preventing conflicts, every device descriptor must have a valid Vendor ID in this field.

idProduct is a Product ID that identifies the vendor's device. The owner of the Vendor ID assigns the Product ID. Both the device descriptor and the device's INF file on the host may contain this value, and if so, Windows may use the value to help select a driver for the device. Each Product ID is specific to a Vendor ID, so multiple vendors can use the same Product ID without conflict.

bcdDevice is the device's release number in BCD format. The vendor assigns this value. The host may use this value to help select a driver for the device.

iManufacturer is an index that points to a string describing the manufacturer or zero if there is no manufacturer descriptor.

iProduct is an index that points to a string describing the product or zero if there is no string descriptor.

iSerialNumber is an index that points to a string containing the device's serial number or 00h if there is no serial number. Serial numbers are useful if users may have more than one identical device on the bus and the host needs to remember which device is which even after rebooting. A serial number also enables a host to determine whether a device is the same one used previously or a new installation of a device with the same Vendor ID and Product ID. Devices with the same Vendor ID, Product ID, and device release number should not share a serial number. Mass-storage devices that use the bulk-only protocol must have serial numbers.

bNumConfigurations equals the number of configurations the device supports at the current operating speed.

Device_Qualifier

Devices that support both full and high speeds must have a device_qualifier descriptor (Table 4-4). When a device switches speeds, the values of some fields in the device descriptor may change. The device_qualifier descriptor contains the values for these fields at the speed not currently in use. In other words, the contents of fields in the device and device_qualifier descriptors swap depending on which speed is in use. A host retrieves a device_qualifier descriptor by send-

Table 4-4: In a device that supports both full and high speeds, the device_qualifier descriptor contains information about the device when operating in the speed not currently in use.

Offset (decimal)	Field	Size (bytes)	Description
0	bLength	1	Descriptor size in bytes (0Ah)
1	bDescriptorType	1	The constant DEVICE_QUALIFIER (06h)
2	bcdUSB	2	USB specification release number (BCD)
4	bDeviceClass	1	Class code
5	bDeviceSubclass	1	Subclass code
6	bDeviceProtocol	1	Protocol Code
7	bMaxPacketSize0	1	Maximum packet size for endpoint zero
8	bNumConfigurations	1	Number of possible configurations
9	Reserved	1	For future use

ing a Get Descriptor request with the high byte of the Setup transaction's wValue field equal to 06h.

The Vendor ID, Product ID, device release number, manufacturer string, product string, and serial-number string don't change when the speed changes, so the device_qualifier descriptor doesn't include these fields.

Configuration

After retrieving the device descriptor, a host can retrieve the device's configuration, interface, and endpoint descriptors.

Each device has at least one configuration that specifies the device's features and abilities. Typically a single configuration is enough, but with driver support, a device with multiple uses or multiple options for power use can support multiple configurations. Only one configuration is active at a time. Each configuration requires a descriptor with information about the device's use of power and the number of interfaces supported (Table 4-5). Each configuration descriptor has subordinate descriptors, including one or more interface descriptors and optional endpoint descriptors. A host retrieves a configuration descriptor and its subordinate descriptors by sending a Get Descriptor request with the high byte of the Setup transaction's wValue field equal to 02h and the wLength field equal to wTotalLength.

Table 4-5: The configuration descriptor specifies the maximum amount of bus current the device will require and gives the total length of the subordinate descriptors.

Offset (decimal)	Field	Size (bytes)	Description
0	bLength	1	Descriptor size in bytes (09h)
1	bDescriptorType	1	The constant CONFIGURATION (02h)
2	wTotalLength	2	The number of bytes in the configuration descriptor and all of its subordinate descriptors
4	bNumInterfaces	1	Number of interfaces in the configuration
5	bConfigurationValue	1	Identifier for Set Configuration and Get Configuration requests
6	iConfiguration	1	Index of string descriptor for the configuration
7	bmAttributes	1	Self/bus power and remote wakeup settings
8	bMaxPower	1	Bus power required in units of 2 mA (USB 2.0) or 8 mA (SuperSpeed).

The host selects a configuration with the Set Configuration request and reads the current configuration number with a Get Configuration request.

wTotalLength equals the number of bytes in the configuration descriptor and all of its subordinate descriptors.

bNumInterfaces equals the number of interfaces in the configuration. The minimum is 01h.

bConfigurationValue identifies the configuration for Get Configuration and Set Configuration requests and must be 01h or higher. A Set Configuration request with a value of zero causes the device to enter the Not Configured state.

iConfiguration is an index to a string that describes the configuration. This value is zero if there is no string descriptor.

bmAttributes sets bit 6 = 1 if the device is self-powered and zero if bus powered. Bit 5 = 1 if the device supports the remote wakeup feature, which enables a suspended USB device to tell the host that the device wants to communicate. The other bits in the field are unused. Bits 4..0 must be zero. Bit 7 must equal 1 for compatibility with USB 1.0

bMaxPower. Specifies how much bus current a device requires. For USB 2.0, bMaxPower is in units of 2 mA. If the device requires 200 mA, bMax-Power=64h. For SuperSpeed, bMaxPower is in units of 8 mA. The maximum

Table 4-6: The other_speed_configuration descriptor has the same fields as the configuration descriptor but contains information about the device when it operates in the speed not currently in use.

Offset (decimal)	Field	Size (bytes)	Description
0	bLength	1	Descriptor size in bytes (09h)
1	bDescriptorType	1	The constant OTHER_SPEED_CONFIGURATION (07h)
2	wTotalLength	2	The number of bytes in the configuration descriptor and all of its subordinate descriptors
4	bNumInterfaces	1	Number of interfaces in the configuration
5	bConfigurationValue	1	Identifier for Set Configuration and Get Configuration requests
6	iConfiguration	1	Index of string descriptor for the configuration
7	bmAttributes	1	Self/bus power and remote wakeup settings
8	MaxPower	1	Bus power required in units of 2 mA (USB 2.0) or 8 mA (SuperSpeed).

bus current a device can request is 500 mA for USB 2.0 and 900 mA for Super-Speed. If the requested current isn't available, the host will refuse to configure the device. A driver may then request an alternate configuration if available.

Other_Speed_Configuration

The second descriptor unique to devices that support both full and high speeds is the other_speed_configuration descriptor (Table 4-6). The structure of the descriptor is identical to that of the configuration descriptor. The only difference is that the other-speed_configuration descriptor describes the configuration when the device is operating at the speed not currently in use. The descriptor has subordinate descriptors just as the configuration descriptor does.

A host retrieves an other_speed_configuration descriptor by sending a Get Descriptor request with the high byte of the Setup transaction's wValue field equal to 07h.

Interface Association

An interface association descriptor (IAD) identifies multiple interfaces associated with a function (Table 4-7). In relation to a device and its descriptors, the term *interface* refers to a feature or function a device implements.

Table 4-7: The interface association descriptor can link multiple interfaces to a single function.

Offset (decimal)	Field	Size (bytes)	Description
0	bLength	1	Descriptor size in bytes (08h)
1	bDescriptorType	1	The constant Interface Association (0Bh)
2	bFirstInterface	1	Number identifying the first interface associated with the function
3	bInterfaceCount	1	The number of contiguous interfaces associated with the function
4	bFunctionClass	1	Class code
5	bFunctionSubClass	1	Subclass code
6	bFunctionProtocol	1	Protocol code
8	iFunction	1	Index of string descriptor for the function

Most device classes specify the class at the interface level rather than at the device level. Assigning functions to interfaces enables a single configuration to support multiple functions. When two or more interfaces in a configuration are associated with the same function, the interface association descriptor tells the host which interfaces are associated. For example, a video-camera function may use one interface to control the camera and another to carry video data.

The *Interface Association Descriptor* ECN says that the descriptor must be supported by future implementations of devices that use multiple interfaces to manage a single device function. Devices that comply with the video-class and audio 2.0 specifications must use interface association descriptors. Class specifications that predate the IAD don't require it. For example, the audio 1.0 class specification defines a class-specific descriptor to associate audio interfaces in a function. Hosts that don't support the IAD ignore it. Windows began supporting the descriptor with Windows XP SP2. In USB 3.0 devices, every function with multiple interfaces must use an IAD.

To enable hosts to identify devices that use the Interface Association descriptor, the device descriptor should contain the following values:

> bDeviceClass = EFh (miscellaneous device class)
>
> bDeviceSubClass = 02h (common class)
>
> bDeviceProtocol = 01h (interface association descriptor)

These codes together form the *Multi-interface Function Device Class Codes*.

A host retrieves an interface association descriptor as one of the subordinate descriptors sent in response to a request for a configuration descriptor. The IAD precedes the interface descriptors that the IAD specifies.

bFirstInterface identifies the interface number of the first of multiple interfaces associated with a function. The interface number is the value of bInterface-Number in the interface descriptor. The interface numbers of associated interfaces must be contiguous.

bInterfaceCount equals the number of contiguous interfaces associated with the function.

bFunctionClass is a class code for the function shared by the associated interfaces. For classes that don't specify a value to use, the preferred value is the bInterfaceClass value from the descriptor of the first associated interface. Values from 01h–FEh are reserved for USB-defined classes. FFh indicates a vendor-defined class. Zero is not allowed.

bFunctionSubClass is a subclass code for the function shared by the associated interfaces. For classes that don't specify a value to use, the preferred value is the bInterfaceSubClass value from the descriptor of the first associated interface.

bInterfaceProtocol is a protocol code for the function shared by the associated interfaces. For classes that don't specify a value to use, the preferred value is the bInterfaceProtocol value from the descriptor of the first associated interface.

iInterface is an index to a string that describes the function. This value is zero if there is no string descriptor.

Interface

The interface descriptor provides information about a function or feature that a device implements. The descriptor contains class, subclass, and protocol information and the number of endpoints the interface uses (Table 4-8).

A configuration can have multiple interfaces that are active at the same time. The interfaces may be associated with a single function or they may be unrelated. Each interface has its own interface descriptor and subordinate descriptors. Each of these interfaces can also have one or more alternate interface settings. The settings are mutually exclusive; only one is active at a time. Each setting has an interface descriptor and subordinate descriptors as needed. Devices that use isochronous transfers have alternate interface settings because the default interface can request no isochronous bandwidth.

Table 4-8: The interface descriptor specifies the number of subordinate endpoints and may specify a USB class.

Offset (decimal)	Field	Size (bytes)	Description
0	bLength	1	Descriptor size in bytes (09h)
1	bDescriptorType	1	The constant Interface (04h)
2	bInterfaceNumber	1	Number identifying this interface
3	bAlternateSetting	1	A number that identifies a descriptor with alternate settings for this bInterfaceNumber.
4	bNumEndpoints	1	Number of endpoints supported not counting endpoint zero
5	bInterfaceClass	1	Class code
6	bInterfaceSubclass	1	Subclass code
7	bInterfaceProtocol	1	Protocol code
8	iInterface	1	Index of string descriptor for the interface

A host retrieves interface descriptors as subordinate descriptors sent in response to a request for a configuration descriptor.

bInterfaceNumber identifies the interface. In a composite device, a configuration has multiple interfaces that are active at the same time. Each interface must have a descriptor with a unique value in this field. The default interface is 00h.

bAlternateSetting identifies the default interface setting or an alternate setting. For each bInterfaceNumber, the device provides an interface descriptor with bAlternateSetting = 00h. This is the default setting. A descriptor for an alternate setting has the same value in bInterfaceNumber, a unique value in bAlternateSetting, and different values as needed in the descriptor's final five bytes. For each bInterfaceNumber, only one bAlternateSetting is active at a time. The alternate settings enable the host to request an interface with different bandwidth or other requirements and capabilities. The Get Interface request retrieves the currently active bAlternateSetting. The Set Interface request selects the bAlternateSetting that a specific bInterfaceNumber should use.

bNumEndpoints equals the number of endpoints the interface supports in addition to endpoint zero. For a device that supports only endpoint zero, this field is zero.

bInterfaceClass is similar to bDeviceClass in the device descriptor, but for devices with a class specified by the interface. Table 4-9 shows defined codes.

Table 4-9: The bInterfaceClass field in the interface descriptor can name a class the interface belongs to.

Class Code (hexadecimal)	Description
00	Reserved
01	Audio
02	Communications device class: communication interface
03	Human interface device
05	Physical
06	Image
07	Printer
08	Mass storage
09	Hub
0A	Communications device class: data interface
0B	Smart Card
0D	Content Security
0E	Video
0F	Personal healthcare device (can instead be declared at the device level)
DC	Diagnostic device (can instead be declared at the device level) bInterfaceSubclass= 01h, bInterfaceProtocol = 01h. USB2 compliance device

E0	Wireless controller
	bInterfaceSubclass = 01h
	  bInterfaceProtocol = 01h: Bluetooth programming interface
	  (can also be declared at the device level)
	  bInterfaceProtocol = 02h: UWB Radio control interface (Wireless USB)
	  bInterface bInterfaceProtocol – 03h: remote NDIS
	bInterfaceSubclass = 02h. Host and device wire adapters (Wireless USB)

EF	Miscellaneous
	bInterfaceSubclass = 01h
	  bInterfaceProtocol = 01h: active sync
	  bInterfaceProtocol = 02h: Palm sync
	bInterfaceSubclass = 03h. Cable based association framework (Wireless USB)

FE	Application specific bInterfaceSubclass = 01h. Device firmware upgrade bInterfaceSubclass = 02h. IrDA bridge bInterfaceSubclass = 03h. Test and measurement
FF	Vendor specific (can instead be declared at the device level)

Values 01h–FEh are reserved for USB-defined classes. FFh indicates a vendor-defined class. Zero is reserved.

bInterfaceSubClass is similar to bDeviceSubClass in the device descriptor, but for devices with a class defined by the interface. If bInterfaceClass equals 00h, bInterfaceSubclass must equal 00h. If bInterfaceClass is in the range 01h–FEh, bInterfaceSubclass equals 00h or a code defined for the interface's class. FFh indicates a vendor-defined subclass.

bInterfaceProtocol is similar to bDeviceProtocol in the device descriptor, but for devices whose class is defined by the interface. The field can specify a protocol for the selected bInterfaceClass and bInterfaceSubClass. If bInterfaceClass is in the range 01h–FEh, bInterfaceProtocol must equal 00h or a code defined for the interface's class. FFh indicates a vendor-defined protocol.

iInterface is an index to a string that describes the interface. This value is zero if there is no string descriptor.

Endpoint

Each endpoint specified in an interface descriptor has an endpoint descriptor (Table 4-10). Endpoint zero never has a descriptor because every device must support endpoint zero, the device descriptor contains the maximum packet size, and the USB specification defines everything else about the endpoint. A host retrieves endpoint descriptors as subordinate descriptors sent in response to a request for a configuration descriptor.

Devices in the audio 1.0 class extend the endpoint descriptor with two additional bytes of audio-specific information. This is the only allowed extension that changes the length of a standard descriptor type. Where needed elsewhere, class and other specifications should define separate, subordinate descriptors that return extended information. For example, USB 3.0 defines the endpoint companion descriptor to return SuperSpeed-specific endpoint information.

bEndpointAddress specifies the endpoint number and direction. Bits 3..0 are the endpoint number. Low-speed devices can have a maximum of 3 endpoint numbers (usually in the range 0–2), while full- and high-speed devices can have 16 (0–15). Bit 7 is the direction, with OUT = 0 and IN = 1. Bits 6..4 are unused and must be zero.

bmAttributes sets bits 1..0 to specify the type of transfer the endpoint supports: 00=control, 01=isochronous, 10=bulk, 11=interrupt. Bits 7..6 are reserved and must be zero. The functions of the remaining bits vary with the endpoint type and speed.

Table 4-10: The endpoint descriptor provides information about an endpoint address.

Offset (decimal)	Field	Size (bytes)	Description
0	bLength	1	Descriptor size in bytes (07h)
1	bDescriptorType	1	The constant Endpoint (05h)
2	bEndpointAddress	1	Endpoint number and direction
3	bmAttributes	1	Transfer type and supplementary information
4	wMaxPacketSize	2	Maximum packet size supported
6	bInterval	1	Service interval or NAK rate

For isochronous endpoints, bits 5..2 can indicate a synchronization type and usage type of data or feedback.

For SuperSpeed interrupt endpoints, bits 5..4 indicate a usage type of Notification or Periodic. Interrupt endpoints have two primary uses with differing needs from the host. Some endpoints require quick response or frequent data transfers in consecutive intervals. For example, users don't want a noticeable delay before seeing the effect of pressing a key or moving a mouse. These endpoints should specify the Periodic usage. Other endpoints provide infrequent notifications or data where timing is less critical. An example is hub notifications that inform the host of device attachment, removal, or other events. The endpoints should specify the Notification usage. The host can use the Usage type in deciding whether to place a port in a low-power state that requires more time to exit. Any undefined bits are reserved.

wMaxPacketSize specifies the maximum number of data bytes the endpoint can transfer in a transaction. The allowed values vary with the device speed and type of transfer.

For USB 2.0, bits 10..0 are the maximum packet size with a range of 0–1024. For USB 1.x, the range is 0–1023. In USB 2.0, bits 12..11 indicate how many additional transactions per microframe a high-speed interrupt or isochronous endpoint supports: 00 = no additional transactions (total of 1 / microframe), 01 = one additional (total of 2 / microframe), 10 = 2 additional (total of 3 / microframe), 11 = reserved. In USB 1.x, these bits were reserved and zero. Bits 15..13 are reserved and zero.

For SuperSpeed bulk endpoints, the value is 1024. For SuperSpeed interrupt and isochronous endpoints, the allowed values depend on the value of bMax-Burst in the SuperSpeed endpoint companion descriptor. If bMaxBurst = 0, wMaxPacketSize can be in the range 0–1024 for isochronous endpoints and 1–1024 for interrupt endpoints. If bMaxBurst > 0, wMaxPacketSize = 1024.

bInterval specifies the service interval for interrupt and isochronous endpoints. The service interval is a period within which the host must reserve time for an endpoint's transactions. The period is an integral number of frames (low and full speed), microframes (high speed), or bus intervals (SuperSpeed). The allowed range and usage of bInterval varies with the device's speed, the transfer type, and the USB version.

For low-speed interrupt endpoints, bInterval is the maximum latency in ms in the range 10–255. For all full-speed interrupt endpoints and for full-speed isochronous endpoints on 1.x devices, the interval equals bInterval in ms. For interrupt endpoints, the value may range from 1–255. For isochronous endpoints in USB 1.x devices, the value must be 1. For isochronous endpoints in full-speed USB 2.0 devices, values 1–16 are allowed, and the interval is $2^{bInterval-1}$ in ms, allowing a range from 1 ms to 32.768 seconds.

For high-speed and SuperSpeed endpoints, the value is in units of 125 µs. The value for interrupt and isochronous endpoints may range from 1–16, and the interval is calculated as $2^{bInterval-1}$, allowing a range from 125 µs to 4.096 seconds.

For high-speed bulk and control OUT endpoints, the field can contain a maximum NAK rate used for compliance purposes only. Devices typically set the field to zero. For other bulk transfers and control transfers, the value is reserved.

SuperSpeed Endpoint Companion

Every SuperSpeed endpoint has a companion descriptor to support SuperSpeed capabilities. A host retrieves endpoint companion descriptors as subordinate descriptors sent in response to a request for a configuration descriptor when the configuration has one or more endpoints.

bMaxBurst specifies the maximum number of packets the endpoint can send or receive in a burst minus one. A value of zero means one packet per burst. The maximum value is 15, indicating 16 packets per burst. A Data Packet in a burst can transmit without waiting for an acknowledgement of the previous Data Packet in the burst.

bmAttributes provides information specific to bulk and isochronous endpoints. For bulk endpoints, bits 4..0 are a MaxStreams value that indicates the maximum number of streams the endpoint supports. Zero means the endpoint

Table 4-11: A SuperSpeed endpoint has a companion descriptor to provide a maximum burst value.

Offset (decimal)	Field	Size (bytes)	Description
0	bLength	1	Descriptor size in bytes (06h)
1	bDescriptorType	1	The constant SUPERSPEED_USB_ENDPOINT_COMPANION (30h)
2	bMaxBurst	1	The maximum number of packets the endpoint can send or receive as part of a burst - 1.
3	bmAttributes	1	For bulk endpoints, the maximum number of streams. For isochronous endpoints, the maximum number of packets in a service interval.
4	wBytesPerInterval	2	For periodic interrupt and isochronous endpoints, the maximum number of bytes the endpoint expects to transfer per service interval.

doesn't define streams. For values 1–16, the number of streams equals $2^{MaxStreams}$ for a maximum value of 65,536.

For isochronous endpoints, bits 1..0 are a Mult value that indicates, along with bMaxBurst, the maximum number of packets in a service interval. The maximum number of packets equals (bMaxBurst + 1) × (Mult + 1). Valid values for Mult are 0–2. The maximum allowed number of packets thus equals (15 + 1) × (2 + 1), or 48.

wBytesPerInterval is the maximum number of bytes a periodic interrupt or isochronous endpoint expects to transfer per service interval.

String

A string descriptor (Table 4-12) contains descriptive text. Other descriptors can contain indexes to strings that describe the manufacturer, product, serial number, configuration, and interface. Class- and vendor-specific descriptors can contain indexes to additional string descriptors. Support for string descriptors is optional, though a class may require them. A host retrieves a string descriptor by sending a Get Descriptor request with the high byte of the Setup transaction's wValue field equal to 03h.

When the host requests a string descriptor, the low byte of the wValue field is an index value. An index value of zero has the special function of requesting language IDs, while other index values request strings.

Table 4-12: A string descriptor identifies a supported language or stores a string of text.

Offset (decimal)	Field	Size (bytes)	Description
0	bLength	1	Descriptor size in bytes (variable)
1	bDescriptorType	1	The constant String (03h)
2	bSTRING or wLANGID	varies	For string descriptor zero, an array of one or more Language Identifier codes. For other string descriptors, a Unicode UTF-16LE string.

wLANGID[0...n] is valid for string descriptor zero only. This field contains one or more 16-bit language ID codes that indicate the languages the strings are available in. U.S. English (0409h) is likely to be the only code supported by an operating system. The wLANGID value must be valid for any string to be valid. Devices that return no string descriptors must not return an array of language IDs. The USB-IF's website has a list of defined USB language IDs.

bString is valid for string descriptors one and higher and contains a string in Unicode UTF-16LE format. In this format, most characters are encoded as 16-bit code units with the low byte of the code unit transmitted first. For U.S. English, the low byte of the code unit is the character's ASCII code. For example, the character *A* transmits as the byte 41h followed by 00h. Some rarely used characters are encoded as surrogate pairs consisting of two 16-bit code units. The strings are not null-terminated.

Binary Object Store and Device Capability

Some devices use additional descriptors to store information that is specific to a technology or a device function. To provide a standard way to provide this information, the Wireless USB specification introduced two new descriptor types. The USB 2.0 Link Power Management Addendum and USB 3.0 specification also incorporate these types.

The binary device object store (BOS) descriptor (Table 4-13) functions as a base descriptor for one or more related device capability descriptors. A device capability descriptor (Table 4-14) provides information about a specific capability or technology. These are the defined device capability descriptors:

- Wireless USB provides information about wireless features.
- USB 2.0 Extension indicates that a device supports the Link Power Management protocol when operating at low, full, or high speed. All Super-

Table 4-13: A binary device object store (BOS) descriptor provides a way to support descriptors that store additional information about a device.

Offset (decimal)	Field	Size (bytes)	Description
0	bLength	1	Descriptor size in bytes (05h).
1	bDescriptorType	1	BOS (0Fh)
2	wTotalLength	2	The number of bytes in this descriptor and all of its subordinate descriptors
4	bNumDeviceCaps	1	The number of device capability descriptors subordinate to this BOS descriptor.

Speed devices must provide this descriptor and must support Link Power Management when operating at high speed. USB 2.0 devices that support Link Power Management also provide this descriptor.

• SuperSpeed USB specifies which speeds the device supports, the lowest speed that provides full functionality, and power-management capabilities. All SuperSpeed devices must provide this descriptor.

• Container ID provides a 128-bit universally unique identifier (UUID) that identifies the device instance. The descriptor is mandatory for USB 3.0 hubs and optional for other SuperSpeed devices.

A host retrieves a BOS descriptor and all of its subordinate device capability descriptors by sending a Get Descriptor request with the high byte of the Setup transaction's wValue field set to 0Fh and the wLength field equal to the descriptor's wTotalLength value. There is no request for reading only a device capability descriptor.

Other Standard Descriptors

Other standard descriptor types are OTG and debug.

Devices that support On-The-Go's Host Negotiation Protocol (HNP) or Session Request Protocol (SRP) have an OTG descriptor that indicates the supported protocols. Chapter 20 has more about this descriptor.

Intel's proposed specification *USB2 Debug Device: A Functional Device Specification* defines a debug descriptor. A debug device connects to the optional debug port defined in the EHCI specification for high-speed host controllers. The debug port and device are intended to replace the RS-232 port that PCs have long used for debugging purposes.

Table 4-14: The device capability descriptor can provide information that is specific to a technology or another aspect of a device or its function.

Offset (decimal)	Field	Size (bytes)	Description
0	bLength	1	Descriptor length in bytes (varies).
1	bDescriptorType	1	DEVICE CAPABILITY (10h)
2	bDevCapabilityType	1	01h = Wireless USB 02h = USB 2.0 EXTENSION 03h = SUPERSPEED_USB 04h = CONTAINER ID 00h, 05h–FFH (reserved)
3	Capability-Dependent	varies	Capability-specific data and format.

Microsoft OS Descriptors

Microsoft OS descriptors enable storing Windows-specific information. Placing the information in descriptors means the information is available on attachment instead of requiring users to provide the information on separate media. The Microsoft OS string descriptor has an index of EEh and contains an embedded signature. Windows XP SP1 and later request this string descriptor from a device on first attachment. A device that doesn't support the descriptor should return STALL. On retrieving a Microsoft OS string descriptor, Windows may request one or more Microsoft OS feature descriptors. The extended compat ID feature descriptor contains Microsoft-defined IDs that can help Windows locate a driver for device functions that don't have Windows-provided drivers. The extended properties feature descriptor can provide text, icons, and other device-specific properties.

Updating Descriptors to USB 2.0

To update descriptors for a USB 1.x device to USB 2.0, all except some devices that have isochronous endpoints require just one change: in the device descriptor, bcdUSB must be 0200h or greater. As Chapter 3 explained, a USB 2.0 device's default interface(s) must request no isochronous bandwidth, so an interface that wants to do isochronous transfers must have at least one alternate interface setting, and the alternate interface descriptor will have at least one subordinate endpoint descriptor.

5

Control Transfers: Structured Requests for Critical Data

Of USB's four transfer types, control transfers have the most complex structure. They're also the only transfer type with functions defined by the USB specification. This chapter looks in greater detail at control transfers and the standard requests defined in the specification.

Elements of a Control Transfer

Control transfers enable the host and a device to exchange information about the device's capabilities and other class-specific or vendor-specific information. As Chapter 3 explained, a control transfer consists of a Setup stage, a Data stage (optional for some transfers), and a Status stage. Each stage consists of one or more transactions.

The descriptions below apply to USB 2.0 transfers. SuperSpeed transfers exchange the same information but use USB 3.0's packet structures and protocols as described in Chapter 3.

Setup Stage

The Setup stage consists of a Setup transaction, which identifies the transfer as a control transfer and transmits the request and other information that the device needs to complete the request.

Devices must return ACK for every Setup transaction received without error. An endpoint that is in the middle of another control transfer must abandon that transfer and acknowledge the new Setup transaction.

Token Packet

Purpose: identifies the receiver and identifies the transaction as a Setup transaction.

Sent by: the host.

PID: SETUP

Additional contents: the device and endpoint addresses.

Data Packet

Purpose: transmits the request and related information.

Sent by: the host.

PID: DATA0

Additional contents: eight bytes in five fields:

bmRequestType specifies the direction of data flow, the type of request, and the recipient.

Bit 7 (Direction) names the direction of data flow for data in the Data stage. Host to device (OUT) or no Data stage is zero; device to host (IN) is 1.

Bits 6..5 (Request Type) specify whether the request is one of USB's standard requests (00), a request defined for a specific USB class (01), or a request defined by a vendor-specific driver for use with a particular product or products (10).

Bits 4..0 (Recipient) define whether the request is directed to the device (00000) or to a specific interface (00001), endpoint (00010), or other element (00011) in the device.

bRequest identifies the request.

wValue can pass request-specific information to the device. Each request can define the meaning of these two bytes in its own way. For example, in a Set Address request, wValue contains the device's address.

wIndex can pass request-specific information to the device. A typical use is to pass an index or offset such as an interface or endpoint number, but each request can define the meaning of these two bytes in any way. When passing an endpoint index, bits 3..0 specify the endpoint number, and bit 7 = 0 for a Control or OUT endpoint or 1 for an IN endpoint. When passing an interface index, bits 7..0 are the interface number. All undefined bits are zero.

wLength is two bytes that contain the number of data bytes in the Data stage that follows. For a host-to-device transfer, wLength is the exact number of bytes the host intends to transfer. For a device-to-host transfer, wLength is a maximum, and the device may return this many bytes or fewer. If the field is zero, the transfer has no Data stage.

Handshake Packet

Purpose: transmits the device's acknowledgement.

Sent by: the device.

PID: ACK.

Additional contents: none. The handshake packet consists of the PID alone.

Comments: If the device detects an error in the received Setup or Data packet, the device returns no handshake. The device's hardware typically handles the error checking and sending of the ACK with no firmware support needed.

Data Stage

The Data stage, when present, consists of one or more IN or OUT transactions. A Data stage with IN transactions sends data to the host. An example is the Get Descriptor request, where the device sends a requested descriptor to the host. A Data stage with OUT transactions sends data to the device. An example is the HID-class request Set Report, where the host sends a report to a device. If wLength in the Setup transaction equals 0000h, the transfer has no Data stage. For example, in the Set Configuration request, the host passes a configuration value to the device in the wValue field of the Setup stage's data packet, so the transaction has no need for a Data stage.

If all of the data can't fit in one packet, the stage uses multiple transactions. In the device descriptor, bMaxPacketSize0 specifies the maximum number of data bytes per packet. The transactions in the Data stage are all in the same direction. When the Data stage is present but there is no data to transfer, the data packet is a ZLP.

The host uses split transactions in the Data stage when the device is low or full speed and a hub between the device and host connects upstream at high speed. The host may use the PING protocol when the device is high speed, the Data stage uses OUT transactions, and the stage has more than one data transaction.

Each IN or OUT transaction in the Data stage contains token, data, and handshake packets.

Token Packet

Purpose: identifies the receiver and identifies the transaction as an IN or OUT transaction.

Sent by: the host.

PID: If the request requires the device to send data to the host, the PID is IN. If the request requires the host to send data to the device, the PID is OUT.

Additional contents: the device and endpoint addresses.

Data Packet

Purpose: transfers all or a portion of the data specified in the wLength field of the Setup transaction's data packet.

Sent by: the device if the token packet's PID is IN or the host if the token packet's PID is OUT.

PID: The first packet is DATA1. Any additional packets in the Data stage alternate DATA0/DATA1.

Additional contents: The host sends data or a ZLP. A device may send data, a ZLP, STALL (unsupported request or halted endpoint), or NAK.

Handshake Packet

Purpose: the data packet's receiver returns status information.

Sent by: the receiver of the Data stage's data packet. If the token packet's PID is IN, the host sends the handshake packet. If the token packet's PID is OUT, the device sends the handshake packet.

PID: A device may return ACK (data received without error), NAK (endpoint busy), or STALL (unsupported request or halted endpoint). A high-speed device that is receiving multiple data packets may return NYET to indicate that the current transaction's data was accepted but the endpoint isn't yet ready for another data packet. A host can return only ACK.

Additional contents: none. The handshake packet consists of the PID alone.

Comments: If the receiver detected an error in the token or data packet, the receiver returns no handshake packet.

Status Stage

The Status stage completes the transfer. In some cases (such as after receiving the first packet of a device descriptor during enumeration), the host may begin the Status stage before the Data stage has completed, and the device must detect the token packet of the Status stage, abandon the Data stage, and complete the Status stage.

Token Packet

Purpose: identifies the receiver and indicates the direction of the Status stage's data packet.

Sent by: the host.

PID: the opposite of the direction of the previous transaction's data packet. If the Data stage's PID was OUT or if there was no Data stage, the Status stage's PID is IN. If the Data stage's PID was IN, the Status stage's PID is OUT.

Additional contents: the device and endpoint addresses.

Data Packet

Purpose: enables the receiver of the Data stage's data to indicate the status of the transfer.

Sent by: the device if the Status stage's token packet's PID is IN or the host if the Status stage's token packet's PID is OUT.

PID: DATA1

Additional contents: The host sends a ZLP. A device may send a ZLP (success), NAK (busy), or STALL (unsupported request or halted endpoint).

Comments: For most requests, a ZLP from the device indicates that the device has performed the requested action (if any). An exception is Set Address, where the device takes the requested action after the Status stage has completed.

Handshake Packet

Purpose: The sender of the Data stage's data indicates the status of the transfer.

Sent by: the receiver of the Status stage's data packet. If the Status stage's token packet's PID is IN, the host sends the handshake packet; if the token packet's PID is OUT, the device sends the data packet.

PID: A device may return ACK (success), NAK (busy), or STALL (unsupported request or halted endpoint). The host returns ACK in response to a data packet received without error.

Additional contents: none. The handshake packet consists of the PID alone.

Comments: The Status stage's handshake packet is the final transmission in the transfer. If the receiver detected an error in the token or data packet, the receiver returns no handshake packet.

For any request that's expected to take many milliseconds to carry out, the protocol should define an alternate way to determine when the request has completed. Doing so ensures that the host doesn't waste a lot of time asking for an acknowledgement that will take a long time to appear. An example is the Set Port Feature(PORT_RESET) request sent to a hub. The reset signal lasts at least 10 ms. Rather than making the host wait this long for the device to complete the request, the hub acknowledges receiving the request when the hub first places the port in the reset state. When the reset is complete, the hub sets a bit that the host can retrieve at its leisure via a Get Port Status request.

Handling Errors

A device might receive a request that firmware doesn't support. Or a device may be unable to respond because the endpoint is in the Halt condition, the firmware has crashed, or the device is no longer attached to the bus. A host may also decide to end a transfer early for any reason.

An example of an unsupported request is one that uses a request code that the device's firmware doesn't know how to respond to. Or a device may support the request but other information in the Setup stage doesn't match what the device expects or supports. On these occasions, a Request Error condition exists and the device notifies the host by sending STALL. Devices must respond to the

Setup transaction with an ACK, so the STALL transmits in the Data or Status stage. When possible, the device should return STALL in the Data stage.

On failing to get a response or on detecting an error in received data or a Halt condition at the endpoint, the host abandons the transfer. The host then tries to re-establish communications with the endpoint by sending the token packet for a new Setup transaction. If a new token packet doesn't cause the device to recover, the host requests the device's hub to reset the device's port.

The host may also end a transfer early by beginning the Status stage before completing all of the Data stage's transactions. In this case, the device must respond to the Status stage in the same way as if all of the data had transferred.

Device Firmware

USB 2.0 device firmware typically performs the steps below to support control transfers. The implementation details vary with the device architecture and programming language.

Control Write Requests with a Data Stage

To complete a control write request with a Data stage, the device must detect the request in the Setup stage, accept the data in the Data stage, and send a ZLP in the Status stage.

1. Device hardware detects a received Setup packet, stores the contents of the transaction's data packet, returns ACK, and triggers an interrupt.

2. On detecting the interrupt, the device decodes the request and ensures that endpoint zero is ready to accept data that arrives following an OUT token packet. The endpoint must also ACK a new Setup packet if the host decides to abandon the transfer and should return a ZLP in response to an IN token packet, which indicates that the host is ending the transfer early.

3. The Data stage begins when the host sends an OUT token packet to endpoint zero. The endpoint stores the received data and returns ACK in the handshake packet. The hardware triggers an interrupt.

4. On detecting the interrupt, the device processes the received data as needed.

5. If the Data stage has additional data packets, steps 3 and 4 repeat for additional OUT transactions up to the wLength value in the Setup transaction.

6. To complete the transfer, the host sends an IN token packet, the device responds with a ZLP, and the host returns ACK.

Control Write Requests with No Data Stage

To complete a control write request without a Data stage, the device must detect the request in the Setup stage and send a ZLP in the Status stage.

1. The hardware detects a Setup packet, stores the contents of the transaction's data packet, returns ACK, and triggers an interrupt.

2. On detecting the interrupt, the device decodes the request, does what is needed to perform the requested action, and arms endpoint zero to respond to an IN token packet. The endpoint must also ACK a new Setup packet if the host decides to abandon the transfer.

3. To complete the transfer, the host sends an IN token packet, the device responds with a ZLP, and the host returns ACK.

Control Read Requests

To complete a control read request, the device must detect the request in the Setup stage, send data in the Data stage, and acknowledge a received handshake in the Status stage.

1. The hardware detects a Setup packet, stores the contents of the transaction's data packet, returns ACK, and triggers an interrupt.

2. On detecting the interrupt, the device decodes the request and arms endpoint zero to send the requested data on receiving an IN token packet. The endpoint must also ACK a new Setup packet if the host decides to abandon the transfer and must return a ZLP in response to an OUT packet if the host begins the Status stage early.

3. The Data stage begins when the host sends an IN token packet to endpoint zero. The device hardware sends the data, detects the received ACK from the host, and triggers an interrupt.

4. On detecting the interrupt, a device that has more data to send arms the endpoint to send the data on receiving another IN token packet, and steps 3 and 4 repeat.

5. On receiving an OUT token packet followed by a ZLP, the endpoint returns ACK to complete the transfer.

Standard Requests

Table 5-1 summarizes the requests defined in the USB 2.0 and USB 3.0 specifications.

Table 5-1: The USB specification defines these requests for control transfers.

Request Code Request Name	Target	wValue	wIndex	Data Stage	
				Data Source	wLength; Contents
00h Get Status	device, interface, or endpoint	0000h	0000h (device), interface, or endpoint	device	0002h; status
01h Clear Feature	device, interface, or endpoint	feature	0000h (device), interface, or endpoint	none	0000h
03h Set Feature	device, interface, or endpoint	feature	0000h (device), interface, or endpoint	none	0000h
05h Set Address	device	device address	0000h	none	0000h
06h Get Descriptor	device	descriptor type and index	0000h or language ID	device	descriptor length (bytes); descriptor
07h Set Descriptor	device	descriptor type and index	0000h or language ID	host	descriptor length (bytes); descriptor
08h Get Configuration	device	0000h	0000h	device	0001h; configuration
09h Set Configuration	device	configuration	0000h	none	0000h
0Ah Get Interface	interface	0000h	interface	device	0001h; alternate setting
0Bh Set Interface	interface	interface	interface	none	0000h
0Ch Synch Frame	endpoint	0000h	endpoint	device	0002h; frame number
30h Set SEL	device	0000h	0000h	host	0006h; exit latency values
31h Set Isochronous Delay	device	Delay in ns	0000h	none	0000h

Get Status

Purpose: The host requests the status of the features of a device, interface, or endpoint.

Request Number (bRequest): 00h

Source of Data: device

Data Length (wLength): 0002h

Contents of wValue field: 0000h

Contents of wIndex field: For a device, 0000h. For an interface, the interface number. For an endpoint, the endpoint number.

Contents of data packet in the Data stage: the device, interface, or endpoint status.

Supported states: Default: undefined. Address: OK for address zero, endpoint zero. Otherwise the device returns STALL. Configured: OK.

Behavior on error: The device returns STALL if the target interface or endpoint doesn't exist.

Comments: For requests directed to devices operating at USB 2.0 speeds, two status bits are defined. Bit zero is the Self-Powered field: 0 = bus-powered, 1 = self-powered. The host can't change this value. Bit 1 is the Remote Wakeup field. The default on reset is zero (disabled). SuperSpeed devices support the Self-Powered bit and use bits 2–4 for power-management options. Bit 2 = 1 means the device is enabled to initiate U1 entry. Bit 3 = 1 means the device is enabled to initiate U2 entry. Bit 4 = 1 means the device is enabled to send Latency Tolerance Messages.

For request directed to the first interface in a function on a USB 3.0 bus, bit 0 = 1 if the function supports remote wakeup, and bit 1 = 1 if the host has enabled the function for remote wakeup. For requests directed to an interface on a USB 2.0 bus, all bits are reserved.

For requests directed to an endpoint, only bit zero is defined. Bit 0 = 1 indicates a Halt condition.

See Set Feature and Clear Feature for more about Remote Wakeup and Halt. All non-assigned bits are reserved.

Clear Feature

Purpose: The host requests to disable a feature on a device, interface, or endpoint.

Request Number (bRequest): 01h.

Source of Data: no Data stage

Data Length (wLength): 0000h

Contents of wValue field: the feature to disable

Contents of wIndex field: For a device feature, 0000h. For an interface feature, the interface number. For an endpoint feature, the endpoint number.

Supported states: Default: undefined. Address: OK for address zero, endpoint zero. Otherwise the device returns a STALL. Configured: OK.

Behavior on error: If the feature, device, or endpoint specified doesn't exist, or if the feature can't be cleared, the device responds with STALL. Behavior is undefined if wLength > 0000h.

Comments: For USB 2.0, this request can clear the DEVICE_REMOTE_WAKEUP and ENDPOINT_HALT features. The request does not clear the TEST_MODE feature.

For SuperSpeed, this request can clear the ENDPOINT_HALT, LTM_ENABLE, U1_ENABLE, and U2_ENABLE features. (To clear the FUNCTION_SUSPEND feature, see Set Feature.)

Clear Feature(ENDPOINT_HALT) resets a bulk, interrupt, or isochronous data toggle to DATA0 (USB 2.0) or Sequence Number to zero (SuperSpeed) and resets a SuperSpeed bulk endpoint's burst size.

Hubs support additional features.

See also Set Feature and Get Status.

Set Feature

Purpose: The host requests to enable a feature on a device, interface, or endpoint.

Request Number (bRequest): 03h

Source of Data: no Data stage

Data Length (wLength): 0000h

Contents of wValue field: the feature to enable

Contents of wIndex field: The low byte equals 00h for a device, the interface number for an interface, or the endpoint number for an endpoint. For a USB 3.0 FUNCTION_SUSPEND request, the high byte can request the Suspend state (bit 0 = 1) or normal operation (bit 0 = 1) and remote wakeup enabled (bit 1 = 1) or disabled (bit 1 = 0).

Supported states: For features other than TEST_MODE: Default: undefined. Address: OK for address zero, endpoint zero. Otherwise the device returns STALL. Configured: OK. High speed must support the TEST_MODE feature in the Default, Address, and Configured states.

Behavior on error: If the endpoint or interface specified doesn't exist, the device responds with STALL.

Comments: USB 2.0 defines these features:

ENDPOINT_HALT (0000h) applies to endpoints. Bulk and interrupt endpoints must support the Halt condition. Events that cause a Halt condition are transmission errors and the device's receiving a Set Feature request to halt the endpoint. DEVICE_REMOTE_WAKEUP (0001h) applies to devices. When the host has set this feature, a device in the Suspend state can request the host to resume communications. TEST_MODE (0002h) applies to devices. Setting this feature causes an upstream-facing port to enter a test mode. Chapter 18 has more about test mode.

SuperSpeed supports ENDPOINT_HALT and these features:

FUNCTION_SUSPEND (00h) applies to interfaces and can place a function in the Suspend state and enable or disable remote wakeup. U1_ENABLE (30h) and U2_ENABLE (31h) apply to devices and enable the U1 and U2 low-power states. LTM_ENABLE (32h) applies to devices and enables sending Latency Tolerance Messages, where a device provides information the host can use in power management. Chapter 16 has more about power management.

Hubs support additional features. The Get Status request tells the host what features, if any, are enabled. Also see Clear Feature.

Set Address

Purpose: The host specifies an address to use in future communications with the device.

Request Number (bRequest): 05h

Source of Data: no Data stage

Data Length (wLength): 0000h

Contents of wValue field: new device address. Allowed values are 0001h–007Fh. Each device on the bus, including the root hub, has a unique address.

Contents of wIndex field: 0000h

Supported States: Default, Address.

Behavior on error: not specified.

Comments: When a hub enables a port after power-up or attachment, the port uses the default address of 0000h until completing a Set Address request from the host.

This request is unlike most other requests because the device doesn't carry out the request until the device has completed the Status stage of the request by sending a ZLP. The host sends the Status stage's token packet to the default address, so the device must detect and respond to this packet before changing its address.

After completing this request, all communications use the new address.

A device using the default address of 0000h is in the Default state. After completing a Set_ Address request to set an address other than 0000h, the device enters the Address state.

A device must send the handshake packet within 50 ms after receiving the request and must implement the request within 2 ms after completing the Status stage.

Get Descriptor

Purpose: The host requests a specific descriptor.

Request Number (bRequest): 06h

Source of Data: device

Data Length (wLength): the number of bytes to return. If the descriptor is longer than wLength, the device returns up to wLength bytes. If the descriptor is shorter than wLength, the device returns the entire descriptor. If the descriptor is shorter than wLength and is an even multiple of the endpoint's maximum packet size, the device returns a ZLP in response to a request for more data after the device has sent the descriptor. The host detects the end of the data on receiving either the requested amount of data or a data packet containing less than the maximum packet size (including a ZLP).

Contents of wValue field: High byte: descriptor type. Low byte: descriptor index, to specify which descriptor to return when there are multiple descriptors of the same type.

Contents of wIndex field: for String descriptors, Language ID. Otherwise 0000h.

Contents of data packet in the Data stage: the requested descriptor.

Supported states: Default, Address, Configured.

Behavior on error: A device that doesn't support the specified descriptor should return STALL.

Comments: Hosts can request the following standard descriptor types: device, device_qualifier, configuration, other_speed configuration, BOS, and string. On receiving a request for a configuration or other_speed configuration descriptor, the device should return the requested descriptor followed by all of its subordinate interface, endpoint, endpoint companion, and class- and vendor-specific descriptors, up to the number of bytes requested. A class or vendor can define additional descriptors that the host can request, such as the HID-class report descriptor. See also Set Descriptor.

Set Descriptor

Purpose: The host adds a descriptor or updates an existing descriptor.

Request Number (bRequest): 07h

Source of Data: host

Data Length (wLength): The number of bytes the host will transfer to the device.

Contents of wValue field: high byte: descriptor type. (See Get Descriptor). Low byte: a descriptor index that specifies which descriptor the device is sending when it has multiple descriptors of the same type.

Contents of wIndex field: For string descriptors, Language ID. Otherwise 0000h.

Contents of data packet in the Data stage: descriptor length.

Supported states: Address and Configured.

Behavior on error: A device that doesn't support the request or the specified descriptor should return STALL.

Comments: This request makes it possible for the host to add new descriptors or change an existing descriptor. Few devices support this request, which could enable errant code to place incorrect information in a descriptor. See also Get Descriptor.

Get Configuration

Purpose: The host requests the value of the current device configuration.

Request Number (bRequest): 08h

Source of Data: device

Data Length (wLength): 0001h

Contents of wValue field: 0000h

Contents of wIndex field: 0000h

Contents of data packet in the Data stage: Configuration value

Supported states: Address (returns zero), Configured

Behavior on error: not specified.

Comments: A device that isn't configured returns 00h in the Data stage. See also Set Configuration.

Set Configuration

Purpose: The host requests the device to use the specified configuration.

Request Number (bRequest): 09h

Source of Data: no Data stage

Data Length (wLength): 0000h

Contents of wValue field: The low byte specifies a configuration. If the value matches a configuration supported by the device, the device implements the requested configuration. A value of 00h indicates not configured, and the device should enter the Address state and wait for a new Set Configuration request to be configured.

Contents of wIndex field: 0000h

Supported states: Address, Configured.

Behavior on error: If wValue isn't equal to 0000h or a configuration supported by the device, the device returns STALL.

Comments: After completing a Set Configuration request specifying a supported configuration, the device enters the Configured state. Many standard requests require the device to be in the Configured state. See also Get Configuration. This request resets bulk, interrupt, and isochronous data toggles to DATA0 (USB 2.0) or Sequence Numbers to zero (SuperSpeed) and resets the burst size of SuperSpeed bulk endpoints.

Get Interface

Purpose: For interfaces that have alternate, mutually exclusive settings, the host requests the currently active interface setting.

Request Number (bRequest): 0Ah

Source of Data: device

Data Length (wLength): 0001h

Contents of wValue field: 0000h

Contents of wIndex field: interface number (bInterfaceNumber)

Contents of data packet in the Data stage: the current setting (bAlternateSetting)

Supported states: Configured

Behavior on error: If the interface doesn't exist, the device returns STALL.

Comments: The wIndex value refers to the bInterfaceNumber value of an interface descriptor and indicates which interface the request applies to. In the Data stage, the device returns a bAlternateSetting value, which identifies which alternate interface setting the device is currently using. Each alternate interface has an interface descriptor and subordinate descriptors as needed. Many interfaces support only one interface setting. See also Set Interface.

Set Interface

Purpose: For interfaces that have alternate, mutually exclusive, settings, the host requests the device to use a specific interface setting.

Request Number (bRequest): 0Bh

Source of Data: no Data stage

Data Length (wLength): 0000h

Contents of wValue field: alternate setting to select (bAlternateSetting)

Contents of wIndex field: interface number (bInterfaceNumber)

Supported states: Configured

Behavior on error: If the requested interface or setting doesn't exist, the device returns STALL.

Comments: This request resets bulk, interrupt, and isochronous data toggles to DATA0 (USB 2.0) or Sequence Numbers to zero (SuperSpeed) and resets the burst size of SuperSpeed bulk endpoints. See also Get Interface.

Synch Frame

Purpose: The device sets and reports an endpoint's synchronization frame.

Request Number (bRequest): 0Ch

Source of Data: host

Data Length (wLength): 0002h

Contents of wValue field: 0000h

Contents of wIndex field: endpoint number

Contents of data packet in the Data stage: frame number

Supported states: Default: undefined. Address: The device returns STALL. Configured: OK.

Behavior on error: An endpoint that doesn't support the request should return STALL.

Comments: In isochronous transfers, a device endpoint may request data packets that vary in size according to a sequence. For example, an endpoint may send a repeating sequence of 8, 8, 8, 64 bytes. The Synch Frame request enables the host and endpoint to agree on which frame will begin the sequence.

On receiving a Synch Frame request, an endpoint returns the number of the frame that will precede the beginning of a new sequence

This request is rarely used because there is rarely a need for the information it provides.

Set SEL

Purpose: For SuperSpeed devices, sets system exit latencies for power management.

Request Number (bRequest): 31h

Source of Data: host

Data Length (wLength): 0006h

Contents of wValue field: 0000h

Contents of wIndex field: 0000h

Contents of data packet in the Data stage: exit latency values.

Supported states: Address, Configured.

Behavior on error: A device that doesn't support the request should return STALL.

Comments: Chapter 16 has more on SuperSpeed power management.

Set Isochronous Delay

Purpose: For SuperSpeed devices, specifies the amount of time between when a host transmits an isochronous packet and when a device will receive the packet.

Request Number (bRequest): 30h

Source of Data: host

Data Length (wLength): 0000h

Contents of wValue field: Delay in ns.

Contents of wIndex field: 0000h.

Supported states: Default, Address, Configured.

Behavior on error: a device that doesn't support the request should return STALL.

Comments: the wValue field can range from 0000h to FFFFh.

Other Requests

In addition to the requests defined in the USB 2.0 and USB 3.0 specifications, a device may respond to class-specific and vendor-specific control requests.

Class-Specific Requests

A class can define mandatory and optional requests. Class drivers on the host should support the mandatory requests and may support optional requests. Some requests are unrelated to the standard requests, while others build on standard requests by defining class-specific fields. An example of a request that's unrelated to standard requests is the Get_Max_LUN request supported by some mass-storage devices. The host uses this request to find out the number of logical units the interface supports. An example of a request that builds on an existing request is the Get Port Status request for hubs. This request is structured like the standard Get Status request but bits 4..0 = 00011 indicate that the request applies to a unit other than the device, an interface, or an endpoint. (The request applies to a port on a hub.) The wIndex field contains the port number.

Vendor-Defined Requests

Implementing a vendor-defined request in a control transfer requires all of the following:

- Vendor-defined fields as needed in the Setup and Data stages of the request. Bits 6..5 in the Setup stage's data packet are set to 10 to indicate a vendor-defined request.

- In the device, code that detects the request number in the Setup packet and knows how to respond.

- In the host, a vendor-specific device driver that supports the request. The driver can expose a function that enables applications to initiate the request.

6

Chip Choices

This chapter is a guide to selecting a device controller. The chips covered include USB 2.0 controllers with basic USB support as well as more full-featured, high-end chips. Chapter 20 discusses controllers for use in USB On-The-Go devices. For information on USB 3.0 controllers as they become available, visit *www.Lvr.com*

Components of a USB Device

Every USB device must have the intelligence to detect and respond to requests and other events at the USB port. A programmed microcontroller or an application-specific integrated circuit (ASIC) can perform these functions in a device.

Device-controller chips vary in how they implement USB communications and in how much firmware support the communications require. Some controllers require little more than accessing buffers to provide and retrieve USB data. Others require device firmware to handle more of the protocol, including managing the sending of descriptors to the host, setting data-toggle values, and ensuring that endpoints return appropriate handshake packets. In general, low-level firmware isn't portable among chips with different architectures, but chip companies provide example firmware for common tasks and applications.

A USB device controller contains a USB port along with whatever buffers, registers, and other I/O capabilities the controller requires to accomplish its tasks. Some device controllers include a general-purpose CPU and on-chip program and data memory or an interface to these in external memory. Other device controllers must interface to an external CPU that handles non-USB tasks and communicates with the USB controller as needed. These chips are sometimes called USB interface chips to distinguish them from microcontrollers with USB capabilities.

For high-volume products and products that require fast performance, an option is a custom-designed ASIC. Several sources offer synthesizable VHDL and Verilog source code for ASICs that function as USB controllers.

Inside a USB 2.0 Controller

A typical USB 2.0 controller contains a USB transceiver, a serial interface engine, buffers to hold USB data, and registers to store configuration, status, and control information relating to USB communications.

The Transceiver

The USB transceiver is the hardware interface between the device's USB connector and the circuits that control USB communications. The transceiver is typically embedded in the chip, but some controllers allow interfacing to an external transceiver.

The Serial Interface Engine

The circuits that interface to the transceiver form a unit called the serial interface engine (SIE). The SIE handles sending and receiving data in transactions. The SIE doesn't interpret or use the data but just places provided data on the bus and stores any data received. A typical SIE does all of the following:

- Detect incoming packets.
- Send packets.
- Detect and generate Start-of-Packet, EOP, Reset, and Resume signaling.
- Encode and decode data for the bus using NRZI encoding with bit stuffing.
- Check and generate CRC values.

- Check and generate Packet IDs.
- Convert between USB's serial data and parallel data in registers or memory.

Buffers

USB controllers use buffers to store received data and data that's ready to transmit on the bus. In some chips, such as PLX Technology's NET2272, the CPU accesses the buffers by reading and writing to registers, while others, such as Cypress Semiconductor's EZ-USB series, reserve a portion of data memory for the buffers.

To enable faster transfers, some chips have double buffers that can store two full sets of data in each direction. While one block is transmitting, firmware can write the next block of data into the other buffer so the data is ready to go as soon as the first block finishes transmitting. In the receive direction, the extra buffer enables a new transaction's data to arrive before the firmware has retrieved the data from the previous transaction. The hardware automatically switches, or ping-pongs, between the two buffers. Some controllers, such as the Cypress EZ-USB FX2 series, support quadruple buffers.

Configuration, Status, and Control Information

USB controller chips typically have registers that hold information about what endpoints are enabled, the number of bytes received, the number of bytes ready to transmit, Suspend-state status, error-checking information, and other status and control information. The number of registers, their contents, and how to access the registers vary with the chip architecture. These differences are one reason why low-level firmware for USB communications typically isn't portable between chip families.

Clock

USB communications require a timing source, typically provided by a crystal oscillator. Because USB's low speed allows more variation in clock speed, low-speed devices can sometimes use a less expensive ceramic resonator. Some controllers have on-chip oscillators and don't require an external timing source.

Other Device Components

In addition to a USB interface, the circuits in a typical USB device include a CPU, program and data memory, other I/O interfaces, and other features such as timers and counters. These circuits may be in the controller chip or in separate components.

CPU

An on-chip CPU in a microcontroller may be based on a general-purpose architecture such as the 8051, or the CPU may have an architecture developed specifically for USB applications. An interface-only USB controller can communicate with any CPU that has a compatible interface.

Program Memory

The program memory holds the code that the CPU executes, including code for USB communications and whatever other tasks the chip is responsible for. This memory may be in the microcontroller or in a separate chip.

The program storage may use ROM, flash memory, EEPROM, EPROM, or RAM. All except RAM (unless battery-backed) are nonvolatile: the memory retains its data after powering down. Chips that can access memory off-chip may support a megabyte or more of program memory.

Another name for the code stored in program memory is firmware. The term suggests that the memory is nonvolatile and not as easily changed as program code that can be loaded into RAM, edited, and re-saved on disk. This book uses the term firmware to refer to a controller's program code, with the understanding that the code may reside in a variety of memory types, some more volatile than others.

ROM (read-only memory) must be mask-programmed at the factory and can't be erased. ROM is practical only for product runs in the thousands.

Flash memory is electrically erasable and thus is popular for use during project development and for final code storage in low-volume projects or devices that might require firmware updates in the field. Current flash-memory technology enables around 100,000 erase/reprogram cycles.

EPROM (erasable programmable ROM) is reprogrammable but is not electrically erasable and thus has been replaced by flash memory in recent chips.

EEPROM (electrically erasable PROM) tends to have longer access times than flash memory but is useful for storing data that changes occasionally such as configuration data. Cypress' EZ-USB controllers can store firmware in EEPROM and load the firmware into RAM on powering up. EEPROMs are available with parallel interfaces and with synchronous serial interfaces such as

Microwire, I²C, and SPI. Current EEPROM technology enables around 10 million erase/reprogram cycles.

RAM (random-access memory) can be erased and rewritten endlessly, but the stored data disappears when the chip powers down. RAM can store program code if using battery backup or if the code loads from a PC into RAM on each power up. Cypress Semiconductor's EZ-USB chips can use RAM for program storage with special hardware and driver code that loads code from the host computer into the chip on power up or attachment. RAM loaded in this way has no limit on the number of erase/rewrite cycles. For battery-backed RAM, the limit is the battery life. Access time for RAM is fast.

Data Memory

Data memory provides temporary storage during program execution. The contents of data memory may include data received from the USB port, data to be sent to the USB port, values for use in calculations, or anything else the chip needs to remember or keep track of. Data memory is RAM.

Other I/O

To do useful work, virtually every USB controller has an interface to the world outside itself in addition to the USB port. An interface-only chip must have a local bus or other interface to the device's CPU. Most chips also have a series of general-purpose input and output (I/O) pins that can connect to other circuits. A chip may have built-in support for other serial interfaces, such as an asynchronous interface for RS-232, or synchronous serial interfaces. Some chips have dedicated interfaces for special purposes such as accessing drives or audio components.

Other Features

A device-controller chip may have additional features such as hardware timers, counters, analog-to-digital and digital-to-analog converters, and pulse-width-modulation (PWM) outputs. Just about anything that you might find in a general-purpose microcontroller is available in a USB device controller.

Simplifying Device Development

Project development will be easier and quicker if you can find a controller chip with all of the following:

- A chip architecture and compiler you're familiar with.
- Excellent hardware documentation.
- Well-documented, bug-free example firmware for an application similar to yours.
- A development system that enables easy downloading and debugging of firmware.

Also helpful is the ability to use a class driver included with the operating system or a well-documented and bug-free driver provided by the chip company or another source.

These are not trivial considerations. The right choices will save you many hours and much aggravation.

Device Requirements

In selecting a device controller suitable for a project, these are some of the areas to consider:

Speed. A device's rate of data transfer depends on the supported speeds on the device and bus, the transfer type. and how busy the bus is. As a device designer, you don't control how busy a user's bus will be, but you can select a speed and transfer type that give the best possible performance for your application.

If a product requires no more than low-speed interrupt and control transfers, a low-speed chip might save money in circuit-board design, components, and cables. But low-speed devices can transfer only up to eight data bytes per transaction, and the USB specification limits the guaranteed bandwidth for an interrupt endpoint to 800 bytes per second, much less than the bus speed of 1.5 Mbps. Plus, implementing low speed's slower edge rates increases the manufacturing cost of low-speed controller chips, so you may find a full-speed chip that can do the job at the same or lower price.

Compared to low and full speeds, circuit-board design for high-speed devices is more critical and can add to the cost of a product. If possible, devices that support high speed should also support full speed so they will work with USB 1.x hosts and hubs.

Endpoints. Each endpoint address supports a transfer type and direction. A device that uses only control transfers needs just the default endpoint. Interrupt, bulk, or isochronous transfers require additional endpoint addresses. Not all chips support all transfer types. Not every controller supports the maximum possible number of endpoint addresses, but few devices need the maximum.

Firmware upgrades. For firmware upgrades in the field, store program code in flash memory, in EEPROM, or in RAM loaded from the host on attachment. The *Device Firmware Upgrade* USB class specification defines a protocol for loading firmware from a host to a device. Chapter 7 has more about this class.

Cables. One reason why mice are almost certain to be low-speed devices is the less stringent cable requirements that allow thinner, more flexible cables. A cable on a low-speed device has a maximum length of 3 m, while full- and high-speed cables can be 5 m.

Other needs. Additional considerations are the amount and type of other I/O, the size of program and data memory, on-chip timers, and other special features that a particular application might require.

Chip Documentation

Most chip companies supplement their data sheets with technical manuals, application notes, example code, and other documentation. The best way to get a head start on writing firmware is to begin with example code.

Example code can be useful even if it doesn't perfectly match your desired application. Enumeration code is useful for any device and also provides a model for performing control transfers for other purposes. Get Descriptor can serve as a model for other control read transfers. Set Address can serve as a model for control write transfers with no Data stage. Example code for control write transfers with a Data stage is harder to find. The only standard, not-class-specific USB request with a host-to-device Data stage is the rarely supported Set Descriptor. One possibility is in code for the communications device class with support for the class-specific Set Line Coding request, where the host sends serial-port parameters in the Data stage.

From the firmware's point of view, bulk and interrupt transfers are identical (except for SuperSpeed's support for streams in bulk transfers) so code for either type of transfer (such as HID code for exchanging reports via interrupt transfers) can serve as a model for any firmware that uses bulk or interrupt transfers.

Chip and tool vendors vary in the amount and quality of documentation and example code provided. You might also find code examples from others who are willing to share their work.

Driver Choices

If your device fits into a class supported by the operating system(s) that the device's USB hosts use, you don't have to write or obtain a device driver. For example, applications can access a HID-class device using standard API functions that communicate with the HID drivers included with Windows.

Some chip companies provide a generic driver that you can use to exchange data with devices. Cypress Semiconductor, Microchip Technology, and Silicon Laboratories all have general-purpose drivers. Devices for Windows systems also have the option of using Microsoft's generic WinUSB driver. Chapter 7 and Chapter 8 have more about classes and device drivers.

Debugging Tools

Ease of debugging also makes a big difference in how easy it is to get a project up and running. Products that can help include development boards and software offered by chip companies and other sources. A protocol analyzer can save much debugging time. Chapter 17 has more about protocol analyzers.

Boards from Chip Companies

Chip manufacturers offer development boards and debugging software to make it easier for developers to test and debug new designs. A development board enables you to load a program from a PC into a chip's program memory or circuits that emulate the chip's hardware.

Typical debugging software provided with development boards is a monitor program that runs on a PC and enables you to control program execution and view the results. Common features include the ability to step through a program, set breakpoints, and view the contents of the chip's registers and memory. You can run the monitor program and a test application at the same time. You can see exactly what happens inside the chip when it communicates with your application.

USB's timing requirements can limit what you can do with breakpoints. For example, if you halt execution during enumeration, the host will give up, and you'll need to restart the enumeration process. But even so, a monitor program can provide a useful window to the firmware in action.

The Silicon Laboratories C8051F34x controllers include a dedicated 2-wire debugging interface that uses no additional memory or port bits on the chip. With these chips, you can debug without needing to assign other chip resources to debugging.

Boards from Other Sources

If you're on a limited budget, inexpensive printed-circuit boards from a variety of vendors can serve as an alternative to the development kits offered by chip manufacturers. You can also use these boards as the base for one-of-a-kind or small-scale projects, saving the time and expense of designing and making a board for the controller chip. Boards that include firmware and a host driver make it easy to exchange data with the device.

I/O Boards. A typical board contains a USB controller and connector along with I/O pins that you can connect to external circuits of your own design. The EZ-USB family is a natural choice for this type of board because its firmware is downloadable from the host so you don't need additional programming hardware.

Figure 6-1 shows two high-speed USB boards with EZ-USB chips: the USBee EX2 Experimenter's Board from CWAV, Inc. and the QuickUSB Module from Bitwise Systems, Inc. Both boards contain programmed Cypress EZ-USB FX2 controllers. Both companies provide host drivers for generic I/O including accessing a high-speed parallel port, and example applications in multiple programming languages. The USBee FX2's driver enables configuring and reading and writing to an 8-bit port. The QuickUSB's driver and user libraries enable accessing up to five 8-bit ports and provides functions to support a parallel port, asynchronous serial ports, I^2C and SPI communications, and configuring FPGAs. A stacking connector mates with an adapter board with headers for accessing the ports. Two asynchronous serial ports have RS-232 interfaces.

Another option is the USBI2C/IO (Figure 6-2) from DeVaSys Embedded Systems. This board contains a Silicon Laboratories full-speed USB C8051F340 with 63 KB of flash memory. Headers provide access to 31 I/O bits plus an I^2C port. DeVaSys provides firmware, a host driver for accessing ports and I^2C communications, and example applications.

Emulating a Device with a PC. Using a PC to emulate a device is another option for developing. You can use the compilers, debuggers, and other software tools you're familiar with on your PC and compile, run, and debug the device code on the PC. PLX Technology's NET2272 Rapid Development Kit

Figure 6-1. Two development boards for the Cypress EZ-USB FX2 are Bitwise Systems, Inc.'s QuickUSB Module (left, shown with adapter board) and CWAV, Inc.'s USBee EX2 Experimenter's Board (right).

(RDK) enables using a PC as a device when developing code using PLX Technology's NET2272 USB interface chip. The kit includes a PCI card with a header that attaches to a daughter card that contains a NET2272. You can install the PCI card in a PC and write applications that perform the role of device firmware that communicates with the interface chip. The application can run as a console application on the PC.

The USB connector on the PCI card can connect to any USB host. When development on the emulated device is complete, you can port the firmware to run on the CPU that the final design will use. If you want to use the development kit's circuits, you can remove the daughter board from the PCI card and wire the daughter board to your device's hardware.

The emulated device may have timing differences, and the may not have the same hardware architecture as the target device, but the ease of developing on a PC can help in getting the code for enumerating and basic data transfers working quickly.

Figure 6-2. The DeVaSys USB I2C/IO board contains a Silicon Labs C8051F340, which has an on-chip debug port.

USB Microcontrollers

If you have a favorite CPU family, the chances are good that a USB-capable variant is available. The family with the most sources for device controllers is the venerable 8051. Although Intel, the 8051's creator, no longer offers USB-capable 8051s, other manufacturers do. Table 6-1 lists chips that are compatible with this and other microcontroller families.

For common applications such as keyboards, drives, and interface converters, application-specific controllers include hardware to support a particular application. Chapter 7 has more about controllers for specific applications.

The following descriptions of USB controllers with embedded CPUs will give an idea of the range of chips available. The chips described are a sampling, and new chips are being released all the time, so for any new project, check the latest offerings.

Table 6-1: USB controller chips that are compatible with popular microcontroller architectures are available from many sources.

Chip Family	Manufacturer	Chips	Bus Speed
ARM	Atmel	AT91SAM7S	full
		AT91SAM9R64	high
	NXP Semiconductors	LPC292x, LPC214x	full
Atmel AVR	Atmel	AT90USBx, AVR32UC3	low/full
Infineon C166	Infineon	C161U	full
Intel 80C186	AMD	Am186CC	full
Intel 8051	Atmel	AT89C513x	full
	Cypress Semiconductor	CY7C64713 EZ-USB	full
		CY7C6801x EZ-USB	full/high
	Silicon Laboratories	C8051F34x	low/full
	Standard Microsystems Corporation (SMSC)	USB2005, USB222x	full, full/high
	Texas Instruments	TUSB3210/3410	full
		TUSB6250	full/high
Microchip PIC18	Microchip Technology	PIC18F2455/2550/ 4455/4550, PIC18(L)F1xK50	low/full
STMicroelectronics ST7	STMicroelectronics	ST7260	low
		ST7265X	full
		ST7268x	full/high

Microchip PIC18F4550

Microchip Technology's PIC microcontrollers are popular due to their low cost, wide availability, large selection, good performance, and low power consumption. The PIC18F4550 contains a USB controller that can function at low and full speeds. Microchip offers other variants with different combinations of features.

Architecture

The PIC18F4550 is a member of Microchip's high-performance, low-cost, 8-bit PIC18 series. Firmware resides in 32 KB of flash memory. The chip has 2

KB of RAM and 256 bytes of EEPROM. A bootloader routine can upgrade firmware via the USB port.

The chip has 34 I/O pins that include a 10-bit analog-to-digital converter, a USART, a synchronous serial port that can be configured to use I2C or SPI, enhanced PWM capabilities, and two analog comparators.

The USB module and CPU can use separate clock sources, enabling the CPU to use a slower, power-saving clock.

USB Controller

The USB controller supports all four transfer types and up to 30 endpoint addresses plus the default endpoint. The endpoints share 1 KB of buffer memory, and transfers can use double buffering. For isochronous transfers, USB data can transfer directly to and from a streaming parallel port.

For each enabled endpoint address, the firmware must reserve memory for a buffer and a buffer descriptor. The buffer descriptor consists of four registers. Firmware can access the register's contents as a structure, a single 32-bit value, or a byte array (Listing 6-1).

The status register contains status information and the two highest bits of the endpoint's byte count. The byte-count register plus the two bits in the status register contain the number of bytes sent or ready to send in an IN transaction or the number of bytes expected or received in an OUT transaction. The address-low and address-high registers contain the starting address for the endpoint's buffer in RAM.

The microcontroller's CPU and the USB SIE share access to the buffers and buffer descriptors. A UOWN bit in the buffer descriptor's status register determines whether the CPU or SIE owns a buffer and its buffer descriptor. The SIE has ownership when data is ready to transmit or when waiting to receive data on the bus. When the SIE has ownership, the CPU shouldn't attempt to access the buffer or buffer descriptor except to read the UOWN bit. When readying an endpoint to perform a transfer, the last operation the firmware should perform is to update the status register to set UOWN, which passes ownership to the SIE. When a transaction completes, the SIE clears the UOWN bit, passing ownership back to the CPU.

Each endpoint number also has a control register that can enable a control endpoint, an IN endpoint, an OUT endpoint, or a pair of IN and OUT endpoints with the same endpoint number. Other bits in the register can stall the endpoint and disable handshaking (for isochronous transactions).

```
// A buffer descriptor table holds 4 bytes.
// This union enables firmware to access the bytes in different ways.

typedef union __BDT
{
        struct                          // Four 8-bit variables.
        {
                BD_STAT STAT;           // Status byte structure
                BYTE CNT;               // Byte count, bits 0-7
                BYTE ADRL;              // Endpoint address in RAM, low byte
                BYTE ADRH;              // Endpoint address in RAM, high byte
        };

        struct                          // The endpoint address in RAM
        {
                unsigned :8;
                unsigned :8;
                BYTE* ADR;              // Address pointer
        };

        DWORD Val;                      // One 32-bit value.

        BYTE v[4];                      // Byte array.

} BDT_ENTRY;
```

Listing 6-1: Firmware can use structures to represent the contents of an endpoint's buffer descriptor table. (Part 1 of 2)

```
// This union represents the buffer descriptor's 8-bit status register in a variety of ways.

typedef union _BD_STAT
{
        BYTE Val;                       // Byte variable

        struct                          // Bit values if the CPU owns the buffer.
        {
                unsigned BC8:1;         // Byte count, bit 8
                unsigned BC9:1;         // Byte count, bit 9
                unsigned BSTALL:1;      // Buffer stall enable
                unsigned DTSEN:1;       // Data toggle synchronization enable
                unsigned INCDIS:1;      // Address increment disable
                unsigned KEN:1;         // Buffer descriptor keep enable
                unsigned DTS:1;         // Data toggle synchronization value
                unsigned UOWN:1;        // USB ownership
        };

        struct                          // Bit values if the USB module owns the buffer.
        {
                unsigned BC8:1;         // Byte count, bit 8
                unsigned BC9:1;         // Byte count, bit 9
                unsigned PID0:1;        // PID, bit 0
                unsigned PID1:1;        // PID, bit 1
                unsigned PID2:1;        // PID, bit 2
                unsigned PID3:1;        // PID, bit 3
                unsigned :1;
                unsigned UOWN:1;        // USB Ownership
        };

        struct                          // The 4-bit PID
        {
                unsigned :2;
                unsigned PID:4;
                unsigned :2;
        };
} BD_STAT;
```

Listing 6-1: Firmware can use structures to represent the contents of an endpoint's buffer descriptor table. (Part 2 of 2)

Additional registers store the device's bus address and status and control information for USB communications and interrupts.

Devices with simpler I/O needs can use the 20-pin PIC18(L)F1xK50 series.

Microchip provides USB Framework firmware and example applications for USB communications. The firmware is written for Microchip's C compiler for PIC18 CPUs. The Framework handles general USB tasks and some class-specific tasks. The files may require only minor changes and additions for a specific application. Provided example projects include keyboard, mouse, generic HID, mass storage, virtual COM port, WinUSB device, and Microchip generic driver device.

Other C compiler options are the CCS C compiler from CCS, Inc. and the HI-TECH C compiler from HI-TECH Software.

For Basic programmers, microEngineering Labs, Inc. offers the PICBASIC PRO compiler. The compiler's built-in USB support enables developing devices without having to know much about USB protocols. The supported USB capabilities are limited yet sufficient for many applications. The compiler comes with example code for a mouse, generic human interface device, virtual COM port, and Microchip generic-driver device.

PICBASIC PRO programs can use four USB-specific instructions:

USBInit initializes the USB port.

USBService monitors the bus status and manages low-level USB communications. A PICBASIC PRO program must call USBService at least every 10 ms.

USBIn retrieves received data from a bulk or interrupt endpoint.

USBOut writes data to a bulk or interrupt endpoint for transmitting.

Assembly-code files provide behind-the-scenes support for the instructions. The compiler automatically includes the files when needed. Adding new USB capabilities to the compiler requires editing the assembly-language source code.

Cypress EZ-USB

Cypress Semiconductor's EZ-USB family includes full-speed and full/high speed controllers. The chips support a variety of options for storing firmware, including loading firmware from the host on each power-up or attachment.

Architecture

The EZ-USB's architecture is similar to the Maxim Integrated Products DS80C320, which is an 8051 with a redesigned core for enhanced performance. The instruction set is compatible with the 8051's. All of the combined code and data memory is RAM. There is no on-chip, non-volatile memory. However, the chips support non-volatile storage in I^2C serial EEPROM and in external parallel memory.

The EZ-USB family includes the full-speed CY7C64713 in the FX1 series and the full/high speed CY7C6801x chips in the FX2 series. Keil Software has a C compiler with a free evaluation version.

USB Controller

The EZ-USB's many options for storing firmware make the chip very flexible but also make the architecture more complicated compared to other USB controllers.

When an EZ-USB wants to use firmware stored in the host, the device enumerates twice. On boot up or device attachment, the host attempts to enumerate the device. Every EZ-USB contains a core that knows how to respond to enumeration requests and can communicate when the device attaches to the bus. The EZ-USB core is independent from the 8051 core that normally controls the chip after enumeration. The EZ-USB core communicates with the host while holding the 8051 core in the reset state.

The EZ-USB core also responds to vendor-specific requests that enable the chip to receive, store, and run firmware received from the host. For basic testing, the core circuits enable the device to transfer data using all four transfer types without any firmware programming.

A ReNum register bit determines whether the EZ-USB or the 8051 core responds to requests at endpoint zero. On power-up, ReNum is zero and the EZ-USB core controls endpoint zero. When ReNum = 1, the 8051 core controls endpoint zero.

The source of an EZ-USB's firmware depends on two things: the contents of the initial bytes in an external EEPROM and the state of the chip's EA input. On power-up and before enumeration, the EZ-USB core attempts to read bytes from a serial EEPROM on the chip's I^2C interface. The result, along with the state of the chip's EA input, tell the core what to do next: use the default mode, load firmware from the host, load firmware from EEPROM, or boot from code memory on the external parallel data bus (Table 6-2). The values in the first EEPROM locations vary depending on whether the chip is an FX1 or FX2. The description below uses the values for the FX2.

Default Mode. The default mode is the most basic mode of operation and doesn't use the serial EEPROM or other external memory. The EZ-USB core uses this mode if EA is logic low and either the core detects no EEPROM or the first byte read from EEPROM is not C0h or C2h.

When the host enumerates the device, the EZ-USB core responds to requests. During this time, the 8051 core is in the reset state. This reset state is controlled by a register bit in the chip. The host can request to write to this bit to place the chip in and out of reset. This reset affects the 8051 core only and is unrelated to USB's Reset signaling.

The descriptors retrieved by the host identify the device as a Default USB Device. The host matches the retrieved Vendor ID and Product ID with values in a Cypress-provided INF file that instructs the host to load the Cypress CyUSB driver to communicate with the chip. The ReNum bit remains at zero.

This default mode is intended for use in debugging. You can use this mode to get the USB interface up and transferring data. In addition to supporting transfers over endpoint zero, the Default USB Device can use the other three transfer types on other endpoints. All of these transfers are possible without writing any firmware or device drivers.

Load Firmware from the Host. The core can also read identifying bytes from the EEPROM on power up and provide this information to the host during enumeration. If the first value read from the EEPROM is C0h, the core reads EEPROM bytes containing the chip's Vendor ID, Product ID, and release number. On device attachment or system boot up, the host uses these bytes to find a matching INF file that identifies a driver for the device. The driver contains firmware to download to the device before re-enumerating. Cypress provides instructions for building a driver with this ability.

The driver uses the vendor-specific Firmware Load request to download the firmware to the device. The firmware contains a new set of descriptors and the code the device will run. For example, a HID-class device will have report descriptors and code for transferring HID report data.

On completing the download, the driver causes the chip to exit the reset state and run the firmware. By writing to a register that controls the chip's DISCON# pin, the firmware causes the device to electrically emulate removal from, then reattachment to the bus. The pin controls one end of a resistor whose

Table 6-2: An EZ-USB can run firmware from four sources.

| Firmware Source | State of EA pin | First Byte in Serial EEPROM (hex) | |
		FX1	FX2
Load from host on re-enumerating	Don't care	B4	C0
Load from serial EEPROM	Don't care	B6	C2
Default USB Device	logic low	No EEPROM present OR not B4 or B6	No EEPROM present OR not C0 or C2
External parallel memory	logic high	No EEPROM present OR not B4 or B6	No EEPROM present OR not C0 or C2

other end connects to D+. When pulled up, the pin indicates device attachment, and when floating, the pin indicates device removal. The firmware also sets ReNum = 1 to cause the 8051 core, instead of the EZ-USB core, to respond to requests at endpoint zero.

On detecting the emulated re-attachment, the host enumerates the device again, this time retrieving the newly stored descriptors and using the information in them to select a device driver to load.

An advantage to storing firmware on the host is easy updates. To update the firmware, you store the new version on the host and the driver sends the firmware to the device on the next power up or attachment. There's no need to replace the chip or use special programming hardware or software. The down side is a more complicated device driver, the need to have the firmware available on the host, and longer enumeration time.

Load Firmware from EEPROM. A third mode of operation provides a way for the chip to store its firmware in an external serial EEPROM. If the first byte read from the EEPROM is C2h, the core loads the EEPROM's entire contents into RAM on power-up. The EEPROM must contain the Vendor ID, Product ID, and release number as well as all descriptors required for enumeration and whatever other firmware and data the device requires. On exiting the reset state, the device has everything it needs for USB communications. The core sets the ReNum bit to 1 on completing the loading of the code. When enumerating the device, the host reads the stored descriptors and loads the appropriate driver. There is no re-enumeration.

Run Code from External Parallel Memory. If no EEPROM is detected, or if the first byte isn't C0h or C2h, and if EA is a logic high, the chip boots from code memory on the external parallel data bus. ReNum is set to 1. The host enumerates the device and loads a driver, and there is no re-enumeration.

ARM

For high-end applications, many developers turn to ARM microcontrollers, which have a fast, efficient, 32-bit RISC architecture. ARM Holdings licenses intellectual property (IP) cores to chip companies for use in their chips. The ARM family includes a range of cores with different capabilities.

An example of an ARM processor with a USB device port is Atmel's AT91SAM7S321. The chip has a full-speed USB port, 32 KB of flash memory for firmware, and 8 KB of RAM. Other I/O includes an 8-channel, 10-bit analog-to-digital converter and synchronous and asynchronous serial ports. Programming can use the free GNU GCC compiler or a compiler from IAR Systems. NXP Semiconductors is another source for ARM-based device controllers.

Controllers that Interface to CPUs

A controller that interfaces to an external CPU enables adding USB to just about any CPU circuit. A disadvantage is the need to use two chips instead of having the CPU and USB controller on a single chip. Also, example code for USB communications using your CPU might not be available.

Some interface chips support a command set for USB-related communications, while others use a series of registers to store USB data and configuration, status, and control information.

Most interface chips have a local data bus with a parallel interface to communicate with the CPU. For fast transfers with external memory, many chips support direct memory access (DMA). To use DMA, the CPU sets up a transfer that reads or writes a block of data to or from data memory without CPU intervention. For CPUs that don't have external parallel buses, a few controllers can use a synchronous or asynchronous serial interface. An interrupt pin can signal the CPU when the controller has received USB data or is ready for new data to send.

Table 6-3 compares a selection of interface chips. The following descriptions will give an idea of the range of chips available. The chips described are a sampling, and new chips are being released all the time, so for new projects, check the latest offerings.

ST-NXP Wireless ISP1582

The ISP1582 from ST-NXP Wireless is a full/high-speed controller that interfaces to an external CPU over a parallel interface.

Architecture

The chip has a serial interface engine for handling USB traffic, a 16-bit data bus, and an 8-bit address bus. An external CPU can communicate with the controller by accessing a series of registers. The controller supports multiplexed and non-multiplexed address buses and DMA transfers.

USB Controller

The USB controller supports full and high speeds. In addition to endpoint zero, the chip can support up to seven IN endpoint addresses and seven OUT endpoint addresses. All enabled endpoints share 8 KB of buffer memory. The control endpoint has 64-byte buffers. Firmware allocates memory to each of the other endpoint addresses, and any of these endpoint addresses can use double buffering.

Firmware controls when the chip attaches to the bus. An external pull-up resistor connects to the chip's RPU pin and to a pull-up voltage. After a hardware reset, the chip appears detached from the bus until the external CPU sets a register bit that causes the chip to switch the pull-up onto the bus's D+ line. This firmware-controlled connection can give the chip time to initialize on power up before the host begins enumeration.

The ISP1583 adds an ATA/ATAPI interface. The ISP1181B and ISP1183 are options for full-speed devices.

PLX Technology NET2272

PLX Technology, Inc.'s NET2272 is a full/high-speed chip that interfaces to an external CPU over a parallel interface.

Table 6-3: These USB interface chips interface to an external CPU.

Company	Chips	CPU Interface	Bus Speed
FTDI	FT232BM	Asynchronous serial	Full
	FT245BM	Parallel	Full
	FT2232H, FT4232H	Asynchronous serial and parallel	High
ST-NXP Wireless	ISP1181B, ISP1183	Parallel	Full
	ISP1582, ISP1583	Parallel	Full/High
PLX Technology	NET2272	Parallel	Full/High

Architecture

A series of registers hold configuration data and other information. Packet buffers hold USB data that has been received and data that is ready to transmit. The parallel interface has 5 address bits and 16 data bits. Transfers to and from the packet buffers can be 8 or 16 bits.

The registers store status and control information and the data received in the last Setup transaction. The CPU also uses registers to read and write endpoint data from and to the packet buffers.

The NET2272 supports three modes for accessing its registers. In direct address mode, the five address bits specify a register to read or write to. In multiplexed address mode, the CPU places the register address on the data bits and the NET2272 reads the address on the falling edge of the ALE control signal. In indirect address mode, the CPU uses the lowest address bit to distinguish between a register address pointer (0) and data (1). The CPU writes a register address pointer to specify a configuration register and then reads or writes data at the address pointed to. Direct and multiplexed address modes can access only registers 00h–1Fh, which typically contain the information accessed most frequently. Indirect address mode can access all registers. The controller also supports DMA transfers. A CPU can write to the NET2272 at up to 60 MB/s and can read at up to 57 MB/s (in DMA mode).

To access endpoint data in the packet buffers, the CPU selects an endpoint by writing to the Endpoint Page Select register or the DMA Endpoint Select register and then accesses the data by reading or writing to the Endpoint Data register.

USB Controller

The NET2272's USB controller supports full and high speeds and all four transfer types. The controller has three physical endpoints in addition to endpoint zero. A device that needs more endpoints can use virtual endpoints, where one or more logical endpoints share a physical endpoint's resources. The device firmware must switch resources between the logical and physical endpoints as needed.

Endpoint zero has a 128-byte buffer, and the other endpoints share 3 KB of packet buffers. Two of the endpoints can use double buffers. After a failed IN or OUT transaction, an endpoint automatically recovers and waits for the host to retry.

FTDI USB UART and USB FIFO

Future Technology Devices International (FTDI) offers controllers that are useful for virtual COM-port devices and other devices that don't fit a defined USB class and need only bulk or isochronous transfers.

Architecture

FTDI's chips take a different approach to USB design. The controllers handle enumeration and other USB communications entirely in hardware.

The FT232R USB UART interfaces to a device CPU via an asynchronous serial (UART) port. The controller handles all of the USB-specific protocols. Device firmware just reads and writes data on the serial port. To send data to the host computer, firmware writes the data to the asynchronous serial port. To read data from the host computer, firmware reads the asynchronous serial port. The FT245R USB FIFO functions in a similar way except the CPU interface is a bidirectional parallel port. Both chips are full speed. The FT2232H is a high-speed version with two ports that can each function as a UART or parallel port. The FT4232H is high speed with four ports.

USB Controller

Both the FT232R and FT245R have a 128-byte transmit buffer and a 256-byte receive buffer. The chips use bulk transfers by default with one endpoint for each direction. A driver for isochronous transfers is also available.

Figure 6-3. For easy prototyping with FTDI's controllers, use the UM232R and UM245R modules.

On the host computer, the chips use a driver provided by FTDI. The driver enables applications to access a chip as a USB virtual COM port or by using a driver-specific API.

Many USB/RS-232 adapters contain FT232R chips. If you have an existing device that communicates with a PC via RS-232, the FT232R offers a quick way to upgrade to USB. In most cases, using an FT232R to convert an RS-232 device to USB requires no changes to device firmware or host application software. The host accesses the device in the same way as if the device connected via an RS-232 serial port.

Host software can access an FT245R as a COM port even though the chip doesn't have an asynchronous serial port. The host doesn't need to know what lies beyond the device's USB port.

Both controllers contain on-chip EEPROM that can store vendor-specific values for a Vendor ID, Product ID, serial-number string, other descriptive strings, and values that specify whether the device is bus- or self-powered. The controller uses default values for items without stored values in EEPROM. FTDI provides a utility that programs the information into the EEPROM. By default, the chips use FTDI's Vendor ID and Product ID. On request, FTDI will grant the right for your device to use their Vendor ID with a Product ID that FTDI assigns to you. Or you can use your own Vendor ID and Product ID.

Both chips also support a Bit Bang mode, where the chip operates as a basic USB device without requiring a connection to a device CPU. A host computer can monitor and control I/O bits on the chip to control LEDs, relays, or other circuits and read switches and logic-gate outputs.

For easy prototyping, FTDI's UM232R and UM245R modules (Figure 6-3) each consist of a circuit board with a controller chip, USB connector, and related circuits mounted on a 24-pin dual in-line package (DIP). The modules fit breadboards or PC boards. A variety of other modules offer different form factors, connectors, and capabilities. A chip with similar capabilities to the FT232R is the Silicon Laboratories CP2102.

7

Device Classes

This chapter is an introduction to the defined USB classes, including how to decide if a new design fits a defined class.

Elements and Use

Most USB devices have much in common with other devices that perform similar functions. Mice send data about mouse movements and button clicks. Drives transfer files. Printers receive data to print and inform the host when they're out of paper.

When many devices provide or request similar services, it makes sense to define protocols for all of the devices to use. A class specification can serve as a guide for programmers who write device firmware or host drivers. Drivers included with an operating system eliminate the need for vendors to provide drivers with their devices.

When a device in a supported class has features or abilities not included in a class driver, a device sometimes can use a class driver along with a vendor-provided filter driver to support the added features and abilities.

Classes not currently supported by an operating system might be supported in a future edition. Firmware that complies with a class specification for an unsupported class will likely be compatible with a driver added in a future edition of the operating system.

Approved Specifications

The USB-IF sponsors device working groups that develop class specifications. The defined classes cover most common device functions. Table 7-1 shows the classes with approved specifications. The hub class is defined in the main USB 2.0 and USB 3.0 specifications rather than in a separate document. Every host must support the hub class because the host requires a root hub to do any communications. Chapter 4 listed the defined class codes for device and interface descriptors.

Windows provides drivers for many classes. As Windows and the class specifications have evolved, the number of supported classes and the completeness of support for those classes has improved. For some classes, such as the device firmware upgrade class, Windows doesn't provide a driver even though the specification has been available for many years. Table 7-2 shows the support for each class under different Windows editions.

Elements of a Class Specification

A class specification defines the number and type of required and optional endpoints for devices in the class. The document may also define formats for data to be transferred including application data and status and control information. Some class specifications define uses for the data being transferred. For example, the HID class has usage tables that define how to interpret data sent by keyboards, mice, and joysticks. Some classes use USB to transfer data in a format defined by another specification. An example is the SCSI commands used by mass-storage devices.

A class specification can define values for fields in standard descriptors and may also define class-specific descriptors, interfaces, and control requests. For example, the device descriptor for a hub includes a bDeviceClass value of 09h to indicate that the device belongs to the hub class. The hub must have a class-specific hub descriptor with bDescriptorType = 29h. Hubs must also support class-specific requests. For example, when the host sends a Get Port Status request to a hub with a port number in the Index field, the hub responds with status information for the port. A class may also require a device to support specific endpoints or comply with tighter timing for standard requests. Chapter 4 showed how the device or interface descriptor declares a class.

Table 7-1: These classes have approved class specifications.

Class	Version[1]	Date	Descriptor Where Class Is Declared
Audio	2.0	05/06	Interface
Communication (CDC)	1.2	11/07	Device or interface
Content security	1.0	08/00	Interface
Device firmware upgrade (DFU)	1.1	08/04	Interface (subclass of Application Specific Interface)
Human interface (HID)	1.11	06/01	Interface
IrDA bridge	1.0	03/00	Interface (subclass of Application Specific Interface)
Mass storage	1.2	06/03	Interface
Personal healthcare	1.0	11/07	Interface (preferred) or device
Printer	1.1	01/00	Interface
Smart card	1.1	03/01	Interface
Still image capture	1.0	07/00	Interface
Test and measurement	1.0	04/03	Interface (subclass of Application Specific Interface)
Video	1.1	06/05	Interface

[1]The current version of the main specification document at this writing. Some classes have additional, supplementary specifications.

Defined Classes

The following sections introduce the defined classes. The purpose is to serve as a guide to deciding whether a new design can use a defined class and if so, what device controllers to consider and what host drivers are available. For more information about a class, consult the class specification.

Audio

The audio class encompasses devices that send or receive encoded voice, music, or other sounds. Audio functions are often part of a device that also supports video, storage, or other functions. Devices in the audio class can use isochronous transfers for audio streams or bulk transfers for data encoded using the MIDI (Musical Instrument Digital Interface) protocol.

Version 2.0 of the audio class specification retains much of the framework defined in version 1.0 but is not backwards compatible. In other words, an

Table 7-2: Windows provides drivers for many classes.

Class	Windows Edition(s) when Class Driver Was Added
Audio	Windows 98 Gold: audio 1.0 Windows Me: MIDI Windows XP: MIDI (improved)
Communications	Windows 98 SE: modem Windows 2000: Remote NDIS
Content Security	Windows XP: devices with CSM-1 interfaces can provide a serial number
Device Firmware Upgrade	No support
Human Interface	Windows 98 Gold: HID 1.0 Windows 98SE: HID 1.1
IrDA Bridge	No support
Mass Storage	Windows 2000: class driver Windows 2000 XP3: support for multiple LUNs
Personal healthcare	No support
Printer	Windows 2000: class driver
Smart Card	Windows 2000 update: class driver
Still Image	Windows 98SE: class driver (first phase/preliminary) Windows 2000: class driver (improved)
Test and Measurement	No support
Video	Windows 98 Gold: USB camera minidriver library USBCAMD 1.0 (not supported under Windows 2000) Windows Me: USB camera minidriver library USBCAMD 2.0 Windows XP SP2: class driver

audio 2.0 device can't use an audio 1.0 host driver. Version 2.0 adds full support for high speed, mandatory use of the interface association descriptor, and new capabilities and controls.

Documentation

The audio specification consists of the main class specification and supporting documents for audio data formats, terminal types, and MIDI devices. The MIDI standard is available from the MIDI Manufacturers Association at *www.midi.org*.

Overview

Each audio function in a device has an Audio Interface Collection that consists of one or more interfaces. The interfaces include one AudioControl (AC) interface, zero or more AudioStreaming (AS) interfaces and zero or more MIDIStreaming (MS) interfaces (Figure 7-1). In other words, every Audio Interface Collection has an AudioControl interface, while AudioStreaming and MIDIStreaming interfaces are optional.

In audio 2.0 devices, an interface association descriptor (IAD) specifies the interfaces that belong to a collection. In audio 1.0 devices, a class-specific AC interface header descriptor contains this information.

An AudioControl interface can enable accessing controls such as volume, mute, bass, and treble. An AudioStreaming interface transfers audio data in isochronous transfers and may also carry control data related to the streaming data. A MIDIStreaming interface transfers MIDI data.

MIDI is a standard for controlling synthesizers, sound cards, and other electronic devices that generate music and other sounds. A MIDI representation of a sound includes values for pitch, length, volume, and other characteristics. A pure MIDI hardware interface carries asynchronous data at 31.25 kbps. A USB interface that carries MIDI data uses the MIDI data format but not the asynchronous interface. Instead, the MIDI data travels on the bus in bulk transfers.

A device can have multiple Audio Interface Collections that are active at the same time, with each collection controlling an independent audio function.

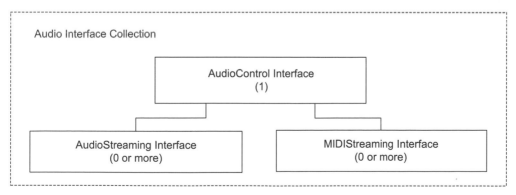

Figure 7-1. Each audio function has an Audio Interface Collection that contains one or more interfaces.

Descriptors

Each audio interface uses standard and class-specific descriptors to enable the host to learn about the interface, its endpoints, and what kinds of data the endpoints transfer. The specification defines a variety of class-specific descriptors that provide information specific to audio functions. Audio 1.0 endpoint descriptors have two additional bytes that follow the 7 bytes defined in the USB 2.0 specification. Audio 2.0 endpoint descriptors use the standard 7-byte structure.

Class-specific Requests

The audio class provides optional class-specific requests for setting and getting the state of audio controls and exchanging generic data.

Chips

Some USB controllers have built-in support for audio functions. The support may include codec (compressor/decompressor) functions, analog-to-digital converters (ADCs), digital-to-analog converters (DACs), and support for Sony/Philips Digital Interface (S/PDIF) encoding for transmitting audio data in digital format.

Texas Instruments has a variety of USB audio chips. The PCM2900 is a stereo audio codec with a full-speed USB port and 16-bit ADC and DAC. The chip has an AudioControl interface, an AudioStreaming interface for each direction, and a HID interface that reports the status of three pins on the chip. The chip requires no user programming but has the option to use a vendor-specific Vendor ID, Product ID, and strings. The PCM2902 adds support for S/PDIF encoding. The PCM2702 is a 16-bit stereo DAC with a full-speed USB interface. The chip can accept data sampled at 48, 44.1, and 32 kHz using either 16-bit stereo or monaural audio data and supports digital attenuation and soft-mute features. The TUSB3200A USB streaming controller contains an 8052-compatible microcontroller that supports up to seven IN endpoints and seven OUT endpoints. The audio support includes a codec port interface, a DMA controller with four channels for streaming isochronous data packets to and from the codec port, and a phase lock loop (PLL) and adaptive clock generator (ACG) to support synchronization modes.

Windows Support

Windows XP and Windows Vista support USB Audio 1.0. Windows Vista implements Microsoft's Universal Audio Architecture (UAA), which improves audio support and defines requirements for devices that will use the operating system's audio drivers. Earlier Windows editions through Windows 2000 can also install the UAA driver. All devices that are compatible with the USB audio class system driver (*usbaudio.sys*) are UAA compliant.

Applications can access USB audio devices using the DirectMusic and Direct-Sound components of the Windows DirectX technology.

Communications

The communications device class (CDC) encompasses a wide range of devices that perform telecommunications and networking functions. Telecommunications devices include analog phones and modems, digital phones (including cell phones), and ISDN terminal adapters as well as virtual COM-port devices. Networking devices include ADSL modems, cable modems, and Ethernet adapters and hubs.

The communications data typically uses an application-specific protocol such as V.250 for modem control or Ethernet for network data.

Documentation

Documentation for the class consists of a main class specification and separate documents for these subclasses:

> Asynchronous transfer mode (ATM)
>
> Ethernet emulation model (EEM)
>
> Ethernet control model (ECM)
>
> ISDN
>
> Public switched telephone network (PSTN)
>
> Wireless mobile communications (WMC)

The V.250 standard (a previous version was V.25ter) defines a derivative of the Hayes AT modem command set and is available from the International Telecommunication Union at *www.itu.int*. The Ethernet standard, IEEE 802.3, is available from *www.ieee.org*.

The Remote Network Driver Interface Specification (NDIS) defines a protocol for using USB and other buses to configure network interfaces and carry Ethernet-framed data. Remote NDIS is based on NDIS, which defines a protocol to manage communications with network adapters and higher-level drivers. Both specifications are from Microsoft and are supported only on Windows.

Overview

A communications device is responsible for device management, call management if needed, and data transmission. Device management includes controlling and configuring a device and notifying the host of events. Call management involves establishing and terminating telephone calls or other connections. Not all devices require call management. Data transmission is the sending and receiving of application data such as phone conversations or files sent over a modem or network.

The communications device class supports six major models for communicating.

- Asynchronous transfer mode (ATM) devices include ADSL modems.
- Ethernet emulation model (EEM) devices exchange Ethernet-framed data. Commands share endpoints, and each packet is preceded by a 2-byte header.
- Ethernet control model (ECM) devices also exchange Ethernet-framed data using an older protocol that is less efficient than EEM. Class-specific requests and notifications manage the interface.
- ISDN devices include terminal adapters for ISDN lines.
- Public switched telephone network (PSTN) devices include voice modems, telephones, and serial-emulation (virtual COM-port) devices. Some devices that exchange Ethernet-framed data use the PSTN model with a vendor-specific protocol.
- Wireless mobile communications (WMC) devices include cell phones and other multi-function devices.

Notifications, which announce events such as ring detect and network connect or disconnect, can travel to the host in an interrupt or bulk pipe. Most devices use interrupt pipes. Each notification consists of an 8-byte header followed by a variable-length data field. Some device types don't require notifications.

Descriptors

The descriptors can specify a communications function at the device or interface level. If specified at the device level, all of the device's interfaces belong to

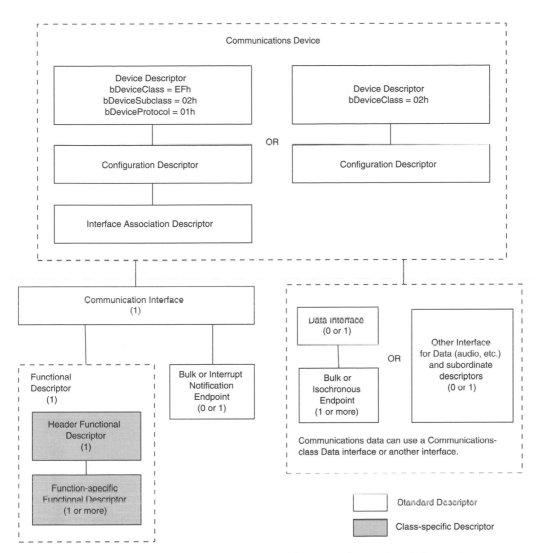

Figure 7-2. A communications device provides interfaces for data and notifications.

the communications function. In the device descriptor, bDeviceClass = 02h to specify CDC (Figure 7-2). In a composite device, which contains multiple functions, an interface association descriptor (IAD) specifies which interfaces belong to the communication function, and bDeviceClass, bDeviceSubclass, and bDeviceProtocol are set as required for the IAD as described in Chapter 4.

Table 7-3: In the interface descriptor for a communication device, the bInterfaceSubClass field indicates the communication model the device supports.

Code	bInterfaceSubClass	Application
00h	RESERVED	–
01h	PSTN Direct Line Control Model	Telephone modem with the host providing any data compression and error correction. The device or host may provide modulation/demodulation of the modem data.
02h	PSTN Abstract Control Model	Telephone modem with the device providing any data compression, error correction, and modulation/demodulation of the modem data.
03h	PSTN Telephone Control Model	Telephone.
04h	ISDN: Multi-Channel Control Model	ISDN device with multiple, multiplexed channels.
05h	ISDN: CAPI Control Model	ISDN device with support for COMMON-ISDN-API (CAPI) commands and messages.
06h	ECM (Ethernet Control Model)	Device that exchanges Ethernet-framed data.
07h	ATM	Asynchronous transfer mode device.
08h	WMC wireless handset control model	Logical handset.
09h	WMC device management model	AT commands only.
0Ah	WMC mobile direct line model	Migrates some functions of wireless terminal adapters to the USB host.
0Bh	WMC OBEX model	Data exchange protocol.
0Ch	EEM (Ethernet Emulation Model)	Device that exchanges Ethernet-framed data.
0Dh–7Fh	Reserved	Future use.
80h–FEh	Vendor specific	Vendor defined.

Every communications device must have an interface descriptor with bInterfaceClass = 02h to indicate a Communication interface that handles device management and call management. The bInterfaceSubClass field specifies a communication model. Table 7-3 shows defined values for the subclasses. The bInterfaceProtocol field can name a protocol supported by a subclass. Table 7-4 shows defined values for protocols.

Table 7-4: In the descriptor for a Communication interface, the bInterfaceProtocol field can indicate a protocol the communications model supports.

Code	Description
00h	No class-specific protocol required
01h	AT commands (specified in ITU V.250)
02h–06h	AT commands used by WMC devices
07h	Ethernet Emulation Model (EEM)
08h–FDh	Future use
FEh	External protocol. The commands are defined by a command set functional descriptor
FFh	Vendor specific

Following the Communication interface descriptor is a class-specific Functional descriptor consisting of a Header Functional descriptor followed by one or more descriptors (also called Functional descriptors) that provide information about a communication function. Table 7-5 shows defined values for these descriptors.

One of these descriptors, the Union Functional descriptor, has the special function of defining a relationship among interfaces that form a functional unit. The descriptor designates one interface as the master or controlling interface, which can send and receive certain messages that apply to the entire group. For example, a Communication interface can be a master interface for a group consisting of a Communication interface and a Data interface. The interfaces that make up a group can include communications-class interfaces as well as other related interfaces such as audio and HID.

If the Communication interface has a bulk or interrupt endpoint for event notifications, the endpoint has a standard endpoint descriptor.

A communications device can also have an interface descriptor with bInterfaceClass = 0Ah to indicate a Data interface. A Data interface can have bulk or isochronous endpoints for carrying application data. Each of these endpoints has a standard endpoint descriptor. Some devices use other class or vendor-specific interfaces for application data. For example, a telephone might use an audio interface to send and receive voice data.

A virtual COM-port device provides serial port emulation. Applications can use COM-port functions to access the device in the same way as if the device con-

Table 7-5: A Functional descriptor consists of a Header functional descriptor followed by one or more function-specific descriptors.

bInterfaceSubClass	Functional Descriptor Type
00h	Header
01h	Call Management
02h	Abstract Control Management
03h	Direct Line Control Management
04h	Telephone Ringer
05h	Telephone Call and Line State Reporting Capabilities
06h	Union
07h	Country Selection
08h	Telephone Operational Modes
09h	USB Terminal
0Ah	Network Channel Terminal
0Bh	Protocol Unit
0Ch	Extension Unit
0Dh	Multi-channel Management
0Eh	CAPI Control Management
0Fh	Ethernet Networking
10h	ATM Networking
11h–18h	WMC Functional Descriptors
19h	OBEX Service Identifier
1Ah–7Fh	Reserved (future use)
80h–FEh	Vendor specific

nected directly to an RS-232 port on the PC. The device may have an asynchronous serial interface that communicates with other circuits, but an asynchronous interface isn't required. The USB host doesn't have to know how the device uses the COM-port data. A virtual COM-port device can use bInterfaceSubClass = 02h to specify the abstract control model and bInterfaceProtocol = 01h to specify AT commands. For compatibility with the Windows driver, the interface should specify this subclass even if the device doesn't use AT commands. The Communication interface has an interrupt endpoint, and the Data interface has a bulk endpoint for each direction. For improved performance, some virtual COM-port devices use vendor-specific drivers and thus don't belong to the communications device class. My book *Serial Port Complete* has more about COM ports and USB virtual COM-port devices.

A USB/Ethernet adapter that functions as a Remote NDIS device consists of a Communication interface and a Data interface. In the Communication interface, bInterfaceSubClass = 02h to specify the abstract control model and bInterfaceProtocol = FFh to specify a vendor-specific protocol. The Communication interface has an interrupt endpoint, and the Data interface has two bulk endpoints. Each endpoint has an endpoint descriptor.

Class-specific Requests

Class-specific requests get and set status and control information. The supported requests vary with the subclass and the device.

Chips

Many communications devices, including virtual COM-port devices, can use just about non-low-speed, general-purpose device controller.

For USB/Ethernet bridges, Asix Electronics Corporation has the AX88172A, which converts between full- or highspeed USB and 10- or 100-Mbps Ethernet. K-Micro has the KLKUSB220 with a 16-bit CPU, full/high-speed USB port, and a 10/100-Mbps Ethernet interface. Freescale Semiconductor's 32-bit MCF5482 ColdFire microprocessor contains a full/high-speed USB device controller and an Ethernet controller.

Windows Support

The modem driver included with Windows 98 SE and later (*usbser.sys*) is compatible with modems and other devices that use the abstract control model. Each device must have an INF file that contains the device's Vendor ID and Product ID. USB virtual COM-port devices can also use the *usbser.sys* driver. Composite CDC devices should use Windows XP SP3 or later, which have updated versions of the *usbser.sys* and *usbccgp.sys* drivers. For mapping Remote NDIS to USB, Windows 2000 and later have the *usb8023.sys* driver.

Several vendors offer drivers for subclasses that Windows doesn't support and enhanced drivers for other subclasses. Belcarra Technologies Corporation has ECM and EEM drivers. Jungo Ltd. has drivers for modems, serial-port emulation, ACM, ECM, and OBEX. MCCI has firmware and driver support for modems, serial-port emulation, WMC, ECM, and OBEX. Thesycon Systemsoftware & Consulting GmbH (yes, that spelling is correct!) has a USBIO Development Kit with an ACM driver.

Content Security

The content security class defines a way to control access to files, music, video, or other data transmitted on the bus. The control can use either of two defined content security methods: basic authorization or digital transmission content protection (DTCP).

Documentation

In addition to the main class specification, each content security method (CSM) has its own specification document. The DTCP specification and license information are available from the Digital Transmission Licensing Administrator (*www.dtcp.com*).

Overview

The class defines a protocol for activating and deactivating a content security method and for associating a content security method to a channel. A channel represents a relationship between an interface or endpoint and one or more CSMs. Only one CSM can be active on a channel at a time.

Basic authorization, also known as Content Security Method 1, or CSM-1, consists only of the class-specific request Get_Unique_ID, which enables a host to request an ID value from a device.

CSM-2 implements DTCP, which prevents unauthorized copying of audio and video entertainment content via USB and other buses. A content provider can use DTCP to specify whether copying is allowed, identify authorized users, and specify an encryption method. A DTCP interface must have an interrupt endpoint in each direction for sending and receiving event notifications. A content provider who wants to use DTCP must sign a license agreement and pay an annual (not trivial) fee.

Two additional CSMs that don't have USB specifications at this writing are open copy protection system (CSM-3) and elliptic curve content protection protocol (CSM-4).

Descriptors

In an interface descriptor, bInterfaceClass = 0Dh declares the content security class. The class has four class-specific descriptors. CSM-2 defines a string descriptor for the string *Digital Transmission Content Protection Version 1.00*.

Class-specific Requests

Two class-specific requests apply to all CSM interfaces. Get_Channel_Settings enables the host to learn what CSM is assigned to a channel. The Set_Channel_Settings request enables the host to assign a CSM to a channel or deactivate a previously assigned CSM. CSM-2 has additional control requests to transfer Authentication and Key Exchange (AKE) commands and responses.

Chips

For a device using content security, the choice of a USB controller depends mainly on the capabilities needed to exchange the content being protected. Adding a content-security function requires only the occasional use of the control endpoint and for CSM-2, two interrupt endpoints.

Windows Support

Windows doesn't include a driver for the content security class except for one function. Under Windows XP and later, if a device has a CSM-1 interface, an application can request the device's serial number by sending a request to the Windows common-class generic parent driver.

The request calls the DeviceIoControl function with the dwIoControlCode parameter set to IOCTL_STORAGE_GET_MEDIA_SERIAL_NUMBER.

Device Firmware Upgrade

The device firmware upgrade (DFU) class defines a protocol for sending firmware enhancements and patches to a device. After receiving the firmware upgrade, the device re-enumerates using its new firmware.

Documentation

The *Device Firmware Upgrade* specification defines the class.

Overview

To perform a firmware upgrade as described in the specification, a device must have two complete sets of descriptors: run time and DFU mode. The run-time descriptors are for normal operation and include descriptors that inform the host that the device is capable of firmware upgrades. The DFU-mode descriptors are for use when a device is upgrading its firmware. For example, a keyboard using its run-time descriptors enumerates as a HID-class device and sends keypress data to the host. During a firmware upgrade, the device suspends normal operations as a keyboard and uses the DFU-mode descriptors to communicate with the DFU driver on the host.

The upgrade process has four phases. In the device-enumeration phase, the device sends its run-time descriptors to the host and operates normally. In the reconfiguration phase, the host sends a Dfu_Detach request and then resets and re-enumerates the device, which returns its DFU-mode descriptors. In the transfer phase, the host sends the firmware upgrade to the device. The manifestation phase begins when the host has completed the transfer. When the device has finished programming the new firmware, device settings determine whether the host resets the device or the device initiates a reset by emulating detach and re-attach. On re-enumerating, the device uses its new, upgraded firmware. During the upgrade process, the device transitions through defined states such as dfuIdle (waiting for DFU requests) and dfuError (an error has occurred).

An upgrade file stored on the host contains the firmware for the upgrade followed by a DFU suffix value that the host can use to help ensure that the firmware is valid and appropriate for a particular device. The suffix contains an error-checking value, a signature consisting of the ASCII text *DFU*, and optional values for the Vendor ID, Product ID, and product release number to identify devices the firmware is appropriate for. The suffix is for the host's use only; the host doesn't send the suffix to the device.

To ensure that the host will load the correct driver for the firmware-upgrade process, the device should use different Product IDs in its run-time and DFU-mode device descriptors.

DFU communications use only the control endpoint.

Descriptors

The DFU function is defined at the interface subclass level. In a device that supports DFU, both the run-time and DFU-mode descriptors include a standard interface descriptor with bInterfaceClass = FEh to indicate an Application

Specific class and bInterfaceSubClass = 01h to indicate the device firmware upgrade class. In DFU mode, the DFU interface must be the only active interface in the device.

Both descriptor sets include a Run-time DFU Functional descriptor that specifies whether the device can communicate on the bus immediately after the manifestation phase, how long to wait for a reset after receiving a DFU_Detach request, and the maximum number of bytes the device can accept in a control Write transfer during a firmware upgrade.

Class-specific Requests

The class defines seven control requests:

Request	Description
DFU_Detach	Detach and re-attach to the bus or wait for bus reset within the time period specified in the DFU Functional descriptor. On reattach or a reset within the specified time, enumerate using the DFU-mode descriptors.
DFU_Dnload	Accept new firmware in the request's Data stage. A request with wLength = 0000h means all of the firmware has been transferred.
DFU_Upload	Send firmware to the host in the request's Data stage.
DFU_GetStatus	Return status and error information. On error, enter the dfuError state.
DFU_ClrStatus	Clear the dfuError state reported in response to a DFU_GetStatus request and enter the dfuIdle state.
DFU_GetState	Same as DFU_GetStatus but with no change in state on error.
DFU_Abort	Return to the dfuIdle state.

Chips

The choice of USB controller depends mainly on the requirements of the device in run-time mode. The device must have enough memory and other resources to store and implement the upgraded firmware. STMicroelectronics has a Windows driver and firmware examples for use with its ST7 microcontrollers.

Windows Support

Windows doesn't provide a driver for this class. Besides STMicroelectonics, another driver source is Jungo Ltd.

Human Interface

The human interface device (HID) class includes keyboards, pointing devices, and game controllers. With these devices, the host reads and acts on human input such as keypresses and mouse movements. Hosts must respond quickly enough so users don't notice a delay between an action and the expected response. Barcode readers can function as HID keyboards with the barcode data emulating keypresses. Other devices with HID interfaces include uninterruptible power supply (UPS) units and display monitors that use HID for user configuration. Some devices that perform vendor-specific functions can also use the HID class.

All HID data travels in reports, which are structures with defined formats. Usage tags in a report tell the host or device how to use received data. For example, a Usage Page value of 09h indicates a button, and a Usage ID value tells which button, if any, was pressed.

Windows and other operating systems have included HID drivers since the earliest editions with USB support. For this reason, the HID class has been popular for devices with a variety of vendor-specific functions. A HID can exchange data for any purpose but can use only control and interrupt transfers. Later chapters have more about using HIDs for vendor-specific functions.

Documentation

The main change from version 1.0 to 1.1 of the HID specification is enabling the host to send reports in interrupt OUT transfers. In a HID 1.0 interface, the host must send all reports in control transfers.

Several documents define Usage-tag values for different device types. *HID Usage Tables* has values for keyboards, pointing devices, various game controllers, displays, telephone controls, and more. Four other device types have their own documents:

Class Definition for Physical Interface Devices (PID) defines values for force-feedback joysticks and other devices that require physical feedback in response to inputs.

The *Monitor Control* specification defines values for user controls and power management for display monitors. The HID interface controls the display's settings only. The image data uses a separate hardware interface.

Usage Tables for HID Power Devices defines values for UPS devices and other devices where the host monitors and controls batteries or other power components.

Point of Sale (POS) Usage Tables defines values for barcode readers, weighing devices, and magnetic-stripe readers.

Additional Usage tables are available from the Gaming Standards Association (*www.gamingstandards.com*) and in Intel's *Open Arcade Architecture Device Data Format Specification* (*www.usb.org*).

Overview

HIDs communicate by exchanging data in reports via control and interrupt transfers. Input and Output reports can use control or interrupt transfers. Feature reports use control transfers. A report descriptor defines the size of each report and Usage values for the report data.

Descriptors

In an interface descriptor, bInterfaceClass = 03h specifies the HID class. The bInterfaceSubClass field indicates whether the HID supports a boot protocol, which a host can use instead of the report protocol defined in the device's report descriptor. A mouse or keyboard can support a boot protocol to enable using the device before the host has loaded the full HID drivers.

Following the interface descriptor is a class-specific HID descriptor, which contains the size of the report descriptor. The report descriptor contains information about the data in the HID reports. An optional physical descriptor that the host requests separately can describe the part(s) of the human body that activate a control.

Class-specific Requests

The class defines six control requests to enable sending and receiving reports, setting and reading the idle rate (how often the device sends a report if the data is unchanged), and setting or reading the currently active protocol (boot or report). To obtain a report descriptor or physical descriptor, the host sends a Get Descriptor request to the interface with the high byte of wValue set to 01h to indicate a class-specific descriptor and the low byte of wValue set to 22h to request a report descriptor or 23h to request a physical descriptor.

Chips

For devices with a human interface, low speed is fast enough to act on received user input with no detectable delay. Some HIDs use low speed because the device needs a flexible or inexpensive cable. A HID can use any speed, however.

Alcor Micro Corporation is a source for controllers with support for interfacing to keyboard matrixes. Cypress Semiconductor's CY7C638xx series supports both USB and PS/2 interfaces to make it easy to design a dual-interface keyboard or mouse.

Code Mercenaries offers programmed chips for use in pointing devices, keyboards, and joysticks. The MouseWarrior series has interfaces for sensors and buttons and supports USB, PS/2, asynchronous serial, and Apple Desktop Bus (ADB). The KeyWarrior series supports USB, PS/2, and ADB and has interfaces to keyboard matrixes and optional support for keyboard macros. The Joy-Warrior series supports a variety of game-controller inputs.

Windows Support

Applications can use API functions to communicate with many HIDs. The functions for exchanging reports include ReadFile and WriteFile as well as HID-specific APIs such HidD_SetFeature and HidD_GetFeature. Documentation for the HID API is in the WDK.

For system keyboards and pointing devices, Windows has exclusive access to Input and Output reports. Attempts to retrieve the reports via API functions trigger the error message *Access Denied*. Applications typically don't need to read the reports that describe keypresses and mouse movements and button clicks. Instead, the operating system reads the reports, and applications use higher-level methods to access the data. For example, a button on a form in a .NET application has a click event that can contain code to execute when a user clicks the button. If a system has multiple keyboards or pointing devices, the application treats them all as a single virtual keyboard or pointing device.

Other options for accessing HIDs include DirectX's DirectInput component and Raw Input. DirectInput provides fast, more direct access to keyboard, mouse, and game-controller data. The raw input API offers a way to read HID data, including keyboard and mouse data, from specific devices, including a specific keyboard when multiple keyboards are attached.

IrDA Bridge

The IrDA (Infrared Data Association) interface defines hardware requirements and protocols for exchanging data over short distances via infrared energy. A USB IrDA bridge converts between USB and IrDA data and enables a host to use USB to monitor, control, and exchange data over an IrDA interface.

Documentation

The specification for USB IrDA bridges is *IrDA Bridge Device Definition*. The IrDA specifications are available from *www.irda.org*.

Overview

The data in an IrDA link uses the Infrared Link Access Protocol (IrLAP), which defines the format of the IrDA frames that carry data, addresses, and status and control information. The IrLAP Payload consists of the address, control, and optional information, or data, fields in an IrLAP frame. In addition to the IrLAP Payload, each frame contains an error-checking value and markers for the beginning and end of the frame.

A USB IrDA bridge uses bulk pipes to exchange data with the host. The host and bridge place status and control information in headers with formats defined in the IrDA bridge specification. On receiving data from the IrDA link, the IrDA bridge extracts the IrLAP Payload, adds a header, and passes the data and header to the host. The header can contain values for the IrDA link's Media_Busy and Link_Speed parameters. On receiving IrDA data from the host, the IrDA bridge removes the header added by the host. The header can specify new values for Link_Speed and the number of beginning-of-frame markers. The bridge then places the IrDA Payload in an IrDA frame for transmitting.

Descriptors

An IrDA-bridge function is defined at the interface subclass level. In the interface descriptor, bInterfaceClass = FEh to indicate an application-specific interface and bInterfaceSubclass 02h to indicate an IrDA Bridge Device. A class-specific descriptor contains IrDA-specific information such as the maximum number of bytes in an IrDA frame and supported baud rates.

Class-specific Requests

The class defines five control requests:

Request	bRequest	Description
Receiving	01h	Is the device currently receiving an IrLAP frame?
Check_Media_Busy	03h	Is infrared traffic present?
Set_IrDA_Rate_Sniff	04h	Accept frames at any speed or at a single speed.
Set_IrDA_Unicast_List	05h	Accept frames from the named addresses only.
Get_Class_Specific_Descriptors	06h	Return the class-specific descriptor.

Chips

To support the IrDA bridge function, a microcontroller must have a non-low-speed USB port with bulk endpoints and an IrDA interface. Micro-controllers can interface to IrDA transceivers and encoder/decoder circuits via asynchronous serial ports. The Texas Instruments TUSB3410 is an 8052 microcontroller with a full-speed USB port and on-chip IrDA encoder/decoder for serial communications via an external IrDA transceiver.

Windows Support

Recent Windows editions include support for IrDA via the *irda.sys* driver and the *irsir.sys* miniport driver for UART-based adapters. Windows doesn't provide a driver for the USB IrDA bridge function.

Mass Storage

The mass storage class is for devices that transfer files and includes hard drives as well as CD, DVD, and flash-memory drives. Cameras can use the mass-storage class to enable accessing picture files in a camera's memory. Under Windows, devices that use the mass-storage driver appear as drives in Windows Explorer and the file system enables users to copy, move, and delete files in the devices. Mass-storage communications is a complex topic. My book *USB Mass Storage* has more about USB protocols, file systems, and the SCSI commands that access storage media.

Documentation

The USB specification for mass storage devices includes an overview and speci-fications for the bulk-only transport protocol, the control/bulk/interrupt (CBI) transport protocol, Universal Floppy Interface (UFI) commands, and the lockable storage devices feature.

The Lockable Storage Devices feature specification defines a protocol to address security and privacy concerns for media contents. With host support, a lockable storage device can require a user-provided passphrase before allowing a host to access the device's media.

Each media type has an industry-standard command-block set to enable controlling devices and reading status information.

Generic SCSI media uses the mandatory commands from *SCSI Primary Command (SPC) Set* and *SCSI Block Command (SBC) Set* from *www.t10.org*.

ATAPI CD/DVD devices use the *ATA/ATAPI* specification from *www.t13.org* and the *MultiMedia Command (MMC) Set* from *www.t10.org*. (An earlier version of the ATA/ATAPI specification was called *SFF 8020i*.)

ATAPI removable media uses *SFF-8070i: ATAPI Removable Rewritable Media Devices*, available from *www.sffcommittee.com*. This document is a supplement to the ATA/ATAPI specification. Floppy drives often belong to this subclass.

UFI uses the *UFI Command Specification* from *www.usb.org*. The commands are based on the SCSI-2 and SFF-8070i command sets.

The USB-IF's USB Attached SCSI Protocol (UASP) working group is developing protocols for efficient mass-storage transfers at SuperSpeed and improved efficiency at lower speeds. The INCITS T10 committee *(www.t10.org)* is developing a related USB Attached SCSI standard to define a transport protocol for USB devices that use SCSI commands.

Overview

Mass-storage devices use bulk transfers to exchange data. Control transfers send class-specific requests and can clear Stall conditions on bulk endpoints. For exchanging other information, virtually all devices use the bulk-only protocol. An alternative, control/bulk/interrupt (CBI), is approved for use only with full-speed floppy drives and not recommended for new devices.

In the bulk-only protocol, a successful data transfer has two or three stages: command transport, data transport (if needed), and status transport. In the command-transport stage, the host sends a command in a structure called a Command Block Wrapper (CBW). In the data-transport stage, the host or device sends the requested data. In the status-transport stage, the device sends

Table 7-6: The CBW contains a command block and other information about the command.

Name	Bits	Description
dCBWSignature	32	The value 43425355h, which identifies the structure as a CBW.
dCBWTag	32	A tag that associates this CBW with the CSW the device will send in response.
dCBWDataTransferLength	32	The number of bytes the host expects to transfer in the data-transport stage.
bmCBWFlags	8	Specifies the direction of the data-transport stage. Bit 7 = 0 for an OUT (host-to-device) transfer. Bit 7 = 1 for an IN (device-to-host) transfer. All other bits are zero. If there is no data-transport stage, bit 7 is ignored.
Reserved	4	Zero
bCBWLUN	4	For devices with multiple LUNs, specifies the LUN the command block is directed to. Otherwise the value is zero.
Reserved	3	Zero
bCBWCBLength	5	The length (1–16) of the command block in bytes
CBWCB	128	The command block for the device to execute.

status information in a structure called a Command Status Wrapper (CSW). Some commands have no data-transport stage.

Table 7-6 shows the fields in the CBW. The meaning of the command-block value in the CBWCB field varies with the command set specified by the interface descriptor's bInterfaceSubClass field.

On receiving a CBW, a device must check that the structure is valid and has meaningful content. A CBW is valid if it is received after a CSW or reset, is 31 bytes, and has the correct value in dCBWSignature. The contents are considered meaningful if no reserved bits are set, bCBWLUN contains a supported LUN value, and bCBWCBLength and CBWCB are valid for the interface's subclass.

Table 7-7 shows the fields in the CSW. On receiving a CSW, the host must check that the structure is valid and has meaningful content. A CSW is valid if it has 13 bytes, has the correct value in dCSWSignature, and has a dCSWTag value that matches dCBWTag of a corresponding CBW. The contents are considered meaningful if bCSWStatus equals 02h or if bCSWStatus equals either

Table 7-7: The CSW contains status and related information about a command.

Name	Bits	Description
dCBWSignature	32	The value 53425355h, which identifies the structure as a CSW.
dCBWTag	32	The value of the dCBWTag in a CBW received from the host.
dCSWDataResidue	32	For OUT transfers, the difference between dCBWDataTransferLength and the number of bytes the device processed. For IN transfers, the difference between dCBWDataTransferLength and the number of bytes the device sent.
bCSWStatus	8	00h = command passed 01h = command failed 02h = phase error

00h or 01h and dCSWDataResidue is less than or equal to dCBWDataTransferLength.

Descriptors

In an interface descriptor, bInterfaceClass = 08h specifies the mass-storage class.

The bInterfaceSubClass field specifies the supported command-block set. Most new designs should set the field to 06h (generic SCSI media). The host then determines the specific device type by issuing a SCSI INQUIRY command. The device's response specifies a peripheral device type (PDT). The SCSI Primary Commands (SPC) specification defines PDT codes. The code for hard drives and flash drives is 00h. The bInterfaceProtocol field indicates the supported transport protocol. Most new designs should set the field to 50h (bulk only).

Every bulk-only mass-storage device must have a serial number in a USB string descriptor. The serial number must be at least 12 characters using only characters in the range *0–9* and *A–F.* A serial number enables the operating system to retain properties such as the drive letter and access policies after a user moves a device to another port or attaches multiple devices with the same Vendor ID and Product ID. The serial number must be different from the serial numbers in other devices that have the same values in the idVendor, idProduct, and bcdDevice fields in the device descriptor.

A mass-storage device must have a bulk endpoint for each direction.

Lockable storage devices have additional descriptors to support the locking capability.

Class-specific Requests

The bulk-only protocol has two defined control requests: Bulk Only Mass Storage Reset (reset the device) and Get Max Lun (get the number of logical units, or partitions, that the device supports). All other commands and status information travel in bulk transfers.

The control/bulk/interrupt (CBI) protocol has one defined control request: Accept Device-Specific Command (ADSC). The Data stage of the request carries the command. A CBI device can use an interrupt transfer to indicate that the device has completed a command's requested action.

Lockable storage devices support additional requests for locking functions.

Chips

A mass-storage device can use just about any non-low-speed controller chip, but several manufacturers have controllers designed specifically for use in mass-storage devices. Prolific Technology and Standard Microsystems Corporation (SMSC) each have chips with interfaces to a variety of mass-storage device types. Controllers with direct interfaces to ATA/ATAPI devices include ST-NXP Wireless' ISP1583, Texas Instruments' TUSB6250, and Cypress Semiconductor's EZUSB AT2LP. Mass storage will likely be an early application for SuperSpeed device.

Windows Support

Windows 2000 and later include a driver that supports bulk-only and CBI devices. The USB storage port driver (*usbstor.sys*) manages communications between the lower-level USB drivers and the Windows storage-class drivers. When a device is formatted using a supported file system, the operating system assigns a drive letter to the device and the device appears in Windows Explorer.

The mass-storage driver in Windows XP and later supports bInterfaceSubClass codes 02h, 05h, and 06h. Support for drives with multiple Logical Unit Numbers (LUNs) was added in Windows 2000 SP3.

One point of confusion relating to the mass-storage support under Windows is the difference between removable devices and removable media. All USB drives are removable devices because they're easily attached and detached from the PC. A removable device may have removable or non-removable media. CD and

DVD drives have removable media. A hard drive has non-removable media because you can't easily remove the disk from the drive. Windows Autoplay applies to devices with removable media. Autoplay enables the operating system to run a program, play a movie, or perform other actions when a disk or other removable media is inserted. To support AutoPlay, some devices with non-removable media emulate devices with removable media.

Personal Healthcare

The personal healthcare device class encompasses devices that help to maintain health and wellness, manage disease, and enable independent living for the elderly. Devices in the class include heart-rate and blood-pressure monitors, glucose meters, pulse oximeters, motion sensors, and pill monitors.

Documentation

The class doesn't define protocols for data or messaging. Devices may use data and messaging standards defined in the ISO/IEEE 11073-20601 Base Exchange Protocol.

Overview

A device may send data that is episodic (at irregular or infrequent intervals) or continuous. A device may collect and store data before transmitting the data to the host, and a device may collect data when detached from the host. For example, a jogger might wear a monitor while out for a run and upload the data on returning home. Devices may support host-to-device communications to receive configuration data and other episodic data from a host.

Descriptors

The preferred location for the class code is in the interface descriptor, but declaring the class in the device descriptor is allowed. The function must have at least one bulk endpoint in each direction. An interrupt IN endpoint and additional endpoints are optional.

Several class-specific descriptors provide class-specific information. A PHDC Class Function descriptor specifies the device's data and messaging protocols. If needed, a Function Extension descriptor follows the PHDC Class Function descriptor. Following each endpoint descriptor is a PHDC QoS descriptor with attributes that describe the latency and reliability of the data channel. If needed, a PHDC MetaData descriptor follows the PHDC QoS descriptor to provide application-specific information.

Class-specific Requests

Set Feature and Clear Feature requests can turn on and off the class-specific Meta-Data Message Preamble feature. A Get Status request can request a bit-map of endpoints that have data.

Chips

Just about any non-low-speed device can support the required endpoints.

Windows Support

Windows doesn't provide a driver for this class.

Printer

The printer class is for devices that convert received data into text, images, or both on paper or other media. The most basic printers print lines of text in a single font. Most laser and inkjet printers understand one or more page description languages (PDLs) and can print text in any font as well as images.

Documentation

The USB Printing Devices specification is for printers of all types. The IEEE-1284 standard (*www.ieee.org*) describes the interface used by parallel-port printers and defines the format for the Device IDs that USB printers use.

Overview

Printer data uses a bulk OUT pipe. The host obtains status information via control requests or an optional bulk IN pipe.

Descriptors

In the interface descriptor, bInterfaceClass = 07h to specify the printer class.

The interface descriptor's bInterfaceProtocol field contains a value that names a type of printer interface:

bInterfaceProtocol	Type
01h	Unidirectional
02h	Bidirectional
03h	IEEE-1284.4-compatible Bidirectional

With all three interface protocols, the host uses the bulk OUT endpoint to send data to the printer. With the unidirectional protocol, the host retrieves status information by sending a class-specific Get Port Status request. With the bidirectional protocol, the host can retrieve status information using Get Port Status or the bulk IN pipe. This method can provide more detailed information. The IEEE-1284.4-compatible bidirectional protocol is similar to the bidirectional protocol but with added support to enable communications with individual functions in a multifunction peripheral.

Class-specific Requests

The printer class has three class-specific requests.

In response to a GET_DEVICE_ID request, the device returns a Device ID in the format specified by the IEEE-1284 standard. The first two bytes of the Device ID are the length in bytes, most significant byte first. Following the length is a string containing a series of keys and their values in this format:

key: value {,value};

All Device IDs must contain the keys MANUFACTURER, COMMAND SET, and MODEL, or their abbreviated forms (MFG, CMD, and MDL). The COMMAND SET key names any PDLs the printer supports, such as Hewlett Packard's Printer Control Language (PCL) or Adobe Postscript. Additional keys, which may be vendor-defined, are optional.

Here is an example Device ID:

MFG:My Printer Company;
MDL:Model 5T;
CMD:MLC,PCL,PML;
DESCRIPTION:My Printer Company Laser Printer 5T;
CLASS.PRINTER,
REV:1.3.2;

In response to the GET_PORT_STATUS request, the device returns a byte that emulates the Status-port byte on a parallel printer port. Three bits in the byte contain status information:

Bit	Name	Meaning When 1	Meaning When 0
3	Not error	no error	error
4	Select	printer selected	printer not selected
5	Paper empty	out of paper	not out of paper

A printer that can't obtain the status byte should respond with 18h to signify *no error, printer selected, not out of paper.* Parallel-port printers use two additional status bits, Busy and Ack, for flow control. These bits don't apply to USB printers.

On receiving a Soft_Reset request, a device should flush all buffers, reset the interface's bulk pipes to their default states, and clear all Stall conditions. In a Soft_Reset request, the bmRequestType value in the Setup transaction should equal 21h to signify a class-specific request that is directed to an interface and has no Data stage. However, version 1.0 of the printer-class specification incorrectly listed the bmRequestType for Soft_Reset as 23h. So to be on the safe side, devices should respond to hosts that use a bmRequestType of 23h with this request, and hosts should try the incorrect value on receiving a STALL in response to this request using the correct value.

Chips

Just about any non-low-speed controller will have the one or two bulk endpoints for a printer function. For converting parallel-port printers to USB, Prolific Technology has the PL-2305 USB-to-IEEE-1284 Bridge Controller. The chip's IEEE-1284 parallel port can interface to an existing parallel port on a printer or other peripheral.

Windows Support

Windows includes drivers that handle tasks for Postscript and non-Postscript printers. A printer manufacturer can customize a driver for a specific printer by providing a printer data file, which is a text file with customization information. The WDK has information on how to create printer data files.

For application programmers, the .NET Framework 3.0 introduced the Windows Presentation Foundation (WPF) subsystem with enhanced printing support.

Smart Card

Smart cards are the familiar plastic cards used for phone cards, gift cards, keyless entry, access to toll roads and mass transit, storing medical and insurance data, enabling satellite TV receivers, and other applications that require storing modest amounts of information with easy and portable access. Alternate terms for smart card are chip card and integrated circuits card (ICC).

Each card contains a module with memory and often a CPU. Many cards allow updating of their contents, for example to change a monetary value or an entry code. Some cards have exposed electrical contacts, while others communicate via embedded antennas.

To access a smart card, you establish a connection to a chip card interface device (CCID), typically by inserting the card into a slot or waving a contactless card near a reader with a wireless interface. Another term for CCID is smart-card reader. (Some CCIDs can also write to cards.) USB enters the picture because some CCIDs have USB interfaces for communicating with USB hosts.

An ICC device (ICCD) is a smart card that has its own USB interface and thus doesn't need a separate CCID. An ICCD uses a vendor-specific USB connector. Another term for ICCD is USB-ICC. If you're thinking that all of these terms are confusingly alike, you're not alone. Table 7-8 summarizes.

Documentation

CCIDs and ICCDs each have a specification document: *Device Class: Smart Card CCID* and *Device Class: Smart Card ICCD*. The INCITS/ISO/IEC 7816 standard (available from *www.ansi.org*) defines physical and electrical characteristics and commands for communicating with smart cards.

Overview

Every CCID must have a bulk endpoint in each direction. All readers with removable cards must also have an interrupt IN endpoint.

The host and device exchange messages on the bulk pipes. A CCID message consists of a 10-byte header followed by message-specific data. The specification defines commands that the host can use to send data and status and control information in messages. Every command requires at least one response message from the CCID. A response contains a message code and status information and may contain additional requested data. The device uses the interrupt endpoint to report errors and the inserting or removal of a card.

An ICCD may have an interrupt IN endpoint, a pair of bulk endpoints, or both endpoint types or may use the control endpoint only.

Descriptors

In an interface descriptor in a CCID or ICCD, bInterfaceClass = 0Bh to declare the CCID class. For ICCDs, bInterfaceProtocol specifies a protocol that indicates what endpoints the device uses. Following the interface descriptor is a

Table 7-8: Smart card terminology can be a challenge to master.

Term	Meaning
Smart card Chip card ICC	The card.
CCID Smart card reader	A device that communicates with cards. May have a USB interface.
ICCD USB-ICC	A card, CCID function, and USB interface in one device.

class-specific CCID Class descriptor with bDescriptorType = 21h. The class descriptor contains parameters such as the number of slots, slot voltages, supported protocols, supported clock frequencies and data rates, and maximum message length. CCIDs and ICCDs use the same class-specific descriptor, but ICCDs ignore some fields.

Class-specific Requests

CCIDs have defined control requests for aborting a transfer, getting clock frequencies, and getting data rates. ICCDs can use class-specific requests to transfer data and other information.

Chips

A CCID can use just about any non-low-speed device controller. Some controllers have support for CCID functions built in. Alcor Micro Corporation has the AU9525 USB smart card reader controller with a full-speed USB interface. Winbond Electronics Corporation's W81E381 is an 8052-compatible microcontroller with USB and smart-card-reader interfaces.

Windows Support

A driver for Windows 2000 and later is available via Windows update. Applications can use DeviceIoControl API functions to communicate with CCIDs.

Still Image Capture

The still image class encompasses cameras that capture still images (in other words, not video) and scanners. The main job of a typical still-image device's USB interface is to transfer image data from the device to the host. Some devices can receive image data from the host as well. If all you need is a way to transfer image files from a camera, another option is to use the mass-storage class.

Documentation

The still-image class specification uses features and commands from *PIMA 15740: 2000 Picture Transfer Protocol* (PTP), which describes requirements for transferring files and controlling digital still cameras. The PIMA document is available from the International Imaging Industry Association (I3A) at *www.i3a.org*.

The USB-IF's *Media Transfer Protocol* specification is an extension of the Picture Transfer Protocol for use with digital cameras and other devices that have significant storage capacity and fulfill their primary purpose while not connected to the bus. For example, a digital camera stores images, and users typically attach the camera to the bus only to transfer images.

Overview

A still-image device has one bulk IN endpoint and one bulk OUT endpoint for transferring both image data and non-image data. The specification also requires an interrupt IN endpoint for event data.

In the bulk and interrupt pipes, information travels in structures called containers. The four container types are the Command Block, Data Block, Response Block, and Event Block. The bulk OUT pipe carries Command and Data Blocks. The bulk IN pipe carries Data and Response Blocks. The interrupt IN pipe carries Event Blocks.

On the bulk pipes, the host communicates by using a protocol with three phases: Command, Data, and Response. A short packet indicates the end of a phase. In the Command phase, the host sends a Command Block that names an operation defined in PIMA 15740. The Command Block contains an operation code that determines if the operation requires a data transfer and if so, the direction of data transfer. In a data transfer, the data travels in a Data Block in the Data phase. The first four bytes of the Data Block are the length in bytes of the data being transferred. Some operations have no Data phase. The final phase is the Response phase, where the device sends a Response Block containing completion information.

On the interrupt pipe, an Event Block can contain up to three Event Codes with status information such as a low-battery warning or a notification that a memory card has been removed. The Check Device Condition Event Code requests the host to send a class-specific Get_Extended_Event_Data request for more information about an event.

A device using the bulk-only protocol cancels a transfer by stalling the bulk endpoints. The host then sends a class-specific Get_Device_Status request and uses the Clear Feature request to clear the stalled endpoints. The host cancels a transfer by sending a class-specific Cancel_Request request. A device is ready to resume data transfers when it returns OK (PIMA 15740 Response Code 2001h) in response to a Get_Device_Status request.

Descriptors

In an interface descriptor, bInterfaceClass = 06h to indicate a still-image device, bInterfaceSubclass = 01h to indicate an image interface, and bInterfaceProtocol = 01h to indicate a still-image capture function. The interface must have descriptors for the bulk IN, bulk OUT, and interrupt IN endpoints.

Class-specific Requests

The class defines four control requests. Cancel_Request requests to cancel the PIMA 15740 transaction named in the request. Get_Extended_Event_Data (optional) requests extended information regarding an event or vendor condition. Device_Reset_Request requests the device to return to the Idle state. The host can use this request after a bulk endpoint has returned a STALL or to clear a vendor-specific condition. Get_Device_Status requests information needed to clear halted endpoints. The host uses this request after a device has canceled a data transfer.

Chips

Just about any non-low-speed USB controller will have the three endpoints required by the still-image class.

Windows Support

Recent Windows editions support the Windows Image Acquisition (WIA) API for communicating with devices in the still-image class. Applications communicate with devices by using ReadFile, WriteFile, and DeviceIoControl commands. The *usbscan.sys* driver adds USB support to WIA in Windows XP and later.

Beginning with Windows XP, cameras that use the Picture Transfer Protocol defined in PIMA 15740 require no vendor-provided driver components, though a vendor can provide a minidriver to support vendor-specific features and capabilities. For scanners, the vendor must provide a microdriver, which is a helper DLL that translates between the driver's communications and a language the scanner understands, or a minidriver that works with the provided drivers to enable communications with the device.

Windows 98 and Windows 2000 use an earlier Still Image architecture (STI). Product vendors must provide a user-mode driver to work with the provided STI driver.

Test and Measurement

The test-and-measurement class (USBTMC) is suited for instrumentation devices where the data on the bus doesn't need guaranteed timing. These devices typically contain components such as ADCs, DACs, sensors, and transducers. A device may be a stand-alone unit or a card in a larger computer.

Before USB, many test-and-measurement devices used the IEEE-488 parallel interface, also known as the General Purpose Interface Bus (GPIB). The USB488 subclass of the test-and-measurement class defines protocols for communicating using IEEE 488's data format and commands.

Documentation

The class's specifications include the main Test and Measurement class specification and a separate document for the USB488 subclass. The IEEE 488 standards are available from *www.ieee.org*.

Overview

A test-and-measurement device requires a bulk OUT endpoint and a bulk IN endpoint. An interrupt IN endpoint is required for devices in the USB488 subclass and otherwise is optional for returning event and status information.

The bulk pipes exchange messages consisting of a header followed by data. The bulk OUT endpoint receives command messages, and the bulk IN endpoint sends response messages. The header for a command message contains a message ID, a bTag value that identifies the transfer, and message-specific information. The header for a response message contains a message ID and bTag values of the command that prompted the response, followed by message-specific information.

Descriptors

The interface subclass specifies the test-and-measurement function. In the interface descriptor, bInterfaceClass = FEh to indicate an application-specific interface and bInterfaceSubClass = 03h to indicate the test-and-measurement class. There are no class-specific descriptors.

Class-specific Requests

The class defines eight control requests for controlling and requesting the status of an interface or transfer and requesting information about the interface's attributes and capabilities.

Chips

Just about any non-low-speed device will have the two or three endpoints this class requires.

Windows Support

Windows doesn't include a driver for this class. National Instruments provides a driver for use with the company's hardware. Other options for test-and-measurement devices that use bulk transfers include the mass-storage class, the WinUSB driver, and vendor-specific drivers. A HID-class device can also perform test and measurement functions. For an existing device with an IEEE-488 interface, a quick solution is to use a commercial IEEE-488/USB converter.

Video

The video class supports digital camcorders, webcams, and other devices that send, receive, or manipulate transient or moving images. The class also supports transferring still images from video devices.

Documentation

Multiple documents make up the video specification. The main class specification defines standard and class-specific descriptors and class-specific control requests for video devices. The video media transport terminal specification defines descriptors and requests for devices such as video cameras and digital VCRs, which stream data stored in sequential media and may require functions such as play, record, rewind, and eject. Separate specifications contain informa-

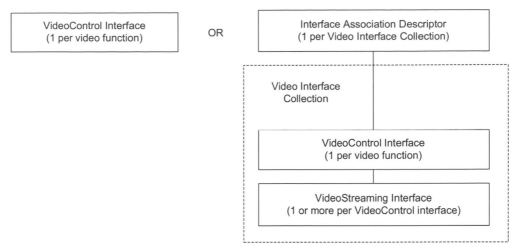

Figure 7-3. A video interface consists of a VideoControl interface and zero or more VideoStreaming interfaces.

tion for MJPEG, MPEG2-TS, and DV formats as well as generic frame-based, stream-based, and uncompressed payloads.

Other specification documents include a video camera example, an FAQ, and an Identifiers document that gathers together identifier values defined in the other video-class specifications.

Overview

Figure 7-3 shows the elements that make up a video function in a USB device. Every function must have a VideoControl interface, which provides information about inputs, outputs, and other components of the function. Most functions also have one or more VideoStreaming interfaces that enable transferring video data. A Video Interface Collection consists of a VideoControl interface and its associated VideoStreaming interfaces. A device can have multiple, independent VideoControl interfaces and Video Interface Collections.

The VideoControl interface uses the control endpoint and may use an interrupt IN endpoint. Each VideoStreaming interface has one isochronous or bulk endpoint for video data and an optional bulk endpoint for still-image data.

Descriptors

The video class defines an extensive set of descriptors that enable devices to provide detailed information about the device's abilities. Each Video Interface Col-

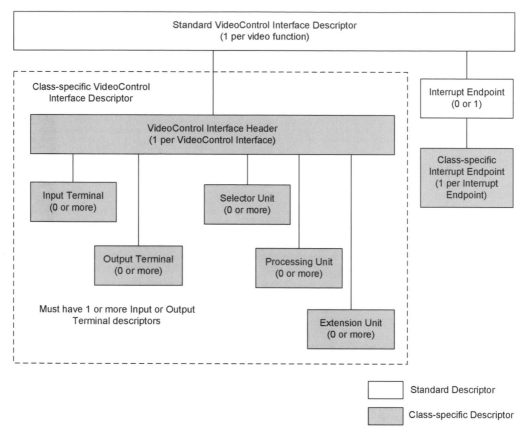

Figure 7-4. The VideoControl interface provides information about inputs, outputs, and other components of a video function.

lection must have an interface association descriptor that specifies the interface number of the first VideoControl interface and the number of VideoStreaming interfaces associated with the function.

The VideoControl Interface. The VideoControl interface (Figure 7-4) has a standard interface descriptor with bInterfaceClass = 0Eh to indicate the video class. The descriptor's iInterface field must reference a string descriptor that contains a function name in U.S. English. (Other languages are optional.) A class-specific VideoControl interface descriptor consists of a VideoControl interface header descriptor followed by one or more Terminal and/or Unit descriptors.

A Terminal is the starting or ending point for information that flows into or out of a function. A Terminal may represent a USB endpoint or another compo-

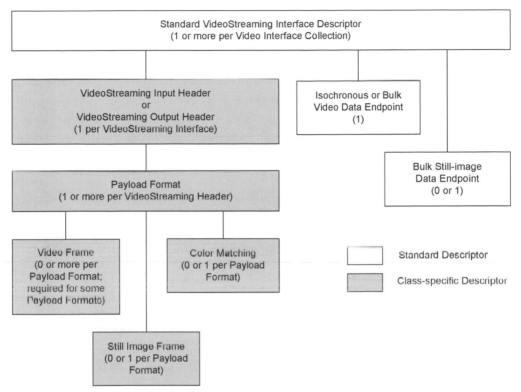

Figure 7-5. A VideoStreaming interface has an endpoint for video data and an optional endpoint for still-image data.

nent such as a CCD sensor, display module, or composite-video input or output.

A Unit transforms data flowing through a function. A Selector Unit routes a data stream to an output, a Processing Unit controls video attributes, and an Extension Unit performs a vendor-defined function.

If the interface has an interrupt endpoint, the endpoint has a standard endpoint descriptor followed by a class-specific endpoint descriptor.

The VideoStreaming Interface. Each VideoStreaming interface (Figure 7-5) has a standard interface descriptor. Following this descriptor, an interface with an IN endpoint has a class-specific VideoStreaming Input Header descriptor, and an interface with an OUT endpoint has a class-specific VideoStreaming Output Header descriptor.

Following the Header descriptor is a Payload Format descriptor for each supported video format. For frame-based formats, the Payload Format descriptor is followed by one or more Video Frame descriptors that describe the dimensions of the video frames and other characteristics specific to a format. Some devices that support still-image capture have a Still Image Frame descriptor. A Payload Format can also have a Color Matching descriptor to describe a color profile. Each VideoStreaming interface has one isochronous or bulk endpoint descriptor for video data and an optional bulk endpoint descriptor for still-image data.

Class-specific Requests

Class-specific control requests enable setting and reading the states of controls in VideoControl and VideoStreaming interfaces.

Chips

Video tends to require a lot of bus bandwidth, so controllers used in video applications are likely to support high speed. Vista Imaging's ViCAM-III chip contains a USB controller and a programmable digital imaging engine that supports video functions. Cypress Semiconductor has partnered with other companies to offer reference designs that use EZ-USB controllers in various video applications. Video will likely be an early application for SuperSpeed chips.

Windows Support

Windows XP SP2 introduced a driver compatible with the video class version 1.0 (*usbvideo.sys*). Vendors of video-class devices that use the driver don't need to provide any driver software but can provide a Control or Streaming extension to support vendor-specific functions or features.

Applications can access video devices using the DirectShow component of DirectX. DirectX version 9.2 added support for the *usbvideo.sys* driver.

For earlier Windows editions, vendors of video devices must provide a minidriver to specify a format for streaming video, implement device-specific functions and properties, and perform bulk transfers if required for video data. The Windows USBCAMD driver manages isochronous data transfers, including synchronizing, starting, and stopping the communications and recovering from errors. The driver communicates with the Windows stream-class driver and with the lower-level USB drivers.

Implementing Non-standard Functions

Some devices perform functions that don't have an obvious match to a USB class. Other functions might fit into a class such as test and measurement or device firmware upgrade, but the lack of a driver in Windows and other operating systems might prompt one to look for a different approach. Many legacy serial- and parallel-port devices perform vendor-specific functions and need to convert to USB. Another function that doesn't fit a defined class is host-to-host communications. USB is flexible enough to accommodate all of these needs.

Choosing a Driver

Class drivers that are suitable for some devices with vendor-defined functions include HID, communications device, and mass storage. HIDs are limited to control and interrupt transfers but can transfer data for any purpose. A virtual COM port in the communications device class can exchange data in bulk transfers. Mass storage is an option for devices that transfer data in files if the host and device support the same file system.

For standard but unsupported classes such as test and measurement and device firmware upgrade, you might be able to obtain a class driver from a third party.

Using a Generic Driver

A generic driver can be a solution for devices that don't fit a standard class. Generic drivers typically enable applications to request control, interrupt, bulk, and isochronous transfers using a driver-specific API.

Microsoft's WinUSB driver is an option if the host systems use Windows XP and later and the device doesn't use isochronous transfers. Chapter 14 has more about WinUSB. Other sources offer generic drivers that have more capabilities and are compatible with earlier Windows editions. Vendors include Andrew Pargeter & Associates, Jungo Ltd., Tetradyne Software, Inc., and Thesycon Systemsoftware & Consulting GmbH. Many of these drivers are in toolkits that generate the required INF file and include example application code. As Chapter 6 explained, some chip companies also provide generic drivers for use with their chips.

Converting from RS-232

The RS-232 serial port was a feature on the very first PCs and persisted for many years on PCs and peripherals. Just about any device that uses RS-232 can use USB instead. There are several approaches to making the switch.

Some RS-232 devices fit into a defined USB class. The communications device class includes modems. The HID class provides usages for pointing devices, uninterruptible power supplies, and point-of-sale devices.

For many other devices, FTDI Chip's FT232R USB UART introduced in Chapter 6 provides a quick way to upgrade a design to USB. The chip can convert an existing RS-232 device to USB with minimal design changes and in most cases no changes to host software or device firmware.

Figure 7-6 shows an example. A typical device with an RS-232 interface contains a UART that converts between the serial data used in RS-232 communications and the parallel data the CPU uses. The signals on the line side of the UART connect to converters that translate between RS-232 voltages and the 5V logic used by the UART. The line side of the converter connects to a cable to the remote computer with an RS-232 interface. To convert from RS-232 to USB, you replace the RS-232 converter with an FT232R. On the host computer, FTDI Chip's Virtual COM port driver enables applications to access the device using the same functions used for RS-232 communications.

Many RS-232/USB adapter modules contain little more than an FT232R or similar chip, an RS-232 interface chip, and connectors for RS-232 and USB. An RS-232 device with an external adapter gives users the choice of using USB or RS-232.

When using a USB/RS-232 adapter, devices that use the status and control signals in unconventional ways and with critical timing requirements may require modifications to device hardware or firmware or application software.

Converting from the Parallel Port

Another port that PCs had from the beginning was the parallel port, which many devices besides printers used. For parallel-port printers, adapter modules are available to enable connecting to a PC via USB.

Devices with other functions may require redesigning for USB. The device might use the WinUSB driver or a generic or custom driver. The device will need new application software to communicate with the driver. A peripheral-side parallel-port interface has 8 bidirectional data pins, 5 status outputs,

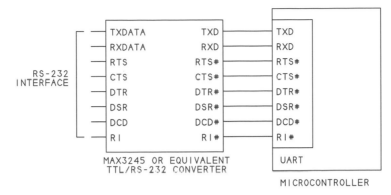

TYPICAL RS-232 DEVICE

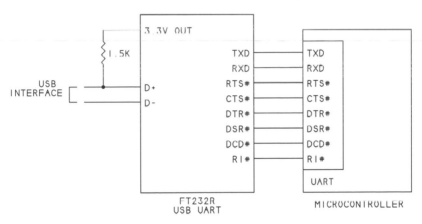

RS-232 DEVICE CONVERTED TO USB

Figure 7-6. FTDI's FT232R USB UART can convert devices with RS-232 interfaces to USB. A driver provided by FTDI causes the device to appear as a COM-port device to host applications.

and 4 control inputs. Thus a USB controller with 17 I/O bits can emulate a parallel port. The device will need vendor-specific firmware to translate between the USB and parallel-port data, plus a host driver and new application software.

PC-to-PC Communications

With one exception, USB doesn't allow hosts to exchange data with each other directly. Every USB communication must be between a host and a device. Yet

205

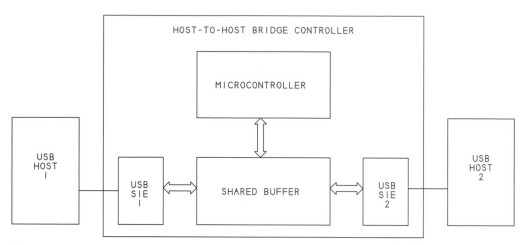

Figure 7-7. To enable two USB hosts to communicate with each other, two USB serial interface engines can share a buffer. Each SIE copies received USB data into the shared buffer, and the other device retrieves the data from the buffer and sends the data to the other host.

because every PC has a USB port, some applications might want to use the interface to communicate between PCs.

If both PCs have Ethernet ports, the cheapest solution is to forget about USB and use Ethernet. Use a crossover cable to connect the PCs directly or connect the PCs via a hub or router.

If Ethernet ports aren't an option, a USB host-to-host bridge cable can do the job. The cable incorporates two USB device controllers (which may reside in a single chip). Each controller represents a USB device. Each device attaches to a different PC, and the devices exchange data via a shared buffer (Figure 7-7). When a PC sends data to its attached device, the device writes the data to the shared buffer. The other device in the bridge retrieves the data from the buffer and sends it on to its attached PC.

Prolific Technology's PL-2501 Hi-Speed USB Host to Host Bridge Controller is a single chip designed for this type of host-to-host application. The chip contains an 8032 microcontroller and two USB SIEs that access a common buffer. Typically, the drivers for bridge cables cause each PC to see the other as a network-connected computer.

Another way to achieve a network connection via USB is to use USB/Ethernet adapters.

An alternate approach for host-to-host communications is to use two FTDI FT232R USB UARTs and cross-connect the asynchronous interfaces in a null-modem configuration. Each PC then has a COM port that communicates with a COM port on the other PC.

The exception to the host-and-device rule is the USB 3.0 Standard-A to USB 3.0 Standard-A cable. With host driver support, SuperSpeed devices will be able to use this cable to communicate with each other. Chapter 19 has more about the cable.

8

How the Host Communicates

This chapter explains how a Windows PC manages communications with USB devices. The driver architecture described applies to Windows XP and Windows Vista, but much of the information also applies to other Windows editions.

Device Drivers

A device driver is a software component that enables applications to access a hardware device. The hardware device may be a printer, modem, keyboard, video display, data-acquisition unit, or just about anything controlled by circuits the CPU can access. Most USB devices are external devices that connect via cables (or wireless links). Some USB devices, such as fingerprint scanners, are in the box with the CPU.

The Layered Driver Model

USB communications under Windows use a layered driver model where each driver in a series, or stack, performs a portion of the communication task. At the top of the stack is a client driver that the operating system has assigned to the device. Another term for client driver is function driver. USB class drivers and vendor-specific device drivers are client drivers. Applications access a USB device by communicating with the client driver. The client driver in turn communicates with lower-level bus and port drivers that access the hardware. One or more filter drivers can supplement a client driver or bus driver.

Dividing communications into layers is efficient because devices that have tasks in common can use the same driver for those tasks. For example, it makes sense to have one set of drivers that handle tasks common to all USB devices. An operating system can provide these drivers so device vendors don't have to do so with much duplication of effort.

User and Kernel Modes

Under Windows, program code runs in either user mode or kernel mode. Each mode allows a different level of privilege in accessing memory and other system resources. Figure 8-1 shows the major components of user and kernel modes in USB communications. Applications run in user mode. A USB device must have a kernel-mode client driver, which can have a supplementary user-mode driver.

User mode has limited access to memory and other system resources. Applications and user-mode client drivers can't access memory that the operating system has designated as protected. Limiting access to memory in this way enables the PC to run multiple applications at the same time. If an application crashes, other applications shouldn't be affected.

Kernel-mode code has unrestricted access to system resources, including the ability to execute memory-management instructions and control access to I/O ports. A kernel-mode driver can allow any application to use a device or allow a single application to have exclusive use. Other abilities that Windows reserves for kernel-mode drivers include DMA transfers and responding to hardware interrupts.

The specifics vary with the driver, but in general, ways that applications may communicate with kernel-mode drivers include Windows API functions, other functions exposed by a user-mode driver, and the properties, methods, and events of classes defined by the .NET Framework. To communicate with a USB device, an application often doesn't have to know anything about the USB protocol or whether a device uses USB at all.

Kernel-mode drivers communicate using structures called I/O request packets (IRPs) supported by the operating system. Each IRP requests a single input or

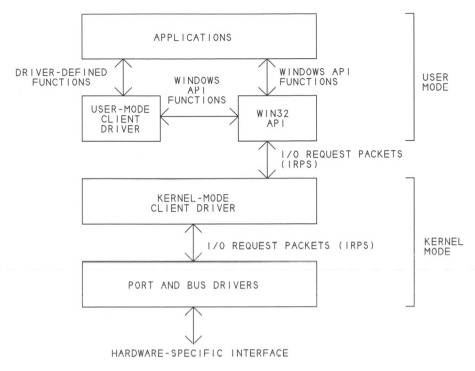

Figure 8-1. USB uses a layered driver model under Windows, with separate drivers for devices and the buses they connect to.

output action. A kernel-mode client driver for a USB device uses IRPs to communicate with the bus drivers that handle USB communications.

Drivers create *device objects* to handle I/O requests. A DEVICE_OBJECT structure represents the device object. A physical device object (PDO) represents a device to a bus driver. A functional device object (FDO) represents a device to a client driver. A filter device object (filter DO) represents a device to a filter driver.

The Windows PnP manager requests the bus driver to create a PDO for each device on a bus. For each PDO, the PnP manager may load and call client and filter drivers that in turn create FDOs and filter DOs.

Inside the Layers

The components involved in accessing USB devices include applications, user-mode client drivers, kernel-mode client drivers, and bus drivers.

Applications

Before an application can communicate with a device, several things must happen. On power up or device attachment, the operating system enumerates the device as described in Chapter 4. To identify which driver to use, Windows compares the retrieved descriptors with the information in the system's INF files. Chapter 9 has more about INF files. When enumeration is complete and the driver is loaded, applications can access the device.

Some drivers cause the host to continuously request data from a device whether or not an application has requested data. For example, a host requests keypress data at intervals from a keyboard.

The Windows API

Applications written in Visual Basic, C and its variants, Delphi, and other languages can access many devices by calling Windows API functions. The supported functions vary with the driver, but an application typically opens communications with CreateFile, exchanges data using a combination of Read-File or ReadFileEx, WriteFile or WriteFileEx, and DeviceIoControl, and closes communications with CloseHandle. Microsoft's Windows Software Development Kit (SDK) documents these functions.

Although the names suggest that the functions are for use with files, ReadFile and WriteFile (and their variants ReadFileEx and WriteFileEx) can communicate with drivers that access many device types via handle-based operations. The function calls pass pointers to buffers to store data being read or data to be written. Depending on the driver, a call to ReadFile might request data from a device or return data that a driver has already requested and stored in the driver's buffer.

DeviceIoControl offers another way to transfer data. Included in each Device-IoControl request is a control code that identifies a specific command. For example, IOCTL_STORAGE_GET_MEDIA_TYPES requests the types of media a mass-storage device supports. Because a function call sends codes to a specific driver, multiple drivers can use the same codes.

Using .NET's Classes

For easier and safer programming, Microsoft's .NET Framework provides classes that eliminate the need to call many API functions from application code. Instead, applications communicate with a Common Language Runtime (CLR) component that in turn may call API functions. The CLR simplifies application programming by handling memory management and other low-level tasks. For example, instead of using ReadFile and WriteFile to access files on drives, applications can use methods in .NET's Directory and File classes. The CLR works with other components in the .NET Framework to translate the application code to API calls that access the files.

The .NET classes don't implement every API function, however. For example, .NET doesn't provide methods for detecting device attachment and removal via WM_DEVICECHANGE messages.

User-mode Client Drivers

A user-mode client driver can define a driver-specific API that applications can use to access devices. The driver is in a dynamic link library (DLL). An example of a user-mode USB driver is *winusb.dll*, which exposes routines for accessing devices that use the WinUSB kernel-mode driver. These routines make up the WinUSB API. In a similar way, *hid.dll* is a user-mode driver that exposes HID API routines for accessing devices that use the HID kernel-mode class driver.

A user-mode driver translates between the driver-defined functions and the Windows API. For example, when an application calls the Hid_GetFeature API function, the user-mode HID driver calls the DeviceIoControl API function, which causes the kernel-mode HID driver to request a HID Feature report from a device.

Kernel-mode Client Drivers

A kernel-mode client driver manages communications between user-mode code and lower-level USB drivers. Kernel-mode client drivers must conform to the Windows Driver Model (WDM) defined by Microsoft for use under Windows 98 and later. These drivers have the extension *.sys*. (Other driver types may also use this extension.) Examples of kernel-mode client drivers are *winusb.sys* (WinUSB) and *hidclass.sys* (HID).

A kernel-mode client driver can be a class driver included with Windows or a vendor-provided driver. The driver manages communications that are specific to a device or a class of devices. A class driver may also communicate with a miniclass driver that manages communications with a subset of devices in a class.

A client driver or miniclass driver can have one or more upper and lower filter drivers (Figure 8-2). An upper-level filter driver can monitor and modify communications between applications and a client driver. A lower-level filter driver

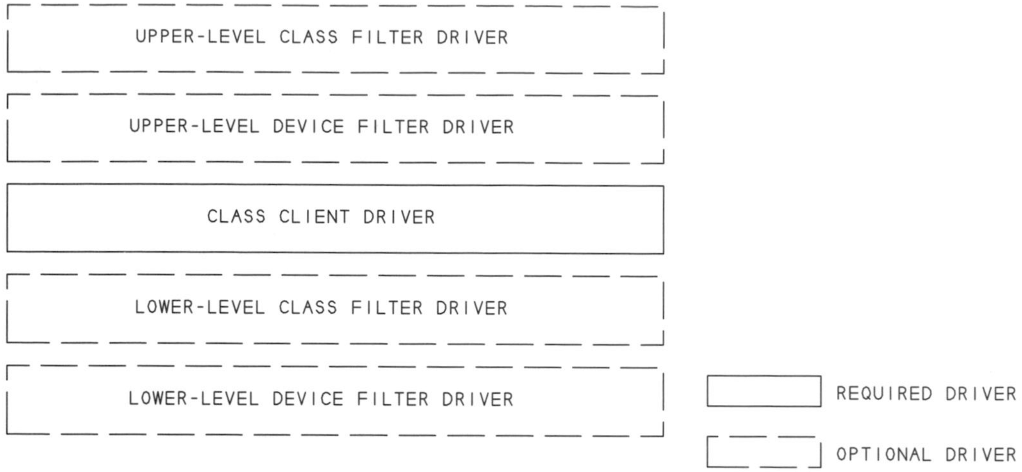

Figure 8-2. A client driver can have one or more filter drivers that monitor or modify communications with devices.

can monitor and modify communications between a client driver and the bus drivers.

For some composite devices, Windows loads a USB common-class generic parent driver (*usbccgp.sys*) between the bus drivers and the client drivers for the device's interfaces. The generic parent driver handles synchronization, Plug-and-Play (PnP), and power-management functions for the device as a whole and manages communications between the lower-level USB drivers and client drivers for the composite device's interfaces.

User-mode programmers have a choice of programming languages, including Visual Basic, Delphi, and C/C++/C#. For kernel-mode drivers, C has the needed capabilities, including portability to multiple Windows platforms. The WDK provides C header files that define data types and constants for drivers to use. While C++ is feasible for some kernel-mode drivers, Microsoft documents problems and risks with using C++.

USB communications use IRPs that contain structures called USB Request Blocks (URBs). The URBs enable a driver to configure devices and transfer data. The WDK documents the URBs. A kernel-mode client driver requests a transfer by creating an URB and submitting it in an IRP to a lower-level driver. The bus and host-controller drivers handle the details of scheduling transactions on the bus. For interrupt and isochronous transfers, if there is no out-

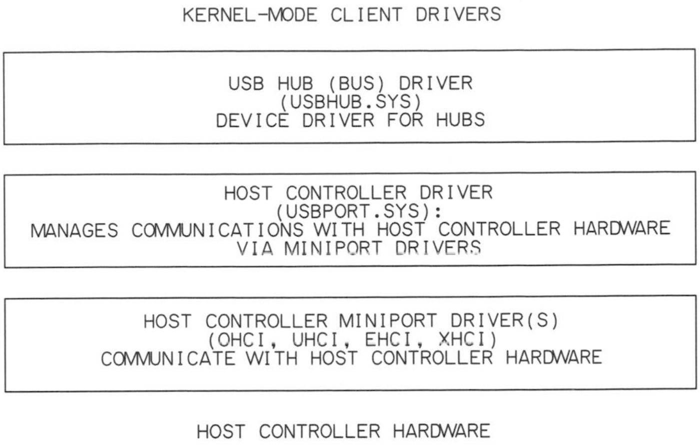

KERNEL-MODE CLIENT DRIVERS

```
┌────────────────────────────────────────────────────────────┐
│                                                            │
│                 USB HUB (BUS) DRIVER                       │
│                    (USBHUB.SYS)                            │
│               DEVICE DRIVER FOR HUBS                       │
│                                                            │
└────────────────────────────────────────────────────────────┘

┌────────────────────────────────────────────────────────────┐
│                                                            │
│               HOST CONTROLLER DRIVER                       │
│                   (USBPORT.SYS):                           │
│     MANAGES COMMUNICATIONS WITH HOST CONTROLLER HARDWARE   │
│                  VIA MINIPORT DRIVERS                      │
│                                                            │
└────────────────────────────────────────────────────────────┘

┌────────────────────────────────────────────────────────────┐
│                                                            │
│            HOST CONTROLLER MINIPORT DRIVER(S)              │
│               (OHCI, UHCI, EHCI, XHCI)                     │
│          COMMUNICATE WITH HOST CONTROLLER HARDWARE         │
│                                                            │
└────────────────────────────────────────────────────────────┘
```

HOST CONTROLLER HARDWARE

Figure 8-3. USB communications under Windows involve a hub, or bus, driver, a host controller driver, and a driver for each host-controller type.

standing IRP for an endpoint when its scheduled time comes up, the host controller skips the transaction.

In USB communications, an URB requests a USB transfer that can consist of one or more transactions. The lower-level drivers schedule the transfer's transactions without requiring further communications with the client driver.

If you're using an existing client driver (rather than writing your own), you need to understand how to access the driver's application-level interface, but you don't have to concern yourself with IRPs and URBs. If you're writing a client driver, you need to provide the IRPs that communicate with the system's USB drivers.

Bus and Host-Controller Drivers

The lower-level USB drivers consist of the hub, or bus, driver, the host-controller driver, and one or more miniport drivers (Figure 8-3). The hub driver (*usbhub.sys*) identifies devices on the bus, creates device objects for the devices, and acts as a client driver for the bus as a whole. The host-controller driver consists of a port driver (*usbport.sys*) that manages tasks that are common to all host controllers plus one or more miniport drivers that each manage communications with a specific type of host-controller hardware.

Windows provides the hub and host-controller drivers. Application and device-driver writers don't have to know the details about how they work, and Microsoft provides little documentation for these drivers. If you want to know more about how to implement low-level communications, one source of information is the source code and other documentation from the Linux USB Project.

Host Controller Types

To access low- and full-speed devices, a USB 1.x or USB 2.0 host can use a controller that conforms to the Open Host Controller Interface (OHCI) standard or the Universal Host Controller Interface (UHCI) standard. To access high-speed devices, a USB 2.0 host uses a host controller that conforms to the Enhanced Host Controller Interface (EHCI) standard. USB 3.0 hosts use a single Extensible Host Controller Interface (xHCI) controller for all speeds. The USB-IF's website has links to the specifications.

For information about which host-controller types are in a PC, in Windows Device Manager, look under *Universal Serial Bus controllers*. To view a driver's name, right-click a host controller's entry and select Properties > Driver > Driver Details. One of the drivers listed should have *ohci*, *uhci*, or *ehci* in the name. Chapter 9 has more about the Device Manager.

OHCI and UHCI Differences

OHCI and UHCI controllers both provide a way for the low- and full-speed USB hardware to communicate with higher-level drivers, but each takes a different approach. UHCI places more of the communications burden on software and thus can use simpler, cheaper hardware. OHCI places more of the burden on the hardware and allows simpler software control. UHCI was developed by Intel, and OHCI was developed by Compaq, Microsoft, and National Semiconductor. Motherboards tend to have UHCI controllers, and expansion cards tend to have OHCI controllers.

The differences between host controllers should be transparent to driver developers and application programmers. Both controller types comply fully with the USB specification. Their performance can differ, however. Developers shouldn't assume a device works fine based on tests with one host-controller type.

An OHCI controller can schedule more than one stage of a control transfer in a single frame, while a UHCI controller always schedules each stage in a different frame. For bulk endpoints with a maximum packet size less than 64 bytes, a UHCI driver attempts no more than one transaction per frame, while an OHCI driver may schedule additional transactions in a frame. An OHCI controller will poll an interrupt endpoint at least once every 32 ms even if the endpoint descriptor requests a maximum latency of 255 ms, while UHCI controllers can, but don't have to, support less-frequent polling.

Developers who use UHCI hosts are sometimes surprised when their devices fail when connected to an OHCI host. The failure occurs because the device isn't expecting to see multiple stages of a control transfer in a frame. Every device should work with both controller types.

Supporting Multiple Speeds

An EHCI controller handles high-speed communications only. The EHCI specification says that a host that supports EHCI must also support low and full speeds except for the unusual situation where every port has a permanently attached high-speed device. To support low and full speeds, the host must have a companion OHCI or UHCI host controller or a USB 2.0-compliant hub, which performs the function of a host controller for low- and full-speed devices. Just about every PC with an EHCI controller has a companion OHCI or UHCI controller that shares the bus.

In general, users and application programmers don't have to know or care which host controller is communicating with a device. To ensure the best performance, Windows warns if the system has high-speed-capable ports and a user attaches a high-speed-capable device to a port that doesn't support high speed.

Writing Drivers

To support vendor-specific functions, a device can use a vendor-specific kernel-mode driver or a vendor-specific user-mode driver that communicates with a kernel-mode driver provided by the operating system or a vendor.

Writing drivers has long been an arcane and difficult art. To help ease the process, Microsoft provides the Windows Driver Foundation (WDF) framework for WDM drivers. When developing a WDF driver, you start with a functioning driver that provides default processing for PnP, power-management, and device I/O events. To support device-specific behavior, you add code that overrides the default processing. The framework hides much of the driver's complexity and results in a more stable product.

This section will help you decide whether you need a device-specific driver and if so, how to get started. For a detailed guide to driver writing, see the WDK documentation and examples and the book *Developing Drivers with the Windows Driver Foundation* by Penny Orwick and Guy Smith (Microsoft Press).

Kernel-mode Drivers

Writing a kernel-mode client driver requires the WDK, which includes a C compiler, a linker, build utilities, and documentation including example source code.

Kernel-mode drivers for Windows 2000 and later can use the Kernel-Mode Driver Framework (KMDF) library included in the WDK for Windows Vista and later. The KMDF isolates the driver code from the details of creating and passing IRPs and managing PnP and power functions.

A KMDF driver creates a framework driver object to represent the driver and a framework device object for each device. Instead of creating and passing IRPs, KMDF drivers perform driver functions via properties, methods, and events of the framework device objects. Instead of handling PnP and power management directly, the framework manages these functions with callback functions providing event notifications as needed.

The framework defines additional object types to represent resources that drivers can use. USB communications use objects that represent USB devices, interfaces, and pipes. Other framework objects can represent files, timers, strings, and other resources.

User-mode Drivers

User-mode drivers for Windows XP and Windows Vista can use the User-Mode Driver Framework (UMDF) library included in the WDK for Windows Vista and later. UMDF drivers communicate via the Windows API instead of kernel-mode functions. Developers of UMDF drivers can program in C++ and debug with user-mode debuggers.

An example of an application that might use a UMDF driver is a device that uses the WinUSB kernel-mode driver but needs to support multiple open handles to a device interface. The user-mode WinUSB driver component limits interfaces to one open handle at a time, while a vendor-provided UMDF driver can allow multiple open handles.

Testing Tools

The WDK's Device Simulation Framework (DSF) can help with driver testing. The framework can simulate an EHCI host controller and devices in software.

Instead of having to attach a physical device to a physical bus for testing, you can use a simulated host controller and device.

Using GUIDs

A Globally Unique Identifier (GUID) is a 128-bit value that uniquely identifies a class or other entity. Windows uses GUIDs in identifying two types of device classes. A device setup GUID identifies a device setup class, which encompasses devices that Windows installs in the same way. A device interface GUID identifies a device interface class, which provides a mechanism for applications to communicate with a driver assigned to devices in the class. In many cases, devices that belong to a particular device setup class also belong to the same device interface class. Some SetupDi_ API functions accept either type of GUID. But each type of GUID provides access to different types of information used for different purposes.

The conventional format divides the GUID into five sets of hex characters with the sets separated by hyphens.

This is the GUID for the HIDCLASS device setup class:

    745a17a0-74d3-11d0-b6fe-00a0c90f57da

This is the GUID for the HID device interface class:

    4d1e55b2-f16f-11cf-88cb-001111000030

Driver writers and others who need to provide a custom GUID can generate one using the *guidgen* utility provided with Visual Studio and also available as a free download from Microsoft. The utility uses an algorithm that makes it extremely unlikely that someone else will create an identical GUID. To create a GUID in Visual Studio Professional edition or better, select Tools > Create GUID.

Device Setup GUIDs

A device setup GUID identifies devices that Windows sets up and configures in the same way and using the same class installer and co-installers. The system file *devguid.h* defines device setup GUIDs for many classes. The WDK provides the file.

Most devices should use a device setup class that corresponds to the device's function, such as printer or disk drive. A single device can belong to multiple setup classes, such as HID and mouse. The USB class is appropriate for USB hosts and hubs and other devices whose installation and configuration requirements or capabilities don't fit another class. A vendor-specific class is another option for such devices, but Microsoft discourages creating vendor-specific classes.

Each device setup GUID corresponds to a Class key in the system registry. Each Class key has a subkey for each instance of a device in the class. Chapter 9 has more about Class keys.

Applications can use device setup GUIDs to retrieve information and perform various installation functions on devices. The *devcon* example in the WDK shows how to use device setup GUIDs to detect and retrieve information about devices and perform functions such as enabling, disabling, restarting, updating drivers for, and removing devices. These functions are the same as those performed by the Device Manager.

Device Interface GUIDs

A class or device driver can register one or more device interface classes to enable applications to learn about and communicate with devices that use the driver. Each device interface class has a device interface GUID.

Using a device interface GUID and SetupDi_ functions, an application can find all attached devices in a device interface class. On detecting a device, the application can obtain a device path name to pass to the CreateFile function. CreateFile returns a handle that the application can use to access the device. Applications can also use device interface GUIDs to request to be notified when a device is attached or removed. Chapter 10 has more about using GUIDs for this purpose.

Unlike device setup GUIDs, device interface GUIDs aren't stored in one file. A driver package may include a C header file or a Visual Basic or a Visual C# variable or constant that defines a device interface GUID. An application that uses the WinUSB driver can define a GUID for accessing a specific device. For the HID class, applications can retrieve the GUID with the function HidD_GetHidGuid.

Device interface GUIDs are useful for finding devices that use the WinUSB driver, devices with vendor-specific drivers, and HID-class devices that perform vendor-specific functions.

For many other devices that perform standard peripheral functions, applications have other ways to find and gain access to devices. For example, to access a drive, the .NET Framework's Directory class includes a GetLogicalDrives method that enables applications to find all of the logical drives on a system (whether or not they use USB). A vendor-specific driver can also define an API to enable applications to access devices without having to provide a GUID.

Some older drivers define a symbolic link for each device they control. For example, the first device attached might be \\.\mydevice0, followed by \\.\mydevice1, \\.\mydevice2, and so on up as needed. Applications access these devices using the symbolic links instead of device interface GUIDs.

9

Matching a Driver to a Device

On detecting a newly attached USB device, the operating system needs to decide what driver to assign to the device. This chapter shows how Windows uses INF files to select a driver and how the Device Manager and system registry store information about devices and their drivers. The information in this chapter applies to Windows XP through Windows Vista with some comments on earlier Windows editions.

Using the Device Manager

The Windows Device Manager displays information about all installed devices and presents a user interface for enabling, disabling, and uninstalling devices and updating or changing a device's assigned driver. For developers, the Device Manager is useful for viewing the driver assigned to a device and for providing a user interface for making Window forget what it knows about a device and start fresh.

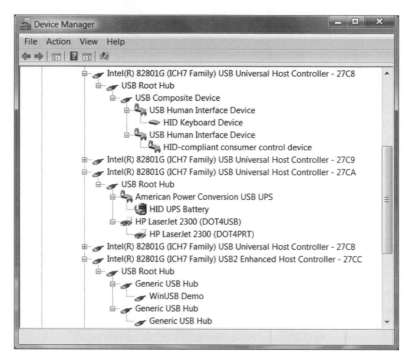

Figure 9-1. Viewing devices by connection in the Device Manager shows which devices connect to which hubs and host controllers.

Viewing Devices

To view the Device Manager, right-click Computer, click Manage, and in the Computer Management pane, select Device Manager. Or from Start, select Settings > Control Panel > System > Hardware > Device Manager. Or save clicks by creating a shortcut to the file *devmgmt.msc* in *Windows\System32*.

The Device Manager's View menu offers options for viewing device information. Viewing devices by connection (Figure 9-1) shows the physical connections from each host controller and root hub, through any additional hubs, to the attached devices. To view information about a device, including its driver(s) and any problem the operating system has detected with the device, right-click the device's listing and select Properties (Figure 9-2).

Viewing devices by type (Figure 9-3) groups devices according to their functions with little regard to hardware interface. The USB class lists host controllers and hubs. A device with a vendor-specific driver can define its own class or use the USB class.

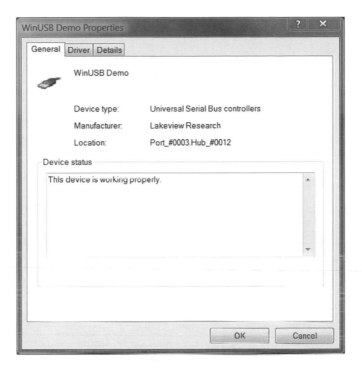

Figure 9-2. Device Manager's Properties screens provide more information about a device, including what driver the operating system has assigned to the device.

By default, the Device Manager shows only attached USB devices. To view devices that have been removed but whose drivers are still installed, set the following system environment variable:

DEVMGR_SHOW_NONPRESENT_DEVICES=1

To set the variable, in the Windows Control Panel, select System > Advanced > Environment Variables, enter the variable's name, and set its value. Then in Device Manager, click View and check the option to Show Hidden Devices. You may need to reboot after setting the environment variable.

Property Pages

Each listing in the Device Manager has property pages that provide additional information about a device and an interface for configuring the device and its driver. To view the property pages, double-click the device's entry. You can request to enable or disable the device or view, update, roll back, or uninstall the device's driver. A Details page provides additional information, including

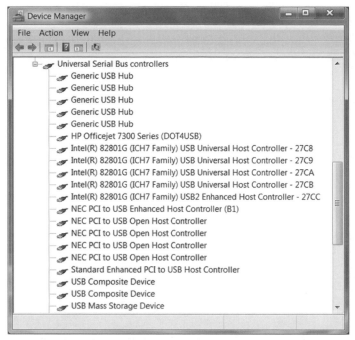

Figure 9-3. Device Manager also has an option to view devices grouped by type, or function.

various system IDs, any filter drivers or coinstallers the device uses, and power capabilities. For example, the Device Instance ID contains the device's Vendor ID (VID) and Product ID (PID). A driver can provide custom property pages when needed.

Device Information in the Registry

The system registry is a database that Windows maintains for storing critical information about the hardware and software installed on a system. The registry stores information about devices that have been installed, including devices not currently attached. After enumerating a new device, Windows stores information about the device in the registry. The registry obtains some of its information from the bus drivers, which in turn obtain the information from the devices. Other information is from the INF file that the operating system selects when assigning a driver to a device.

You can view the registry's contents using Windows' *regedit* utility (Start > Run > *regedit*). You can also use regedit to edit the registry's contents, but making registry changes this way isn't recommended and is seldom necessary. The Windows SDK documents API functions that enable applications to read and write to the registry. Device installation adds or changes device information in the registry. A request to uninstall a device via the Device Manager or another application also results in registry changes.

The system registry is so important that Windows maintains multiple backup copies in case the current copy becomes unusable. Windows' System Restore utility can restore the registry to an earlier state.

The registry's data has a tree structure. Each node on the tree is a registry key. Each key can have entries with assigned values and subkeys that in turn may have entries and subkeys. Information about the system's hardware and installed software is under the HKEY_LOCAL_MACHINE key. Information about USB devices is under several subkeys: the hardware key, the class key, the driver key, and the service key.

The Hardware Key

The hardware key, also called the instance key or device key, stores information about an instance of a specific device. Hardware keys are under the enumerator (Enum) key:

    HKEY_LOCAL_MACHINE\System\CurrentControlSet\Enum

Under the Enum key is a USB key. Each subkey of the USB key contains the Vendor ID and Product ID of a USB device. Figure 9-4 shows the entry for a device with a Vendor ID of 0925h and Product ID or 1234h. Under each of these keys may be one or more hardware keys, with each hardware key identifying an instance of the device. Table 9-1 lists some of the entries under the hardware key.

A device without a USB serial number gets a new hardware key every time the device attaches to a port the device hasn't been attached to previously. If you physically remove the device from the bus and attach a different device with identical descriptors to the same port, the operating system doesn't know the difference and thus doesn't create a new hardware key. Devices with USB serial numbers have one hardware key per physical device without regard to what port the device attaches to.

A USB device may also have one or more keys for additional enumerators such as HID, USBPRINT, and USBSTOR. For example, a UPS back-up device with a HID interface can have a key in the Enum\USB branch for the HidUsb service and a key in the Enum\HID branch for the HidBatt service.

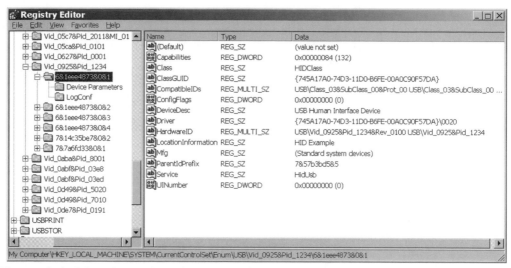

Figure 9-4. A hardware key contains information about an instance of a device with a specific Vendor ID and Product ID.

Table 9-1: These are some of the entries in a USB device's hardware key.

Key	Description	Source of Information
Class	Name of the device's setup class	INF file (from *devguid.h*)
ClassGUID	GUID of the device's setup class	INF file (from *devguid.h*)
DeviceDesc	Device Description	INF file, Models section, device description entry
HardwareID	ID string containing the device's Vendor ID and Product ID	Device descriptor
CompatibleIDs	ID string(s) containing the device's class and (optional) subclass and protocol	Device and interface descriptors
Mfg	Device manufacturer	INF file, Manufacturer section, manufacturer name entry
Driver	Name of the device's driver key	System registry, under CurrentControlSet\Control\Class
Location Information	"USB Device" or iProduct string	Bus driver or string descriptor
Service	Name of the device's Service key	System registry under HKLM\System\ CurrentControlSet\Services

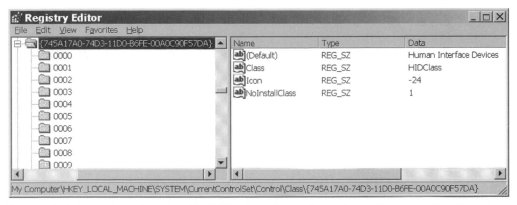

Figure 9-5. The class key for the HID class includes a friendly name for the class and an index to an icon.

The Class Key

The class key stores information about a device setup class and the devices that belong to it. The class keys are under this registry key:

HKEY_LOCAL_MACHINE\System\CurrentControlSet\Control\Class

The name of a class key is the device setup GUID for the class and is the same as the value stored in the hardware key for devices in the class, under Class-GUID. Figure 9-5 shows the class key for the HID class. The class key contains a friendly name for the setup class, the class name from the header file that defines the GUID, and an index value that specifies the icon to use in the Device Manager and other windows that display setup information. Applications can retrieve the index of the mini-icon for a class by calling Setup-DiGetClassBitmapIndex. A vendor-specific class installer or co-installer can provide a vendor-specific icon.

Optional entries in the class key can affect what users see on device installation. If NoInstallClass is present and not equal to zero, users will never need to manually install devices in the class. If SilentInstall is present and not equal to zero, the PnP manager will install devices in the class without displaying dialog boxes or requiring user interaction. If NoDisplayClass is present and not equal to zero, the Device Manager doesn't display the class's devices.

UpperFilters and LowerFilters entries can specify upper filter and lower filter drivers that apply to all devices in the class.

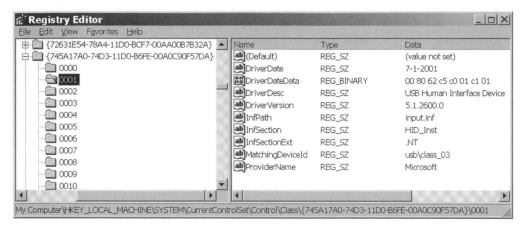

Figure 9-6. The driver keys under each class key have information about the drivers assigned to instances of devices in the class.

Table 9-2: The driver key contains information about the driver assigned to a device.

Key	Description	Source of Information
DriverDate	Date of the driver file	INF file, Version section, DriverVer directive
DriverDesc	Driver description	INF file
DriverVer	Driver version	INF file, Version section, DriverVer directive
InfPath	Name of INF file	INF file name
InfSection	Name of the driver's DDInstall section	INF file
InfSectionExt	"Decorated" extension used in INF file (.NT, etc.)	INF file
MatchingDeviceID	The hardware or compatible ID used to assign the driver	Device descriptor and INF file
ProviderName	The provider of the driver	INF file, Provider string

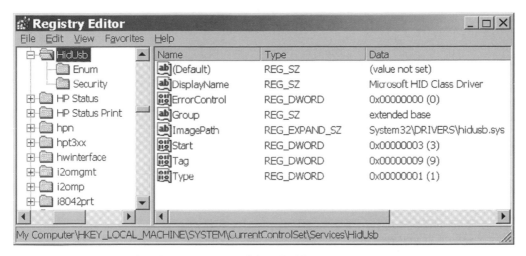

Figure 9-7. The service key names a driver's file.

The Driver Key

Under the class key, each device in a class has a driver key, also called a software key. In the hardware key for a device instance, the Driver entry names a device setup GUID that matches a class key and a device instance number that matches a driver subkey under the class key. Figure 9-6 shows the key for a generic HID-class device. Table 9-2 lists some of the entries for a driver key.

The driver key contains the name of the INF file that in turn names the device's driver files.

The Service Key

A service key has information about a driver's files, including where they are and how to load them. Service keys are in this branch:

HKEY_LOCAL_MACHINE\System\CurrentControlSet\Services

Service keys exist for each host controller type, hubs, classes such as storage (USBSTOR) and printers (USBPRINT), and HID functions (HidBatt, HidServ, HidUsb). Figure 9-7 shows the Service key for HidUsb.

Inside INF Files

A device-setup information file, or INF file, is a text file that contains information about one or more devices in a device setup class. The devices can be from one or more companies. The file tells system Setup components what driver or drivers to use and contains information to store in the registry. Windows includes INF files for the drivers provided with the operating system. The files are in the *%windir%\inf* folder. The operating system copies any new INF files for user-added devices to this folder.

By default, the INF folder is hidden. If you don't see it in Windows Explorer, select Tools > Folder Options > View, then under Hidden Files, select *Show hidden files and folders*. Do not select *Hide file extensions for known file types*.

On first attachment, after retrieving descriptors from a USB device, Windows looks for a match between the information in the descriptors and the information in the system's INF files.

The WDK has a detailed reference on INF files and many examples. Often you can begin with an example and customize it as needed. Listing 9-1 shows an INF file for a device that uses the WinUSB driver.

Structure and Syntax

The contents of an INF file follow these rules.

- The information is arranged in sections, with each section containing one or more items. The section name is in square brackets [ ]. Some of the sections (Version, Manufacturer) are standard sections that every INF file contains. Other sections have names defined in other sections. For example, the CopyFiles directive defines a section that contains names of files for the installation process to copy. The sections can be in any order, but the order of the items within a section can be critical.

- A semicolon (;) indicates a comment.

- Text enclosed in percent symbols (*%sampletext%*) is a token that refers to a string. For example, you might have the following item:

    DisplayName = %WinUSB_SvcDesc%

  with an item in the Strings section that defines the string:

    WinUSB_SvcDesc="WinUSB Demo"

- Windows defines Dirid values that can refer to system paths. The value for the Windows directory (typically *Windows*) is 10. Other ways to represent the Windows directory are the environment variables *%windir%* and *%SystemRoot%*. The System directory (*%windir%\system32*) is 11. The Drivers directory (*%windir%\system32\drivers*) is 12.

```
[Version]
Signature = "$Windows NT$"
Class = USB
ClassGUID={36FC9E60-C465-11CF-8056-444553540000}
Provider = %ProviderName%
DriverVer=02/07/2008,1.0.0
;CatalogFile=MyCatFile.cat

; Manufacturer

[Manufacturer]
%ProviderName% = MyDevice_WinUSB,NTx86,NTamd64

[MyDevice_WinUSB.NTx86]
%USB\MyDevice.DeviceDesc% =USB_Install, USB\VID_0925&PID_1456

[MyDevice_WinUSB.NTamd641]
%USB\MyDevice.DeviceDesc% =USB_Install, USB\VID_0925&PID_1456

; Installation

[USB_Install]
Include=winusb.inf
Needs=WINUSB.NT

[USB_Install.Services]
Include=winusb.inf
AddService=WinUSB,0x00000002,WinUSB_ServiceInstall

[WinUSB_ServiceInstall]
DisplayName    = %WinUSB_SvcDesc%
ServiceType    = 1
StartType      = 3
ErrorControl   = 1
ServiceBinary  = %12%\WinUSB.sys

[USB_Install.Wdf]
KmdfService=WINUSB, WinUsb_Install
UmdfServiceOrder=WINUSB
```

Listing 9-1: This INF file is for a device that uses the WinUSB driver. (Part 1 of 3).

```
[WinUSB_Install]
KmdfLibraryVersion=1.7

[USB_Install.HW]
AddReg=Dev_AddReg

[Dev_AddReg]
HKR,,DeviceInterfaceGUIDs,0x10000,"{42CA71EC-CE1C-44c2-82DE-87D8D8FF6C1E}"

[USB_Install.CoInstallers]
AddReg=CoInstallers_AddReg
CopyFiles=CoInstallers_CopyFiles

[CoInstallers_AddReg]
HKR,,CoInstallers32,0x00010000,"WinUSBCoInstaller.dll","WUDFUpdate_01007.dll","WdfCoInstal
    ler01007.dll,WdfCoInstaller"

[CoInstallers_CopyFiles]
WinUSBCoInstaller.dll
WdfCoInstaller01007.dll
WUDFUpdate_01007.dll

[DestinationDirs]
CoInstallers_CopyFiles=11

; Source Media

[SourceDisksNames.x86]
1 = %DISK_NAME%,,,\i386

[SourceDisksNames.amd64]
2 = %DISK_NAME%,,,\amd64

[SourceDisksFiles.x86]
WinUSBCoInstaller.dll=1
WdfCoInstaller01007.dll=1
WUDFUpdate_01007.dll=1
```

Listing 9-1: This INF file is for a device that uses the WinUSB driver. (Part 2 of 3).

```
[SourceDisksFiles.amd64]
WinUSBCoInstaller.dll=2
WdfCoInstaller01007.dll=2
WUDFUpdate_01007.dll=2

; Copy Files

[_CopyFiles_sys]
winusb.sys

; Destination Directories

[DestinationDirs]
DefaultDestDir = 12 ; %SystemRoot%\system32\drivers
 _CopyFiles_sys - 12

; Strings

[Strings]
ProviderName-"Lakeview Research"
USB\MyDevice.DeviceDesc="WinUSB Demo"
WinUSB_SvcDesc="WinUSB Demo"
DISK_NAME="My Install Disk"
```

Listing 9-1: This INF file is for a device that uses the WinUSB driver. (Part 3 of 3).

- Some section names can use extensions to specify which operating systems and/or CPUs the item applies to. For example, NTx86 means the item applies only to systems with x86-based CPUs under Windows XP or later:

    [MyDevice_WinUSB.NTx86]

Other extensions are NTamd64 for 64-bit CPUs based on the x86 architecture and NTia64 for Itanium-based CPUs. A section name with this type of extension is called a *decorated* section name.

Device-specific Values

A device that uses the WinUSB driver can use Listing 9-1's INF file with the following edits to customize the file for a specific device.

Two Models sections ([MyDevice_WinUSB.NTx86] and [MyDevice_WinUSB.NTamd64]) each contain a device hardware ID value. In the example, this value is USB\VID_0925&PID_1456. The hardware ID contains the Vendor ID (0925h) and Product ID (1456h) from the device descriptor in the device.

The KmdfLibraryVersion directive specifies a version number for the KMDF library, which provides redistributable co-installer files used in installing the driver. The version number can vary with the WDK build and must match the version of the framework library used to develop the driver. The files *WdfCoInstaller01007.dll* and *WUDFUpdate_01007.dll* also incorporate the version number in their names and change with the library version. Chapter 14 has more about these files.

In the Dev_AddReg section, a WinUSB device should have a vendor-defined device interface GUID as described in Chapter 8.

The Strings section can provide device-specific strings for the company name, descriptions of the device and the driver service, and a name for the installation media.

A catalog file contains cryptographic hash values that function as digital thumbprints that identify the files in a driver package. The catalog file can also contain a digital signature that the operating system uses to determine whether the driver files have been altered since the signature was created. You can create an unsigned catalog file with the Inf2Cat tool in the WDK. Chapter 17 has more about digital signatures. The example INF file includes a commented-out reference to the file *MyCatFile.cat*.

Using Device Identification Strings

To identify possible drivers for a device, Windows searches the system's INF files for a device identification string that matches a string created from information in the device's descriptors. Types of device identification strings include hardware IDs and compatible IDs.

Identification Strings Obtained from a Device

Every USB device has a device ID, which is a hardware ID that the hub driver creates from the Vendor ID, Product ID, bcdDevice, and as appropriate, other values in the device descriptor. When assigning a driver, the device ID is the best match. A device ID for a USB device has this form:

USB\Vid_xxxx&Pid_yyyy&Rev_zzzz

The values in xxxx, yyyy, and zzzz are four characters each, with *xxxx* = idVendor, *yyyy* = idProduct, and *zzzz* = bcdDevice. The *xxxx* and *yyyy* values are hexadecimal except for Windows Me, which uses decimal, and *zzzz* is in BCD format.

For example, a device with Vendor ID = 0925h, Product ID = 1234h, and bcd-Device = 0310 has this device ID:

USB\Vid_0925&Pid_1234&Rev_0310

Composite devices can specify a driver for each function. In this case, the device has a device ID for each interface that represents a function. A device ID for an interface has this form:

USB\Vid_xxxx&Pid_yyyy&Rev_zzzz&MI_ww

The 2-character value in ww equals bInterfaceNumber in the interface descriptor for one of the device's interfaces.

A HID-class device whose report descriptor contains more than one top-level collection can have a device ID for each collection. A device ID for a collection has this form with *hh* indicating the collection number:

USB\Vid_xxxx&Pid_yyyy&Rev_zzzz&MI_ww&Colbb

In addition to a device ID, some drivers create one or more hardware IDs and compatible IDs for devices. A hardware ID has a similar format to a device ID but represents a less precise match. For example, the ID may omit the bcdDevice value:

USB\Vid_xxxx&Pid_yyyy

A hardware ID for a CDC device can use a Cdc_ value to specify a subclass. This device ID specifies CDC subclass 08h (WMC wireless handset control model):

USB\Vid_0925&Pid_0902&Rev_0210&Cdc_08

A compatible ID identifies a device by class and optional subclass and protocol codes and may have any of the following forms:

USB\Class_aa&SubClass_bb&Prot_cc
USB\Class_aa&SubClass_bb
USB\Class_aa

The values *aa*, *bb*, and *cc* match values in the device descriptor or an interface descriptor and are two characters each: *aa* is bDeviceClass or bInterfaceClass, *bb* is bDeviceSubclass or bInterfaceSubclass, and *cc* is bDeviceProtocol or bInterfaceProtocol. The values are expressed in hexadecimal, except for Windows Me, which uses decimal.

For example, the class code for HIDs is 03h, so HID-class devices have the following compatible ID:

USB\Class_03

Mass-storage devices and printers have additional class-specific compatible IDs defined in the WDK documentation.

A compatible ID in an INF file indicates a less desirable but acceptable match. Compatible IDs enable Windows to find and load a driver if the installation can't find an INF file with a matching device ID. A vendor's INF file should not contain a compatible ID.

Obtaining Identification Strings from an INF File

In an INF file, each entry in a Models section has one or more hardware IDs. The first hardware ID should be a device ID. Following the device ID may be one or more hardware and compatible IDs separated by commas.

Finding a Match

In looking for the best match between the information retrieved from a device and the information in INF files, the installer assigns a rank to every possible match, with a lower numerical value indicating a better match. NT-based Windows editions give more favorable ranks to signed drivers, and 64-bit Windows editions require signed drivers. Windows 98 doesn't check for signed drivers.

A signed driver has a catalog file with a digital signature that indicates that the driver has passed Windows Hardware Quality Labs (WHQL) testing. Chapter 17 has more about WHQL testing. The best match is a device ID that matches a hardware ID in a signed driver's INF file. An installer that can't find a match starts the Found New Hardware wizard and gives the user a chance to specify a location to look for the INF file.

Composite devices, which have multiple interfaces, are a special case. Because each interface may require a different driver, selecting a driver using only the Vendor ID and Product ID isn't sufficient. Windows XP and later can use the compatible ID USB\COMPOSITE, which loads the USB common class generic parent driver. This driver creates device and compatible IDs for each interface, and the installer assigns a driver to each interface. In earlier Windows editions, the bus or hub driver handles this task.

Windows provides INF files for many devices and device classes, and devices may provide their own INF files. To speed up searching, Windows creates a precompiled INF (PNF) file during device installation and stores the file in the same folder as the device's INF file. The PNF file contains much of the same information as the INF file but in a format that enables quicker searching.

When to Provide an INF File

Not every device requires its own INF file. Many devices that use the system's class drivers can use the INF file that Windows provides for the class. These are some INF files for USB classes included with Windows XP:

Class	INF File
audio	wdmaudio.inf
human interface device (HID)	input.inf (hiddev.inf in Windows 98)
hub	usb.inf
mass storage	usbstor.inf
printer	usbprint.inf
smart card	smartcrd.inf
still image	sti.inf

Because Windows XP and later prefer signed drivers, if you provide an unsigned driver for a device in a supported class, Windows XP and later won't use your driver and instead will select a compatible ID from the class's INF file. An INF file is considered part of the driver package, so Windows XP and later prefer a system-provided INF file for a system driver over an unsigned, vendor-provided INF file for the same driver even if the vendor's INF file contains a matching hardware ID.

When the best match is an unsigned driver, operating-system settings can affect whether Windows blocks installation, installs the driver with a warning, or installs with no warning. To change the setting, in Windows Control Panel, select System > Hardware > Driver Signing.

A device that uses a class driver can have a custom, signed INF file with vendor-specific strings that display in the Device Manager. For example, the entry for a HID can be a vendor-specific string instead of the default *USB Human Interface Device*.

Many INF files provided with Windows contain sections with manufacturer-specific information. When a device passes WHQL tests, Microsoft can add the device's sections to an existing INF file or add a manufacturer-specific INF file to the files distributed with Windows.

Modems and USB virtual COM ports in the communications device class must provide their own INF files even if they use system-supplied drivers. A device that uses the WinUSB driver must have an INF file that contains the device's Vendor ID and Product ID. A device with a vendor-specific driver must have an INF file.

Tools and Diagnostic Aids

Microsoft provides tools to help in creating and testing INF files. The ChkINF utility tests a file's structure and syntax. Log files record events that occur during device installation.

ChkINF is a Perl script that requires a Perl interpreter, available free from *www.activeware.com* and other sources. The script runs from a command prompt and creates an HTML page that annotates an INF file with errors and warnings.

During device installation, the PnP manager and the Windows Setup and Device Installer Services (SetupAPI) log events and errors to a text file. The log can be very helpful when debugging problems with device installations. In Windows XP, the data is in *%windir%\setupapi.log*. In Windows Vista, the data is in *%windir%\inf\SetupAPI.dev.log*. The WDK documentation has more about how to use the logging capability.

Tips for Using INF Files

Here are some tips for using INF files during and after product development:

Use a Valid Vendor ID

Firmware that you make available outside of a controlled environment must use a Vendor ID assigned by the USB-IF. My example code uses the Vendor ID of 0925h, which is assigned to my company, Lakeview Research. The owner of the Vendor ID is responsible for ensuring that each product and version has a unique Vendor ID/Product ID pair. Borrowing someone else's Vendor ID can lead to conflicts if the owner of the ID uses the same values for a different device.

Finding INF Files

On installing a device with a new INF file, Windows copies the INF file to *%windir%\inf* and may rename the file *oem*.inf* and create a .PNF file named *oem*pnf*, where * is a number. Using numbered *oem* file names eliminates conflicts if multiple vendors provide INF files with the same name. To find INF files that contain a specific Vendor ID and Product ID, go to Start > Search > For Files or Folders, browse to *%windir%\inf* and search for the text *VID_xxxx&PID_yyyy*, where *xxxx* is the device's Vendor ID and *yyyy* is the Product ID.

Removing Device Information

When experimenting with different settings in an INF file, you may find that the operating system remembers information stored in the system registry from a previous version of the INF file. If you want the installation to use a different or changed INF file for a device (because you've changed the driver or device firmware, for example), you may need to tell the operating system to forget what it knows about the device. With the device installed, right-click its listing in the Device Manager, and select Uninstall. In the *inf* directory, remove (but save in another location if needed) any INF and PNF files that contain your device's Vendor ID and Product ID. You can then detach and reattach the device, and installation will start fresh in searching for a driver.

What the User Sees

What the user sees on attaching a USB device varies with the Windows edition, the contents of the device's INF file, the driver's location, whether the driver has a co-installer and is digitally signed, and whether the device has been attached and enumerated previously and has a serial number.

Device and Class Installers

Device and class installers are DLLs that provide functions relating to device installation. Windows provides default installers for devices in supported device setup classes. On NT-based Windows editions, a device vendor can provide a device co-installer that works along with a class co-installer to support operations specific to one or more devices in a class. A device co-installer can add information to the registry, request additional configuration information from the user, provide device-specific Property pages for the Device Manager to display, and perform other tasks relating to device installation. The WDK includes the Driver Install Frameworks (DIFx) tools for creating Windows Installer packages.

Searching for a Driver

On boot up or device attachment, after retrieving a device's descriptors, the operating system searches for a hardware key that matches information in the descriptors. On success, the operating system can assign a driver to the device. The hardware key's Driver entry points to the driver key, which names the INF file. The hardware key's Service entry points to the service key, which has information about the driver files.

On first attachment, no matching hardware key exists so Windows searches for a match in the INF files. On finding none, the New Device Wizard starts. For signed drivers, an installation program can use the SetupCopyOEMInf API to copy the provided INF file to the INF folder on the user's system. On finding a matching INF file, Windows copies the file to *%windir%\inf* (if the file isn't already present), loads the driver(s) specified in the file if necessary, and adds the appropriate keys to the system registry. The device then displays in the Device Manager.

After installing a device, when installing additional devices that are identical except for the serial number, Windows behaves differently depending on whether the driver is digitally signed. When the driver is signed, Windows uses administrative privileges to install the driver for additional devices after the first, even if the current user doesn't have these privileges. If the driver is unsigned, Windows uses the privileges of the current user in deciding whether to install the driver for additional devices.

When re-attaching a previously attached device, whether Windows finds a driver key can depend on whether the device's descriptors include a USB serial number string. If the device doesn't have a serial number, Windows finds the hardware key only if the device is re-attached to a port where the device was attached previously. If the device has a serial number, Windows finds the hardware key no matter which port the device attaches to.

10

Detecting Devices

This chapter shows how applications can obtain information about attached devices, request a handle for communicating with a device, and detect when a device is attached or removed. Each of these tasks involve using Windows API functions and the device interface GUIDs introduced in Chapter 8. Because many .NET programmers have limited experience with API functions, I begin with a short tutorial on the topic.

A Brief Guide to Calling API Functions

You can do a lot of programming without ever calling a Windows API function. Microsoft's .NET Framework provides classes that support common tasks including creating user interfaces, accessing files, manipulating text and graphics, accessing common peripheral types, networking, security functions, and exception handling. Internally, a class's methods are likely to call API functions, but the classes offer a safer, more secure, and more modular, object-oriented way for programmers to accomplish the tasks. Languages that can use the .NET Framework include Visual Basic, Visual C#, and Visual C++.

But .NET's classes don't handle every task. Some applications must do things that require calling API functions. A .NET application can use .NET classes where possible and API calls where needed.

Because calling API functions can be an obscure art at times, this section includes an introduction to the topic.

The code examples in this chapter assume the following Imports and using statements:

VB
```
Imports Microsoft.Win32.SafeHandles
Imports System.Runtime.InteropServices
```
Instead of Imports statements, you can provide references to the namespaces in the project's properties, in the References tab. A reference to the System namespace is in the properties by default.

VC#
```
using Microsoft.Win32.SafeHandles;
using System;
using System.Runtime.InteropServices;
```

Managed and Unmanaged Code

Managed code is program code that accesses properties, methods, and events of the .NET Framework's classes. Managed code compiles to the Microsoft Intermediate Language (MSIL). When the application runs, .NET's common language runtime (CLR) environment executes the MSIL code.

Because all .NET languages use the same CLR, components written in different .NET languages can easily interoperate. For example, a Visual Basic application can call a function written in Visual C# without worrying about differences in calling conventions. The CLR also simplifies programming by implementing garbage collection to manage memory. In contrast, Windows API functions are unmanaged code whose DLLs contain compiled machine code that executes directly on the target CPU.

A Visual C++ application can compile to managed code, unmanaged code, or a combination. The language incorporates a technology that enables managed code to call API functions exactly as unmanaged code does.

For other .NET languages, managed code can call API functions by using methods of the System.Runtime.InteropServices namespace. The namespace supports the Platform Invocation Services, also known as PInvoke and

P/Invoke. The process of calling unmanaged functions from managed code is called Interop.

The DLLs

The DLLs included with Windows are typically stored in *%System-Root%\system32*. The operating system searches this folder when an application calls a DLL function. Header files and documentation for Windows API functions are in the Windows Driver Kit (WDK) and Windows Software Development Kit (SDK):

Function	DLL	Documentation
Find devices	setupapi.dll	WDK under Device Installation
Access devices that support handle-based operations	kernel32.dll	SDK under File Management
Receive notifications of device attachment and removal	user32.dll	SDK under Device Management

Header files contain declarations in C for the DLLs' functions and define constants, variables, structures, and other components the functions access. The declarations enable applications to find the functions and pass parameters to them.

A Visual Basic or Visual C# application must translate the declarations in the header files from C to Visual Basic or Visual C# syntax and data types. Translating from C is more complicated than simple syntax changes because many of the variable and structure types don't have one-to-one equivalents in .NET. The .NET code may also requires marshaling to enable passing data between managed and umanaged code.

Marshaling

Visual Basic and Visual C# applications must take special care to ensure that any data passed to an unmanaged function survives the trip from managed to unmanaged code, and back if needed. The .NET Framework provides the Marshal class to help. Marshaling means doing whatever is needed to make the data available. The class provides methods for allocating memory for variables to pass to unmanaged code, copying data between unmanaged and managed memory, and converting between managed and unmanaged data types. For example, the PtrToStringAuto method accepts a pointer to a string in unmanaged memory and returns the string being pointed to. This code retrieves a string from the pointer (IntPtr pDevicePathName) returned by an API function:

VB
```
Dim devicePathName as String = ""
devicePathName = Marshal.PtrToStringAuto(pDevicePathName)
```

VC#
```
String devicePathName = "";
devicePathName = Marshal.PtrToStringAuto(pDevicePathName);
```

The MarshalAs attribute defines an array's size to enable accessing the array in a structure returned by unmanaged code. This example declares a 16-byte array parameter that will hold a GUID from a structure returned by an API function:

VB
```
<MarshalAs(UnmanagedType.ByValArray, _
    ArraySubType:=UnmanagedType.U1, SizeConst:=16)> _
    Public dbcc_classguid() _
    As Byte
```

VC#
```
[ MarshalAs( UnmanagedType.ByValArray,
    ArraySubType=UnmanagedType.U1, SizeConst=16 ) ]
    public Byte[] dbcc_classguid;
```

The GUID is marshaled into the byte array as an UnmanagedType.ByValArray. The ArraySubType field defines the array's elements as unsigned, 1-byte (U1) values and the SizeConst field sets the array's size as 16 bytes.

In an asynchronous read or write operation, an application may need to ensure that a variable or structure passed to an unmanaged function remains in the same memory location after the function returns. Doing so enables other unmanaged functions to access the variable or structure when completing the asynchronous operation. The Marshal.AllocHGlobal method can help by allocating memory that the garbage collector won't move:

VB
```
Dim inputReportBuffer(2) As Byte
Dim unManagedBuffer As IntPtr

unManagedBuffer = Marshal.AllocHGlobal(inputReportBuffer.Length)
```

VC#
```
Byte[] inputReportBuffer = {0,0,0};
IntPtr unManagedBuffer = IntPtr.Zero;
```

unManagedBuffer = Marshal.AllocHGlobal(inputReportBuffer.Length);

The Marshal.FreeHGlobal method frees allocated memory when the application no longer needs to access the memory:

VB   Marshal.FreeHGlobal(unManagedBuffer)

VC#   Marshal.FreeHGlobal(unManagedBuffer);

To ensure that code to free memory or other resources executes, place the code in the Finally block of a Try...Catch...Finally statement. The examples in this book omit the Try statements.

Declaring a Function

This is an example declaration for the API function HidD_GetNumInputBuffers, which applications can use to learn the number of Input reports that the driver for a HID-class device can store:

VB
```
<DllImport("hid.dll", SetLastError:=True)>
        Shared Function HidD_GetNumInputBuffers _
        (ByVal HidDeviceObject As SafeFileHandle, _
        ByRef NumberBuffers As Int32) _
        As Boolean
End Function
```

VC#
```
[ DllImport( "hid.dll", SetLastError=true ) ]
internal static extern Boolean HidD_GetNumInputBuffers
        ( SafeFileHandle HidDeviceObject,
        ref Int32 NumberBuffers );
```

The declaration contains this information:

- A DllImport attribute that names the file that contains the function's executable code (*hid.dll*). The optional SetLastError field is set to true to enable retrieving error codes using the GetLastWin32Error method. Instead of DllImport, Visual Basic applications can use a Declare statement, but Dllimport offers more control.
- The function's name (HidD_GetNumInputBuffers).
- The parameters the function will pass to the operating system (HidDeviceObject, NumberBuffers).
- The data types of the values passed (SafeFileHandle, Int32).

- Whether the function passes parameters by value or by reference. The default is by value. Visual Basic supports the optional ByVal modifier. To pass by reference, precede the parameter name with ByRef (Visual Basic) or ref (Visual C#). The function passes HidDeviceObject by value and NumberBuffers by reference.

- The data type of the value returned for the function (Boolean). A few API calls have no return value, and Visual Basic can declare these functions as subroutines.

In Visual Basic, the declaration must be in the Declarations section of a file.

In Visual C#, the *extern* modifier indicates that the function resides in a different file.

Calling a Function

After declaring a function and any parameters to be passed, an application can call the function. This is a call to the HidD_GetNumInputBuffers function declared above:

VB
```
Dim success As Boolean

success = HidD_GetNumInputBuffers _
        (hidDeviceObject, _
        numberOfInputBuffers)
```

VC#
```
Boolean success = false;

success = HidD_GetNumInputBuffers
        (hidDeviceObject,
        ref numberOfInputBuffers);
```

The hidDeviceObject parameter is a SafeFileHandle returned previously by the CreateFile function, and numberOfInputBuffers is an Int32. The Visual C# code must use the ref modifier to pass numberOfInputBuffers by reference. If the function returns with success = True, numberOfInputBuffers contains the number of Input buffers.

Managing Data

Understanding how to pass data to API functions and use data returned by API functions requires understanding .NET's data types and how the CLR passes them to unmanaged code. The explanations below provide a background to understand the example code in this and later chapters. If the details seem obscure at this point, you can skip ahead and come back as needed.

Data Types

The header files for API functions use many data types that the .NET Framework doesn't support. To specify a variable's type for an API call, in many cases you can use a .NET type of the same length. For example, a DWORD is a 32-bit integer, so a .NET application can declare a DWORD as an Int32. A GUID translates to .NET's System.Guid type. For pointers, .NET provides the IntPtr type, whose size adjusts as needed to 32 or 64 bits depending on the platform. IntPtr.Zero is a null pointer.

A parameter defined in C as a HANDLE can use an IntPtr, but a safer and more reliable option for some handles is a SafeHandle object. With an IntPtr reference to a handle, in some situations, an exception can "leak" a handle, and a finalizer can corrupt a handle still in use in an asynchronous operation. Recycling of IntPtr handles can expose data that belongs to another resource. SafeHandle objects don't have these vulnerabilities.

The SafeHandle class is abstract. To use a SafeHandle object, you can use one of the provided classes derived from SafeHandle or derive a new class from SafeHandle. Devices accessed via ReadFile and WriteFile can use the SafeFileHandle class.

Passing Variables

Every parameter passed to a function has both an element type and a passing mechanism. The element type is *value* or *reference,* and the passing mechanism is *by value* or *by reference.* The element type determines in part the effect of the passing mechanism.

A value type contains data. For example, a Byte variable assigned a value of 3 consists of one byte with the value 00000011_b. Value types include all numeric data types; the Boolean, Char, and Date types; structures, even if their members are reference types; and enumerations. A reference type contains a reference, or pointer, that specifies the location of the variable's data, which resides elsewhere in memory. A 2-byte array variable contains the location where the array's 2 bytes are stored. Reference types include Strings; arrays, even if their elements are value types; classes; and delegates.

For help in determining if a variable is a value or reference types, Visual Basic provides the IsReference function. The function returns true if a variable is a reference type or false if a value type.

Whether to pass a parameter by value or by reference depends on what information the function expects, the element type being passed, and in some cases whether the type is blittable (defined below). Sometimes multiple ways can achieve the same result.

Passing a value type by value passes a copy of the variable's value. If the called function changes the value of the variable or its members, the calling function doesn't see the change. For example, when calling ReadFile to read data from a device, the application passes an Int32 variable that contains the number of bytes requested from the device. The called function uses the passed value but doesn't have to return the value to the calling application, so the application can pass the variable, which is a value type, by value.

Passing a value type by reference passes a pointer to the variable's data. If the called function changes the variable or its members, the calling application sees the changes. An example, again using ReadFile, is passing an Int32 variable by reference to hold the number of bytes the function returns. The called function writes a value to the variable, and when the function returns, the calling application sees the value written.

Passing a reference type by value also passes a pointer to the variable's data, but the effect varies depending on whether the type is *blittable*. A blittable type is a .NET data type that managed and unmanaged code represent in the same way. Blittable types include Byte, SByte, Int16, UInt16, Int32, UInt32, Int64, UInt64, IntPtr, UIntPtr, Single, Double, and IntPtr as well as SafeHandles used as IN parameters.

When an application passes a blittable, reference type by value to an unmanaged function, the application passes a reference to the original variable. To prevent the garbage collector from moving the variable while the function executes, the CLR pins the variable in memory. The calling application sees changes to the variable's value but not changes to the variable's instance. Passing a reference to the original variable in this way reduces overhead and improves performance compared to passing the variable by value.

An example of passing a blittable, reference type by value is passing a Byte array in a synchronous call to ReadFile, which expects a pointer to an array that the function will fill with data read from the device. Because a Byte array is a reference type and a Byte is a blittable type, if the application passes the array by value, the called function receives a pointer to the original array. The function writes the data to the array, and when the function returns, the calling application can access the new data. (For non-blittable types, the CLR converts the data to a format the function accepts and passes a pointer to the converted data.)

The calling application doesn't see changes the called function makes to the variable's instance, only changes to its value. For example, if the called function sets the variable to Nothing/null, the calling application doesn't see the change.

Passing a reference type by reference passes a pointer that points to a pointer to the variable's data. The calling application sees changes to the variable and to the variable's instance. The examples in this book don't use this passing mechanism.

Passing Structures

Some API functions pass and return structures that can contain multiple items of different types. The header files contain declarations for the structures in C syntax.

A .NET application can usually declare an equivalent structure (a Visual Basic Structure or Visual C# struct) or a class that contains the items in the structure. To ensure that the managed and unmanaged code agree on the layout and alignment of the structure's members, a structure's declaration or class definition can set the StructLayout attribute to LayoutKind.Sequential.

VB   `<StructLayout(LayoutKind.Sequential)>`

VC#   `[ StructLayout( LayoutKind.Sequential ) ]`

The Visual Basic and Visual C# compilers always specify LayoutKind.Sequential for value types, which include structures but not classes, so specifying LayoutKind.Sequential in code is optional for structures.

The optional CharSet field can determine whether strings are converted to ANSI or Unicode before being passed to unmanaged code. CharSet.Auto selects 8-bit ANSI or 16-bit Unicode characters depending on the target platform. A DllImport attribute can also use the CharSet field.

VB   `<StructLayout(LayoutKind.Sequential, CharSet:=CharSet.Auto)>`

VC#   `[ StructLayout( LayoutKind.Sequential, CharSet=CharSet.Auto ) ]`

Some structures are difficult or impractical to duplicate in Visual Basic or Visual C#. A solution is to use a generic buffer of the expected size. The application can fill the buffer before passing it and extract returned data from the buffer as needed.

Finding Your Device

The Windows API provides a series of SetupDi_ API functions that enable applications to find all devices in a device interface class and to obtain a device path name for each device. The CreateFile function can use the device path name to obtain a handle for accessing the device. As Chapter 8 explained, these functions can be useful in finding devices that use the WinUSB driver, HID-class devices that perform vendor-specific functions, and some devices with vendor-specific drivers.

Obtaining a device path name requires these steps:

1. Obtain the device interface GUID.

2. Request a pointer to a device information set with information about all installed and present devices in the device interface class.

3. Request a pointer to a structure that contains information about a device interface in the device information set.

4. Request a structure containing a device interface's device path name.

5. Extract the device path name from the structure.

The application can then use the device path name to open a handle for communicating with the device.

Table 10-1 lists the API functions that applications can use to perform these tasks.

The following code shows how to use API functions to find a device and obtain its device path name. For complete Visual C# and Visual Basic applications that demonstrate how to use these functions, visit *www.Lvr.com*.

Obtaining the Device Interface GUID

As Chapter 8 explained, for many drivers, applications can obtain a device interface GUID from a C header file or other declaration provided with a driver. The device's INF file should contain the same GUID.

For the HID class, Windows provides an API function to obtain the GUID defined in *hidclass.h*.

Table 10-1: Applications use these functions to find devices and obtain device path names to enable accessing devices.

API Function	DLL	Purpose
HidD_GetHidGuid	hid	Retrieve the device interface GUID for the HID class.
SetupDiDestroyDeviceInfoList	setupapi	Free resources used by SetupDiGetClassDevs.
SetupDiGetClassDevs	setupapi	Retrieve a device information set for the devices in a specified class.
SetupDiGetDeviceInterfaceDetail	setupapi	Retrieve a device path name.
SetupDiEnumDeviceInterfaces	setupapi	Retrieve information about a device in a device information set.

VB **Definitions**

```
<DllImport("hid.dll", SetLastError:=True)>
Sub HidD_GetHidGuid (ByRef HidGuid As System.Guid)
End Sub
```

Use

```
Dim hidGuid As System.Guid
HidD_GetHidGuid(hidGuid)
```

VC# **Definitions**

```
[ DllImport( "hid.dll", SetLastError=true ) ]
public static extern void HidD_GetHidGuid( ref System.Guid HidGuid );
```

Use

```
System.Guid hidGuid;
HidD_GetHidGuid( ref hidGuid );
```

For other GUIDs, you can specify a a constant GUID value as a string and convert the string to a System.Guid object.

VB **Definitions**

```
Public Const WINUSB_DEMO_GUID_STRING As String = _
   "{42CA71EC-CE1C-44c2-82DE-87D8D8FF6C1E}"
```

Use

```
Dim myGuid As New System.Guid(WINUSB_DEMO_GUID_STRING)
```

Definitions

public const string WINUSB_DEMO_GUID_STRING =
  "{42CA71EC-CE1C-44c2-82DE-87D8D8FF6C1E}";

Use

System.Guid myGuid = new System.Guid(WINUSB_DEMO_GUID_STRING);

Requesting a Pointer to a Device Information Set

The SetupDiGetClassDevs function can return a pointer to an array of structures containing information about all devices in the device interface class specified by a GUID.

VB **Definitions**

<DllImport("setupapi.dll", SetLastError:=True, CharSet:=CharSet.Auto)> _
Shared Function SetupDiGetClassDevs _
        (ByRef ClassGuid As System.Guid, _
        ByVal Enumerator As IntPtr, _
        ByVal hwndParent As IntPtr, _
        ByVal Flags As Int32) _
        As IntPtr
End Function

Use

Public Const DIGCF_PRESENT As Int32 = 2
Public Const DIGCF_DEVICEINTERFACE As Int32 = &H10

Dim deviceInfoSet As IntPtr

deviceInfoSet = SetupDiGetClassDevs _
        (myGuid, _
        IntPtr.Zero, _
        IntPtr.Zero, _
        DIGCF_PRESENT Or DIGCF_DEVICEINTERFACE)

VC# **Definitions**

[DllImport("setupapi.dll", SetLastError = true, CharSet = CharSet.Auto)]
internal static extern IntPtr SetupDiGetClassDevs
        (ref System.Guid ClassGuid,
        IntPtr Enumerator,
        IntPtr hwndParent,
        Int32 Flags);

Use

```
internal const Int32 DIGCF_PRESENT = 2;
internal const Int32 DIGCF_DEVICEINTERFACE = 0X10;

IntPtr deviceInfoSet;

deviceInfoSet = SetupDiGetClassDevs
        ( ref myGuid,
        IntPtr.Zero,
        IntPtr.Zero,
        DIGCF_PRESENT | DIGCF_DEVICEINTERFACE );
```

Details

For HID-class devices, the ClassGuid parameter is the HidGuid value returned by HidD_GetHidGuid. For other drivers, the application can pass a reference to the appropriate GUID. The example passes null pointers for Enumerator and hwndParent. The Flags parameter uses system constants defined in *setupapi.h*. The flags in the example cause the function to look for device interfaces that are currently attached and enumerated members of the class identified by the ClassGuid parameter.

The returned deviceInfoSet value is a pointer to a device information set that contains information about all attached and enumerated devices in the specified device interface class. The device information set contains a device information element for each device in the set, or array. Each device information element contains a handle to a device's devnode (a structure that represents the device) and a linked list of device interfaces associated with the device.

When finished using the device information set, the application should free the resources used by calling SetupDiDestroyDeviceInfoList as described later in this chapter.

Identifying a Device Interface

A call to SetupDiEnumDeviceInterfaces retrieves a pointer to a structure that identifies a device interface in the previously retrieved deviceInfoSet array. The call passes an array index that specifies a device interface. To retrieve information about all devices in an array, an application can increment the index until the function returns zero, indicating that the array has no more interfaces.

In some cases, such as when looking for a HID-class device with a specific Vendor ID and Product ID, the application may need to request more information before deciding whether a retrieved device interface is the desired one.

Definitions

```
Public Structure SP_DEVICE_INTERFACE_DATA
        Dim cbSize As Int32
        Dim InterfaceClassGuid As Guid
        Dim Flags As Int32
        Dim Reserved As IntPtr
End Structure

<DllImport("setupapi.dll", SetLastError:=True)> _
Shared Function SetupDiEnumDeviceInterfaces _
        (ByVal DeviceInfoSet As IntPtr, _
        ByVal DeviceInfoData As IntPtr, _
        ByRef InterfaceClassGuid As System.Guid, _
        ByVal MemberIndex As Int32, _
        ByRef DeviceInterfaceData As SP_DEVICE_INTERFACE_DATA) _
        As Boolean
End Function
```

Use

```
Dim memberIndex As Int32 = 0
Dim MyDeviceInterfaceData As SP_DEVICE_INTERFACE_DATA
Dim success As Boolean

MyDeviceInterfaceData.cbSize = Marshal.SizeOf(MyDeviceInterfaceData)

success = SetupDiEnumDeviceInterfaces _
        (deviceInfoSet, _
        IntPtr.Zero, _
        myGuid, _
        memberIndex, _
        MyDeviceInterfaceData)
```

Definitions

```
internal struct SP_DEVICE_INTERFACE_DATA
{
        internal Int32 cbSize;
        internal Guid InterfaceClassGuid;
        internal Int32 Flags;
        internal IntPtr Reserved;
}
[DllImport("setupapi.dll", SetLastError = true)]
internal static extern Boolean SetupDiEnumDeviceInterfaces
        (IntPtr DeviceInfoSet,
        IntPtr DeviceInfoData,
        ref System.Guid InterfaceClassGuid,
        Int32 MemberIndex,
        ref SP_DEVICE_INTERFACE_DATA DeviceInterfaceData);
```

Use

```
Int32 memberIndex = 0;
MyDeviceInterfaceData = new SP_DEVICE_INTERFACE_DATA();
Boolean success = false;

MyDeviceInterfaceData.cbSize = = Marshal.SizeOf( MyDeviceInterfaceData );

success = SetupDiEnumDeviceInterfaces
        (deviceInfoSet,
        IntPtr.Zero,
        ref myGuid,
        memberIndex,
        ref MyDeviceInterfaceData);
```

Details

In the SP_DEVICE_INTERFACE_DATA structure, the cbSize parameter is the size of the structure in bytes. The Marshal.SizeOf method returns the structure's size.

The myGuid and deviceInfoSet parameters are values retrieved previously. The DeviceInfoData parameter can be a pointer to an SP_DEVINFO_DATA structure that limits the search to a particular device instance or a null pointer. The memberIndex parameter is an index to a structure in the deviceInfoSet array. The MyDeviceInterfaceData parameter is a pointer to the SP_DEVICE_INTERFACE_DATA structure that the function returns. The structure identifies a device interface of the requested type. The function returns true on success.

Requesting a Structure with the Device Path Name

The SetupDiGetDeviceInterfaceDetail function returns a structure that contains a device path name for a device interface identified in an SP_DEVICE_INTERFACE_DATA structure.

When calling this function for the first time, you don't know the size in bytes of the DeviceInterfaceDetailData structure to pass in the DeviceInterfaceDetail-DataSize parameter. Yet the function won't return the structure unless the function call passes the correct size. The solution is to call the function twice. The first time, GetLastError returns the error *The data area passed to a system call is too small,* but the RequiredSize parameter contains the correct value for Device-InterfaceDetailDataSize. The second call passes the returned size value, and the function returns the structure.

The code below doesn't pass a structure for the DeviceInterfaceDetailData parameter. Instead, the code reserves a generic buffer, passes a pointer to the buffer, and extracts the device path name directly from the buffer. The code thus doesn't require a structure declaration, but I've included one to show the contents of the returned buffer.

VB **Definitions**

```
Public Structure SP_DEVICE_INTERFACE_DETAIL_DATA
        Dim cbSize As Int32
        Dim DevicePath As String
End Structure

<DllImport("setupapi.dll", SetLastError:=True, CharSet:=CharSet.Auto)> _
Shared Function SetupDiGetDeviceInterfaceDetail _
        (ByVal DeviceInfoSet As IntPtr, _
        ByRef DeviceInterfaceData As SP_DEVICE_INTERFACE_DATA, _
        ByVal DeviceInterfaceDetailData As IntPtr, _
        ByVal DeviceInterfaceDetailDataSize As Int32, _
        ByRef RequiredSize As Int32, _
        ByVal DeviceInfoData As IntPtr) _
        As Boolean
End Function
```

Use

```
Dim bufferSize As Int32
Dim detailDataBuffer As IntPtr
Dim success As Boolean

success = SetupDiGetDeviceInterfaceDetail _
        (deviceInfoSet, _
        MyDeviceInterfaceData, _
        IntPtr.Zero, _
        0, _
        bufferSize, _
        IntPtr.Zero)

detailDataBuffer = Marshal.AllocHGlobal(bufferSize)

Marshal.WriteInt32 _
        (detailDataBuffer,
        ConvertToInt32(IIf((IntPtr.Size = 4), 4 + Marshal.SystemDefaultCharSize, 8)))

success = SetupDiGetDeviceInterfaceDetail _
        (deviceInfoSet, _
        MyDeviceInterfaceData, _
        detailDataBuffer, _
        bufferSize, _
        bufferSize, _
        IntPtr.Zero)
```

VC#

Definitions

```
internal struct SP_DEVICE_INTERFACE_DETAIL_DATA
{
        internal Int32 cbSize;
        internal String DevicePath;
}

[DllImport("setupapi.dll", SetLastError = true, CharSet = CharSet.Auto)]
internal static extern Boolean SetupDiGetDeviceInterfaceDetail
        (IntPtr DeviceInfoSet,
        ref SP_DEVICE_INTERFACE_DATA DeviceInterfaceData,
        IntPtr DeviceInterfaceDetailData,
        Int32 DeviceInterfaceDetailDataSize,
        ref Int32 RequiredSize,
        IntPtr DeviceInfoData);
```

Use

```
Int32 bufferSize = 0;
IntPtr detailDataBuffer;
Boolean success = false;

success = SetupDiGetDeviceInterfaceDetail
    (deviceInfoSet,
    ref MyDeviceInterfaceData,
    IntPtr.Zero,
    0,
    ref bufferSize,
    IntPtr.Zero);

detailDataBuffer = Marshal.AllocHGlobal( bufferSize );

Marshal.WriteInt32
    (detailDataBuffer, (IntPtr.Size == 4) ? (4 + Marshal.SystemDefaultCharSize) : 8);

success = SetupDiGetDeviceInterfaceDetail
    (deviceInfoSet,
    ref MyDeviceInterfaceData,
    detailDataBuffer,
    bufferSize,
    ref bufferSize,
    IntPtr.Zero);
```

Details

After calling SetupDiGetDeviceInterfaceDetail, bufferSize contains the value to pass in the DeviceInterfaceDetailDataSize parameter in the next call. But before calling the function again, the code needs to take care of a few things.

The second function call returns a pointer (detailDataBuffer) to an SP_DEVICE_INTERFACE_DETAIL_DATA structure in unmanaged memory. The Marshal.AllocGlobal method uses the returned bufferSize value to allocate memory for the structure.

The cbSize member of the structure passed in detailDataBuffer equals four bytes for cbSize plus the width of one character for the device path name (which is empty when passed to the function). The Marshal.WriteInt32 method copies the cbSize value into the first member of detailDataBuffer. The IIf function (Visual Basic) or "?" conditional operator (Visual C#) selects the correct value for 32- and 64-bit systems.

The second call to SetupDiGetDeviceInterfaceDetail passes the pointer to detailDataBuffer and sets the deviceInterfaceDetailDataSize parameter equal to the bufferSize value returned previously in RequiredSize.

When the function returns after the second call, detailDataBuffer points to a structure containing a device path name.

Extracting the Device Path Name

In detailDataBuffer, the first four bytes are the cbSize member. The string containing the device path name begins at the fifth byte.

VB
```
Dim devicePathName As String = ""
Dim pDevicePathName As IntPtr = New IntPtr(detailDataBuffer.ToInt32 + 4)

devicePathName = Marshal.PtrToStringAuto(pDevicePathName)

Marshal.FreeHGlobal(detailDataBuffer)
```

VC#
```
String devicePathName = "";
IntPtr pDevicePathName = new IntPtr( detailDataBuffer.ToInt32() + 4 );

devicePathName = Marshal.PtrToStringAuto(pDevicePathName);

Marshal.FreeHGlobal(detailDataBuffer);
```

Details

The pDevicePathName variable points to the string in the buffer. The Marshal.PtrToString method retrieves the string from the buffer. When finished with the buffer, Marshal.FreeHGlobal frees the memory previously allocated for the buffer.

Closing Communications

When finished using the DeviceInfoSet returned by SetupDiGetClassDevs, the application should call SetupDiDestroyDeviceInfoList to free resources.

VB **Definitions**
```
<DllImport("setupapi.dll", SetLastError:=True)> _
Shared Function SetupDiDestroyDeviceInfoList _
     (ByVal DeviceInfoSet As IntPtr) _
     As Int32
End Function
```

Table 10-2: Applications can use CreateFile to request a handle to a device and CloseHandle to free the resources used by a handle.

API Function	DLL	Purpose
CloseHandle	kernel32	Free resources reserved by CreateFile. To close handles for the SafeHandle and derived classes, use the Close method, which calls CloseHandle internally.
CreateFile	kernel32	Retrieve a handle for communicating with a device.

Use

SetupDiDestroyDeviceInfoList (deviceInfoSet)

VC# **Definitions**

[DllImport("setupapi.dll", SetLastError = true)]
internal static extern Int32 SetupDiDestroyDeviceInfoList
        (IntPtr DeviceInfoSet);

Use

SetupDiDestroyDeviceInfoList(deviceInfoSet);

Obtaining a Handle

An application can use a retrieved device path name to obtain a handle that enables communicating with the device. Table 10-2 shows API functions related to requesting a handle.

Requesting a Communications Handle

After retrieving a device path name, an application is ready to open communications with the device. The CreateFile function requests a handle to an object, which can be a file or another resource managed by a driver that supports handle-based operations. For example, applications can request a handle to use in exchanging reports with HID-class devices. For devices that use the WinUSB driver, CreateFile obtains a handle the application uses to obtain a WinUSB device handle for accessing a device.

The call to CreateFile can pass a SECURITY_ATTRIBUTES structure that can limit access to the handle or IntPtr.Zero if the function doesn't need to limit access.

VB **Definitions**

```
Friend Const FILE_ATTRIBUTE_NORMAL As Int32 = &H80
Friend Const FILE_FLAG_OVERLAPPED As Int32 = &H40000000
Friend Const FILE_SHARE_READ As Int32 = 1
Friend Const FILE_SHARE_WRITE As Int32 = 2
Friend Const GENERIC_READ As UInt32 = &H80000000UL
Friend Const GENERIC_WRITE As UInt32 = &H40000000
Friend Const OPEN_EXISTING As Int32 = 3


<DllImport("kernel32.dll", CharSet:=CharSet.Auto, SetLastError:=True)> _
Shared Function CreateFile _
        (ByVal lpFileName As String, _
        ByVal dwDesiredAccess As UInt32, _
        ByVal dwShareMode As Int32, _
        ByVal lpSecurityAttributes As IntPtr, _
        ByVal dwCreationDisposition As Int32, _
        ByVal dwFlagsAndAttributes As Int32, _
        ByVal hTemplateFile As Int32) _
        As SafeFileHandle
End Function
```

Use

```
Dim deviceHandle As SafeFileHandle

deviceHandle = CreateFile _
        (devicePathName, _
        GENERIC_WRITE Or GENERIC_READ, _
        FILE_SHARE_READ Or FILE_SHARE_WRITE, _
        IntPtr.Zero, _
        OPEN_EXISTING, _
        FILE_ATTRIBUTE_NORMAL Or FILE_FLAG_OVERLAPPED, _
        0)
```

VC# **Definitions**

```
internal const Int32 FILE_ATTRIBUTE_NORMAL = 0X80;
internal const Int32 FILE_FLAG_OVERLAPPED = 0X40000000;
internal const Int32 FILE_SHARE_READ = 1;
internal const Int32 FILE_SHARE_WRITE = 2;
internal const UInt32 GENERIC_READ = 0X80000000;
internal const UInt32 GENERIC_WRITE = 0X40000000;
internal const Int32 OPEN_EXISTING = 3;
```

```
[DllImport("kernel32.dll", SetLastError = true, CharSet = CharSet.Auto)]
internal static extern SafeFileHandle CreateFile
        (String lpFileName,
        UInt32 dwDesiredAccess,
        Int32 dwShareMode,
        IntPtr lpSecurityAttributes,
        Int32 dwCreationDisposition,
        Int32 dwFlagsAndAttributes,
        Int32 hTemplateFile);
```

Use

```
internal SafeFileHandle deviceHandle;

deviceHandle = CreateFile
        (devicePathName,
        (GENERIC_WRITE | GENERIC_READ),
        FILE_SHARE_READ | FILE_SHARE_WRITE,
        IntPtr.Zero,
        OPEN_EXISTING,
        FILE_ATTRIBUTE_NORMAL | FILE_FLAG_OVERLAPPED,
        0);
```

Details

The function passes a pointer to the devicePathName string returned by Setup-DiGetDeviceInterfaceDetail. The dwDesiredAccess parameter requests read/write access to the device. The dwShareMode parameter allows other processes to access the device while the handle is open. The lpSecurityAttributes parameter is a null pointer (or a pointer to a SECURITY_ATTRIBUTES structure). The dwCreationDisposition parameter must be OPEN_EXISTING for devices. For use with the WinUSB driver, the dwFlagsAndAttributes parameter must use FILE_FLAG_OVERLAPPED. The FILE_ATTRIBUTE_NORMAL attribute indicates that no other attributes such as hidden, read-only, or encrypted are set. The example passes zero for the unused hTemplate parameter. The function returns a SafeFileHandle object.

Closing the Handle

When finished communicating with a device, the application should free the resources reserved by CreateFile.

VB   deviceHandle.Close()

VC#   deviceHandle.Close();

Details

SafeFileHandle objects support the Close method, which marks the handle for releasing and freeing resources. The method calls the CloseHandle API function internally.

Detecting Attachment and Removal

Many applications find it useful to know when a device has been attached or removed. On detecting when a device is attached, the application can begin communicating with the device. On detecting when a device has been removed, the application can stop attempting to communicate until detecting reattachment. Windows provides device-notification functions for this purpose.

About Device Notifications

To request to be informed when a device is attached or removed, an application's form can register to receive notification messages for devices in a device interface class. The operating system passes WM_DEVICECHANGE messages to the form's WndProc method (called WindowProc in C). An application can override WndProc in a form's base class with a method that processes the messages and then passes them to the base class's WndProc method. (The code below shows how to do this.) Each notification contains a device path name that the application can use to identify the device that the notification applies to. Table 10-3 lists the API functions used in registering for device notifications. The example that follows shows how to use the functions.

Registering for Device Notifications

Applications use the RegisterDeviceNotification function to request to receive notification messages. The function requires a handle for the window or service that will receive the notifications, a pointer to a DEV_BROADCAST_DEVICEINTERFACE structure that holds information about the request, and flags to indicate whether the handle is for a window or service.

In the DEV_BROADCAST_DEVICEINTERFACE structure passed to RegisterDeviceNotification, the dbcc_devicetype member is set to DBT_DEVTYP_DEVICEINTERFACE to specify that the application wants

Table 10-3: These functions enable an application to request to receive or stop receiving notifications about device attachment and removal.

API Function	DLL	Purpose
RegisterDeviceNotification	user32	Request to receive device notifications
UnregisterDeviceNotification	user32	Request to stop receiving device notifications

to receive notifications about a device interface class, and classguid is the GUID of the device interface class (myGuid in the example).

When the WM_DEVICECHANGE messages are no longer of interest, the application should call UnregisterDeviceNotification as described later in this chapter.

VB **Definitions**

```
Friend Const DBT_DEVTYP_DEVICEINTERFACE As Int32 = 5
Friend Const DEVICE_NOTIFY_WINDOW_HANDLE As Int32 = 0
Friend Const DIGCF_PRESENT As Int32 = 2
Friend Const DIGCF_DEVICEINTERFACE As Int32 = &H10
Friend Const WM_DEVICECHANGE As Int32 = &H219

<StructLayout(LayoutKind.Sequential)> _
Friend Class DEV_BROADCAST_DEVICEINTERFACE
        Friend dbcc_size As Int32
        Friend dbcc_devicetype As Int32
        Friend dbcc_reserved As Int32
        Friend dbcc_classguid As Guid
        Friend dbcc_name As Int16
End Class

<DllImport("user32.dll", CharSet:=CharSet.Auto, SetLastError:=True)> _
Shared Function RegisterDeviceNotification _
        (ByVal hRecipient As IntPtr, _
        ByVal NotificationFilter As IntPtr, _
        ByVal Flags As Int32) _
        As IntPtr
End Function
```

Use

Place this statement in the _Load event for the form that will receive device-change messages:

```
frmMy = Me

Dim devBroadcastDeviceInterface As DEV_BROADCAST_DEVICEINTERFACE = _
       New DEV_BROADCAST_DEVICEINTERFACE()
Dim devBroadcastDeviceInterfaceBuffer As IntPtr
Dim deviceNotificationHandle As IntPtr
Dim size As Int32

' frmMy is the form that will receive device-change messages.

Friend frmMy As frmMain

size = Marshal.SizeOf(devBroadcastDeviceInterface)

devBroadcastDeviceInterface.dbcc_size = size
devBroadcastDeviceInterface.dbcc_devicetype = DBT_DEVTYP_DEVICEINTERFACE
devBroadcastDeviceInterface.dbcc_reserved = 0
devBroadcastDeviceInterface.dbcc_classguid = myGuid

devBroadcastDeviceInterfaceBuffer = Marshal.AllocHGlobal(size)

Marshal.StructureToPtr _
       (devBroadcastDeviceInterface, _
       devBroadcastDeviceInterfaceBuffer, _
       True)

deviceNotificationHandle = RegisterDeviceNotification _
       (frmMy.Handle, _
       devBroadcastDeviceInterfaceBuffer, _
       DEVICE_NOTIFY_WINDOW_HANDLE)

Marshal.FreeHGlobal (devBroadcastDeviceInterfaceBuffer)
```

VC#

Definitions

```
internal const Int32 DBT_DEVTYP_DEVICEINTERFACE = 5;
internal const Int32 DEVICE_NOTIFY_WINDOW_HANDLE = 0;
internal const Int32 DIGCF_PRESENT = 2;
internal const Int32 DIGCF_DEVICEINTERFACE = 0X10;
internal const Int32 WM_DEVICECHANGE = 0X219;
```

```
[ StructLayout( LayoutKind.Sequential ) ]
internal class DEV_BROADCAST_DEVICEINTERFACE
{
        internal Int32 dbcc_size;
        internal Int32 dbcc_devicetype;
        internal Int32 dbcc_reserved;
        internal Guid dbcc_classguid;
        internal Int16 dbcc_name;
}
[DllImport("user32.dll", CharSet = CharSet.Auto, SetLastError = true)]
internal static extern IntPtr RegisterDeviceNotification
        (IntPtr hRecipient,
        IntPtr NotificationFilter,
        Int32 Flags);
```

Use

Place this statement in the _Load event for the form that will receive device-change messages:

```
frmMy = this;

DEV_BROADCAST_DEVICEINTERFACE devBroadcastDeviceInterface =
    new DEV_BROADCAST_DEVICEINTERFACE();
IntPtr devBroadcastDeviceInterfaceBuffer;
IntPtr deviceNotificationHandle;
Int32 size = 0;

// frmMy is the form that will receive device-change messages.

internal frmMain frmMy;

size = Marshal.SizeOf( devBroadcastDeviceInterface );

devBroadcastDeviceInterface.dbcc_size = size;
devBroadcastDeviceInterface.dbcc_devicetype = DBT_DEVTYP_DEVICEINTERFACE;
devBroadcastDeviceInterface.dbcc_reserved = 0;
devBroadcastDeviceInterface.dbcc_classguid = myGuid;

devBroadcastDeviceInterfaceBuffer = Marshal.AllocHGlobal( size );

Marshal.StructureToPtr
        ( devBroadcastDeviceInterface,
        devBroadcastDeviceInterfaceBuffer,
        true );
```

```
deviceNotificationHandle = RegisterDeviceNotification
    ( frmMy.Handle,
    devBroadcastDeviceInterfaceBuffer,
    DEVICE_NOTIFY_WINDOW_HANDLE );

Marshal.FreeHGlobal( devBroadcastDeviceInterfaceBuffer );
```

Details

The device-notification functions use several constants defined in header files. The Marshal.SizeOf method retrieves the size of the DEV_BROADCAST_DEVICEINTERFACE structure for passing to the structure's dbcc_size member.

Marshal.AllocGlobal allocates memory for a buffer that will hold the DEV_BROADCAST_DEVICEINTERFACE structure.

The Marshal.StructureToPointer method copies the structure into the buffer. The application is then ready to call RegisterDeviceNotification, passing the handle to a form that will receive the notifications and a pointer to the buffer.

When finished using devBroadcastDeviceInterfaceBuffer, the application can use Marshal.FreeHGlobal to free the memory allocated for it by AllocHGlobal.

Capturing Device Change Messages

The WndProc function processes messages received by a form, dialog box, or other window.

VB

```
Protected Overrides Sub WndProc(ByRef m As Message)

    If m.Msg = WM_DEVICECHANGE Then

        OnDeviceChange(m)

    End If

    MyBase.WndProc(m)

End Sub
```

```
VC#    protected override void WndProc( ref Message m )
       {
              if ( m.Msg == WM_DEVICECHANGE )
              {
                     OnDeviceChange( m );
              }
              base.WndProc( ref m );
       }
```

On receiving a WM_DEVICECHANGE message, the method calls the application's OnDeviceChange method, which can examine the message and take action, and then passes the message to the WndProc method in the form's base class.

Reading Device Change Messages

A device-change message contains two pointers: lParam and wParam. The wParam property is a code that indicates device arrival, removal, or another event. The lParam property is a device management structure. There are several defined types of device-management structures, but each begins with the same DEV_BROADCAST_HDR structure. The structure's dbch_devicetype member indicates the type of device-management structure that lParam points to.

If dbch_devicetype = DBT_DEVTYP_DEVICEINTERFACE, the structure is a DEV_BROADCAST_DEVICEINTERFACE and the application can retrieve the complete structure, read the device path name in the dbcc_name member, and compare the name to the device path name of the device of interest.

This example detects device arrival and removal:

VB   **Definitions**

```
Friend Const DBT_DEVICEARRIVAL As Int32 = &H8000
Friend Const DBT_DEVICEREMOVECOMPLETE As Int32 = &H8004
```

Use

Friend Sub OnDeviceChange(ByVal m as Message)

    If (m.WParam.ToInt32 = DBT_DEVICEARRIVAL) Then

        ' Find out if the device path name matches wParam.
        ' If yes, perform any tasks required on device arrival.

    ElseIf (m.WParam.ToInt32 = DBT_DEVICEREMOVECOMPLETE) Then

        ' Find out if the device path name matches wParam.
        ' If yes, perform any tasks required on device removal.

    End If

End Sub

VC# **Definitions**

internal const Int32 DBT_DEVICEARRIVAL = 0X8000;
internal const Int32 DBT_DEVICEREMOVECOMPLETE = 0X8004;

Use

```
internal void OnDeviceChange( Message m )
{
        if ( ( m.WParam.ToInt32() == DBT_DEVICEARRIVAL ) )
        {
                // Find out if the device path name matches wParam.
                // If yes, perform any tasks required on device arrival.
        }
        else if ( ( m.WParam.ToInt32() == DBT_DEVICEREMOVECOMPLETE ) )
        {
                // Find out if the device path name matches wParam.
                // If yes, perform any tasks required on device removal.
        }
}
```

Retrieving the Device Path Name in the Message

If the message indicates a device arrival or removal (or another event of interest), the application can investigate further.

In the structure that lParam points to, if dbch devicetype contains DBT_DEVTYP_DEVICEINTERFACE, the event relates to a device interface.

Thus lParam contains a DEV_BROADCAST_DEVICEINTERFACE structure, which begins with a DEV_BROADCAST_HDR structure. The dbcc_name member contains the device path name of the device the message applies to. The application can compare this device path name with the device path name of the device of interest. On a match, the application can take any desired actions.

This example code uses two declarations for the DEV_BROADCAST_DEVICEINTERFACE structure. The first declaration, presented earlier, is used when calling RegisterDeviceNotification. A second declaration, DEV_BROADCAST_DEVICEINTERFACE_1, enables marshaling the data in dbcc_name and classguid.

VB **Definitions**

```
<StructLayout(LayoutKind.Sequential)> _
Friend Class DEV_BROADCAST_HDR
        Friend dbch_size As Int32
        Friend dbch_devicetype As Int32
        Friend dbch_reserved As Int32
End Class


<StructLayout(LayoutKind.Sequential, CharSet:=CharSet.Auto)> _
        Friend Class DEV_BROADCAST_DEVICEINTERFACE_1
        Friend dbcc_size As Int32
        Friend dbcc_devicetype As Int32
        Friend dbcc_reserved As Int32
        <MarshalAs(UnmanagedType.ByValArray, _
                ArraySubType:=UnmanagedType.U1, _
                SizeConst:=16)> _
                Friend dbcc_classguid() As Byte
        <MarshalAs(UnmanagedType.ByValArray,
                sizeconst:=255)> _
                Friend dbcc_name() As Char
End Class
```

Use

```
Dim devBroadcastDeviceInterface As New DEV_BROADCAST_DEVICEINTERFACE_1()
Dim devBroadcastHeader As New DEV_BROADCAST_HDR()

Marshal.PtrToStructure(m.LParam, devBroadcastHeader)
```

```
If (devBroadcastHeader.dbch_devicetype = DBT_DEVTYP_DEVICEINTERFACE) Then

    Dim stringSize As Int32 =
        Convert.ToInt32((devBroadcastHeader.dbch_size - 32) / 2)

    Array.Resize(devBroadcastDeviceInterface.dbcc_name, stringSize)

    Marshal.PtrToStructure (m.LParam, devBroadcastDeviceInterface)

    Dim deviceNameString As _
        New String(devBroadcastDeviceInterfacc.dbcc_name, 0, stringSize)

    If (String.Compare (deviceNameString, devicePathName, True) = 0) Then
            'The name matches.
    Else
            'It's a different device.
    End If
End If
```

Definitions

```
[ StructLayout( LayoutKind.Sequential ) ]
internal class DEV_BROADCAST_HDR
{
    internal Int32 dbch_size;
    internal Int32 dbch_devicetype;
    internal Int32 dbch_reserved;
}

[ StructLayout( LayoutKind.Sequential, CharSet=CharSet.Auto ) ]
internal class DEV_BROADCAST DEVICEINTERFACE_1
{
    internal Int32 dbcc_size;
    internal Int32 dbcc_devicetype;
    internal Int32 dbcc_reserved;
    [ MarshalAs( UnmanagedType.ByValArray,
            ArraySubType=UnmanagedType.U1,
            SizeConst=16 ) ]
            internal Byte[] dbcc_classguid;
    [MarshalAs(UnmanagedType.ByValArray,
            SizeConst = 255)]
            intcrnal Char[] dbcc_name;
}
```

Use

```
DEV_BROADCAST_DEVICEINTERFACE_1 devBroadcastDeviceInterface =
        new DEV_BROADCAST_DEVICEINTERFACE_1();
DEV_BROADCAST_HDR devBroadcastHeader = new DEV_BROADCAST_HDR();

Marshal.PtrToStructure( m.LParam, devBroadcastHeader );

if ( ( devBroadcastHeader.dbch_devicetype == DBT_DEVTYP_DEVICEINTERFACE ) )
{
        Int32 stringSize = Convert.ToInt32( ( devBroadcastHeader.dbch_size - 32 ) / 2 );

        Array.Resize(ref devBroadcastDeviceInterface.dbcc_name, stringSize);

        Marshal.PtrToStructure( m.LParam, devBroadcastDeviceInterface );

        String DeviceNameString =
                new String(devBroadcastDeviceInterface.dbcc_name, 0, stringSize);

        if ( ( String.Compare( deviceNameString, devicePathName, true ) == 0 ) )
        {
                // The name matches.;
        }
        else
        {
                // It's a different device.;
        }
}
```

Details

MarshalPtrToStructure copies the message's lParam property into a DEV_BROADCAST_HDR structure. If the message relates to a device interface, the application retrieves the device path name.

The name is in a Char array in unmanaged memory. The application needs to retrieve the array and convert it to a String.

The dbch_size member of DEV_BROADCAST_HDR contains the number of bytes in the complete DEV_BROADCAST_DEVICEINTERFACE structure. To obtain the number of characters in the device path name stored in dbch_name, subtract the 32 bytes in the structure that are not part of the name and divide by 2 because there are 2 bytes per character.

The Array.Resize method trims dbcc_name to the size of the device path name. Marshal.PtrToStructure copies the data from the unmanaged block in lParam to the devBroadcastDeviceInterface structure. The Char array containing the device path name is then stored as a String in deviceNameString, and the String.Compare method looks for a match.

Stopping Device Notifications

To stop receiving device notifications, an application calls UnregisterDeviceNotification.

VB **Definitions**

```
<DllImport("user32.dll", SetLastError:=True)> _
Shared Function UnregisterDeviceNotification _
    (ByVal Handle As IntPtr) _
        As Boolean
End Function
```

Use

```
UnregisterDeviceNotification(deviceNotificationHandle)
```

VC# **Definitions**

```
[DllImport("user32.dll", SetLastError = true)]
internal static extern Boolean UnregisterDeviceNotification(IntPtr Handle);
```

Use

```
UnregisterDeviceNotification( deviceNotificationHandle );
```

11

Human Interface Devices: Using Control and Interrupt Transfers

The human interface device (HID) class was one of the first USB classes supported under Windows. On PCs running Windows 98 or later, applications can communicate with HIDs using the drivers built into the operating system. Because the HID class supports exchanging data for application-specific purposes, many special-purpose devices use the HID class.

Chapter 7 introduced the class. This chapter shows how to determine whether a device can use the human-interface class, introduces HID-specific requests, and discusses HID firmware options. Chapter 12 describes the reports that HIDs use to exchange information and Chapter 13 shows how to access HIDs from applications.

What is a HID?

The name *human interface device* suggests that HIDs interact directly with people, and many HIDs do just that. A mouse detects when someone moves it or presses a key. A host may send data that translates to an effect that a user senses on a joystick. Besides keyboards, mice, and joysticks, devices with HID interfaces include remote controls; telephone keypads; game controls such as data gloves and steering wheels; barcode readers; and UPS units. Devices with physical control panels can use a HID interface to send control-panel input to the host. Devices with virtual control panels on the host can use a HID interface to send control-panel data to the device. A virtual control panel can be cheaper to implement than traditional physical controls on a device.

A HID doesn't have to have a human interface. The device just needs to be able to function within the limits of the HID class specification. These are the major abilities and limits of HID-class devices:

- All data exchanged resides in fixed-length structures called reports. The host sends and receives data by sending and requesting reports in control or interrupt transfers. The report format is flexible and can handle just about any type of data.

- A HID must have an interrupt IN endpoint for sending Input reports.

- A HID can have at most one interrupt IN endpoint and one interrupt OUT endpoint. A device that requires more interrupt endpoints can be a composite device with multiple HID interfaces. An application obtains separate handles for each HID in the device.

- The interrupt IN endpoint enables the HID to send information to the host at unpredictable times. For example, there's no way for the host computer to know when a user will press a key on the keyboard, so the host's driver uses interrupt transactions to poll the device periodically to obtain new data. SuperSpeed devices can send ERDY Transaction Packets to request communications with the host.

- The rate of data exchange is limited. As Chapter 3 explained, a host can guarantee a low-speed interrupt endpoint a maximum data transfer rate of 800 bytes/sec. For full-speed endpoints, the maximum is 64 kB/s. High-speed and SuperSpeed endpoints support faster rates, but to comply with the USB 2.0 and USB 3.0 specifications, the endpoints in the default interface should request no more than 64 kB/s. Under Windows, supporting an alternate HID interface requires a vendor-provided driver, which eliminates the advantage of using Windows-provided drivers. Control transfers have no guaranteed bandwidth except for the bandwidth reserved for all control transfers on the bus.

- Windows 98 Gold (original edition) supports USB 1.0, so interrupt OUT transfers aren't supported and all host-to-device reports must use control transfers.

A HID may be just one of multiple interfaces in a device. For example, a USB speaker might use isochronous transfers for audio and a HID interface for controlling volume, balance, treble, and bass.

Hardware Requirements

To comply with the HID specification, the interface's endpoints and descriptors must meet several requirements.

Endpoints

All HID transfers use either the control endpoint or an interrupt endpoint. Every HID must have an interrupt IN endpoint for sending data to the host. An interrupt OUT endpoint is optional. Table 11-1 shows the transfer types and their typical use in HIDs.

Reports

The requirement for an interrupt IN endpoint suggests that every HID must have at least one Input report defined in the HID's report descriptor. Output and Feature reports are optional.

Control Transfers

The HID specification defines six class-specific requests. Two requests, Set Report and Get Report, provide a way for the host and device to transfer reports to and from the device using control transfers. Set Idle and Get Idle set and read the Idle rate, which determines whether or not a device resends data that hasn't changed since the last report. Set Protocol and Get Protocol set and read a protocol value, which can enable a device to function with a simplified protocol when the full HID drivers aren't loaded on the host, such as during boot up.

Table 11-1: The transfer type used in a HID transfer depends on the chip's abilities and the requirements of the data being sent.

Transfer Type	Source of Data	Typical Data	Required Pipe?	WIndows Support
Control	Device (IN transfer)	Data that doesn't have critical timing requirements.	yes	Windows 98 Gold and later
	Host (OUT transfer)	Data that doesn't have critical timing requirements, or any data if there is no OUT interrupt pipe.		
Interrupt	Device (IN transfer)	Periodic or low-latency data.	yes	
	Host (OUT transfer)	Periodic or low-latency data.	no	Windows 98 SE and later

Interrupt Transfers

Interrupt endpoints provide another way to exchange data, especially when the receiver must get the data periodically and with minimum delay. Control transfers can be delayed if the bus is very busy, while the bandwidth for interrupt transfers is guaranteed to be available after successful enumeration.

The ability to do Interrupt OUT transfers was added in USB 1.1, and the option to use an interrupt OUT pipe was added to version 1.1 of the HID specification. Windows 98 SE was the first Windows edition to support USB 1.1 and HID 1.1.

Firmware Requirements

The device's descriptors must include an interface descriptor for the HID class, a class-specific HID descriptor, and an interrupt IN endpoint descriptor. An interrupt OUT endpoint descriptor is optional. The firmware must also contain a class-specific report descriptor with information about the format and use of the report data.

A HID can support one or more reports. The report descriptor specifies the size and contents of the data in a device's report(s) and may also include information about how the receiver of the data should use the data. Values in the descriptor define each report as an Input, Output, or Feature report. The host receives data in Input reports and sends data in Output reports. A Feature report can travel in either direction.

Every device should support at least one Input report that the host can retrieve using interrupt transfers or control requests. Output reports are optional. To be compatible with Windows 98 Gold, devices that use Output reports should support sending the reports using control transfers. Using interrupt transfers for Output reports is optional. Feature reports always use control transfers and are optional.

Descriptors

As with any USB device, a HID's descriptors tell the host what it needs to know to communicate with the device. Listing 11-1 shows example device, configuration, interface, class, and endpoint descriptors for a HID with a vendor-specific function.

The host learns about the HID interface during enumeration by sending a Get Descriptor request for the configuration containing the HID interface. An interface descriptor specifies the HID interface. A HID class descriptor specifies the combined number of report and physical descriptors supported by the interface. During enumeration, the HID driver requests the report descriptor and any physical descriptors.

PBP   In PICBASIC PRO, descriptor tables are in assembly code. Each table is a list of values with each preceded by a retlw instruction, which places the literal value that follows in the working register and returns to the calling code. You don't have to know assembly code to compose a descriptor. Start with an example and edit the values as needed.

Device Descriptor

12	bLength	Descriptor size in bytes
01	bDescriptorType	Descriptor type (Device)
0200	bcdUSB	USB Specification release number (BCD) (2.00)
00	bDeviceClass	Class Code (class is specified in interface descriptor)
00	bDeviceSubClass	Subclass code
00	bDeviceProtocol	Protocol code
08	bMaxPacketSize0	Endpoint zero maximum packet size
0925	idVendor	Vendor ID (Lakeview Research)
1234	idProduct	Product ID
0100	bcdDevice	Device release number (BCD)
01	iManufacturer	Manufacturer string index
02	iProduct	Product string index
00	iSerialNumber	Device serial number string index
01	bNumConfigurations	Number of configurations

Configuration Descriptor

09	bLength	Descriptor size in bytes
02	bDescriptorType	Descriptor type (Configuration)
0029	wTotalLength	Total length of this and subordinate descriptors
01	bNumInterfaces	Number of interfaces in this configuration
01	bConfigurationValue	Index of this configuration
00	iConfiguration	Configuration string index
A0	bmAttributes	Attributes (bus powered, remote wakeup supported)
32	bMaxPower	Maximum power consumption (100 mA)

Interface Descriptor

09	bLength	Descriptor size in bytes
04	bDescriptorType	Descriptor type (Interface)
00	bInterfaceNumber	Interface Number
00	bAlternateSetting	Alternate Setting Number
02	bNumEndpoints	Number of endpoints in this interface
03	bInterfaceClass	Interface class (HID)
00	bInterfaceSubclass	Interface subclass
00	bInterfaceProtocol	Interface protocol
00	iInterface	Interface string index

Listing 11-1: Example descriptors for a vendor-specific HID. All values are in hexadecimal. (Part 1 of 2)

HID Descriptor

09	bLength	Descriptor size in bytes
21	bDescriptorType	Descriptor type (HID)
0110	bcdHID	HID Spec. release number (BCD) (1.1)
00	bCountryCode	Country code
01	bNumDescriptors	Number of subordinate class descriptors
22	bDescriptorType	Descriptor type (report)
002F	wDescriptorLength	Report descriptor size in bytes

Interrupt IN Endpoint Descriptor

07	bLength	Descriptor size in bytes
05	bDescriptorType	Descriptor type (Endpoint)
81	bEndpointAddress	Endpoint number and direction (1 IN)
03	bmAttributes	Transfer type (interrupt)
0040	wMaxPacketSize	Maximum packet size
0A	bInterval	polling interval (milliseconds)

Interrupt OUT Endpoint Descriptor

07	bLength	Descriptor size in bytes
05	bDescriptorType	Descriptor type (Endpoint)
01	bEndpointAddress	Endpoint number and direction (1 OUT)
03	bmAttributes	Transfer type (interrupt)
0040	wMaxPacketSize	Maximum packet size
0A	bInterval	polling interval (milliseconds)

Listing 11-1: Example descriptors for a vendor-specific HID. All values are in hexadecimal. (Part 2 of 2)

Here is Listing 11-1's device descriptor for use in PICBASIC PRO:

```
DeviceDescriptor
        retlw   (EndDeviceDescriptor-DeviceDescriptor)/2; bLength
        retlw   0x01            ; bDescriptorType
        retlw   0x00            ; bcdUSB low byte
        retlw   0x02            ; bcdUSB high byte
        retlw   0x00            ; bDeviceClass
        retlw   0x00            ; bDeviceSubClass
        retlw   0x00            ; bDeviceProtocol
        retlw   0x08            ; bMaxPacketSize0
        retlw   0x25            ; idVendor low byte
        retlw   0x09            ; idVendor high byte
        retlw   0x34            ; idProduct low byte
        retlw   0x12            ; idProduct high byte
        retlw   0x00            ; bcdDevice low byte
        retlw   0x01            ; bcdDevice high byte
        retlw   0x01            ; iManufacturer
        retlw   0x02            ; iProduct
        retlw   0x00            ; iSerialNumber
        retlw   0x01            ; bNumConfigurations
EndDeviceDescriptor
```

C18   For Microchip's MPLAB C18 compiler, descriptors can reside in structures. This structure holds a device descriptor:

```
typedef struct __attribute__ ((packed)) _USB_DEVICE_DESCRIPTOR
{
        BYTE            bLength;
        BYTE            bDescriptorType;
        WORD            bcdUSB;
        BYTE            bDeviceClass;
        BYTE            bDeviceSubClass;
        BYTE            bDeviceProtocol;
        BYTE            bMaxPacketSize0;
        WORD            idVendor;
        WORD            idProduct;
        WORD            bcdDevice;
        BYTE            iManufacturer;
        BYTE            iProduct;
        BYTE            iSerialNumber;
        BYTE            bNumConfigurations;
} USB_DEVICE_DESCRIPTOR;
```

This is Listing 11-1's device descriptor stored in a structure:

```
ROM USB_DEVICE_DESCRIPTOR device_dsc=
{
        0x12,           // bLength
        0x01,           // bDescriptorType
        0x0200,         // bcdUSB
        0x00,           // bDeviceClass
        0x00,           // bDeviceSubClass
        0x00,           // bDeviceProtocol
        0x08,           // bMaxPacketSize0
        0x0925,         // idVendor
        0x1234,         // idProduct
        0x0100,         // bcdDevice
        0x01,           // iManufacturer
        0x02,           // iProduct
        0x00,           // iSerialNumber
        0x01            // bNumConfigurations
};
```

The HID Interface

In the interface descriptor, bInterfaceclass = 03h to identify the interface as a HID. Other fields that contain HID-specific information in the interface descriptor are the bInterfaceSubclass and bInterfaceProtocol fields, which can specify a boot interface.

If bInterfaceSubclass = 01h, the device supports a boot interface. A HID with a boot interface can communicate with the host even when the host hasn't loaded its HID drivers. This situation might occur when the computer boots directly to DOS or when viewing the system setup screens that you can access on bootup, or when using Windows Safe mode for system troubleshooting.

A keyboard or mouse with a boot interface can use a simplified protocol supported by the BIOS in many hosts. The BIOS loads from ROM or other non-volatile memory on bootup and is available in any operating-system mode. The HID specification defines boot-interface protocols for keyboards and mice. If a device has a boot interface, bInterfaceProtocol indicates if the HID supports a keyboard (01h) or mouse (02h) function.

The HID Usage Tables document defines the report format for keyboards and mice that use the boot protocol. The BIOS understands the boot protocol and assumes that a boot device will support the protocol, so the BIOS doesn't need to read a report descriptor from the device. Before sending or requesting reports, the BIOS sends the HID-specific Set Protocol request to request to use the boot protocol. When the full HID drivers have been loaded, the driver can use Set Protocol to cause the device to switch from the boot protocol to the report protocol, which uses the report formats defined in the report descriptor.

If the HID doesn't support a boot protocol, bInterfaceSubclass = 00h.

HID Class Descriptor

The HID class descriptor (Table 11-2) identifies additional descriptors for HID communications. The class descriptor has seven or more fields depending on the number of additional descriptors.

Report Descriptors

A report descriptor defines the format and use of the data in the HID's reports. If the device is a mouse, the data reports mouse movements and button clicks. If the device is a relay controller, the data specifies which relays to open and close. The descriptor format is flexible enough for use with devices with varied functions.

A report descriptor is a class-specific descriptor. The host retrieves the descriptor by sending a Get Descriptor request to the interface with the wValue field containing 22h in the high byte.

Listing 11-2 is a basic report descriptor that defines an Input report, an Output report, and a Feature report. The device sends two bytes of vendor-defined data in the Input report. The host sends two bytes of vendor-defined data in the Output report. The Feature report is two bytes of vendor-defined data that the host can send to the device or request from the device.

Basic report descriptors similar to this example can serve many HIDs with vendor-specific functions. For a loop-back test, device firmware can copy received data from an Input report into an Output report to send back to the host. For a "lights and switches" application, firmware can use received Input report data to control LEDs and use Output reports to send logic states read at switches.

Each item in the report descriptor consists of a byte that identifies the item and one or more bytes containing the item's data. The HID specification defines item types that a report can contain. Here is the function of each item in the example report descriptor:

The **Usage Page** item (06h) specifies the general function of the device, such as generic desktop control, game control, or alphanumeric display. In the example

Table 11-2: The HID class descriptor specifies the length of the report descriptor.

Offset (decimal)	Field	Size (bytes)	Description
0	bLength	1	Descriptor size in bytes.
1	bDescriptorType	1	This descriptor's type: 21h to indicate the HID class.
2	bcdHID	2	HID specification release number (BCD).
4	bCountryCode	1	Numeric expression identifying the country for localized hardware (BCD) or 00h.
5	bNumDescriptors	1	Number of subordinate report and physical descriptors.
6	bDescriptorType	1	The type of a class-specific descriptor that follows. (A report descriptor (required) is type 22h.)
7	wDescriptorLength	2	Total length of the descriptor identified above.
9	bDescriptorType	1	Optional. The type of a class-specific descriptor that follows. A physical descriptor is type 23h
10	wDescriptorLength	2	Total length of the descriptor identified above. Present only if bDescriptorType is present immediately above. May be followed by additional wDescriptorType and wDescriptorLength fields to identify additional physical descriptors.

descriptor, the Usage Page is the vendor-defined value FFA0h. The HID Usage Tables document provides values for different Usage Pages. Vendor-defined Usage Pages use the range FF00h–FFFFh.

The **Usage** item (09h) specifies the function of an individual report in a Usage Page. For example, Usages available for generic desktop controls include mouse, joystick, and keyboard. Because the example's Usage Page is vendor-defined, all of the Usages in the Usage Page are vendor-defined also. In the example, the Usage is 01h.

The **Collection (Application)** item (A1h) begins a group of items that together perform a single function, such as keyboard or mouse. Each report descriptor must have an application collection.

The Collection contains three reports. Each report has these items:

A vendor-defined Usage applies to the data in the report.

A Logical Minimum and Logical Maximum specify the range of values that the report can contain.

06	FFA0	Usage Page (vendor-defined)
09	01	Usage (vendor-defined)
A1	01	Collection (Application)
09	03	Usage (vendor-defined)
15	00	Logical Minimum (0)
26	00FF	Logical Maximum (255)
95	02	Report Size (8 bits)
75	08	Report Count (2)
81	02	Input (Data, Variable, Absolute)
09	04	Usage (vendor-defined)
15	00	Logical Minimum (0)
26	00FF	Logical Maximum (255)
75	08	Report Size (8 bits)
95	02	Report Count (2)
91	02	Output (Data, Variable, Absolute)
09	05	Usage (vendor-defined)
15	00	Logical Minimum (0)
26	00FF	Logical Maximum (255)
75	08	Report Size (8 bits)
95	02	Report Count (2)
B1	02	Feature (Data, Variable, Absolute)
C0		End Collection

Listing 11-2: This report descriptor defines an Input report, an Output report, and a Feature report. Each report transfers two vendor-defined bytes. All values are hexadecimal.

The Report Size item indicates how many bits are in each reported data item. In the example, each data item is eight bits.

The Report Count item indicates how many data items the report contains. In the example, each report contains two data items.

In the final item, the first byte specifies whether the report is an Input report (81h), Output report (91h), or Feature report (B1h). The second byte contains additional information about the report data, such as whether the values are relative or absolute.

An **End Collection** item (C0h) closes the Application Collection.

These are the basics. Chapter 12 has more about report formats.

HID-specific Requests

The HID specification defines six HID-specific requests (Table 11-3).

Table 11-3: The HID class defines six HID-specific requests.

Request Number	Request	Data Source (Data stage)	wValue (high byte, low byte)	wIndex	Data Length (bytes) (wLength)	Data Stage Contents	Required?
01h	Get Report	device	report type, Report ID	interface	report length	report	yes
02h	Get Idle	device	00h, Report ID	interface	0001h	idle duration	no
03h	Get Protocol	device	0000h	interface	0001h	protocol	yes for HIDs that support a boot protocol
09h	Set Report	host	report type, Report ID	interface	report length	report	no
0Ah	Set Idle	no Data stage	idle duration, Report ID	interface	–	–	no, except for keyboards using the boot protocol
0Bh	Set Protocol	no Data stage	00h, protocol	interface	–	–	yes for HIDs that support a boot protocol

Get Report

Purpose: The host requests an Input or Feature report from a HID using a control transfer.

Request Number (bRequest): 01h

Source of Data: device

Data Length (wLength): length of the report

Contents of wValue field: The high byte contains the report type (01h = Input, 03h = Feature), and the low byte contains the Report ID. The default Report ID is zero.

Contents of wIndex field: the number of the interface the request is directed to.

Contents of data packet in the Data stage: the report

Comments: The HID specification says that all HIDs must support this request. A host may enumerate and communicate with a HID that doesn't support the request, but future editions of the operating system might enforce the requirement. See also Set Report.

Get Idle

Purpose: The host reads the current Idle rate from a HID.

Request Number (bRequest): 02h

Source of Data: device

Data Length (wLength): 0001h

Contents of wValue field: The high byte is 00h. The low byte indicates the Report ID the request applies to. If the low byte is 00h, the request applies to all of the HID's Input reports.

Contents of wIndex field: the number of the interface that supports this request.

Contents of data packet in the Data stage: the Idle rate, expressed in units of 4 ms.

Comments: HIDs aren't required to support this request. See Set Idle for more details.

Get Protocol

Purpose: The host learns whether the boot or report protocol is currently active in the HID.

Request Number (bRequest): 03h

Source of Data: device

Data Length (wLength): 0001h

Contents of wValue field: 0000h

Contents of wIndex field: the number of the interface that supports this request.

Contents of data packet in the Data stage: the protocol (00h = boot protocol, 01h = report protocol).

Comments: Boot devices must support this request. See also Set Protocol.

Set Report

Purpose: The host sends an Output or Feature report to a HID using a control transfer.

Request Number (bRequest): 09h

Source of Data: host

Data Length (wLength): length of the report

Contents of wValue field: The high byte contains the report type (02h = Output, 03h = Feature), and the low byte contains the Report ID. The default Report ID is zero.

Contents of wIndex field: the number of the interface the request is directed to.

Contents of data packet in the Data stage: the report.

Comments: If a HID interface doesn't have an Interrupt OUT endpoint or if the host complies only with version 1.0 of the HID specification, this request is the only way the host can send data to the HID. HIDs aren't required to support this request. See also Get Report.

Set Idle

Purpose: saves bandwidth by limiting the reporting frequency of an interrupt IN endpoint when the data hasn't changed since the last report.

Request Number (bRequest): 0Ah

Data Length (wLength): 0000h

Contents of wValue field: The high byte sets the duration, or the maximum amount of time between reports. A value of 00h means that the HID will send a report only when the report data has changed. The low byte indicates the Report ID that the request applies to. If the low byte is 00h, the request applies to all of the HID's Input reports.

Contents of wIndex field: the number of the interface that supports this request.

Comments: The duration is in units of 4 ms, which gives a range of 4–1,020 ms. No matter what the duration value, if the report data has changed since the last Input report sent, on receiving an interrupt IN token packet, the HID sends the data. If the data hasn't changed and the duration time hasn't elapsed since the last report, the HID returns NAK. If the data hasn't changed and the duration time has elapsed since the last report, the HID sends report data. A duration value of 00h indicates an infinite duration: the HID sends a report only if the report data has changed and otherwise returns NAK. On enumerating a HID, the Windows HID driver attempts to set the idle rate to 00h. HIDs aren't required to support this request except for keyboards using the boot protocol. Not all device controllers have hardware support for the Idle rate though firmware can support the feature with help from a hardware timer. A HID can refuse the request by returning STALL. See also Get Idle.

Set Protocol

Purpose: The host specifies whether the HID should use the boot or report protocol.

Request Number (bRequest): 0Bh

Data Length (wLength): 0000h

Contents of wValue field: the protocol (0000h = boot protocol, 0001h = report protocol).

Contents of wIndex field: the number of the interface that supports this request.

Comments: Boot devices must support this request. See also Get Protocol.

Transferring Data

When enumeration is complete, the host has identified the device interface as a HID, established pipes with the interface's endpoints, and learned the report formats for sending and receiving data.

The host can then request reports using interrupt IN transfers and control transfers with Get Report requests. The device also has the option to support receiving reports using interrupt OUT transfers and control transfers with Set Report requests.

Writing Firmware

Many firmware compilers provide HID examples, perhaps because all major operating systems provide host HID drivers and HID firmware is less complex than what's required for many other classes.

PBP PIC BASIC PRO includes code for a mouse and a generic HID that sends and receives reports using interrupt transfers. Supporting the HID Get Report or Set Report requests would require added support in assembly code.

C18 Microchip provides HID example code for the PIC18F4550 and other Microchip microcontrollers for the MPLAB C18 compiler. Microchip's USB Framework includes mouse and generic HID examples. The code supports sending and receiving reports using interrupt transfers. See *www.Lvr.com* for a generic HID example that supports exchanging reports via both interrupt and control transfers.

Tools

Another option for users of Microchip controllers is HIDmaker FS from Trace Systems, Inc. A software wizard asks questions about your device and generates firmware to implement the Input, Output, and Feature reports you specify. The wizard supports the PICBASIC PRO compiler as well as the Microchip MPLAB C18, CCS C, and HI-TECH C compilers. The wizard can generate PC application code to access the HID in several programming languages.

The HIDmaker Test Suite includes two other tools. The AnyHID application displays report descriptors and enables exchanging data with attached and enumerated HIDs (except system mice and keyboards). USBwatch is a low-budget USB analyzer for HIDs. To use the analyzer, you add the provided code to your device firmware and connect the device's asynchronous serial port to a PC's serial port via RS-232 or a USB/COM-port adapter. The firmware writes debugging data to the serial port for display by the USBwatch application. USBwatch can display enumeration and application data. You can also define your own messages for firmware to send at locations you select in your code.

12

Human Interface Devices: Reports

Chapter 11 introduced the reports that HIDs use to exchange data. A report can be a basic buffer of bytes or a complex assortment of items with assigned functions and units. This chapter shows how to create reports to fit specific applications.

Report Structure

The report descriptor provides information about the data the HID sends and receives. The descriptor identifies the device's function and can specify uses and units for the report data. Controls and data items describe values to be transferred in one or more reports. A control is a button, switch, or other physical entity that operates or regulates an aspect of a device. Everything else is a data item.

For vendor-specific devices intended for use with a single application, the application often knows in advance the type, size, and order of the data in a report so there's no need to obtain this information from the device. For example, when the vendor of a data-acquisition unit creates an application for use with the unit, the vendor already knows the data format the device uses in its reports. At most, the application might check the Product ID and release number from the device descriptor to learn whether the application can request a particular setting or action. For applications like these, the host and device can exchange data in vendor-defined buffers without relying on the report descriptor to define what the buffers contain.

Using the HID Descriptor Tool

The HID Descriptor Tool (Figure 12-1) is a free utility from the USB-IF. The tool helps create report descriptors and flags errors. Instead of having to look up the values that correspond to each item in your report, you can select the item from a list and enter the value you want to assign to it, and the tool adds the item to the descriptor. You can also add items manually. The Parse Descriptor function displays the raw and interpreted values in your descriptor and comments on any errors found. When you have an error-free descriptor, you can convert it to the syntax your firmware requires. The tool has limited support for vendor-specific items, however, and may flag these as errors.

Control and Data Item Values

Several documents define values that reports may contain. The first place to look is the USB-IF's *HID Usage Tables*, which defines values for generic desktop controls, simulation controls, game controls, LEDs, buttons, telephone devices, and more. Other values are defined in the main HID specification and the HID specifications for monitor, power, and point-of-sale devices.

Item Format

The HID specification defines two report item types: short items and long items. As of HID 1.11, there are no defined Long items.

A Short item's 1-byte prefix specifies the item type, item tag, and item size. These are the elements that make up the prefix byte:

Bit Number	Contents	Description
1..0	Item size	Number of bytes in the item
3..2	Item type	Item scope: Main, Global, or Local
7..4	Item tag	Item function

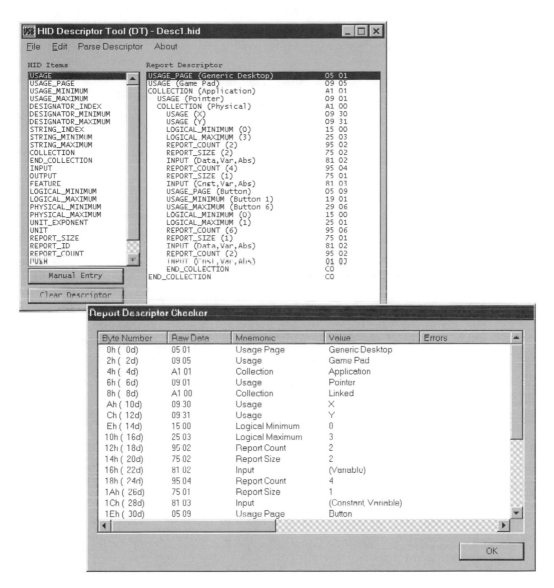

Figure 12-1. The HID Descriptor Tool helps in creating and testing HID report descriptors.

The item size specifies how many data bytes the item contains. Note that an item size of 11_b corresponds to 4 data bytes (not 3):

Item Size (binary)	Number of Data Bytes
00	0
01	1
10	2
11	4

The item type specifies the scope of the item: Main (00), Global (01), or Local (10). This chapter has more information about these item types.

The item tag specifies the item's function.

The Main Item Type

A Main item defines or groups data items within a report descriptor. There are five Main item types. Input, Output, and Feature items each define fields in a type of report. Collection and End Collection items group related items within a report. The default for all Main items is zero.

Input, Output, and Feature Items

Table 12-1 shows supported values for Input, Output, and Feature items. Each item has a 1-byte prefix followed by 1 or 2 bytes that describe the report data.

An Input item applies to data a device sends to the host. An Input report contains one or more Input items. The host uses interrupt IN transfers or Get Report requests to request Input reports.

An Output item applies to information that the host sends to the device. An Output report contains one or more Output items. Hosts can send Output reports via interrupt OUT transfers and Set Report requests.

A Feature report contains one or more Feature items. The report can travel in either direction. Feature reports typically contain configuration settings that affect the overall behavior of the device or one of its components. For example, the host may have a virtual (on-screen) control panel to enable users to select and control a device's settings. The host uses control transfers with Set Report and Get Report requests to send and receive Feature reports.

Following each Input, Output, or Feature item prefix are up to 9 bits that describe the item's data. (An additional 23 bits are reserved.) An Input item pre-

Table 12-1: The bits that follow Input, Output, and Feature Item prefixes describe the data in a report.

Prefix	Item Data		
	Bit Number	**Meaning if bit = 0**	**Meaning if bit = 1**
Input (100000nn, where nn=the number of bytes in the data following the prefix) For example, use 81h for 1 byte of item data. Use 82h for 2 bytes of item data.	0	Data	Constant
	1	Array	Variable
	2	Absolute	Relative
	3	No wrap	Wrap
	4	Linear	Non-linear
	5	Preferred state	No preferred state
	6	No null position	Null state
	7	Reserved	
	8	Bit field	Buffered bytes
	9-31	Reserved	
Output (100100nn, where nn=the number of bytes in the data following the prefix) For example, use 91h for 1 byte of item data. Use 92h for 2 bytes of item data.	0	Data	Constant
	1	Array	Variable
	2	Absolute	Relative
	3	No wrap	Wrap
	4	Linear	Non-linear
	5	Preferred state	No preferred state
	6	No null position	Null state
	7	Non-volatile	Volatile
	8	Bit field	Buffered bytes
	9-31	Reserved	
Feature (101100nn, where nn=the number of bytes in the data following the prefix) For example, use B1h for 1 byte of item data. Use B2h for 2 bytes of item data.	0	Data	Constant
	1	Array	Variable
	2	Absolute	Relative
	3	No wrap	Wrap
	4	Linear	Non-linear
	5	Preferred state	No preferred state
	6	No null position	Null state
	7	Non-volatile	Volatile
	8	Bit field	Buffered bytes
	9-31	Reserved	

fix followed by 8 bits of item data has the value 81h. The high four bits equal 8h to indicate an Input item, and the low four bits equal 1h to indicate that the item data uses 1 byte. An Input item prefix followed by 9 bits of data has the value 82h, with the high four bits set to 8h to indicate an Input item and the low four bits set to 2h to indicate that the item data uses 2 bytes.

The bit functions are the same for Input, Output, and Feature items, except that Input items don't support the volatile/non-volatile bit. These are the uses for each bit:

Data | Constant. Data means that the contents of the item are modifiable (read/write). Constant means the contents are not modifiable (read-only).

Array | Variable. This bit specifies whether the data reports the state of every control (Variable) or just reports the states of controls that are asserted, or active (Array). Reporting only the asserted controls results in a more compact report for devices such as keyboards that have many controls (keys) but where only one or a few controls are asserted at the same time.

For example, if a keypad has eight keys, setting this bit to Variable would mean that the keypad's report would contain a bit for each key. In the report descriptor, the report size would be one bit, the report count would be eight, and the total amount of data sent would be eight bits. Setting the bit to Array would mean that each key has an assigned index, and the keypad's report would contain only the indexes of keys that are pressed. With eight keys, the report size would be three bits, which can report a key number in the range 0–7. The report count would equal the maximum number of simultaneous keypresses that could be reported. If the user can press only one key at a time, the report count would be 1 and the total amount of data sent would be just 3 bits. If the user can press all of the keys at once, the report count would be 8 and the total amount of data sent would be 24 bits.

An out-of-range value reported for an Array item indicates that no controls are asserted.

Absolute | Relative. Absolute means that the value is based on a fixed origin. Relative means that the data indicates the change from the last reading. A joystick normally reports absolute data (the joystick's current position), while a mouse reports relative data (how far the mouse has moved since the last report).

No Wrap | Wrap. Wrap indicates that the value rolls over to the minimum if the value continues to increment after reaching its maximum and rolls over to the maximum if the value continues to decrement after reaching its minimum.

An item specified as No Wrap that exceeds the specified limits may report a value outside the limits. This bit doesn't apply to Array data.

Linear | Non-linear. Linear indicates that the measured data and the reported value have a linear relationship. In other words, a graph of the reported data and the property being measured forms a straight line. In non-linear data, a graph of the reported data and the property being measured forms a curve. This bit doesn't apply to Array data.

Preferred State | No Preferred State. Preferred state indicates that the control will return to a particular state when the user isn't interacting with it. A momentary pushbutton has a preferred state (not pushed, or out) when no one is pressing the button. A toggle switch has no preferred state and remains in the last state selected by a user. This bit doesn't apply to Array data.

No Null Position | Null State. Null state indicates that the control supports a state where the control isn't sending meaningful data. A control indicates that it's in the null state by sending a value outside the range defined by its Logical Minimum and Logical Maximum. No Null Position indicates that any data sent by the control is meaningful data. A hat switch on a joystick is in a null position when it isn't being pressed. This bit doesn't apply to Array data.

Non-volatile | Volatile. The Volatile bit applies only to Output and Feature report data. Volatile means the device may change the value on its own, without host interaction, as well as when the host sends a report requesting the device to change the value. For example, users might request to change the value of a control by pressing a button on the device or by clicking a button on a virtual control panel to cause the host to send a report to the device. Non-volatile means that the device changes the value only when the host requests a new value in a report.

When the host is sending a report and doesn't want to change a volatile item, the value to assign to the item depends on whether the data is defined as relative or absolute. If a volatile item is defined as relative, a report that assigns a value of zero should result in no change. If a volatile item is defined as absolute, a report that assigns an out-of-range value should result in no change. This bit doesn't apply to Array data.

Bit Field | Buffered Bytes. Bit Field means that each bit or a group of bits in a byte can represent a separate piece of data. Buffered Bytes means that the data consists of one or more byte-wide values. The report size for Buffered Byte items must be eight. This bit doesn't apply to Array data. Note that this bit is bit 8 in the item's data so setting this bit requires two bytes of item data.

Table 12-2: Data values for the Collection and End Collection Main Item Tags.

Value	Type	Description
00h	Physical	Data at a single geometric point.
01h	Application	Items that have a common purpose or carry out a function.
02h	Logical	Items that describe a data structure.
03h	Report	Wraps the fields in a report.
04h	Named array	Array of selector usages.
05h	Usage switch	Modifies the purpose or function of Usages in a collection.
06h	Usage modifier	Modifies the purpose or function of a Usage.
07h–7Fh	Reserved	–
80h–FFh	Vendor defined	–

Collections

All of the report types use Collection and End Collection items to group related items. Following each Collection item (A1h) in the report descriptor is a value indicating the collection type (Table 12-2). The End Collection item is a single byte (C0h).

All report items must be in an application collection. Use of the other collection types is optional. All Main items between a Collection item and its End Collection item are part of the collection. Each collection must have a Usage tag (described below). Collections can be nested.

A top-level collection is a collection that isn't nested within another collection. A HID interface can have multiple top-level application collections with each representing a different HID function. For example, a keyboard with an embedded pointing device can have a single HID interface with two top-level collections, one for the pointing device's reports and one for the keyboard's reports. Unlike HIDs in separate interfaces in a composite device, these HID functions share interrupt endpoints.

The Global Item Type

Global items identify reports and describe the data in them, including characteristics such as the data's function, maximum and minimum allowed values, and the size and number of report items. A Global item tag applies to every item that follows until the next Global item tag. Thus a report descriptor

Table 12-3: There are twelve defined Global items.

Item Type	Value (nn holds the number of bytes that follow)	Description
Usage Page	000001nn	Specifies the data's usage or function.
Logical Minimum	000101nn	Smallest value that an item will report.
Logical Maximum	001001nn	Largest value that an item will report.
Physical Minimum	001101nn	The logical minimum expressed in physical units.
Physical Maximum	010001nn	The logical maximum expressed in physical units.
Unit exponent	010101nn	Base 10 exponent of units.
Unit	011001nn	Unit values.
Report Size	011101nn	Size of an item's fields in bits.
Report ID	100001nn	Prefix that identifies a report.
Report Count	100101nn	The number of data fields for an item.
Push	101001nn	Places a copy of the global item state table on the stack.
Pop	101101nn	Replaces the item state table with the last structure pushed onto the stack.
Reserved	110001nn–111101nn	For future use.

doesn't have to repeat values that don't change from one item to the next. Table 12-3 shows the defined Global items.

Identifying the Report

Report ID. A HID can support multiple reports of the same type, with each report having its own Report ID and contents. This way, each report doesn't have to include every piece of data. Sometimes the simplicity of using a single report outweighs the need to reduce the bandwidth used by longer reports, however.

In the report descriptor, a Report ID item applies to all items that follow until the next Report ID. If there is no Report ID item, the report uses the default ID of 00h. A descriptor should not declare a Report ID of 00h. Report IDs are specific to each report type, so a HID can have one report of each type with the default Report ID. However, if one report type uses multiple Report IDs, every report in the HID must have a declared Report ID. For example, if a descriptor declares Report IDs 01h and 02h for Feature reports, any Input or Output reports must also have a Report ID greater than 00h.

In a transfer that uses a Set Report or Get Report request, the host specifies a Report ID in the Setup transaction in the low byte of the wValue field. In an interrupt transfer, if the interface supports more than one Report ID, the Report ID precedes the report data on the bus. If the interface supports only the default Report ID of 00h, the Report ID doesn't travel on the bus with the report in interrupt transfers.

For Windows applications, the report buffer provided to an API function must be large enough to hold the report plus one byte for the Report ID even if using only Report ID zero. When a HID supports multiple Report IDs for Input reports of different sizes, the Windows HID driver requires applications to pass a buffer large enough to hold the longest report.

When a HID supports multiple reports of the same type and different sizes and the HID is sending a report whose data is a multiple of the endpoint's maximum packet size, the HID indicates the end of the report by sending a ZLP for all but the HID's longest report.

For interrupt transfers that retrieve Input reports from HIDs with multiple Input Report IDs, the host's driver has no way to request a specific report from the device. The device firmware decides which report to place in the endpoint buffer to send to the host. At the host, the HID driver stores the received Report ID and report data.

Describing the Data's Use

The Global items that describe the data and how to use it are the Usage Page, Logical Minimum and Maximum, Physical Minimum and Maximum, Unit, and Unit Exponent. Each of these items helps the receiver of the report interpret the report's data. All but the Usage Page are involved with converting raw report data to values with units attached. The items make it possible for a report to contain data in a compact form, with the receiver of the data responsible for converting the data to meaningful values.

Usage Page. An item's Usage is a 32-bit value that identifies a function that a device performs. A Usage contains two values: the upper 16 bits are a Global Usage Page item and the lower 16 bits are a Local Usage item. The value in the Local Usage item is a Usage ID. The term *Usage* can refer to either the 32-bit value or the 16-bit Local value. To prevent confusion, some sources use the term Extended Usage to refer to the 32-bit value. Microsoft defines a USAGE type that is a 16-bit value that can contain a Usage Page or a Usage ID.

Multiple items can share a Usage Page while having different Usage IDs. After a Usage Page appears in a report, all Usage IDs that follow are in that Usage Page until the descriptor declares a new Usage Page.

The HID Usage Tables document defines many Usage Pages. There are Usage Pages for common device types including generic desktop controls (mouse, keyboard, joystick), digitizer, barcode scanner, camera control, and various game controls. A vendor can define Usage Pages using values from FF00h to FFFFh.

Logical Minimum and Logical Maximum. The Logical Minimum and Logical Maximum define limits for reported values. The limits are expressed in logical units, which means that they use the same units as the values they apply to. For example, if a device reports values of up to 500 mA in units of 2 mA, the Logical Maximum is 250.

If the most significant bit of the highest byte is 1, the value is negative and is expressed as a two's complement. (To express a negative value as a two's complement, complement each bit and add 1 to the result. Perform the same operations to obtain the negative value represented by a two's complement.) Using 1-byte values, 00h to 7Fh represent the decimal values zero through +127, and FFh to 80h represent the decimal values -1 through -128.

The HID specification says that if both the Logical Minimum and Logical Maximum are considered positive, there's no need for a sign bit. But the report-descriptor test in the USB-IF Compliance Tool assumes that if the most-significant bit is 1, the value is negative. These values will fail the compliance test because the Logical Minimum (0) is greater than the Logical Maximum (-1):

```
0x15 0x00    // Logical Minimum
0x25 0xFF    // Logical Maximum - WRONG!
```

If the desired result is a minimum of zero and a maximum of 255, the solution is to use a 2-byte value for the maximum:

```
0x15 0x00    // Logical Minimum
0x26 0x00FF  // Logical Maximum
```

Note that the Logical Maximum item tag is now 26h to indicate that the data that follows the tag is two bytes. Because the most-significant bit of the Logical Maximum is zero, the value is assumed positive and the compliance test accepts the values as valid.

Converting Units

The Physical Minimum, Physical Maximum, Unit Exponent, and Unit items define how to convert reported values into more meaningful units.

Physical Minimum and Physical Maximum. The Physical Minimum and Physical Maximum define the limits for a value when expressed in the units defined by the Units tag. In the earlier example of values of zero through 250 in units of 2 mA, the Physical Minimum is zero and the Physical Maximum is 500. The receiving device uses the logical and physical limit values to obtain the value in the desired units. In the example, reporting the data in units of 2 mA means that the value can transfer in a single byte, with the receiver of the data using the Physical Minimum and Maximum values to translate to mA. The price is a loss in resolution, compared to reporting 1 bit per mA. If the report descriptor doesn't specify these items, they default to the Logical Minimum and Logical Maximum.

Unit Exponent. The Unit Exponent specifies what power of 10 to apply to the value obtained after using the logical and physical limits to convert the value into the desired units. The exponent can range from -8 to +7. A value of zero causes the value to be multiplied by 10^0, which is the same as applying no exponent. These are the codes:

Exponent	0	1	2	3	4	5	6	7	-8	-7	-6	-5	-4	-3	-2	-1
Code	00h	01h	02h	03h	04h	05h	06h	07h	08h	09h	0Ah	0Bh	0Ch	0Dh	0Eh	0Fh

For example, if the value obtained is 1234 and the Unit Exponent is 0Eh, the final value is 12.34.

Unit. The Unit tag specifies what units to apply to the report data after the value is converted using the Physical and Unit Exponent items. The HID specification defines codes for the basic units of length, mass, time, temperature, current, and luminous intensity. Most other units can be derived from these.

Specifying a Unit value can be more complicated than you might expect. Table 12-4 shows values to work from. A value can be as long as four bytes, with each nibble having a defined function. Nibble 0 (the least significant nibble) specifies the measurement system, either English or SI (International System of Units) and whether the measurement is in linear or angular units. Each of the nibbles that follow represents a quality to be measured with the value of the nibble representing the exponent to apply to the value. For example, a nibble

Table 12-4: The units to apply to a reported value are a function of the measuring system and exponent values specified in the Unit item.

Nibble Number	Quality Measured	Measuring System (Nibble 0 value)				
		None (0h)	SI Linear (01h)	SI Rotation (2h)	English Linear (3h)	English Rotation (4h)
1	Length	None	Centimeter	Radian	Inch	Degree
2	Mass	None	Gram		Slug	
3	Time	None	Second			
4	Temperature	None	Kelvin		Fahrenheit	
5	Current	None	Ampere			
6	Luminous Intensity	None	Candela			
7	Reserved	None				

with a value of 2h means that the corresponding value is in units squared. A nibble with a value of Dh, which represents -3, means that the units are expressed as $1/units^3$. These exponents are separate from the Unit Exponent value, which is a power of ten applied to the data, rather than an exponent applied to the units.

Note that the basic SI units for length and temperature are meters and kilograms, but the HID specification uses centimeters and grams as basic units for the Unit tag.

Converting Raw Data

To convert raw data to values with units attached, three things must occur. The firmware's report descriptor must contain the information needed for the conversion. The sender must provide data that matches the report descriptor's specifications. And the receiver of the data must apply the conversions specified in the report descriptor.

Below are examples of descriptors and raw and converted data. Just because a tag exists in the HID specification doesn't mean you have to use it. If the application knows what format and units to use for the values it's going to send or receive, the firmware doesn't have to specify these items.

To specify time in seconds, up to a minute, the report descriptor might include this information:

Logical Minimum: 00h

Logical Maximum: 3Ch

Physical Minimum: 00h

Physical Maximum: 3Ch

Unit: 1003h. Nibble 0 = 3 to select the English Linear measuring system (though in this case, any value from 1 to 4 would work). Nibble 3 = 1 to select time in seconds.

Unit Exponent: 00h

With this information, the receiver knows that the value sent equals a number of seconds.

To specify time in tenths of seconds up to a minute, increase the Logical Maximum and Physical Maximum and change the Unit Exponent:

Logical Minimum: 00h

Logical Maximum: 0258h

Physical Minimum: 00h

Physical Maximum: 0258h

Unit: 1003h. Nibble 0 = 3h to select the English Linear measuring system. Nibble 3 = 1h to select time in seconds.

Unit Exponent: 0Fh. This represents an exponent of -1 to indicate that the value is expressed in tenths of seconds rather than seconds.

Sending values as large as 600 requires 2 bytes, which the firmware specifies in the Report Size tag.

To send a temperature value using one byte to represent temperatures from -20 to 110°F, the report descriptor might contain the following:

Logical Minimum: 80h (-128 decimal expressed as a hexadecimal two's complement)

Logical Maximum: 7Fh (127 decimal)

Physical Minimum: ECh (-20 expressed as a hexadecimal two's complement)

Physical Maximum: 6Eh (110 decimal)

Unit: 10003h. Nibble 0 is 3h to select the English Linear measuring system. Nibble 4 is 1h to select degrees Fahrenheit.

Unit Exponent: 00h

These values ensure the highest possible resolution for a single-byte report item, because the transmitted values can span the full range from 0 to 255.

In this case the logical and physical limits differ, so converting is required. This function accepts decimal values and returns the number of bits per logical unit:

VB
```
Private Function BitsPerLogicalUnit _
        (ByVal logical_maximum As Int32, _
        ByVal logical_minimum As Int32, _
        ByVal physical_maximum As Int32, _
        ByVal physical_minimum As Int32, _
        ByVal unit_exponent As Int32) _
        As Single

        Dim calculatedBitsPerLogicalUnit As Single = Convert.ToSingle _
                ((logical_maximum - logical_minimum) / _
                ((physical_maximum - physical_minimum) * _
                (Math.Pow(10, unit_exponent)))))

        Return calculatedBitsPerLogicalUnit

End Function
```

VC#
```
private Single BitsPerLogicalUnit
        (Int32 logical_maximum,
        Int32 logical_minimum,
        Int32 physical_maximum,
        Int32 physical_minimum,
        Int32 unit_exponent)
{
        Single calculatedBitsPerLogicalUnit = Convert.ToSingle
                ((logical_maximum - logical_minimum) /
                ((physical_maximum - physical_minimum) *
                (Math.Pow(10, unit_exponent))));

        return calculatedBitsPerLogicalUnit;
}
```

With the example values, the resolution is 1.96 bits per degree, or 0.51 degree per bit.

This function converts a logical value to the specified physical units:

```
VB      Private Function ValueInPhysicalUnits _
                (ByVal value As Int32, _
                ByVal logical_maximum As Int32, _
                ByVal logical_minimum As Int32, _
                ByVal physical_maximum As Int32, _
                ByVal physical_minimum As Int32, _
                ByVal unit_exponent As Int32) _
                As Single

                Dim calculatedValueInPhysicalUnits As Single = _
                        Convert.ToSingle _
                        (value * _
                        ((physical_maximum - physical_minimum) * _
                        (Math.Pow(10, unit_exponent)))/ _
                        (logical_maximum - logical_minimum))

                Return calculatedValueInPhysicalUnits
        End Function
```

```
VC#     private Single ValueInPhysicalUnits
                (Int32 value,
                Int32 logical_maximum,
                Int32 logical_minimum,
                Int32 physical_maximum,
                Int32 physical_minimum,
                Int32 unit_exponent)
        {
                Single calculatedValueInPhysicalUnits = Convert.ToSingle
                        (value *
                        ((physical_maximum - physical_minimum) *
                        (Math.Pow(10, unit_exponent))) /
                        (logical_maximum - logical_minimum));

                return calculatedValueInPhysicalUnits;
        }
```

If the value in logical units (the raw data) is 63, the converted value in the specified units is 32° F.

Describing the Data's Size and Format

Two Global items describe the size and format of the report data.

Report Size specifies the size in bits of a field in an Input, Output, or Feature item. Each field contains one piece of data.

Report Count specifies how many fields an Input, Output, or Feature item contains.

For example, if a report has two 8-bit fields, Report Size is 08h and Report Count is 02h. If a report has one 16-bit field, Report Size is 10h and Report Count is 01h.

A single Input, Output, or Feature report can contain multiple items, each with its own Report Size and Report Count.

Saving and Restoring Global Items

The final two Global items enable saving and restoring sets of Global items. These items allow flexible report formats while using minimum storage space in the device.

Push places a copy of the Global-item state table on the CPU's stack. The Global-item state table contains the current settings for all previously defined Global items.

Pop is the complement to Push. It restores the saved states of the previously pushed Global item states.

The Local Item Type

Local items specify qualities of the controls and data items in a report. A Local item's value applies to all items that follow within a Main item until the descriptor assigns a new value. Local items don't carry over to the next Main item; each Main item begins fresh with no Local items defined.

Local items relate to general usages, body-part designators, and strings. A Delimiter item enables grouping sets of Local items. Table 12-5 shows the values and meaning of each of the items.

Usage. The Local Usage item is the Usage ID that works together with the Global Usage Page to describe the function of a control, data, or collection.

The HID Usage Tables document lists many Usage IDs. For example, the Buttons Usage Page uses Local Usage IDs from 0001h to FFFFh to identify which button in a set is pressed, with a value of 000h meaning no button pressed.

Table 12-5: Local items can provide information about Usages, body parts, and strings.

Local Item Type	Value (nn indicates the number of item bytes that follow)	Description
Usage	000010nn	The use for an item or collection.
Usage Minimum	000110nn	The starting Usage associated with the elements in an array or bitmap.
Usage Maximum	001010nn	The ending Usage associated with the elements in an array or bitmap.
Designator Index	001110nn	A Designator value in a physical descriptor. Indicates what body part applies to a control.
Designator Minimum	010010nn	The starting Designator associated with the elements in an array or bitmap.
Designator Maximum	010110nn	The ending Designator associated with the elements in an array or bitmap.
String Index	011110nn	Associates a string with an item or control.
String Minimum	100010nn	The first string index when assigning a group of sequential strings to controls in an array or bitmap.
String Maximum	100110nn	The last string index when assigning a group of sequential strings to controls in an array or bitmap.
Delimiter	101010nn	The beginning (1) or end (0) of a set of Local items.
Reserved	101011nn to 111110nn	For future use.

If a single Usage precedes a series of controls or data items, that Usage applies to all of the controls or data items. If multiple Usages precede controls or data items and the number of controls or data items equals the number of Usages, each Usage applies to one control or data item, with the Usages and the controls or data items pairing up in sequence.

In this example, the report contains two bytes. The first byte's Usage is X, and the second byte's Usage is Y.

Usage (X),
Usage (Y),
Report Count (02h),
Report Size (08h),
Input (Data, Variable, Absolute),

If multiple Usages preceded a series of controls or data items and the number of controls or data items is greater than the number of Usages, each Usage pairs up with one control or data item in sequence, and the final Usage applies to all of the remaining controls or data items.

In the following example, the report is 16 bytes. Usage X applies to the first byte, Usage Y applies to the second byte, and a vendor-defined Usage applies to the third through 16th bytes.

Usage (X)
Usage (Y)
Usage (vendor defined)
Report Count (10h),
Report Size (08h),
Input (Data, Variable, Absolute)

Usage Minimum and Maximum. The Usage Minimum and Usage Maximum can assign a series of Usage IDs to the elements in an array or bitmap. The following example describes a report that contains the state (0 or 1) of each of three buttons. The Usage Minimum and Usage Maximum specify that the first button has a Usage ID of 01h, the second button has a Usage ID of 02h, and the third button has a Usage ID of 03h:

Usage Page (Button Page)
Logical Minimum (09h)
Logical Maximum (01h)
Usage Minimum (01h)
Usage Maximum (03h)
Report Count (03h)
Report Size (01h)
Input (Data, Variable, Absolute)

Designator Index. For items with a physical descriptor, the Designator Index specifies a Designator value in a physical descriptor. The Designator specifies what body part the control uses.

Designator Minimum and Designator Maximum. When a report contains multiple Designator Indexes that apply to the elements in a bitmap or array, a

Designator Minimum and Designator Maximum can assign a sequential Designator Index to each bit or array item.

String Index. An item or control can include a String Index to associate a string with the item or control. The strings are stored in the same format described in Chapter 4 for product, manufacturer, and serial-number strings.

String Minimum and Maximum. When a report contains multiple string indexes that apply to the elements in a bitmap or array, a String Minimum and String Maximum can assign a sequential String Index to each bit or array item.

Delimiter. A Delimiter defines the beginning (01h) or end (00h) of a local item. A delimited local item may contain alternate usages for a control. Different applications can thus define a device's controls in different ways. For example, a button may have a generic use (Button 1) and a specific use (Send, Quit, etc.).

Physical Descriptors

A physical descriptor specifies the part or parts of the body intended to activate a control. For example, each finger might have its own assigned control. Similar physical descriptors are grouped into a physical descriptor set. A set consists of a header, followed by the physical descriptors. A physical descriptor is a HID-specific descriptor. The host can retrieve a physical descriptor set by sending a Get Descriptor request to the HID interface with 23h in the high byte of the wValue field and the number of the descriptor set in the low byte of the wValue field. Physical descriptors are optional. For most devices, these descriptors either don't apply or the information they provide has no practical use. The HID specification has more information on how to use physical descriptors.

Padding

To pad a descriptor so it contains a multiple of eight bits, a descriptor can include a Main item with no assigned Usage. This excerpt from a keyboard's report descriptor specifies an Output report that transfers five bits of data and three bits of padding:

```
Usage Page (LEDs)
Usage Minimum (01h)
Usage Maximum (05h)
Output (Data, Variable, Absolute) (five 1-bit LEDs)
Report Count (01h)
Report Size (03h)
Output (Constant) (3 bits of padding)
```

13

Human Interface Devices: Host Application

Chapter 10 showed how to obtain a handle to communicate with a device. This chapter shows how Visual Basic and Visual C# applications can use handles to access HID-class devices.

HID API Functions

The Windows HID API provides an extensive set of functions that applications can use to learn about a HID's reports and to send and receive report data. The WDK documents the functions.

The HID API considers each report item to be either a button or value. A button is a control or data item that has a discrete, binary value, such as ON (1) or OFF (0). Buttons include items represented by unique Usage IDs in the Buttons, Keyboard, and LED Usage pages. Any report item that isn't a button is a value usage. The report descriptor defines the range for each value usage.

Table 13-1: Applications can use these API functions to obtain information about a HID and its reports.

Function	Purpose
HidD_FreePreparsedData	Free resources used by HidD_GetPreparsedData.
HidD_GetAttributes	Retrieve a pointer to a structure containing the HID's Vendor ID, Product ID, and device release number.
HidD_GetPhysicalDescriptor[1]	Retrieve a physical descriptor.
HidD_GetPreparsedData	Return a handle to a buffer with information about the HID's reports.
HidP_GetButtonCaps	Retrieve an array with information about the buttons in a top-level collection for a specified report type.
HidP_GetCaps	Retrieve a structure describing a HID's reports.
HidP_GetExtendedAttributes[1]	Retrieve a structure with information about Global items the HID parser didn't recognize.
HidP_GetLinkCollectionNodes	Retrieve a structure with information about collections within a top-level collection.
HidP_GetSpecificButtonCaps	Like HidP_GetButtonCaps but can specify a Usage Page, Usage ID, and link collection.
HidP_GetSpecificValueCaps	Like HidP_GetValueCaps but can specify a Usage Page, Usage ID, and link collection.
HidP_GetValueCaps	Retrieve an array with information about the values in a top-level collection for a specified report type.
HidP_IsSameUsageAndPage	Determine if two Usages (each consisting of a Usage Page and Usage ID) are equal.
HidP_MaxDataListLength	Retrieve the maximum number of HIDP_DATA structures that HidP_GetData can return for a HID report type and top-level collection.
HidP_MaxUsageListLength	Retrieve the maximum number of Usage IDs that HidP_GetUsages can return for a report type and top-level collection.
HidP_TranslateUsagesToI8042ScanCodes	Map Usages on the HID_USAGE_PAGE_KEYBOARD Usage Page to PS/2 scan codes.
HidP_UsageAndPageListDifference	Retrieve the differences between two arrays of Usages (Usage Page and Usage ID).
HidP_UsageListDifference	Retrieve the differences between two arrays of Usage IDs.

[1]Not supported under Windows 98 Gold.

Table 13-2: Applications can use these API functions to retrieve strings from a HID.

Function	Purpose
HidD_GetIndexedString[1]	Retrieve a specified string.
HidD_GetManufacturerString[1]	Retrieve a manufacturer string
HidD_GetProductString[1]	Retrieve a product string.
HidD_GetSerialNumberString[1]	Retrieve a serial-number string.

[1]Not supported under Windows 98 Gold.

Requesting Information about the HID

Table 13-1 lists API functions that request information about a HID and its reports. Many applications use only a few of these functions. HidD_GetPreparsedData retrieves a pointer to a buffer that contains information about the HID's reports. HidP_GetCaps uses the pointer to retrieve a HIDP_CAPS structure that specifies what report types a device supports and provides information about the type of information in the reports. For example, the structure specifies the number of HIDP_BUTTON_CAPS structures that have information about a button or set of buttons. The application can call HidP_GetButtonCaps to retrieve these structures. For values, the structure specifies the number of HIDP_VALUE_CAPS structures, and the application can call HidP_GetValueCaps to retrieve these structures.

The HID API also includes functions for retrieving strings, including one to retrieve a serial number. Table 13-2 lists these functions.

Sending and Receiving Reports

Table 13-3 lists functions that applications can use to send and receive reports.

The Windows HID driver causes the host controller to request Input reports. The driver stores received reports in a buffer. ReadFile retrieves one or more reports from the buffer. If the buffer is empty, ReadFile waits for a report to arrive. In other words, ReadFile doesn't cause a device to send a report but just reads reports that the driver has requested.

WriteFile sends an Output report. The function uses an interrupt transfer if the HID has an interrupt OUT endpoint and the operating system is later than Windows 98 Gold. Otherwise, WriteFile uses a control transfer with a Set Report request. If using interrupt transfers, WriteFile will wait if the device

Table 13-3: Applications can use these API functions to send and receive reports.

Function	Purpose
HidD_GetFeature	Read a Feature report.
HidD_GetInputReport[1]	Read an Input report using a control transfer.
HidD_SetFeature	Send a Feature report.
HidD_SetOutputReport[1]	Send an Output report using a control transfer.
ReadFile	Read an Input report obtained via an interrupt transfer.
WriteFile	Send an Output report. Use an interrupt transfer if possible, otherwise use a control transfer.

[1]Requires Windows XP or later.

NAKs. If using control transfers, WriteFile returns with an error code on failure or a timeout.

HidD_GetInputReport requests an Input report using a control transfer with a Get Report request. The function bypasses the Input report buffer. HidD_SetOutputReport provides a way to send an Output report using a control transfer with a Set Report request even if the HID and operating system support using interrupt transfers.

For Feature reports, HidD_GetFeature retrieves a report using a control transfer and Get Report request and HidD_SetFeature sends a report using a control transfer and Set Report request. Note that HidD_SetFeature is not the same thing as the standard USB request Set Feature.

All of the functions that use control transfers return with an error code on failure or a timeout.

Providing and Using Report Data

After retrieving a report, an application can use the raw data directly from the buffer or use API functions to extract button or value data. In a similar way, an application can write data to be sent directly into a report's buffer or use API functions to place the data in a buffer for sending.

Table 13-4 lists API functions that extract information in received reports and store information in reports to be sent. For example, an application can find out what buttons have been pressed by calling HidP_GetButtons, which returns a buffer containing the Usage IDs of all buttons that belong to a speci-

Table 13-4: Applications can use these API functions to extract information in retrieved reports and store information in reports to be sent.

Function	Purpose
HidP_GetButtons	Same as HidP_GetUsages.
HidP_GetButtonsEx	Same as HidP_GetUsagesEx.
HidP_GetData	Retrieve an array of structures with each structure identifying either the data index and state of a button control that is set to ON (1) or the data index and data for a value control.
HidP_GetScaledUsageValue	Retrieve a signed and scaled value from a report.
HidP_GetUsages	Retrieve a list of all of the buttons that are on a specified Usage Page and are set to ON (1).
HidP_GetUsagesEx	Retrieve a list of all of the buttons that are set to ON (1).
HidP_GetUsageValue	Retrieve the data for a specified value.
HidP_GetUsageValueArray	Retrieve data for an array of values with the same Usage ID.
HidP_InitializeReportForID[1]	Set all buttons to OFF (0) and set all values to their null values if defined and otherwise to zero.
HidP_SetButtons	Same as HidP_SetUsages.
HidP_SetData	Sets the states of buttons and data in values in a report.
HidP_SetScaledUsageValue	Convert a signed and scaled physical number to a Usage's logical value and set the value in a report.
HidP_SetUsages	Set one or more buttons in a report to ON (1).
HidP_SetUsageValue	Set the data for a specified value.
HidP_SetUsageValueArray	Set the data for an array of values with the same Usage ID.
HidP_UnsetButtons	Same as HidP_UnsetUsages.
HidP_UnsetUsages	Set one or more buttons in a report to OFF (0).

[1]Not supported under Windows 98 Gold.

fied Usage Page and are set to ON. An application can set and clear buttons in a report to be sent by calling HidP_SetButtons and HidP_UnsetButtons. Applications can retrieve and set values in a report using HidP_GetUsageValue and Hid_Set_UsageValue.

Managing HID Communications

Table 13-5 lists API functions that applications can use in managing HID communications.

Table 13-5: Applications can use these API functions in managing HID communications.

Function	Purpose
HidD_FlushQueue	Delete all Input reports in the buffer.
HidD_GetHidGuid	Retrieve the device interface GUID for HID-class devices.
HidD_GetNumInputBuffers[1]	Retrieve the number of reports the Input report buffer can hold.
HidD_SetNumInputBuffers[1]	Set the number of reports the Input report buffer can hold.
HidRegisterMinidriver	HID mini-drivers call this function during initialization to register with the HID class driver.

[1]Not supported under Windows 98 Gold.

Chapter 10 showed how to use HidD_GetHidGuid to obtain the device interface GUID for the HID class. HidD_SetNumInputBuffers requests to change the size of the HID driver's buffer for Input reports. A larger buffer can be helpful if the application might be too busy at times to read reports before the buffer overflows. The value set is the number of reports the buffer will hold, not the number of bytes. HidD_FlushQueue deletes any Input reports in the buffer.

Identifying a Device

After obtaining a handle to a HID as described in Chapter 10, an application can use API functions to find out whether the HID is a device that the application wants to communicate with. The application can identify a device by its Vendor ID and Product ID, or by searching for a device with a specific Usage, such as a game controller.

The code examples in this chapter assume the following Imports and using statements:

VB
```
Imports Microsoft.Win32.SafeHandles
Imports System.Runtime.InteropServices
Imports System.Threading
```

VC#
```
using Microsoft.Win32.SafeHandles;
using System.Runtime.InteropServices;
using System;
using System.Threading;
```

Reading the Vendor ID and Product ID

For vendor-specific devices that don't have standard Usages, searching for a device with a specific Vendor ID and Product ID is often useful. The API function HidD_GetAttributes retrieves a pointer to a structure containing the Vendor ID, Product ID, and device release number.

VB **Definitions**

```
Friend Structure HIDD_ATTRIBUTES
        Friend Size As Int32
        Friend VendorID As Int16
        Friend ProductID As Int16
        Friend VersionNumber As Int16
        End Structure

<DllImport("hid.dll", SetLactError:=Truc)> _
Shared Function HidD_GetAttributes _
        (ByVal HidDeviceObject As SafeFileHandle, _
        ByRef Attributes As HIDD_ATTRIBUTES)
        As Boolean
        End Function
```

Use

```
Dim DeviceAttributes As HIDD_ATTRIBUTES
Dim success As Boolean

DeviceAttributes.Size =  Marshal.SizeOf(DeviceAttributes)

success = HidD_GetAttributes _
        (deviceHandle, _
        DeviceAttributes)
```

```vb
' Compare the Vendor ID and Product ID to the desired values.
' Example values:

Dim myProductID As Int16  = &h0925
Dim myVendorID As Int16 = &h1234

If (DeviceAttributes.VendorID = myVendorID) And _
        (DeviceAttributes.ProductID = myProductID) Then

        Debug.WriteLine("My device detected")

Else
        Debug.WriteLine("Not my device")

        deviceHandle.Close()
End If
```

VC#   **Definitions**
```csharp
internal struct HIDD_ATTRIBUTES
{
        internal Int32 Size;
        internal Int16 VendorID;
        internal Int16 ProductID;
        internal Int16 VersionNumber;
}
[ DllImport( "hid.dll", SetLastError=true ) ]
internal static extern Boolean HidD_GetAttributes
        ( SafeFileHandle HidDeviceObject,
        ref HIDD_ATTRIBUTES Attributes );
```

Use
```csharp
HIDD_ATTRIBUTES DeviceAttributes;
Boolean success = false;

DeviceAttributes.Size = Marshal.SizeOf( DeviceAttributes );

success = HidD_GetAttributes(
        deviceHandle,
        ref DeviceAttributes);
```

```
// Compare the Vendor ID and Product ID to the desired values.
// Example values:

Int16 myProductID = 0x1234;
Int16 myVendorID = 0x0925;

if ( ( DeviceAttributes.VendorID == myVendorID ) &&
( DeviceAttributes.ProductID == myProductID ) )
{
        Debug.WriteLine( "My device detected" );
}
 else
{
        Debug.WriteLine( "Not my device." );

        deviceHandle.Close(),
}
```

Details

The deviceHandle parameter is a handle returned by CreateFile. A call to HidD_GetAttributes passes a HIDD_ATTRIBUTES structure with the Size member set to the structure's length. If the function returns true, the structure filled without error. The application can then compare the retrieved values with the desired Vendor ID and Product ID and device release number.

If the attributes don't indicate the desired device, the application should close the handle to the interface. The application can then move on to test the next HID in the device information set retrieved with SetupDiGetClassDevs as described in Chapter 10.

Getting a Pointer to Device Capabilities

Another way to find out more about a device is to examine its capabilities. The first task is to call HidD_GetPreparsedData to get a pointer to a buffer with information about the device's capabilities.

VB **Definitions**

```
<DllImport("hid.dll", SetLastError:=True)> _
Shared Function HidD_GetPreparsedData _
        (ByVal HidDeviceObject As SafeFileHandle, _
        ByRef PreparsedData As IntPtr) _
        As Boolean
        End Function
```

Use

```
Dim preparsedData As IntPtr
Dim success As Boolean

success = HidD_GetPreparsedData(deviceHandle, preparsedData)
```

VC# **Definitions**

```
[ DllImport( "hid.dll", SetLastError=true ) ]
internal static extern Boolean HidD_GetPreparsedData
        ( SafeFileHandle HidDeviceObject,
        ref IntPtr PreparsedData );
```

Use

```
IntPtr preparsedData = new IntPtr();
Boolean success = false;

success = HidD_GetPreparsedData( deviceHandle, ref preparsedData );
```

Details

The deviceHandle parameter is the handle returned by CreateFile. The preparsedData variable points to the buffer containing the data. The application doesn't need to access the buffer's data directly. The code just needs to pass the pointer to another API function.

When finished using the PreparsedData buffer, the application should free system resources by calling HidD_FreePreparsedData as described later in this chapter.

Getting the Device's Capabilities

HidP_GetCaps returns a pointer to a structure that contains information about the device's capabilities. The structure contains the HID's Usage Pages, Usages, report lengths, and the number of button-capabilities structures, value-capabilities structures, and data indexes that identify specific controls and data items in

Input, Output, and Feature reports. An application can use the capabilities information to identify a specific HID and learn about its reports and report data. Not every item in the structure applies to all devices.

VB

Definitions

```
Friend Structure HIDP_CAPS
        Friend Usage As Int16
        Friend UsagePage As Int16
        Friend InputReportByteLength As Int16
        Friend OutputReportByteLength As Int16
        Friend FeatureReportByteLength As Int16
        <MarshalAs(UnmanagedType.ByValArray, SizeConst:=17)> _
                Friend Reserved() As Int16
        Friend NumberLinkCollectionNodes As Int16
        Friend NumberInputButtonCaps As Int16
        Friend NumberInputValueCaps As Int16
        Friend NumberInputDataIndices As Int16
        Friend NumberOutputButtonCaps As Int16
        Friend NumberOutputValueCaps As Int16
        Friend NumberOutputDataIndices As Int16
        Friend NumberFeatureButtonCaps As Int16
        Friend NumberFeatureValueCaps As Int16
        Friend NumberFeatureDataIndices As Int16
        End Structure

<DllImport("hid.dll", SetLastError:=True)> _
Shared Function HidP_GetCaps _
        (ByVal PreparsedData As IntPtr, _
        ByRef Capabilities As HIDP_CAPS) _
        As Int32
        End Function
```

Use

```
Dim Capabilities As HIDP_CAPS
Dim result As Int32

result = HidP_GetCaps(preparsedData, Capabilities)
```

Definitions

```
internal struct HIDP_CAPS
{
        internal Int16 Usage;
        internal Int16 UsagePage;
        internal Int16 InputReportByteLength;
        internal Int16 OutputReportByteLength;
        internal Int16 FeatureReportByteLength;
        [ MarshalAs( UnmanagedType.ByValArray, SizeConst=17 ) ]
                internal Int16[] Reserved;
        internal Int16 NumberLinkCollectionNodes;
        internal Int16 NumberInputButtonCaps;
        internal Int16 NumberInputValueCaps;
        internal Int16 NumberInputDataIndices;
        internal Int16 NumberOutputButtonCaps;
        internal Int16 NumberOutputValueCaps;
        internal Int16 NumberOutputDataIndices;
        internal Int16 NumberFeatureButtonCaps;
        internal Int16 NumberFeatureValueCaps;
        internal Int16 NumberFeatureDataIndices;
}
[ DllImport( "hid.dll", SetLastError=true ) ]
internal static extern Int32 HidP_GetCaps
        ( IntPtr PreparsedData,
        ref HIDP_CAPS Capabilities );
```

Use

```
internal HIDP_CAPS Capabilities;
Int32 result = 0;

result = HidP_GetCaps( preparsedData, ref Capabilities );
```

Details

The preparsedData parameter is the pointer returned by HidD_GetPreparsedData. When the function returns, the application can examine and use whatever values are of interest in the Capabilities structure. For example, to look for a joystick, look for UsagePage = 0001h and Usage = 0004h.

The ReportByteLength items are useful when setting buffer sizes for sending and receiving reports.

Table 13-6: The transfer type used to send or receive a report can vary with the API function, operating system edition, and available endpoints.

Report Type	API Function	Transfer Type
Input	ReadFile	Interrupt IN
	HidD_GetInputReport (Windows XP and later)	Control with Get Report request
Output	WriteFile	Interrupt OUT if available; otherwise control with Set Report request
	HidD_SetOutputReport (Windows XP and later)	Control with Set Report request
Feature IN	HidD_GetFeature	Control with Get Report request
Feature OUT	HidD_SetFeature	Control with Set Report request

Getting the Capabilities of the Buttons and Values

An application can also retrieve the capabilities of each button and value in a report. HidP_GetValueCaps returns a pointer to an array of structures containing information about the values in a report. The NumberInputValueCaps property of the HIDP_CAPS structure is the number of structures returned by HidP_GetValueCaps.

The items in the structures include many values obtained from the HID's report descriptor as described in Chapter 12. The items include the Report ID, whether a value is absolute or relative, whether a value has a null state, and logical and physical minimums and maximums. A LinkCollection identifier distinguishes between controls with the same Usage and Usage Page in the same collection. In a similar way, the HidP_GetButtonCaps function can retrieve information about a report's buttons. The information is stored in a HidP_ButtonCaps structure. Not every application needs to retrieve this information.

Sending and Receiving Reports

The previous API functions help in finding and learning about a device that matches what the application is looking for. On finding a device of interest, the application and device are ready to exchange data in reports.

Table 13-3 showed API functions for exchanging reports. Table 13-6 summarizes the transfer types the host uses with different report types. The application doesn't have to know or care which transfer type or endpoint the driver uses.

Sending an Output Report to the Device

On obtaining a handle and learning the number of bytes in an Output report, an application can send a report to the HID. The application places the data to send in a buffer and calls WriteFile.

VB   Definitions

```
<DllImport("kernel32.dll", SetLastError:=True)> _
Shared Function WriteFile _
        (ByVal hFile As SafeFileHandle, _
        ByVal lpBuffer() As Byte, _
        ByVal nNumberOfBytesToWrite As Int32, _
        ByRef lpNumberOfBytesWritten As Int32, _
        ByVal lpOverlapped As IntPtr) _
        As Boolean
        End Function
```

Use

```
Dim numberOfBytesWritten As Int32 = 0
Dim outputReportBuffer() As Byte = Nothing
Dim success As Boolean

' Set the size of the Output report buffer.

Array.Resize(outputReportBuffer, Capabilities.OutputReportByteLength)

' Store the Report ID in the first byte of the buffer:

outputReportBuffer(0) = 0

' Store the report data following the Report ID. Example:
outputReportBuffer(1) = 85
outputReportBuffer(2) = 83
outputReportBuffer(3) = 66

' Send the report.

success = WriteFile _
        (deviceHandle, _
        outputReportBuffer, _
        outputReportBuffer.Length, _
        numberOfBytesWritten, _
        IntPtr.Zero)
```

VC#   **Definitions**

```
[ DllImport( "kernel32.dll", SetLastError=true ) ]
internal static extern Boolean WriteFile
        ( SafeFileHandle hFile,
        Byte[] lpBuffer,
        Int32 nNumberOfBytesToWrite,
        ref Int32 lpNumberOfBytesWritten,
        IntPtr lpOverlapped );
```

Use

```
Int32 numberOfBytesWritten = 0;
Byte[] outputReportBuffer = null;
Boolean success = false;

// Set the size of the Output report buffer.

Array.Resize(ref outFeatureReportBuffer, Capabilities.FeatureReportByteLength);

// Store the Report ID in the first byte of the buffer:

outputReportBuffer[ 0 ] = 0;

// Store the report data following the Report ID. Example:

outputReportBuffer[ 1 ] = 85;
outputReportBuffer[ 2 ] = 83;
outputReportBuffer[ 3 ] = 66;

// Send the report.

success = WriteFile
        (deviceHandle,
        outputReportBuffer,
        outputReportBuffer.Length,
        ref numberOfBytesWritten,
        IntPtr.Zero);
```

Details

In the call to WriteFile, the hFile parameter is a handle returned by CreateFile. The lpBuffer parameter is a byte array that contains the report ID followed by the report data. The nNumberOfBytesToWrite parameter specifies how many bytes to write and should equal the OutputReportByteLength property of the

HIDP_CAPS structure retrieved with HidP_GetCaps. This value is the report size in bytes plus one byte for the Report ID.

The lpOverlapped parameter is a null pointer in this example, but WriteFile can use overlapped I/O as described in the following section on ReadFile. Overlapped I/O can prevent the application's thread from hanging if the HID's interrupt OUT endpoint NAKs endlessly. In normal operation, the endpoint should accept received data with little delay.

On success, the function returns true with lpNumberOfBytesWritten pointing to the number of bytes the function wrote to the HID.

If the interface supports only the default Report ID of zero, the Report ID doesn't transmit on the bus, but the Report ID must always be the first byte in the buffer the application passes to WriteFile.

When sending a report to an interrupt endpoint, WriteFile returns on success or error and will wait endlessly if the endpoint continues to NAK the report data. When sending a report via the control endpoint, WriteFile returns on success, an error, or a timeout if the endpoint continues to NAK the report data.

A returned error message of *CRC Error* indicates that the host controller attempted to send the report, but the device didn't respond as expected. Despite the message, the problem isn't likely to be due to an error detected in a CRC calculation. The error is more likely to be due to a firmware problem that keeps the endpoint from accepting the report data. If WriteFile doesn't return at all, the interrupt OUT endpoint possibly isn't configured to ACK the report data.

Reading an Input Report from the Device

The complement to WriteFile is ReadFile. After obtaining a handle to the HID interface and learning the size of the largest Input report, an application can use ReadFile to read an Input report from a device.

When called using non-overlapped I/O, ReadFile is a blocking call. If an application calls the function when the HID driver's Input buffer is empty, the calling thread waits until a report is available, the user closes the application from the Task Manager, or the user removes the device from the bus. An overlapped, or asynchronous, read operation can keep an application's main thread from hanging as it waits for a report.

With an overlapped read, ReadFile returns immediately whether a report is available or not. If the function doesn't return a report, the application can call WaitForSingleObject with a specified timeout. WaitForSingleObject returns when a report is available or on a timeout or other error. On a timeout or error, the application can try again or call the CancelIo function to cancel the read operation. This approach works well if reports are normally available without delay but the application needs to regain control if for some reason there is no report.

To prevent long delays waiting for WaitForSingleObject to return, an application can set the timeout to zero and call the function repeatedly in a loop or at intervals, triggered by a timer. The function returns immediately whether or not a report is available, and the application can perform other tasks in the loop or between timer events.

To improve performance, an application can call ReadFile in a separate thread that notifies the main thread when a report is available. A .NET application can define an asynchronous delegate and use the BeginInvoke method to call a method that calls ReadFile in a different thread. BeginInvoke can specify a callback routine that executes in the application's main thread when the method that has called ReadFile returns. The callback routine can retrieve the returned report and use the received data as needed.

This example uses overlapped reads with a timeout:

VB

Definitions
```
Friend Const FILE_FLAG_OVERLAPPED As Int32 = &H40000000
Friend Const GENERIC_READ As UInt32 = &H80000000UL
Friend Const GENERIC_WRITE As UInt32 = &H40000000
Friend Const WAIT_OBJECT_0 As Int32 = 0
Friend Const WAIT_TIMEOUT As Int32 = &H102


<DllImport("kernel32.dll", SetLastError:=True)> _
Shared Function CancelIo _
        (ByVal hFile As SafeFileHandle) _
        As Int32
        End Function


<DllImport("kernel32.dll", CharSet:=CharSet.Auto, SetLastError:=True)> _
Shared Function CreateEvent _
        (ByVal SecurityAttributes As IntPtr, _
        ByVal bManualReset As Boolean, _
        ByVal bInitialState As Boolean, _
        ByVal lpName As String) _
        As IntPtr
        End Function
```

```
<DllImport("kernel32.dll", CharSet:=CharSet.Auto, SetLastError:=True)> _
    Shared Function GetOverlappedResult _
    (ByVal hFile As SafeFileHandle, _
    ByVal lpOverlapped As IntPtr, _
    ByRef lpNumberOfBytesTransferred As Int32, _
    ByVal bWait As Boolean) _
    As Boolean
    End Function

<DllImport("kernel32.dll", SetLastError:=True)> _
Shared Function ReadFile _
    (ByVal hFile As SafeFileHandle, _
    ByVal lpBuffer As IntPtr, _
    ByVal nNumberOfBytesToRead As Int32, _
    ByRef lpNumberOfBytesRead As Int32, _
    ByVal lpOverlapped As IntPtr) _
    As Boolean
    End Function

 <DllImport("kernel32.dll", SetLastError:=True)> _
Shared Function WaitForSingleObject _
    (ByVal hHandle As IntPtr, _
    ByVal dwMilliseconds As Int32) _
    As Int32
    End Function
```

Use

```
Dim eventObject As IntPtr
Dim HidOverlapped As New NativeOverlapped
Dim inputReportBuffer() As Byte = Nothing
Dim numberOfBytesRead As Int32
Dim result As Int32
Dim success As Boolean
Dim unManagedBuffer As IntPtr
Dim unManagedOverlapped As IntPtr

Array.Resize(inputReportBuffer, Capabilities.InputReportByteLength)
```

```
eventObject = CreateEvent
      (IntPtr.Zero,
      False,
      False,
      String.Empty)

HidOverlapped.OffsetLow = 0
HidOverlapped.OffsetHigh = 0
HidOverlapped.EventHandle = eventObject

unManagedBuffer = Marshal.AllocHGlobal(inputReportBuffer.Length)
unManagedOverlapped = Marshal.AllocHGlobal(Marshal.SizeOf(HidOverlapped))
Marshal.StructureToPtr(HidOverlapped, unManagedOverlapped, False)

readHandle = CreateFile _
      (devicePathName, _
      GENERIC_READ, _
      FILE_SHARE_READ Or FILE_SHARE_WRITE, _
      IntPtr.Zero, _
      OPEN_EXISTING, _
      FILE_FLAG_OVERLAPPED, _
      0)

success = ReadFile _
      (readHandle, _
      unManagedBuffer, _
      inputReportBuffer.Length, _
      numberOfBytesRead, _
      unManagedOverlapped)
```

```
' If ReadFile returned True, a report is available. Otherwise, check for completion.

If Not (success) Then

        result = WaitForSingleObject(eventObject, 3000)

        Select Case result

                Case WAIT_OBJECT_0
                        success = True
                        GetOverlappedResult _
                                (readHandle, _
                                unManagedOverlapped, _
                                numberOfBytesRead, _
                                False)

                Case WAIT_TIMEOUT
                        CancelIo(readHandle)

                Case Else
                        CancelIo(readHandle)

        End Select
End If

If success Then

        ' A report was received.
        ' Copy the received data to inputReportBuffer for the application to use.

        Marshal.Copy _
                (unManagedBuffer, inputReportBuffer, 0, numberOfBytesRead)
End If

Marshal.FreeHGlobal(unManagedOverlapped)
Marshal.FreeHGlobal(unManagedBuffer)
```

VC# **Definitions**

```
internal const Int32 FILE_FLAG_OVERLAPPED = 0X40000000;
internal const UInt32 GENERIC_READ = 0X80000000;;
internal const UInt32 GENERIC_WRITE = 0X40000000;
internal const Int32 WAIT_OBJECT_0 = 0;
internal const Int32 WAIT_TIMEOUT = 0X102;
```

```
[ DllImport( "kernel32.dll", SetLastError=true ) ]
internal static extern Int32 CancelIo
        ( SafeFileHandle hFile );

[ DllImport( "kernel32.dll", CharSet=CharSet.Auto, SetLastError=true ) ]
internal static extern IntPtr CreateEvent
        ( IntPtr SecurityAttributes,
        Boolean bManualReset,
        Boolean bInitialState,
        String lpName );

[DllImport("kernel32.dll", CharSet = CharSet.Auto, SetLastError = true)]
internal static extern Boolean GetOverlappedResult
        (SafeFileHandle hFile,
        IntPtr lpOverlapped,
        ref Int32 lpNumberOfBytesTransferred,
        Boolean bWait);

[ DllImport( "kernel32.dll", SetLastError=true ) ]
internal static extern Boolean ReadFile
        ( SafeFileHandle hFile,
        IntPtr lpBuffer,
        Int32 nNumberOfBytesToRead,
        ref Int32 lpNumberOfBytesRead,
        IntPtr lpOverlapped );

[ DllImport( "kernel32.dll", SetLastError=true ) ]
internal static extern Int32 WaitForSingleObject
        ( IntPtr hHandle,
        Int32 dwMilliseconds );
```

Use

```
IntPtr eventObject= IntPtr.Zero;
NativeOverlapped HidOverlapped = new NativeOverlapped();
Byte[] inputReportBuffer = null;
Int32 numberOfBytesRead = 0;
Int32 result = 0;
Boolean success = false;
IntPtr unManagedBuffer = IntPtr.Zero;
IntPtr unManagedOverlapped = IntPtr.Zero;

Array.Resize(ref inputReportBuffer, Capabilities.InputReportByteLength);
```

```
eventObject = CreateEvent
        (IntPtr.Zero,
        false,
        false,
        String.Empty);

HidOverlapped.OffsetLow = 0;
HidOverlapped.OffsetHigh = 0;
HidOverlapped.EventHandle = eventObject;

unManagedBuffer = Marshal.AllocHGlobal(inputReportBuffer.Length);
unManagedOverlapped = Marshal.AllocHGlobal(Marshal.SizeOf(HidOverlapped));
Marshal.StructureToPtr(HidOverlapped, unManagedOverlapped, false);

readHandle = CreateFile
        (devicePathName,
        GENERIC_READ,
        FILE_SHARE_READ | FILE_SHARE_WRITE,
        IntPtr.Zero,
        OPEN_EXISTING,
        FILE_FLAG_OVERLAPPED,
        0);

success = ReadFile
        (readHandle,
        unManagedBuffer,
        inputReportBuffer.Length,
        ref numberOfBytesRead,
        unManagedOverlapped);
```

```
// If ReadFile returned true, a report is available. Otherwise, check for completion.

if (!success)
{
        result = WaitForSingleObject
                (eventObject,
                3000);

        switch ( result )
        {
                case WAIT_OBJECT_0:

                        success = True;
                        GetOverlappedResult
                                (readHandle,
                                unManagedOverlapped,
                                ref numberOfBytesRead,
                                false);
                        break;

                case WAIT_TIMEOUT:

                        CancelIo(readHandle);
                        break;

                default:

                        CancelIo(readHandle);
                        break;
        }
}
if (success)
{
        // A report was received.
        // Copy the received data to inputReportBuffer for the application to use.

        Marshal.Copy(unManagedBuffer, inputReportBuffer, 0, numberOfBytesRead);
}
Marshal.FreeHGlobal(unManagedOverlapped);
Marshal.FreeHGlobal(unManagedBuffer);
```

Details

The buffer passed to ReadFile should be at least the size reported in the InputReportByteLength property of the HIDP_CAPS structure returned by HidP_GetCaps.

The CreateEvent function returns a pointer to an event object that will be set to the signaled state when the read operation succeeds or the function times out or returns another error. The call to ReadFile passes the returned pointer in the HidOverlapped structure. Marshaling allocates memory for the overlapped structure and the report buffer to ensure that their contents remain accessible for the life of the overlapped operation.

CreateFile obtains a handle for overlapped I/O by setting the dwFlagsAndAttributes parameter to FILE_FLAG_OVERLAPPED.

The call to ReadFile passes the handle returned by CreateFile, an array to store the returned report, the report's length, a pointer to a variable to hold the number of bytes read, and a pointer to a NativeOverlapped structure. The structure's EventHandle member is the handle returned by CreateEvent.

ReadFile returns immediately. A return value of true indicates that the function has retrieved one or more reports. False means that a report wasn't available. To detect when a report arrives, the application calls WaitForSingleObject, passing a pointer to the event object and a timeout value in milliseconds.

If WaitForSingleObject returns success (WAIT_OBJECT_0), GetOverlappedResult returns the number of bytes read. The Marshal.Copy method copies the report data to the managed inputReportBuffer array. The application can then use the report data as desired and free the memory previously allocated and no longer needed.

The first byte in inputReportBuffer is the Report ID, and the following bytes are the report data. If the interface supports only the default Report ID of zero, the Report ID doesn't transmit on the bus but is still present in the buffer returned by ReadFile.

A call to ReadFile doesn't initiate traffic on the bus. The host begins requesting reports when the HID driver loads during enumeration, and the driver stores received reports in a ring buffer. When the buffer is full and a new report arrives, the buffer drops the oldest report. A call to ReadFile reads the oldest report in the buffer. If the driver's buffer is empty, ReadFile waits for a report to arrive.

Under Windows 98 SE and later, HidD_SetNumInputBuffers can set the buffer size. Different Windows editions have different default buffer sizes, ranging from 2 under Windows 98 Gold to 32 under Windows XP.

Each handle with read access to the HID has its own Input buffer, so multiple applications can read the same reports.

If the application doesn't request reports as frequently as the endpoint sends them, some reports will be lost. One way to keep from losing reports is to increase the size of the report buffer passed to ReadFile. If multiple reports are available, ReadFile returns as many as will fit in the buffer. If you need to be absolutely sure not to lose a report, use Feature reports instead. Also see the tips in Chapter 3 about performing time-critical transfers.

The Idle rate introduced in Chapter 11 determines whether or not a device sends a report if the data hasn't changed since the last transfer.

If ReadFile isn't returning, these are possible reasons:

- The HID's interrupt IN endpoint is NAKing the IN token packets because the endpoint hasn't been armed to send report data. An endpoint's interrupt typically triggers only after endpoint sends data, so the device must arm the endpoint to send the first report before the first interrupt.

- The number of bytes the endpoint is sending doesn't equal the number of bytes in a report (for HIDs that use the default Report ID) or the number of bytes in a report + 1 (for HIDs that use other Report IDs).

- For HIDs with multiple Report IDs, the first byte doesn't match a valid Report ID.

Writing a Feature Report to the Device

To send a Feature report to a device, use HidD_SetFeature, which sends a Set Report request and a report in a control transfer.

VB **Definitions**

```
<DllImport("hid.dll", SetLastError:=True)> _
Shared Function HidD_SetFeature _
        (ByVal HidDeviceObject As SafeFileHandle, _
        ByVal lpReportBuffer() As Byte, _
        ByVal ReportBufferLength As Int32) _
        As Boolean
        End Function
```

Use

```
Dim outFeatureReportBuffer() As Byte = Nothing
Dim success As Boolean

Array.Resize(outFeatureReportBuffer, Capabilities.FeatureReportByteLength)

' Store the Report ID in the first byte of the buffer:

outFeatureReportBuffer(0) = 0

' Store the report data following the Report ID. Example:

outFeatureReportBuffer(1) = 79
outFeatureReportBuffer(2) = 75

success = HidD_SetFeature _
        (deviceHandle, _
        outFeatureReportBuffer, _
        outFeatureReportBuffer.Length)
```

VC# **Definitions**

```
[ DllImport( "hid.dll", SetLastError=true ) ]
internal static extern Boolean HidD_SetFeature
        ( SafeFileHandle HidDeviceObject,
        Byte lpReportBuffer[],
        Int32 ReportBufferLength );
```

Use

```
Byte[] outFeatureReportBuffer = null;
Boolean success = false;

Array.Resize(ref outFeatureReportBuffer, Capabilities.FeatureReportByteLength);
```

```
// Store the Report ID in the first byte of the buffer:

outFeaturetReportBuffer[ 0 ] = 0;

// Store the report data following the Report ID. Example:

outFeatureReportBuffer[ 1 ] =  79;
outFeatureReportBuffer[ 2 ] =  75;

success = HidD_SetFeature
     (deviceHandle,
     outFeatureReportBuffer,
     outFeatureReportBuffer.Length);
```

Details

HidD_SetFeature requires a handle to the HID, an array to write, and the array's length. The first byte in the outFeatureReportBuffer array is the Report ID. The array's length is in the HIDP_CAPS structure retrieved by HidP_GetCaps.

The function returns true on success. If the device continues to NAK the report data, the function times out and returns.

A call to HidD_SetOutputReport works in much the same way to send an Output report using a control transfer. The function passes a handle to the HID, a pointer to a byte array containing an Output report, and the number of bytes in the report plus one byte for the Report ID.

Reading a Feature Report from a Device

To read a Feature report from a device, use HidD_GetFeature, which sends a Get_Feature request in a control transfer. The endpoint returns the report in the Data stage.

VB   **Definitions**
```
<DllImport("hid.dll", SetLastError:=True)> _
Shared Function HidD_GetFeature _
     (ByVal HidDeviceObject As SafeFileHandle, _
     ByVal lpReportBuffer() As Byte, _
     ByVal ReportBufferLength As Int32) _
     As Boolean
     End Function
```

Use

```
Dim inFeatureReportBuffer() As Byte = Nothing
Dim success As Boolean

Array.Resize(inFeatureReportBuffer, Capabilities.FeatureReportByteLength)

'The first byte in the report buffer is the Report ID:

InFeatureReportBuffer(0) = 0

success = HidD_GetFeature _
        (deviceHandle, _
        inFeatureReportBuffer, _
        inFeatureReportBuffer.Length)
```

VC#

Definitions

```
[ DllImport( "hid.dll", SetLastError=true ) ]
internal static extern Boolean HidD_GetFeature
        ( SafeFileHandle HidDeviceObject,
        Byte[] lpReportBuffer,
        Int32 ReportBufferLength );
```

Use

```
Byte[] inFeatureReportBuffer = null;
Boolean success = false;

Array.Resize(ref inFeatureReportBuffer, Capabilities.FeatureReportByteLength);

// The first byte in the report buffer is the Report ID:

inFeatureReportBuffer[0] = 0;

success = HidD_GetFeature
        (deviceHandle,
        inFeatureReportBuffer,
        inFeatureReportBuffer.Length);
```

Details

HidD_GetFeature requires a handle to the HID, an array to hold the retrieved report(s), and the array's length. The inFeatureReportBuffer array holds the retrieved report. The first byte in the array is the Report ID. The array's length is in the HIDP_CAPS structure retrieved by HidP_GetCaps.

The function returns true on success. If the device continues to return NAK in the Data stage of the transfer, the function times out and returns.

A call to HidD_GetInputReport works in much the same way to request an Input report using a control transfer. The function passes a handle to the HID, an array to hold the Input report, and the number of bytes in the report plus one byte for the Report ID.

Closing Communications

When finished communicating, the application should call the Close method to close any SafeFileHandles opened by CreateFile as described in Chapter 10. When finished using the PreparsedData buffer that HidD_GetPreparsedData returned, the application should call HidD_FreePreparsedData.

VB

Definitions

```
<DllImport("hid.dll", SetLastError:=True)> _
Shared Function HidD_FreePreparsedData _
        (ByVal PreparsedData As IntPtr) _
        As Boolean
        End Function
```

Use

```
Dim success As Boolean

success = HidD_FreePreparsedData(preparsedData)
```

VC#

Definitions

```
[ DllImport( "hid.dll", SetLastError=true ) ]
internal static extern Boolean HidD_FreePreparsedData
        ( IntPtr PreparsedData );
```

Use

```
Boolean success = false;

success = HidD_FreePreparsedData( preparsedData );
```

14

Using WinUSB for Vendor-Defined Functions

An option for devices that perform vendor-specific functions is Microsoft's WinUSB driver. This chapter shows how to develop a device that uses the WinUSB driver and how to use the WinUSB API to access the device from applications.

Capabilities and Limits

A device is a candidate for using the WinUSB driver if the device and its host computer(s) meet the requirements below.

Device Requirements

The device:

- Exchanges application data using any combination of control, interrupt, and bulk endpoints. (The driver doesn't support isochronous transfers.)

- Has descriptors that specify a vendor-specific class.

Host Requirements

The host:

- Is Windows XP SP2 or later.

- Needs no more than one open handle to the device at once.

- Has an INF file that contains the device's Vendor ID and Product ID and a vendor-defined device interface GUID.

- Has the WinUSB driver and installation files. For Windows XP, the device vendor can provide the files, which are a free, redistributable download from Microsoft. Windows Vista systems include the files.

- Has a vendor-provided application to communicate with the device. Programming languages for the application can include Visual Basic, Visual C#, and other languages that can call Windows API functions.

Device Firmware

A WinUSB device has an interface descriptor with bInterfaceClass = FFh to indicate a vendor-specific class. Listing 14-1 shows descriptors for an example WinUSB device. Following the interface descriptor are endpoint descriptors for interrupt IN, interrupt OUT, bulk IN, and bulk OUT endpoints as needed. A device can also use vendor-specific control transfers. Unlike HID data, WinUSB data doesn't have to be in defined-length reports.

Device firmware can respond to vendor-specific requests in control transfers. Firmware handles these transfers in much the same way as the HID Get Report and Set Report requests. The Setup packet can use any values for the wValue, wIndex, and wLength fields. In the bmRequestType field, bits 6..5 equal 10 to indicate a vendor-defined request. The bRequest field is a vendor-defined request number.

For all of the transfer types, the host application and device firmware must agree on the data format. For example, for a data-acquisition device, firmware might define a vendor-specific control request with bRequest = 01h to identify the request, wIndex indicating which sensor reading to return, and wLength equal to the number of bytes the device should return with the requested data. Or the firmware might send sensor data in a defined format on an interrupt or bulk endpoint. In a similar way, a host application can send data to a device using control, bulk, or interrupt transfers.

Device Descriptor

12	bLength	Descriptor size in bytes
01	bDescriptorType	Descriptor type (Device)
0200	bcdUSB	USB Specification release number (BCD) (2.00)
00	bDeviceClass	Class Code
00	bDeviceSubClass	Subclass code
00	bDeviceProtocol	Protocol code
08	bMaxPacketSize0	Endpoint 0 maximum packet size
0925	idVendor	Vendor ID (Lakeview Research)
1456	idProduct	Product ID
0100	bcdDevice	Device release number (BCD)
00	iManufacturer	Manufacturer string index
00	iProduct	Product string index
00	iSerialNumber	Device serial number string index
01	bNumConfigurations	Number of configurations

Configuration Descriptor

09	bLength	Descriptor size in bytes
02	bDescriptorType	Descriptor type (Configuration)
002E	wTotalLength	Total length of this and subordinate descriptors
01	bNumInterfaces	Number of interfaces in this configuration
01	bConfigurationValue	Index of this configuration
00	iConfiguration	Configuration string index
E0	bmAttributes	Attributes (self powered, remote wakeup supported)
32	bMaxPower	Maximum power consumption (100 mA)

Interface Descriptor

09	bLength	Descriptor size in bytes
04	bDescriptorType	Descriptor type (Interface)
00	bInterfaceNumber	Interface number
00	bAlternateSetting	Alternate setting number
04	bNumEndpoints	Number of endpoints in this interface
FF	bInterfaceClass	Interface class (vendor specific)
00	bInterfaceSubclass	Interface subclass
00	bInterfaceProtocol	Interface protocol
00	iInterface	Interface string index

Listing 14-1: Example descriptors for a WinUSB device. All values are in hexadecimal. (Part 1 of 2)

Interrupt IN Endpoint Descriptor

07	bLength	Descriptor size in bytes
05	bDescriptorType	Descriptor type (Endpoint)
81	bEndpointAddress	Endpoint number and direction (1 IN)
03	bmAttributes	Transfer type (interrupt)
0008	wMaxPacketSize	Maximum packet size
0A	bInterval	polling interval (milliseconds)

Interrupt OUT Endpoint Descriptor

07	bLength	Descriptor size in bytes
05	bDescriptorType	Descriptor type (Endpoint)
01	bEndpointAddress	Endpoint number and direction (1 OUT)
03	bmAttributes	Transfer type (interrupt)
0008	wMaxPacketSize	Maximum packet size
0A	bInterval	polling interval (milliseconds)

Bulk IN Endpoint Descriptor

07	bLength	Descriptor size in bytes
05	bDescriptorType	Descriptor type (Endpoint)
82	bEndpointAddress	Endpoint number and direction (2 IN)
02	bmAttributes	Transfer type (bulk)
0040	wMaxPacketSize	Maximum packet size
00	bInterval	polling interval (ignored)

Bulk OUT Endpoint Descriptor

07	bLength	Descriptor size in bytes
05	bDescriptorType	Descriptor type (Endpoint)
02	bEndpointAddress	Endpoint number and direction (2 OUT)
02	bmAttributes	Transfer type (bulk)
0040	wMaxPacketSize	Maximum packet size
00	bInterval	polling interval (ignored)

Listing 14-1: Example descriptors for a WinUSB device. All values are in hexadecimal. (Part 2 of 2)

PBP   For PICBASIC PRO firmware for WinUSB, visit my website (*www.Lvr.com*).

C18   The Microchip USB Framework provides WinUSB firmware for the PIC18F4550 and other Microchip microcontrollers. The code supports sending and receiving data using bulk and interrupt transfers. For code that also supports control transfers, visit *www.Lvr.com*.

Assigning the WinUSB Driver

Installing a USB device that uses the WinUSB driver requires an INF file that identifies the device. Chapter 9 showed an INF file for a WinUSB device. Windows XP installations also require a free, redistributable coinstaller files from the WDK.

The WinUSB coinstaller file is:

WinUsbCoinstaller.dll

located in:

<winddk_home>\<build_number>\redist\winusb\<arch>

where *<winddk_home>* and *<build_number>* are the home directory and subdirectory of the WDK and *<arch>* indicates a PC architecture such as x86 for 32-bit systems, amd64 for AMD 64-bit systems, or ia64 for Itanium 64-bit systems. For example, a 32-bit file for WDK build 6001 might be stored here:

c:\winddk\6001\redist\winusb\x86

The coinstaller contains the *winusb.sys* driver so you don't need to provide this file separately. The coinstaller installs the driver.

The other needed WDK files are:

WdfCoinstallerxxx.dll
WUDFUpdate_xxx.dll

where xxx represents the edition of the file.

For WDK build 6001, the file names are:

WdfCoinstaller01007.dll
WudfUpdate_01007.dll

For other WDK builds, the file editions and file names may differ. Check the directories for the correct file names for your WDK.

The files are located here:

<winddk_home>\<build_number>\redist\wdf\<arch>

where again *<winddk_home>* and *<build_number>* are the WDK's home directory and subdirectory and *<arch>* indicates a PC architecture.

The value of KmdfLibraryVersion in the INF file must correspond to the version numbers of *WdfCoInstaller01xxx.dll* and *WUDFUpdate_01xxx.dll*. For WDK build 6001, which contains *WdfCoInstaller01007.dll* and *WUDFUpdate_01007.dll*, set KmdfLibraryVersion=1.7.

If using WDK build 6000, make these changes to the example INF file: the WudfUpdate and WdfCoinstaller file names are *WudfUpdate_01005.dll* and *WdfCoinstaller01005.dll*, and KmdfLibraryVersion=1.5. Later WDK editions may require similar changes to these items.

Accessing the Device

Accessing a WinUSB device requires finding the device, initializing communications, and exchanging data using bulk, interrupt, and control transfers as needed. The WinUSB driver provides *Winusb.dll*, which exposes WinUSB-specific functions that applications can call to obtain access to devices and to configure, and exchange data with them.

The code examples in this chapter assume the following Imports and using statements:

VB
```
Imports Microsoft.Win32.SafeHandles
Imports System.Runtime.InteropServices
```

VC#
```
using Microsoft.Win32.SafeHandles;
using System;
using System.Runtime.InteropServices;
```

Obtaining a WinUSB Handle

Before exchanging data with a WinUSB device, an application obtains a device pathname using SetupDi_ functions and the device interface GUID from the device's INF file. The application can then use CreateFile to obtain a handle. In the call to CreateFile, the dwFlagsandAttributes parameter must be set to FILE_FLAG_OVERLAPPED.

Chapter 8 discussed how to generate a GUID. Chapter 10 showed how to obtain a handle with CreateFile and use the handle to detect when a device is attached and removed.

After calling CreateFile to obtain a handle, the application calls WinUsb_Initialize to obtain a WinUSB interface handle. The application uses this handle for all communications with the interface.

VB **Definitions**

```
Friend Structure devInfo
        Friend deviceHandle As SafeFileHandle
        Friend winUsbHandle As IntPtr
        Friend bulkInPipe As Byte
        Friend bulkOutPipe As Byte
        Friend interruptInPipe As Byte
        Friend interruptOutPipe As Byte
        Friend devicespeed As UInt32
End Structure

<DllImport("winusb.dll", SetLastError:=True)> Friend Shared Function WinUsb_Initialize _
        (ByVal DeviceHandle As SafeFileHandle, _
        ByRef InterfaceHandle As IntPtr)
        As Boolean
End Function
```

Use

```
Dim success As Boolean

Friend myDevInfo As New devInfo

success = WinUsb_Initialize _
        (myDevInfo.deviceHandle, _
        myDevInfo.winUsbHandle)
```

VC# **Definitions**

```
internal struct devInfo
{
        internal SafeFileHandle deviceHandle;
        internal InPtr winUsbHandle;
        internal Byte bulkInPipe;
        internal Byte bulkOutPipe;
        internal Byte interruptInPipe;
        internal Byte interruptOutPipe;
        internal UInt32 devicespeed;

[DllImport("winusb.dll", SetLastError = true)]
internal static extern Boolean WinUsb_Initialize
        (SafeFileHandle DeviceHandle,
        ref IntPtr InterfaceHandle);
```

Use

```
Boolean success;

internal devInfo myDevInfo = new devInfo();

success = WinUsb_Initialize
        (myDevInfo.deviceHandle,
        ref myDevInfo.winUsbHandle);
```

Details

The application can create a devInfo structure to hold information about a device and its endpoints. The myDevInfo.deviceHandle parameter is the handle returned by CreateFile. On success, the function returns True and myDevInfo.winUsbHandle is a pointer to a WinUSB handle that the application can use to access the device.

Requesting an Interface Descriptor

The WinUsb_QueryInterfaceSettings function returns a structure with information about a WinUSB interface.

VB **Definitions**

```
Friend Structure USB_INTERFACE_DESCRIPTOR
        Friend bLength As Byte
        Friend bDescriptorType As Byte
        Friend bInterfaceNumber As Byte
        Friend bAlternateSetting As Byte
        Friend bNumEndpoints As Byte
        Friend bInterfaceClass As Byte
        Friend bInterfaceSubClass As Byte
        Friend bInterfaceProtocol As Byte
        Friend iInterface As Byte
End Structure

<DllImport("winusb.dll", SetLastError:=True)> _
Friend Shared Function WinUsb_QueryInterfaceSettings _
        (ByVal InterfaceHandle As IntPtr, _
        ByVal AlternateInterfaceNumber As Byte, _
        ByRef UsbAltInterfaceDescriptor As USB_INTERFACE_DESCRIPTOR) _
        As Boolean
End Function
```

Use

```
Dim ifaceDescriptor As USB_INTERFACE_DESCRIPTOR
Dim success As Boolean

success = WinUsb_QueryInterfaceSettings _
        (myDevInfo.winUsbHandle, _
        0, _
        ifaceDescriptor)
```

VC#   **Definitions**

```
internal struct USB_INTERFACE_DESCRIPTOR
{
        internal Byte bLength;
        internal Byte bDescriptorType;
        internal Byte bInterfaceNumber;
        internal Byte bAlternateSetting;
        internal Byte bNumEndpoints;
        internal Byte bInterfaceClass;
        internal Byte bInterfaceSubClass;
        internal Byte bInterfaceProtocol;
        internal Byte iInterface;
}

[DllImport("winusb.dll", SetLastError = true)]
internal static extern Boolean WinUsb_QueryInterfaceSettings
        (IntPtr InterfaceHandle,
        Byte AlternateInterfaceNumber,
        ref USB_INTERFACE_DESCRIPTOR UsbAltInterfaceDescriptor);
```

Use

```
USB_INTERFACE_DESCRIPTOR ifaceDescriptor;
Boolean success;

success = WinUsb_QueryInterfaceSettings
        (myDevInfo.winUsbHandle,
        0,
        ref ifaceDescriptor);
```

Details

The function accepts a pointer to a WinUsb handle and a bAlternateSetting number from the interface descriptor to indicate which interface setting to query. On success, the function returns True and a pointer to a USB_INTERFACE_DESCRIPTOR structure containing information from the requested interface descriptor.

Identifying the Endpoints

For each endpoint in the interface descriptor, an application can call WinUsb_QueryPipe to learn the endpoint's transfer type and direction. The myDevInfo structure can store the information.

VB **Definitions**

```
Friend Enum USBD_PIPE_TYPE
        UsbdPipeTypeControl
        UsbdPipeTypeIsochronous
        UsbdPipeTypeBulk
        UsbdPipeTypeInterrupt
End Enum

Friend Structure WINUSB_PIPE_INFORMATION
        Friend PipeType As USBD_PIPE_TYPE
        Friend PipeId As Byte
        Friend MaximumPacketSize As UShort
        Friend Interval As Byte
End Structure

<DllImport("winusb.dll", SetLastError:=True)> _
Friend Shared Function WinUsb_QueryPipe _
        (ByVal InterfaceHandle As IntPtr, _
        ByVal AlternateInterfaceNumber As Byte, _
        ByVal PipeIndex As Byte, _
        ByRef PipeInformation As WINUSB_PIPE_INFORMATION) _
        As Boolean
End Function
```

Use

The UsbEndpointDirectionIn and UsbEndpointDirectionOut functions enable querying the direction of an endpoint:

```
Private Function UsbEndpointDirectionIn(ByVal addr As Int32) As Boolean

        If ((addr And &H80) = &H80) Then
                UsbEndpointDirectionIn = True
        Else
                UsbEndpointDirectionIn = False
        End If

End Function

Private Function UsbEndpointDirectionOut(ByVal addr As Int32) As Boolean

        If ((addr And &H80) = 0) Then
                UsbEndpointDirectionOut = True
        Else
                UsbEndpointDirectionOut = False
        End If

End Function
```

The application can request and store information about each of the interface's endpoints in turn.

```
For i As Int32 = 0 To ifaceDescriptor.bNumEndpoints - 1

        WinUsb_QueryPipe _
                (myDevInfo.winUsbHandle, _
                0, _
                Convert.ToByte(i), _
                pipeInfo)

        If ((pipeInfo.PipeType = _
                USBD_PIPE_TYPE.UsbdPipeTypeBulk) And _
                UsbEndpointDirectionIn(pipeInfo.PipeId)) Then
                myDevInfo.bulkInPipe = pipeInfo.PipeId

        ElseIf ((pipeInfo.PipeType = _
                USBD_PIPE_TYPE.UsbdPipeTypeBulk) And _
                UsbEndpointDirectionOut(pipeInfo.PipeId)) Then
                myDevInfo.bulkOutPipe = pipeInfo.PipeId

        ElseIf (pipeInfo.PipeType = _
                USBD_PIPE_TYPE.UsbdPipeTypeInterrupt) And _
                UsbEndpointDirectionIn(pipeInfo.PipeId) Then
                myDevInfo.interruptInPipe = pipeInfo.PipeId

        ElseIf (pipeInfo.PipeType = _
                USBD_PIPE_TYPE.UsbdPipeTypeInterrupt) And _
                UsbEndpointDirectionOut(pipeInfo.PipeId) Then
                myDevInfo.interruptOutPipe = pipeInfo.PipeId

        End If
Next i
```

VC#   **Definitions**

```
internal enum USBD_PIPE_TYPE
{
        UsbdPipeTypeControl,
        UsbdPipeTypeIsochronous,
        UsbdPipeTypeBulk,
        UsbdPipeTypeInterrupt,
}
```

```
[StructLayout(LayoutKind.Sequential)]
internal struct WINUSB_PIPE_INFORMATION
{
        internal USBD_PIPE_TYPE PipeType;
        internal Byte PipeId;
        internal ushort MaximumPacketSize;
        internal Byte Interval;
}


[DllImport("winusb.dll", SetLastError = true)]
internal static extern Boolean WinUsb_QueryPipe
        (IntPtr InterfaceHandle,
        Byte AlternateInterfaceNumber,
        Byte PipeIndex,
        ref WINUSB_PIPE_INFORMATION PipeInformation);
```

Use

The UsbEndpointDirectionIn and UsbEndpointDirectionOut functions enable querying the direction of an endpoint:

```
private Boolean UsbEndpointDirectionIn(Int32 addr)
{
        Boolean directionIn;

        if (((addr & 0X80) == 0X80))
                { directionIn = true; }

        else
                { directionIn = false; }
}
        return directionIn;
}
private Boolean UsbEndpointDirectionOut(Int32 addr)
{
        Boolean directionOut;

        if (((addr & 0X80) == 0))
                { directionOut = true; }

        else
                { directionOut = false; }

        return directionOut;
}
```

The application can request and store information about each of the interface's endpoints in turn.

```
for ( Int32 i=0; i <= ifaceDescriptor.bNumEndpoints - 1; i++ )
{
        WinUsb_QueryPipe
                (myDevInfo.winUsbHandle,
                0,
                Convert.ToByte(i),
                ref pipeInfo);

        if (((pipeInfo.PipeType ==
                USBD_PIPE_TYPE.UsbdPipeTypeBulk) &&
                UsbEndpointDirectionIn(pipeInfo.PipeId)))
        {
                myDevInfo.bulkInPipe = pipeInfo.PipeId;
        }
        else if (((pipeInfo.PipeType ==
                USBD_PIPE_TYPE.UsbdPipeTypeBulk) &&
                UsbEndpointDirectionOut(pipeInfo.PipeId)))
        {
                myDevInfo.bulkOutPipe = pipeInfo.PipeId;
        }
        else if ((pipeInfo.PipeType ==
                USBD_PIPE_TYPE.UsbdPipeTypeInterrupt) &&
                UsbEndpointDirectionIn(pipeInfo.PipeId))
        {
                myDevInfo.interruptInPipe = pipeInfo.PipeId;
        }
        else if ((pipeInfo.PipeType ==
                USBD_PIPE_TYPE.UsbdPipeTypeInterrupt) &&
                UsbEndpointDirectionOut(pipeInfo.PipeId))
        {
                myDevInfo.interruptOutPipe = pipeInfo.PipeId;
        }
}
```

Details

The PipeId value equals bEndpointAddress in the endpoint descriptor. A valid endpoint has a PipeId greater than zero. The USBD_PIPE_TYPE enumerator includes an entry for isochronous pipes, but the WinUSB driver doesn't support isochronous transfers.

Setting Pipe Policies

After identifying an endpoint, an application can set vendor-specific policies for transfers at the endpoint. Table 14-1 shows the policies.

VB **Definitions**

```
Friend Enum POLICY_TYPE As UInt32
        SHORT_PACKET_TERMINATE = 1
        AUTO_CLEAR_STALL
        PIPE_TRANSFER_TIMEOUT
        IGNORE_SHORT_PACKETS
        ALLOW_PARTIAL_READS
        AUTO_FLUSH
        RAW_IO
End Enum


' Use this definition when the returned Value parameter is a Byte
' (all except PIPE_TRANSFER_TIMEOUT):

<DllImport("winusb.dll", SetLastError:=True)> _
Friend Shared Function WinUsb_SetPipePolicy _
        (ByVal InterfaceHandle As IntPtr, _
        ByVal PipeID As Byte, _
        ByVal PolicyType As UInt32, _
        ByVal ValueLength As UInt32, _
        ByRef Value As Byte) _
        As Boolean
End Function


' Use this alias when the returned Value parameter
' is a UInt32 (PIPE_TRANSFER_TIMEOUT only):

<DllImport("winusb.dll", EntryPoint:="WinUsb_SetPipePolicy", SetLastError:=True)> _
Friend Shared Function WinUsb_SetPipePolicy1 _
        (ByVal InterfaceHandle As IntPtr, _
        ByVal PipeID As Byte, _
        ByVal PolicyType As UInt32, _
        ByVal ValueLength As UInt32, _
        ByRef Value As UInt32) _
        As Boolean
End Function
```

Table 14-1: The WinUsb_SetPipePolicy function can specify how the driver responds to various conditions when performing a transfer and whether data bypasses WinUSB's queuing and error handling.

Parameter	Value	Default	Description
SHORT_PACKET_TERMINATE	01h	False	If True, terminate a write transfer that is a multiple of wMaxPacketSize with a ZLP.
AUTO_CLEAR_STALL	02h	False	If True, clear a stall condition automatically.
PIPE_TRANSFER_TIMEOUT	03h	Zero	Set a transfer timeout interval in milliseconds. Zero = never time out.
IGNORE_SHORT_PACKETS	04h	False	If True, complete a read operation only on receiving the specified number of bytes. If False, complete a read operation on receiving the specified number of bytes or a short packet.
ALLOW_PARTIAL_READS	05h	True	Sets the policy if the endpoint returns more data than requested. If True, complete the read operation and save or discard the extra data as specified by AUTO_FLUSH. If False, fail the read request.
AUTO_FLUSH	06h	False	If True and ALLOW_PARTIAL_READS is also True, discard extra data. If False and ALLOW_PARTIAL_READS is True, save extra data and return it in the next read operation. If ALLOW_PARTIAL_READS is False, ignore.
RAW_IO	07h	False	Determines whether calls to WinUsb_ReadPipe bypasses WinUSB's queuing and error handling, If True, calls pass directly to the USB stack, and the read buffer must be a multiple of wMaxPacketSize and less than the host controller's maximum per transfer. If False, calls don't pass directly to the USB stack, and the buffers don't have the size restrictions.

Use

With these overloaded functions, you can call SetPipePolicy to set a policy with a Byte or UINT32 value as needed.

```
Private Function SetPipePolicy _
        (ByVal pipeId As Byte, ByVal policyType As UInt32, ByVal value As Byte) _
        As Boolean

        Dim success As Boolean = WinUsb_SetPipePolicy _
                (myDevInfo.winUsbHandle, _
                pipeId, _
                policyType, _
                1, _
                value)

        Return success

End Function

Private Function SetPipePolicy _
        (ByVal pipeId As Byte, ByVal policyType As UInt32, ByVal value As UInt32) _
        As Boolean

        Dim success As Boolean = WinUsb_SetPipePolicy1 _
                (myDevInfo.winUsbHandle, _
                pipeId, _
                policyType, _
                4, _
                value)

        Return success

End Function
```

Call the functions to set policies for an endpoint:

```
Dim success As Boolean

SetPipePolicy _
        (myDevInfo.bulkInPipe, _
        POLICY_TYPE.IGNORE_SHORT_PACKETS, _
        Convert.ToByte(False))

Dim pipeTimeout As UInt32 = 2000
```

```
        success = SetPipePolicy _
            (myDevInfo.bulkInPipe, _
            POLICY_TYPE.PIPE_TRANSFER_TIMEOUT, _
            pipeTimeout)
```

VC#   **Definitions**
```
internal enum POLICY_TYPE
{
        SHORT_PACKET_TERMINATE = 1,
        AUTO_CLEAR_STALL,
        PIPE_TRANSFER_TIMEOUT,
        IGNORE_SHORT_PACKETS,
        ALLOW_PARTIAL_READS,
        AUTO_FLUSH,
        RAW_IO,
}
// Use this definition when the returned Value parameter is a Byte
// (all except PIPE_TRANSFER_TIMEOUT):

[DllImport("winusb.dll", SetLastError = true)]
internal static extern Boolean WinUsb_SetPipePolicy
        (IntPtr InterfaceHandle,
        Byte PipeID,
        UInt32 PolicyType,
        UInt32 ValueLength,
        ref Byte Value);

//  Use this alias when the returned Value parameter is a UInt32
// (PIPE_TRANSFER_TIMEOUT only):

[DllImport("winusb.dll", SetLastError = true, EntryPoint = "WinUsb_SetPipePolicy")]
internal static extern Boolean WinUsb_SetPipePolicy1
        (IntPtr InterfaceHandle,
        Byte PipeID,
        UInt32 PolicyType,
        UInt32 ValueLength,
        ref UInt32 Value);
```

Use

With these overloaded functions, you can call SetPipePolicy to set a policy with a Byte or UINT32 value as needed.

```
private Boolean SetPipePolicy( Byte pipeId, UInt32 policyType, Byte value )
{
        Boolean success = WinUsb_SetPipePolicy
                ( myDevInfo.winUsbHandle,
                pipeId,
                policyType,
                1,
                ref value ;

        return success;
}

private Boolean SetPipePolicy( Byte pipeId, UInt32 policyType, UInt32 value )
{
        Boolean success = WinUsb_SetPipePolicy1
                ( myDevInfo.winUcbHandlo,
                pipeId,
                policyType,
                4,
                ref value );

        return success;
}
```

Call the functions to set policies for an endpoint:

```
Boolean success;

success = SetPipePolicy
        ( myDevInfo.bulkInPipe,
        Convert.ToUInt32(POLICY_TYPE.IGNORE_SHORT_PACKETS),
        Convert.ToByte(false));

UInt32 pipeTimeout = 2000;

success = SetPipePolicy
        (myDevInfo.bulkInPipe,
        Convert.ToUInt32(POLICY_TYPE.PIPE_TRANSFER_TIMEOUT),
        pipeTimeout);
```

Details

The WinUsb_SetPipePolicy function accepts a Byte for the value parameter for all policies except PIPE_TRANSFER_TIMEOUT, which requires a UINT32. To handle both types, the code provides a definition that accepts a Byte value and an alias that accepts a UINT32. Two overloaded SetPipePolicy functions accept different value parameter types and pass the parameter to WinUsb_SetPipePolicy.

The Byte parameters have true/false meanings, so for readability, the SetPipePolicy function accepts a Boolean value, and the Convert.ToByte method converts to a Byte for passing to WinUsb_SetPipePolicy.

The example sets two policies for the bulk IN endpoint. In a similar way, you can set policies for all of the interface's endpoints. A companion function for reading pipe policies is WinUsb_GetPipePolicy.

Writing Data via Bulk and Interrupt Transfers

The WinUsb_WritePipe function can write data using bulk or interrupt transfers.

VB

Definitions

```
<DllImport("winusb.dll", SetLastError:=True)> _
Friend Shared Function WinUsb_WritePipe _
        (ByVal InterfaceHandle As IntPtr, _
        ByVal PipeID As Byte, _
        ByVal Buffer() As Byte, _
        ByVal BufferLength As UInt32, _
        ByRef LengthTransferred As UInt32, _
        ByVal Overlapped As IntPtr) _
        As Boolean
End Function
```

Use

```
Dim buffer(1) As Byte
Dim bytesToWrite As UInt32 = 2
Dim bytesWritten As UInt32
Dim success As Boolean
```

```
' Place data in the buffer to send. Example:

buffer(0) = 72
buffer(1) = 105
bytesToWrite = Convert.ToUInt32(buffer.Length)

success = WinUsb_WritePipe _
        (myDevInfo.winUsbHandle, _
        myDevInfo.bulkOutPipe, _
        buffer, _
        bytesToWrite, _
        bytesWritten, _
        IntPtr.Zero)
```

VC#

Definitions

```
[DllImport("winusb.dll", SetLastError = true)]
internal static extern Boolean WinUsb_WritePipe
        (IntPtr InterfaceHandle,
        Byte PipeID,
        Byte[] Buffer,
        UInt32 BufferLength,
        ref UInt32 LengthTransferred,
        IntPtr Overlapped);
```

Use

```
Byte[] buffer = new Byte[2];
UInt32 bytesToWrite = 2;
UInt32  bytesWritten = 0;
Boolean success;

// Place data in the buffer to send. Example:
buffer[0] = 72;
buffer[1] - 105;

bytesToWrite = Convert.ToUInt32( buffer.Length);

success = WinUsb_WritePipe
        (myDevInfo.winUsbHandle,
        myDevInfo.bulkOutPipe,
        buffer,
        bytesToWrite,
        ref bytesWritten,
        IntPtr.Zero);
```

Details

The WinUsb_WritePipe function accepts a pointer to a WinUSB handle, an endpoint address, a buffer with data to send, and the number of bytes to write. On success, the function returns True with the number of bytes written in bytesWritten. If the function uses overlapped I/O, the Overlapped parameter contains a pointer to an OVERLAPPED structure. To send data via an interrupt transfer, change myDevInfo.bulkOutPipe to myDevInfo.interruptOutPipe.

To cause the driver to terminate transfers that are exact multiples of wMaxPacketSize with ZLPs, call WinUsb_SetPipePolicy with SHORT_PACKET_TERMINATE = True. This option can be useful if the device firmware needs a way to identify the end of a transfer of unknown length.

Reading Data via Bulk and Interrupt Transfers

The WinUsb_ReadPipe function can read data via bulk or interrupt transfers.

VB **Definitions**

```
<DllImport("winusb.dll", SetLastError:=True)> _
Friend Shared Function WinUsb_ReadPipe _
        (ByVal InterfaceHandle As IntPtr, _
        ByVal PipeID As Byte, _
        ByVal Buffer() As Byte, _
        ByVal BufferLength As UInt32, _
        ByRef LengthTransferred As UInt32, _
        ByVal Overlapped As IntPtr) _
        As Boolean
End Function
```

Use

```
Dim buffer(63) As Byte
Dim bytesRead As UInt32
Dim bytesToRead As UInt32 = 64
Dim success As Boolean
```

```
success = WinUsb_ReadPipe _
      (myDevInfo.winUsbHandle, _
      myDevInfo.bulkInPipe, _
      buffer, _
      bytesToRead, _
      bytesRead, _
      IntPtr.Zero)
```

VC#

Definitions

```
[DllImport("winusb.dll", SetLastError = true)]
internal static extern Boolean WinUsb_ReadPipe
      (IntPtr InterfaceHandle,
      Byte PipeID,
      Byte[] Buffer,
      UInt32 BufferLength,
      ref UInt32 LengthTransferred,
      IntPtr Overlapped);
```

Use

```
Byte[] buffer = new Byte[ 64 ];
UInt32 bytesRead = 0;
UInt32 bytesToRead =  64;
Boolean success = false;

success = WinUsb_ReadPipe
      (myDevInfo.winUsbHandle,
      myDevInfo.bulkInPipe,
      buffer,
      bytesToRead,
      ref bytesRead,
      IntPtr.Zero);
```

Details

The WinUsb_ReadPipe function accepts a pointer to a WinUSB handle, an endpoint address, the buffer that will store the received data, and the maximum number of bytes to read. On success, the function returns True with the received data in the passed buffer and the number of bytes read in bytesRead. If the function uses overlapped I/O, the Overlapped parameter contains a pointer to an OVERLAPPED structure. To send data via an interrupt transfer, change bulkInPipe to interruptInPipe.

The number of bytes read can depend on the policies set by WinUsb_SetPipePolicy.

Using Vendor-defined Control Transfers

Another option for transferring data is to use vendor-defined requests sent via control transfers directed to the interface.

VB **Definitions**

```
Friend Structure WINUSB_SETUP_PACKET
        Friend RequestType As Byte
        Friend Request As Byte
        Friend Value As UShort
        Friend Index As UShort
        Friend Length As UShort
        End Structure


<DllImport("winusb.dll", SetLastError:=True)> _
Friend Shared Function WinUsb_ControlTransfer _
        (ByVal InterfaceHandle As IntPtr, _
         ByVal SetupPacket As WINUSB_SETUP_PACKET, _
         ByVal Buffer() As Byte, _
         ByVal BufferLength As UInt32, _
         ByRef LengthTransferred As UInt32, _
         ByVal Overlapped As IntPtr) _
         As Boolean
End Function
```

Use

```
Dim bytesReturned As UInt32
Dim dataStage(1) As Byte
Dim setupPacket As WINUSB_SETUP_PACKET
Dim success As Boolean

' Use this for a vendor-specific request to an interface with a device-to-host Data stage.

' setupPacket.RequestType = &HC1

' Use this for a vendor-specific request to an interface with host-to-device Data stage:

setupPacket.RequestType = &H41

' The number that identifies the specific request.

setupPacket.Request = 1
```

```
' Vendor-defined values to send to the device.

setupPacket.Index = 2
setupPacket.Value = 3

' For control Write transfers (host-to-device Data stage), provide data for the Data stage.
' Example:

dataStage(0) = 65
dataStage(1) = 66

' The number of bytes in the request's Data stage.

setupPacket.Length = Convert.ToUInt16(dataStage.Length)

success = WinUsb_ControlTransfer _
        (myDevInfo.winUsbHandle, _
        setupPacket, _
        dataStage, _
        setupPacket.Length, _
        bytesReturned, _
        IntPtr.Zero)
```

VC#   **Definitions**

```
internal struct WINUSB_SETUP_PACKET
{
        internal Byte RequestType;
        internal Byte Request;
        internal ushort Value;
        internal ushort Index;
        internal ushort Length;
}

[DllImport("winusb.dll", SetLastError = true)]
internal static extern Boolean WinUsb_ControlTransfer
        (IntPtr InterfaceHandle,
        WINUSB_SETUP_PACKET SetupPacket,
        Byte[] Buffer,
        UInt32 BufferLength,
        ref UInt32 LengthTransferred,
        IntPtr Overlapped);
```

Use

```
UInt32  bytesReturned = 0;
Byte[] dataStage = new Byte[ 2 ];
WINUSB_SETUP_PACKET setupPacket;
Boolean success;

// Use this for a vendor-specific request to an interface with a device-to-host Data stage.

// setupPacket.RequestType = 0XC1;

// Use this for a vendor-specific request to an interface with host-to-device Data stage.

setupPacket.RequestType = 0X41;

// The request number that identifies the specific request.

setupPacket.Request = 1;

// Vendor-specific values to send to the device.

setupPacket.Index = 2;
setupPacket.Value = 3;

// For control Write transfers  (host-to-device Data stage), provide data for the Data stage.
// Example:

dataStage[0] = 65;
dataStage[1] = 66;

// The number of bytes in the request's Data stage.

setupPacket.Length = Convert.ToUInt16( dataStage.Length );

success = WinUsb_ControlTransfer
        (myDevInfo.winUsbHandle,
        setupPacket,
        dataStage,
        setupPacket.Length,
        ref bytesReturned,
        IntPtr.Zero);
```

Details

The WINUSB_SETUP_PACKET structure holds the contents of the fields in the Setup stage's data packet as described in Chapter 2. The application sets RequestType to the bmRequestType value for a vendor-specific request directed to an interface with bit 7 indicating the direction of the Data stage. The Request, Value, and Index fields are the desired values for bRequest, wValue, and wIndex in the request.

For a control write request, the application places the data to send to the device in an array. For a control read request, the application provides an array to hold data received from the device.

The WinUsb_ControlTransfer function initiates a control transfer. The function passes a pointer to a WinUSB handle to the interface, a WINUSB_SETUP_PACKET structure, a byte array that contains data to send or space for received data, and the number of bytes to read or write. On success, the function returns True with the number of bytes read or written in the LengthTransferred parameter.

Closing Communications

When finished communicating with a device, the application should free reserved resources.

VB **Definitions**

```
<DllImport("winusb.dll", SetLastError:=True)> Friend Shared Function WinUsb_Free _
     (ByVal InterfaceHandle As IntPtr) _
     As Boolean
     End Function
```

Use

```
WinUsb_Free(myDevInfo.winUsbHandle)
myDevInfo.deviceHandle.Close()
```

VC# **Definitions**

```
[DllImport("winusb.dll", SetLastError = true)]
internal static extern Boolean WinUsb_Free
     (IntPtr InterfaceHandle);
```

Use

```
WinUsb_Free(myDevInfo.winUsbHandle);
myDevInfo.deviceHandle.Close();
```

Details

WinUsb_Free frees the resources allocated by WinUsb_Initialize, and the Close method marks the SafeFileHandle obtained with CreateFile for releasing and freeing.

15

All About Hubs

A hub is an intelligent device that provides attachment points for devices and manages each device's connection to the bus. Devices that plug directly into the host computer connect to the system's root hub. Other devices can connect to external hubs downstream from the root hub.

A hub manages power use, helps initiate communications with newly attached devices, and passes traffic up and down the bus. To manage power, a hub provides current to attached devices and limits current on detecting an over-current condition. To help initiate communications with devices, the hub detects and informs the host of newly attached devices and carries out requests that apply to the devices' ports. The hub's role in passing traffic up and down the bus varies with the speeds of the host, device, and hubs between them.

This chapter presents essentials about hub communications. You don't need to know every detail about hubs in order to design a USB peripheral. But some understanding of what the hub does can help in understanding how devices are detected and communicate on the bus.

Figure 15-1. This hub has an upstream-facing port with a Standard-B receptacle (left), four downstream-facing ports with Standard-A receptacles (center), and a power connection (right).

USB 2.0

Each external USB 2.0 hub has one port, or attachment point, that connects in the upstream direction (toward the host) (Figure 15-1). This upstream-facing port may connect directly to the host's root hub, or the port may connect to a downstream-facing port on another external hub. Each hub has one or more downstream-facing ports. Most downstream ports have a receptacle for attaching a cable. An exception is hubs in compound devices, whose downstream-facing ports connect to functions embedded in the device. Hubs with one, two, four, and seven downstream ports are common. A hub may be self powered or bus powered. As Chapter 16 explains, bus-powered hubs are limited because you can't attach high-power devices to them.

A USB 2.0 hub acts as a remote processor with store-and-forward capabilities. The hub converts between high-speed upstream communications and low- and full-speed downstream communications as needed and performs other functions that help make efficient use of bus time. In contrast, a USB 1.x hub doesn't convert between speeds; it just passes received traffic up or down the bus. For traffic to and from low-speed devices, a USB 1.x hub changes the edge rate and signal polarity but not the bit rate. The added intelligence of USB 2.0 hubs is a major reason why the high-speed bus remains compatible with USB 1.x devices.

Controller chips for hubs contain dedicated silicon to perform hub functions. Due to timing requirements, implementing a hub function with a general-purpose device controller chip isn't feasible. For single-chip compound devices,

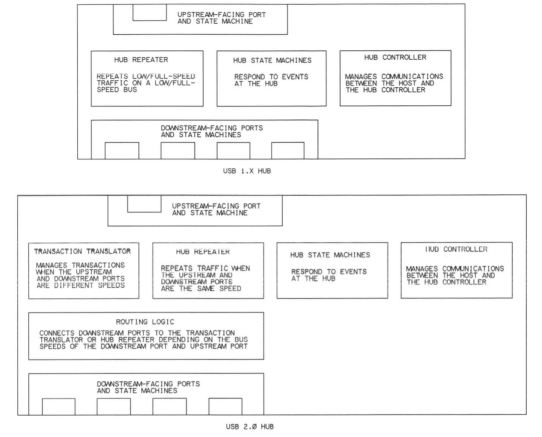

Figure 15-2. A USB 2.0 hub contains one or more transaction translators and routing logic that enable a hub on a high-speed bus to communicate with low- and full-speed devices. A USB 1.x hub doesn't convert between bus speeds. (Adapted from _Universal Serial Bus Specification Revision 2.0._)

chips that contain an embedded hub and a generic device controller are available.

An external USB 2.0 hub contains a hub repeater and a hub controller (Figure 15-2). The hub repeater passes USB traffic between the upstream hub (which may be on the host) and attached and enabled downstream devices. The hub controller manages communications between the host and the hub repeater. State machines control the hub's response to events at the hub repeater and upstream and downstream ports. A USB 2.0 hub also has one or more transaction translators and routing logic that enable low- and full-speed devices to communicate on a high-speed bus.

The host's root hub is a special case. The host controller performs many of the functions that the hub repeater and hub controller perform in an external hub, so a root hub may contain little more than routing logic and downstream ports.

The Hub Repeater

The hub repeater re-transmits the packets it receives, sending them on their way up or down stream with minimal changes. The hub repeater also detects when a device is attached and removed, establishes the connection of a device to the bus, detects bus faults such as over-current conditions, and manages power to the device.

A USB 2.0 hub repeater has two modes of operation depending on the upstream bus speed. When the hub connects upstream to a full-speed bus segment, the repeater functions as a low- and full-speed repeater. When the hub connects upstream to a high-speed bus segment, the repeater functions as a high-speed repeater. The repeaters in USB 1.x hubs always function as low- and full-speed repeaters.

The Low- and Full-speed Repeater

The hub repeater in a USB 1.x hub handles low- and full-speed traffic. A USB 2.0 hub also uses this type of repeater when its upstream port connects to a full-speed bus. In this case, the USB 2.0 hub doesn't send or receive high-speed traffic but instead functions identically to a USB 1.x hub.

A low- and full-speed repeater re-transmits all low- and full-speed packets received from the host, including data that has passed through one or more additional hubs, to all enabled, full-speed, downstream ports. Enabled ports include all ports with attached devices that are ready to receive communications from the hub. Devices with ports that aren't enabled include devices that the host controller has stopped communicating with due to errors or other problems, devices in the Suspend state, and devices that aren't yet ready to communicate because they have just been attached or are in the process of exiting the Suspend state.

The hub repeater doesn't translate, examine the contents of, or process the traffic to or from full-speed ports. The repeater just regenerates the edges of the signal transitions and passes the traffic on.

Low-speed devices never see full-speed traffic. A USB 1.x hub repeats only low-speed packets to low-speed devices. The hub identifies a low-speed packet by the PRE packet identifier that precedes the packet. The hub repeats the low-speed packets, and only these packets, to any enabled low-speed ports. The hub also repeats low-speed packets to its full-speed downstream ports because a full-speed port may connect to a hub that in turn connects to a low-speed device. To give hubs time to make their low-speed ports ready to receive data, the host adds a delay of at least four full-speed bit widths between the PRE packet and the low-speed packet.

Compared to full speed, traffic in a low-speed cable segment varies not only in speed, but also in edge rate and polarity. A hub whose downstream port connects directly to a low-speed device uses low speed's edge rate and polarity when communicating with the device. When communicating upstream, the hub uses full-speed's faster edge rate and an inverted polarity compared to low speed. The hub repeater converts between the edge rates and polarities as needed. Chapter 18 has more on the signal polarities, and Chapter 19 has more about edge rates.

The High-speed Repeater

A USB 2.0 hub uses a high-speed repeater when the hub's upstream port connects to a high-speed bus segment. In this case, the hub sends and receives all upstream traffic at high speed even if the traffic is to or from a low- or full-speed device. Routing logic in the hub determines whether traffic to or from a downstream port passes through a transaction translator.

Unlike a low- and full-speed repeater, a high-speed repeater re-clocks received data to minimize accumulated jitter. In other words, instead of just repeating received transitions, a high-speed repeater uses its own local clock to time the transitions when retransmitting. The edge rate and polarity don't change. An elasticity buffer allows for small differences between the hub's clock frequency and the timing of the received data. When the buffer is half full, the received data begins clocking out.

The Transaction Translator

Every USB 2.0 hub must have a transaction translator to manage communications with low- and full-speed devices. The transaction translator communicates upstream at high speed while enabling low- and full-speed devices to continue to communicate at low and full speeds. The transaction translator

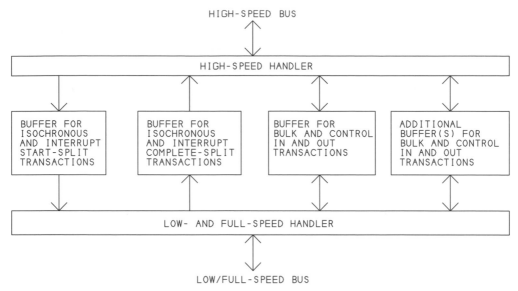

Figure 15-3. A transaction translator contains a high-speed handler for upstream traffic, buffers for storing information in split transactions, and a low- and full-speed handler for downstream traffic to low- and full-speed devices.

stores received data and forwards, or transmits, the data toward its destination at the appropriate speed.

The transaction translator frees bus time by enabling other communications to use the bus while a hub completes a low- or full-speed transaction with a device. Transaction translators can also enable low- and full-speed devices to have more bandwidth than the host could allocate on a shared low/full-speed bus.

For traffic to and from low- and full-speed devices, the high-speed repeater communicates with the transaction translator, which manages transactions with the devices.

Sections

The transaction translator contains three sections (Figure 15-3). The high-speed handler communicates with the host at high speed. The low/full-speed handler communicates with devices at low and full speeds. Buffers store data used in transactions with low- and full-speed devices. Each transaction translator has to have at least four buffers: one for interrupt and isochronous start-split transactions, one for interrupt and isochronous complete-split transactions, and two or more for control and bulk transfers.

1. THE HOST INITIATES AND COMPLETES THE START-SPLIT TRANSACTION WITH THE HUB.

2. THE HUB INITIATES AND COMPLETES THE TRANSACTION WITH THE DEVICE.

3. THE HOST INITIATES AND COMPLETES THE COMPLETE-SPLIT TRANSACTION WITH THE HUB.

Figure 15-4. In a transfer that uses split transactions, the host communicates at high speed with a USB 2.0 hub, and the hub communicates at low or full speed with the device. Isochronous transactions may use multiple start-split or complete-split transactions.

Managing Split Transactions

When a USB 2.0 host wants to communicate with a low- or full-speed device that connects to a hub on a high-speed bus, the host initiates a split transaction with the USB 2.0 hub that is nearest the device and communicating upstream at high speed. Figure 15-4 shows the transactions that make up a split transaction.

One or more start-split transactions contain the information the hub needs to complete the transaction with the device. The transaction translator stores the information received from the host and completes the start-split transaction with the host.

On completing a start-split transaction, the hub performs the function of a host controller in carrying out the transaction with the device. The transaction translator initiates the transaction in the token phase, sends data or stores returned data or status information as needed in the data phase, and sends or

379

receives a status code as needed in the handshake phase. The hub uses low or full speed as needed in its communications with the device.

After the hub has had time to exchange data with the device, in all transactions except isochronous OUTs, the host initiates one or more complete-split transactions to retrieve the information returned by the device and stored in the transaction translator's buffer. The hub performs these transactions at high speed.

Table 15-1 compares the structure and contents of transactions with low- and full-speed devices at different bus speeds.

Bulk and control transfers don't have the timing constraints of interrupt and isochronous transfers and thus use a simpler protocol. In the start-split transaction, the USB 2.0 host sends the start-split token packet (SSPLIT), followed by the usual low- or full-speed token packet and any data packet destined for the device. The USB 2.0 hub that is nearest the device and communicating upstream at high speed returns ACK or NAK. The host is then free to use the bus for other transactions. The device knows nothing about the transaction yet.

On returning ACK in a start-split transaction, the hub has two responsibilities. The hub must complete the transaction with the device and must continue to handle any other bus traffic received from the host or other attached devices.

To complete the transaction, the hub converts the packet or packets received from the host to the appropriate speed, sends them to the device and stores the data or handshake returned by the device. Depending on the transaction, the device may return data, a handshake, or nothing. For IN transactions, the hub returns a handshake packet to the device. To the device, the transaction has proceeded at the expected low or full speed and is now complete. The device has no knowledge that the transaction is a split transaction. The host hasn't yet received the device's response.

While the hub is completing the transaction with the device, the host may initiate other bus traffic that the device's hub must handle as well. Separate hardware modules within the hub handle the two functions. When the hub has had enough time to complete the transaction with the device, the host begins a complete-split transaction with the hub.

In a complete-split transaction, the host sends a complete-split token packet (CSPLIT), followed by a low- or full-speed token packet to request the data or status information the hub has received from the device. The hub returns the information. The transfer is now complete at the host. The host doesn't return an ACK to the hub. If the hub doesn't have the packet ready to send, the hub

Table 15-1: When a low- or full-speed device has a transaction on a high-speed bus, the host uses start-split (SSPLIT) and complete-split (CSPLIT) transactions with the USB 2.0 hub nearest the device and communicating upstream at high speed.

Bus Speed	Transaction Type	Transaction Phase		
		Token	Data	Handshake
Low/Full-speed communications with the device	Setup, OUT	PRE if low speed, LS/FS token	PRE if low speed, data	status (except for isochronous)
	IN	PRE if low speed, LS/FS token	data or status	PRE if low speed, status (except for isochronous)
High-speed communications between a USB 2.0 hub and host in transactions with a low- or full-speed device	Setup, OUT (isochronous OUT has no CSPLIT transaction)	SSPLIT, LS/FS token	data	status (bulk and control only)
		CSPLIT, LS/FS token	–	status
	IN	SSPLIT, LS/FS token	–	status (bulk and control only)
		CSPLIT, LS/FS token)	data or status	–

returns NYET, and the host retries later. The device is unaware of the complete-split transaction.

In split transactions in interrupt and isochronous transfers, the process is similar but with stricter timing. The goals are to transfer data to the host as soon as possible after the device has data available to send and to transfer data to the device just as the device is ready to receive new data. To achieve this timing, isochronous transactions with large packets use multiple start splits or complete splits and transfer a portion of the data in each.

Unlike with bulk and control transfers, start-split transactions in interrupt and isochronous transfers have no handshake phase, just the start-split token followed by an IN, OUT, or Setup token and OUT or Setup transactions, data.

In an interrupt transaction, the hub schedules the start split in the microframe just before the earliest time that the hub is expected to begin the transaction with the device. For example, assume that the microframes in a frame are numbered in sequence, 0–7. If the start split is in microframe 0, the transaction with the device can occur as early as microframe 1. The device may have data or a handshake response to return to the host as early as microframe 2, and the host schedules time for three complete-split transactions in microframes 2, 3, and 4. If the hub doesn't yet have the information to return in a complete split, the hub returns NYET and the host retries.

Full-speed isochronous transactions can transfer up to 1023 bytes. To ensure that the data transfers as soon as the device has data to send or is ready to receive data, transactions with large packets use multiple start splits or complete splits with up to 188 data bytes in each. This amount is the maximum quantity of full-speed data that fits in a microframe. A single transaction's data can require up to eight start-split or complete-split transactions.

In an isochronous IN transaction, the host schedules complete-split transactions in every microframe where the host expects the device to have at least a portion of the data to return. Requesting the data in smaller chunks ensures that the host receives the data as quickly as possible. The host doesn't have to wait for all of the data to transfer from the device at full speed before beginning to retrieve the data.

In an isochronous OUT transaction, the host sends the data in one or more start-split transactions. The host schedules the transactions so the hub's buffer will never be empty but will contain as few bytes as possible. Each SPLIT packet contains bits that indicate the data's position in the low- or full-speed data packet (beginning, middle, end, or all). There is no complete-split transaction.

Bandwidth Use of Low- and Full-speed Devices

Because a USB 2.0 hub acts as a host controller in managing transactions, low- and full-speed devices share low/full-speed bandwidth only with devices that use the same transaction translator. Most hubs provide one transaction translator for all ports, but a single hub can provide a transaction translator for each port that connects to a low- or full-speed device.

If two full-speed devices each have a dedicated transaction translator on a high-speed bus, each device can use all of the transaction translator's downstream, full-speed bandwidth. When the hub(s) convert to high speed, the full-speed traffic uses little of the high-speed bandwidth.

For bulk transactions, the extra transaction with the host in each split transaction can result in lower throughput for a full-speed device that connects to a hub on a busy bus that is also carrying high-speed bulk traffic.

The Hub Controller

A USB 2.0 hub controller manages communications between the host and the hub. As it does for all devices, the host enumerates a newly detected hub to learn about it. The hub descriptor retrieved during enumeration tells the host the number of ports on the hub. After enumerating the hub, the host requests the hub to report whether the hub has any attached devices. If so, the host enumerates these as well.

The host finds out if a device is attached to a port by sending the hub-class request Get Port Status. This is similar to a Get Status request but is directed to a hub and has a port number in the wIndex field. The hub returns two 16-bit values that indicate whether a device is attached and other information such as whether the device is in the Suspend state.

The hub controller is also responsible for disabling any port that was responsible for loss of bus activity or babble. Loss of bus activity occurs when a packet doesn't end with the expected EOP. Babble occurs when a device continues to transmit beyond the EOP.

Each hub has a Status Change endpoint configured for Interrupt IN transfers. A USB 2.0 host polls the endpoint to find out if the hub has any changes to report. On each poll, the hub controller returns NAK if there have been no changes or data that indicates a specific port or the hub itself as the source of the change. After a reported change, the host sends requests to find out more about the change and take whatever action is needed. For example, if the hub reports attachment of a new device, the host attempts to enumerate the device.

Speed

An external USB 2.0 hub's downstream ports must support low, full, and high speeds. In the upstream direction, if a USB 2.0 hub's upstream segment is high speed, the hub communicates at high speed. Otherwise, the hub communicates upstream at low and full speeds.

A USB 1.x hub's upstream port must support low- and full-speed communications. All downstream ports with connectors must support both low- and full-speed communications. USB 1.x hubs never support high speed.

Filtering Traffic according to Speed

Low-speed devices aren't capable of receiving full-speed data so hubs don't repeat full-speed traffic to low-speed devices. Otherwise, a low-speed device

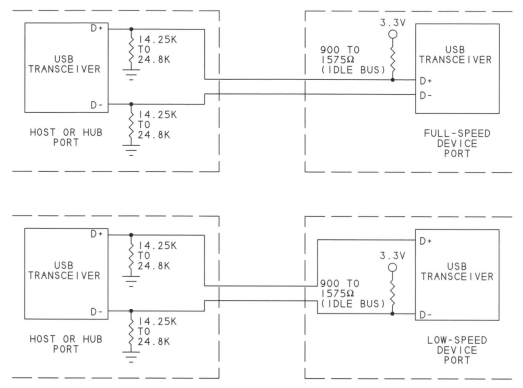

Figure 15-5. The device's port has a stronger pull-up than the hub's. The location of the pull-up tells the hub whether the device is low or full speed. High-speed devices are full speed at attachment.

would try to interpret full-speed traffic as low-speed data and might even mistakenly see what looks like valid data. Full- or high-speed data on a low-speed cable could also cause problems due to radiated electromagnetic interference (EMI). In the other direction, hubs repeat received low-speed data upstream.

Low- and full-speed devices aren't capable of receiving high-speed data, so USB 2.0 hubs don't repeat high-speed traffic to these devices, including USB 1.x hubs.

Detecting Device Speed

On attachment, every USB 2.0 device must support either low or full speed. A hub detects whether an attached device is low or full speed by detecting which signal line is more positive on an idle line. Figure 15-5 illustrates. As Chapter 4 explained, the hub has pull-down resistors of 14.25k–24.8kΩ on D+ and D-. A newly attached device has a pull-up of 900–1575Ω on either D+ for a full-speed device or D- for a low-speed device. When a device attaches to a port, the line with the pull-up is more positive than the hub's logic-high input threshold. The hub detects the voltage, assumes a device is attached, and determines the speed by detecting which line is pulled up.

After detecting a full-speed device, a USB 2.0 hub determines whether the device supports high speed by using the high-speed detection handshake. The handshake occurs during the Reset state that the hub initiates during enumeration. If the handshake succeeds, the device removes its pull-up and communications are at high speed. A USB 1.x hub ignores the attempt to handshake, and the failure of the handshake informs the device that it must use full speed. Chapter 18 has more details about the handshake.

Maintaining Active Links

SOF packets keep full- and high-speed devices from entering the Suspend state on an otherwise idle bus. On an idle, full-speed bus, the host continues to send an SOF once per frame, and hubs pass these packets on to their full-speed devices. On an otherwise idle, high-speed bus, the host continues to send an SOF once per microframe, and hubs pass these packets on to their high-speed devices. A full-speed device that connects to a USB 2.0 hub that communicates upstream at high speed will also receive an SOF once per frame from the hub.

Low-speed devices don't see the SOFs. Instead, at least once per frame, hubs must send their low-speed devices a low-speed End-of-Packet (EOP) signal (defined in Chapter 18). This signal functions as a keep-alive signal that keeps a device from entering the Suspend state on a bus with no low-speed activity. A host can also request a hub to suspend the bus at a single port. Chapter 16 has more on how hubs manage the Suspend state.

USB 3.0

A USB 3.0 hub contains both a USB 2.0 hub that supports low, full, and high speeds and a SuperSpeed hub (Figure 15-6). The hubs operate independently except for sharing logic to control VBUS. The host enumerates a USB 3.0 hub as two devices. Hubs are the only devices with ports that can communicate upstream at the same time at both SuperSpeed and high speed.

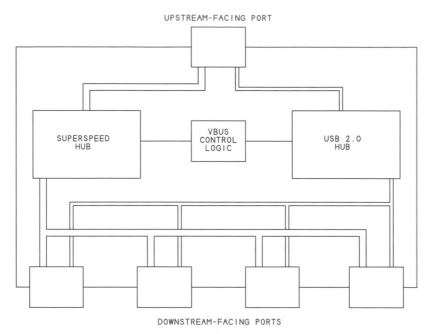

UPSTREAM-FACING PORT

SUPERSPEED HUB

VBUS CONTROL LOGIC

USB 2.0 HUB

DOWNSTREAM-FACING PORTS

Figure 15-6. A USB 3.0 hub contains a USB 2.0 hub and a hub for SuperSpeed. (Adapted from *Universal Serial Bus 3.0 Specification*.)

Bus Speeds

The speed of a hub's upstream port determines what bus speeds are available to downstream ports. If the upstream port connects at SuperSpeed, the hub can communicate with downstream devices at any speed. If the upstream port connects at high speed, the hub can communicate downstream at low, full, and high speeds. If a USB 3.0 hub's upstream port connects at full speed, the hub can communicate downstream at low and full speeds. A downstream-facing port that connects internally to an embedded device can support a single speed. At the hub's upstream port, traffic to and from downstream SuperSpeed devices uses the SuperSpeed wires, and traffic to and from downstream low-, full-, and high-speed devices uses the USB 2.0 wires. As with USB 2.0 hubs, all upstream traffic on the USB 2.0 wires uses high speed (unless a USB 1.x hub is upstream from the hub).

Components

The SuperSpeed portion of a USB 3.0 hub consists of a repeater/forwarder and a hub controller. Like the hub repeater in a USB 2.0 hub, the repeater/forwarder re-transmits received packets, detects device attachment and removal, establishes the connection of a device to the bus, detects bus faults such as over-current conditions, and manages power to the device. A hub may partially store a Data Packet before beginning to forward it, and the hub stores and forwards all other packets. Buffers help to manage the traffic that passes through the hub. Buffers enable storing packet headers for later delivery to a downstream device that must exit a low-power mode before receiving traffic. Buffers also enable receiving asynchronous messages from multiple downstream devices at once and holding received payload data to repeat. To enable retrying, after transmitting a Data Packet, the buffer retains the packet until receiving a link-level acknowledgement.

As in a USB 2.0 hub, a USB 3.0 hub controller manages communications between the host and the hub. The hub sends status information via an interrupt IN Status Change endpoint. A hub with information to report sends an ERDY Transaction Packet to the host.

Managing Traffic

The hub stores and forwards header packets and repeats Data Packets. The hub must be able to store eight header packets directed to the same downstream port and eight header packets received at a downstream port.

During hub enumeration, the host sends a Set Hub Depth request to assign a hub-depth value to the hub. The value equals the number of additional upstream hubs that lie in the path between the hub and the root hub. Hubs that connect directly to the root hub have a hub depth of zero. Any hubs that connect to downstream ports on those hubs have a hub depth of one. Any hubs that connect to those hubs have a hub depth of two, and so on up to a maximum hub depth of four. The USB 2.0 specification defines the root hub as tier 1 in the bus topology, so hub depth equals the hub's tier - 2.

Unlike USB 2.0 hubs, USB 3.0 hubs don't broadcast downstream traffic but instead direct traffic only toward the target device. Using routing instead of broadcasting enables ports to enter a low-power state when not communicating with the host even if the bus is carrying traffic to other device. In the upstream direction, hubs route all traffic to the host as with USB 2.0. On receiving a packet from the host, a hub uses its hub-depth value and a Route String in the packet header to determine whether the hub should process the packet or route the packet to a downstream port. The Route String has five 4-bit fields. Each field contains information that applies to one of up to five external hubs in the path that the packet travels. The hub-depth value identifies which 4-bit field in a received Route String applies to the hub. The field contains either a port number to route the packet to or zero if the packet's destination is the hub itself. Because the Route String's fields are four bits, a USB 3.0 hub can have at most 15 downstream ports. A hub that isn't configured assumes all packets are directed to itself.

The Hub Class

Hubs are members of the hub class, which is the only class defined in the main USB specification.

Hub Descriptors

The hub descriptor informs the host of hub-specific capabilities such as supported modes for power switching and overcurrent protection. For USB 3.0 hubs, the hub descriptor has additional fields to support USB 3.0 capabilities. A host can request the descriptor with a Get Hub Descriptor control request. A USB 3.0 hub must have a device capability descriptor with a Container ID that identifies the device instance. The Container ID is the same value for the USB 2.0 and USB 3.0 hub functions in a device.

Hub Class Requests

A host can use hub-class requests to obtain status information, set and clear hub and port features, and monitor and control transaction translators.

Port Indicators

The USB 2.0 specification defines optional indicators to indicate port status to the user. The specification assigns standard meanings to the colors and blinking properties of status LEDs or similar indicators. Each downstream port on a hub can have an indicator, which can be a single bi-color green/amber LED or a separate LED for each color:

Green	fully operational
Amber	error condition
Blinking off/green	software attention required
Blinking off/amber	hardware attention required
Off	not operational

16

Managing Power

A convenient feature of USB is the ability to draw power from the bus. But using bus power carries the responsibility to operate within allowed limits, including reducing power in the Suspend state.

This chapter will help you decide if a device can use bus power. Plus, whether your design is bus-powered or self-powered, you'll find out how to ensure that your device follows the USB specification's requirements for managing power. Also covered are new power-saving options for USB 2.0 and USB 3.0.

Power Options

Inside a typical PC is a power supply with amperes to spare. Many hubs also have their own power supplies. Some USB devices can take advantage of these existing supplies rather than providing their own power sources.

Bus power has several advantages. Users don't need an electrical outlet near the device. A device with no internal power supply can be physically smaller, lighter in weight, and less expensive to manufacture. The device can save energy because power supplies in PCs use efficient switching regulators rather than the cheap linear regulators in the power adapters that many peripherals use. (Self-powered hubs may use inefficient supplies, however.)

Voltages

The nominal voltage between the VBUS and GND wires in a USB cable is 5V, but the actual value can vary. VBUS at a host or hub's downstream port can be anywhere in the range 4.45–5.25V. Cable and connector losses further reduce the voltage available at a device's port.

These are the minimum and maximum valid voltages for connectors on downstream-facing ports:

Hub Type	USB Version	Available Current per Port (mA)	VBUS at Hub Port (V)	
			Minimum	Maximum
High Power	USB 2.0	500	4.75	5.25
	USB 3.0	900	4.45	5.25
Low Power	USB 2.0	100	4.4	5.25
	USB 3.0	150	4.45	5.25

High-power USB 2.0 devices must at minimum respond to enumeration requests with at least 4.4V on the B connector. All USB 3.0 devices must at minimum respond to enumeration requests with at least 4.0V on the B connector. Transient conditions can cause the voltage to drop briefly by a few additional tenths of a volt.

USB controller chips typically use a +5V or +3.3V supply. Devices powered at 3.3V can use an inexpensive low-dropout linear regulator to obtain 3.3V from VBUS. If a component needs a higher voltage, the device can contain a step-up switching regulator.

Using Bus Power

Figure 16-1 will help you decide whether a specific device can use bus power. Advances in semiconductor technology have reduced the power required by many circuits. Thanks to CMOS manufacturing processes, lower supply voltages for components, and power-conserving modes in CPUs, you can do a lot with 100 mA.

A device that requires up to 100 mA can be bus powered from any host or hub. A device that requires up to 500 mA can use bus power when attached to a self-powered hub or any host except some battery-powered hosts. A SuperSpeed device on a USB 3.0 bus can draw up to 150 mA from any USB 3.0 hub and up to 900 mA when attached to any host except some battery-powered hosts.

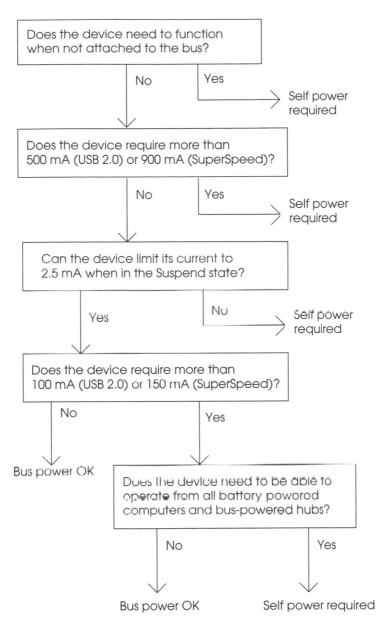

Figure 16-1. Some devices can draw all of their power from the bus.

No device should draw more than 100 mA (USB 2.0) or 150 mA (SuperSpeed) until the host has configured the device for more current. Devices must limit their power consumption further when in the Suspend state. In some cases, battery charging can exceed these limits as described later in this chapter.

Of course, devices such as digital cameras that need to function when not attached to a host will need self power. Self power can use batteries or power from a wall socket. To save battery power, a device can use bus power when connected to the bus and self power otherwise. Because a device in the Suspend state should draw very little current from the bus, some devices need their own supplies to enable operating when the bus is suspended.

Power Needs

USB 2.0 defines a low-power device as a bus-powered device that draws up to 100 mA from the bus and a high-power device as a device that draws up to 500 mA from the bus. A self-powered device can draw up to 100 mA from the bus and as much power as is available from the device's supply.

A high-power device must be able to enumerate at low power. On power-up, a USB 2.0 device can draw up to 100 mA from the bus until the host has configured the device. After retrieving a configuration descriptor, the host examines the amount of current requested in bMaxPower, and if the current is available, the host sends a Set Configuration request to select the configuration. The device can then draw up to the bMaxPower value from the bus. In reality, hosts and hubs are likely to allocate either 100 mA or 500 mA to a device rather than a precise amount requested in bMaxPower.

A self-powered USB 2.0 device may also draw up to 100 mA from the bus any time the device isn't in the Suspend state. This capability enables the device's USB interface to function when the device's power supply is off and the host detects and enumerates the device. Otherwise, if a device's pull-up is bus-powered and the rest of the interface is self-powered, the host will detect the device but won't be able to communicate with it.

The limits are absolute maximums, not averages. Also remember that the bus's power-supply voltage can be as high as 5.25V, and a higher voltage can result in greater current consumption.

A device must never provide upstream power. Even the pull-up must remain unpowered until VBUS is present. A device that provides upstream power can cause problems that include a PC that doesn't boot or doesn't resume from the Suspend state, a hub that doesn't enumerate its downstream devices, and failure of an upstream device. A self-powered device must connect to VBUS to detect its presence even if the device never uses bus power. USB compliance testing includes a back-voltage test to verify that a device doesn't provide upstream power. The test, described in the compliance test documentation, requires just three resistors and a voltmeter.

Hosts in embedded systems may turn off VBUS to save power but may still need the ability to detect device attachment even when VBUS is off. The *Device Capacitance* ECN to the USB 2.0 specification enables device detection by ensuring a change in capacitance on VBUS on device attachment. The ECN mandates a capacitance of 1–10 µF between VBUS and GND on a device's upstream-facing port.

SuperSpeed devices must obey the same rules for using power but with higher limits of 150 mA for low-power and self-powered devices and 900 mA for high-power devices.

Informing the Host

During enumeration, the host learns whether the device is self powered or bus powered and the maximum current the device will draw from the bus. All hubs must have over-current protection that blocks excessive current to a device.

If you connect a high-power device to a low-power hub on a Windows PC, you'll see a message informing you that the hub doesn't have enough power available. If the bus has a low-power device connected to a high-power port, Windows recommends swapping the device with the high-power device (Figure 16-2).

A device can support both bus-powered and self-powered options, using self power when available and bus power (possibly with limited abilities) otherwise.

When a hub's power supply is removed or turned off, the hub must remain in the Configured state, transition its downstream ports to the Powered Off state, and inform the host of the change via the hub's Status Change endpoint.

Battery Charging

USB devices with rechargeable batteries can often recharge the batteries by connecting to a USB host or hub or a dedicated charging unit. The USB 2.0 specification doesn't define a way to draw charging currents greater than 500 mA or use bus current to charge batteries that are too weak to enable a device to enumerate.

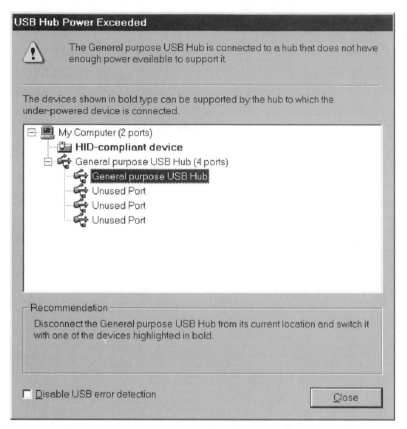

Figure 16-2. Windows warns users when they connect a high-power device to a low-power hub and helps them find an alternate connection.

The USB-IF's *Battery Charging Specification* addresses these needs and defines protocols for efficient and compliant charging of batteries in USB devices. The specification defines requirements for USB hosts, hubs, and dedicated devices that operate as USB chargers. A USB charger contains charger-detection circuits so a device can learn if it's connected to a USB charger.

The description that follows is based on V1.0 of the battery-charging specification. V2.0, in development at this writing, will likely define host protocols for managing the charging process.

Charger Types

The specification defines three types of USB chargers:

- A host charger is a USB 2.0 host that can provide 500 mA to a port at any time and that supports charger detection. A low- or full-speed device must limit the current drawn from a host charger to 1.5A. A high-speed device must limit the current drawn from a host charger to 900 mA. A device that has connected to a host charger by pulling up D+ or D- can draw charging current even if the host has placed the device in the Suspend state.

- A hub charger is a USB 2.0 hub that can provide 500 mA to a downstream port for normal operation and supports charger detection. Devices that connect to hub chargers can draw the same charging currents as permitted for host chargers.

- A dedicated charger provides power from a USB connector but doesn't enumerate the attached device. The charger must connect its D+ and D- lines together via a 200Ω resistor and must limit the charging current to under 1.5A. The ability to use a USB connector is convenient for users and lowers manufacturing cost because the device doesn't need a vendor-specific connector or cable for charging.

Charger Detection

After detecting the presence of VBUS, a device can determine whether it's connected to a USB charger by driving D+ to the VDAT_SRC voltage (0.5V–0.7V) and detecting the voltage on D-. If D- is greater than VDAT_REF (0.4V), the device is attached to a USB charger.

A host or hub charger that detects a voltage between 0.4V and 0.8V on D+ drives D- to VDAT_SRC, which exceeds VDAT_REF. On a dedicated charger, D+ and D- are connected together and thus both exceed VDAT_REF. Hosts and hubs that don't function as USB chargers pull D- to ground via a 15K resistor, which brings D- below VDAT_REF.

A device attached to a USB charger can determine the charger type after pulling up D+ (full speed) or D- (low speed) and detecting the voltage on the line not pulled up:

Device Speed	Action	Detected Voltage	Charger Type
Full	Pull D+ high	D- is low	Host or hub
		D- is high	Dedicated
Low	Pull D- high	D+ is low	Host or hub
		D+ is high	Dedicated

To ensure valid voltages when connecting, a low-speed device must draw less than 100mA when it pulls D- high. The specification provides timing requirements and other details for implementing charger detection.

Charging Dead Batteries

A dead-battery provision allows devices with dead or very weak batteries to draw up to 100 mA from a host or hub until the batteries are charged to a weak battery threshold. A device whose battery has charged to the weak battery threshold is capable of powering up successfully and connecting to the bus by pulling D+ or D- high. The device defines its weak-battery-threshold voltage. The provision also allows the bus to power a device that normally operates on battery power but has no batteries installed.

Hub Power

Power use on hubs has special considerations. A hub must control power to its downstream devices and must monitor power consumption and take action when devices use too much current and present a safety hazard.

Power Sources

The root hub gets its power from the host. Other hubs are either self-powered or bus-powered.

If the host uses AC power from a wall socket or another external source, a USB 2.0 root hub must be capable of supplying 500 mA to each port on the hub. If the host is battery-powered, the hub may supply either 500 or 100 mA to each port. A hub that supplies 500 mA per port is a high-power hub, and a hub that supplies 100 mA per port is a low-power hub.

All of a bus-powered hub's downstream devices must be low power. A USB 2.0 hub can draw no more than 500 mA and the hub itself will use some current, leaving less than 500 mA for all attached devices combined. Thus you shouldn't connect two bus-powered hubs in series. The upstream hub can guarantee no more than 100 mA to each downstream port, and that amount doesn't leave enough current to power a second hub that also has one or more downstream ports that each require 100 mA.

An exception is a bus-powered compound device, which consists of a hub and one or more downstream, non-removable devices. In this case, the hub's configuration descriptor can report the maximum power required by the hub's electronics plus its non-removable device(s). The configuration descriptors for the non-removable device(s) report that the devices are self-powered with bMaxPower = 00h. The hub descriptor indicates whether a hub's ports are removable.

Like other high-power, bus-powered devices, a USB 2.0 bus-powered hub can draw up to 100 mA until configured and up to 500 mA after being configured. During configuration, the hub must manage the available current so its devices and the hub combined don't exceed the allowed current.

Like other self-powered devices, a self-powered USB 2.0 hub may also draw up to 100 mA from the bus so the hub interface can continue to function when the hub's power supply is off. If the hub's power is from an external source such as AC power from a wall socket, the hub is high power and must be capable of supplying 500 mA to each port on the hub. If the hub uses battery power, the hub may supply 100 or 500 mA to each port on the hub.

USB 3.0 raises the current limits. USB 3.0 hubs can provide up to 900 mA per port if high power and 150 mA per port if low power. If the upstream port isn't connected, the hub doesn't provide power to the downstream ports unless the hub supports the USB battery charging specification.

Over-current Protection

As a safety precaution, hubs must be able to detect an over-current condition, which occurs when the current used by the total of all devices attached to the hub exceeds a set value. On detecting an over-current condition, a hub's port circuits limit the current at the port, and the hub informs the host of the problem. Windows warns the user when a device exceeds the current limit of its hub port (Figure 16-3).

The current that triggers the over-current actions must be less than 5A. To allow for transient currents, the over-current value should be greater than the

Figure 16-3. When a device exceeds the current limit of its hub's port, Windows warns the user and offers assistance.

total of the maximum allowed currents for the devices. In the worst case, seven high-power, bus-powered, USB 2.0 downstream devices can legally draw up to 3.5A. So a supply for a self-powered hub with up to seven downstream ports would provide much less than 5A at all times unless something goes very wrong. A hub can implement multiple over-current gangs.

A device can briefly draw a larger inrush current on attachment to the bus. The over-current protection circuits typically don't see the inrush current because a capacitor downstream from the protection provides the stored energy. If the inrush current is too large, the device will fail compliance tests.

Power Switching

A bus-powered hub must support power switching that can provide and cut off power to downstream ports in response to control requests. A single switch may control all ports, or the ports may switch individually. A self-powered hub must support switching its ports to the Powered Off state and may also support power switching via control transfers.

Saving Power

All USB devices must support the low-power Suspend state. Additional low-power states enable conserving power with quicker transitions and less stringent requirements than Suspend. With host support, USB 2.0 devices can use the Sleep state. SuperSpeed devices can support the U1 and U2 low-power states.

USB 2.0 Link Power Management

The *USB 2.0 Link Power Management (LPM) Addendum* to the USB 2.0 specification defines four USB link power management states. SuperSpeed-capable devices must support link power management when operating at high speed. USB 2.0 devices may also support link power management. A link consists of a cable segment and the two ports, or link partners, the cable connects.

The addendum assigns names to conditions described in the USB 2.0 specification and adds the new L1 (Sleep) state:

L0 (On). The link is carrying data or is able to do so. When not carrying data, the link carries SOF (full and high speed) or keep-alive (low speed) signals.

L1 (Sleep). The link doesn't carry data or SOF/keep-alive signals. The device may reduce power consumption.

L2 (Suspend). The link doesn't carry data or SOF/keep-alive signals. The device must reduce power consumption.

L3 (Off). The link is powered off, disconnected, or disabled and isn't capable of performing data signaling.

The *USB 2.0 Phase-locked SOFs* ECN to the USB 2.0 specification can help isochronous devices save power. To comply with the ECN, SOFs issued on exiting the Sleep or selective Suspend states must be in phase lock with the SOFs that preceded the low-power state. Isochronous devices can thus enter a low-power state and maintain synchronization to SOFs on returning to full power.

Suspend State

The Suspend state reduces a device's use of bus power when the host doesn't need to communicate. A USB 2.0 device must enter the Suspend state when the bus has had no activity for 3 ms.

While in the Suspend state, a device must draw no more than 2.5 mA from the bus. A device that needs to function when the host has ceased communicating may need to be self-powered. However, many device controllers can consume very little power while remaining able to detect activity requiring attention on an I/O pin and wake the host as needed.

Global and Selective Suspends

In a global suspend, a USB 2.0 host stops communicating with the entire bus, which carries no traffic or SOFs. When a full-or high-speed device detects that no SOF has arrived for 3 ms, the device enters the Suspend state. Low-speed devices do the same when they haven't received a low-speed keep-alive signal for 3 ms. A device must be in the Suspend state within 10 ms of no bus activity.

A host may also request a selective suspend of an individual port. The host issues the class-specific Set Port Feature request to a hub with wIndex set to a port number and wValue set to PORT_SUSPEND. The request instructs the hub to stop sending any traffic, including SOFs or low-speed keep-alives, to the specified port.

Current Limits for Suspended Devices

A device in the Suspend state should consume maximum of 2.5 mA of bus current averaged over 1 s. The limit includes current through the pull-up on D+ or D-.

The USB 2.0 specification defined a limit of just 500 µA for devices that don't support remote wakeup. However, the limit was difficult for many devices to meet, and in 2008, the USB-IF raised the limit with the ECN *Suspend Current Limit Changes*. USB 3.0 also uses the new limit.

Configured, bus-powered hubs and configured, bus-powered compound devices can draw up to 12.5 mA when suspended. A bus-powered hub can thus consume 2.5 mA while providing 2.5 mA for each of up to four downstream ports.

Resuming Communications

To resume communications on a suspended bus, a host places the bus in the Resume state (the K state, defined in Chapter 18) for at least 20 ms. The host follows the Resume with a low-speed EOP. The host then resumes sending SOFs and any other communications. (For low-speed devices, the nearest hub issues low-speed keep-alive signals instead of sending SOFs.) For selectively suspended devices, a host can request a hub to resume communications on a downstream-facing port by issuing a Clear Port Feature(PORT_SUSPEND) request.

A device that wants to be able to request to resume communications indicates support for remote wakeup in the configuration descriptor's bmAttributes field. The host enables remote wakeup by sending a Set Port Feature(DEVICE_REMOTE_WAKEUP) request to the hub port that is the device's link partner. A suspended device with remote wakeup enabled can request to resume communications by driving the upstream bus segment in the Resume state for 1–15 ms. The device then places its drivers in a high-impedance state to enable receiving traffic from the upstream hub. The resume signaling propagates upstream to the first non-suspended hub, which may be the root hub. When the resume signaling has completed, the device again receives SOFs or low-speed keep-alives and other traffic. A device may initiate a Resume any time after the bus has been idle for at least 5 ms. The host must allow a device at least 10 ms to recover from a Resume.

Some device controllers require firmware support to monitor the bus to determine when to enter the Suspend state, while other controllers handle the task entirely in hardware. The device's serial interface engine typically handles the resume signaling without firmware support.

When a device uses bus power, firmware may need to control power to external circuits, removing power on entering the Suspend state and restoring power on resuming. A power switch with soft-start capability can limit current surges when switching. Micrel Inc. has power-distribution switches suitable for use with USB devices. Each switch contains one or more high-side MOSFET switches with soft-start capability.

Sleep State

The L1 Sleep state provides a way for devices to reduce power consumption without having to meet the Suspend state's stringent requirements. The Sleep state also enables faster transitions to and from the powered state. A major purpose in defining the Sleep state was to provide a more effective mechanism for power conservation on mobile, battery-powered platforms.

In the Sleep state, a device receives no USB traffic including SOFs or keep-alive signaling. The device can reduce power consumption but isn't required to do so.

To place a device in the Sleep state, a host issues a Set_and_Test(PORT_L1) request to the hub that is the device's link partner. A hub that supports the Sleep state then initiates an LPM transaction to the device by issuing a token packet with an EXT Packet ID, followed by an extended token packet with an LPM Packet ID (0011b). (Chapter 2 covered Packet IDs.) In the LPM token packet, the bmAttributes field requests the Sleep state and provides information used in resume signaling (Table 16-1).

A device that receives an EXT token packet followed by an LPM token packet can return ACK (ready to transition to the Sleep state), NYET (not ready to transition to the Sleep state), STALL (requested link state not supported), or no response (the device doesn't support the transaction type or detected an error).

The hub NAKs the Data stage of the Set_and_Test request as needed until the downstream device returns ACK or STALL or fails to respond after three attempts. The hub then returns a completion code in the Data stage of the request.

To resume communications with a device in the Sleep state, a host issues a Clear Port Feature(PORT_L1) request to the device's link partner. The hub then initiates resume signaling with the device. The signaling is identical to a resume from Suspend except for timing. The HIRD value in the LPM token packet indicates how long the hub will hold the line in the Resume state when exiting Sleep. The encoded value can specify a range from 50 μs to 1.2 ms.

In the LPM token packet, if bRemoteWake = 1, the device can request to wake the host by driving the line in the Resume state for 50 μs.

A host that doesn't support the Sleep state will never request it. Devices that don't support the Sleep state can return STALL or no response to token packets that contain the LPM Packet ID.

SuperSpeed Power Management

SuperSpeed offers more ways to conserve power, including new low-power states and latency tolerance messages that help the host manage power on the bus and for the system.

Table 16-1: In an LPM extended token packet, the bmAttributes field provides information about the requested Sleep state.

Bits	Field	Description
10..9	Reserved	For future use.
8	bRemoteWake	1 = the device can wake the host. 0 = the device cannot wake the host.
7..4	HIRD	Host initiated resume duration (encoded value)
3..0	bLinkState	0001 = L1 (Sleep). Other values reserved.

If you're developing a device that must use as little power as possible, you might choose to support SuperSpeed even if the application doesn't require fast performance. With SuperSpeed's extremely fast data transfers and new low-power states, some devices can save significant power by entering a low-power state between transactions.

Link States

SuperSpeed defines four operational link states:

- U0 is normal operation and is the highest link state. (Note that U0 has the lowest number but the highest power and thus is considered the highest link state.) This is the only state where the link can carry packets.
- U1 is a low-power state with fast transitions to U0. The state has no mandated reduction in bus current, but the link carries no signaling and the device can implement power-saving measures.
- U2 is a more aggressive low-power state with slower transitions to U0. The state has no mandated reduction in bus current, but the link carries no signaling, and the device can turn off clock circuits and implement other power-saving measures that require more time to transition to U0.
- U3 is the Suspend state and is the lowest link state. The link carries no signaling, and a device whose port is in U3 can draw up to 2.5 mA of bus current. A device in the Suspend state must detect Warm Reset (defined in Chapter 18) and wakeup signaling. A device that supports remote wakeup must be capable of sending wakeup signaling.

In addition to the above states, which apply to links, a SuperSpeed device can have one or more functions in the function suspend state while the link and other function(s) in the device may remain in a higher-power state.

For each device, the host calculates U1 and U2 System Exit Latency values that are a measure of the time required to transition from U1 or U2 to U0. For devices with interrupt or isochronous endpoints, the host uses these values in determining whether the device can initiate U1 or U2. If the corresponding Latency value plus one bus interval is greater than the shortest service interval on the device, the host doesn't allow the device to initiate the low-power state.

A link that is in U0 and is not transmitting data or other packets is in the logical idle state and transmits encoded zeroes. A link in U1, U2, or U3 is in the electrical idle state and carries no signaling.

Changing States

Link-level communications control the state of a link. The host doesn't need to know the state of every link on the bus. To conserve power, if a link has no pending upstream traffic, a hub transitions its upstream port to the lowest link state possible. In other words, if a hub's downstream ports are in U1 and U2, the hub can place its upstream port in U1. If all of the ports are in U2, the hub can reduce power further by placing its upstream port in U2. Only a host can request a transition to U3. When a host or hub wants to communicate with a device, any links in the communication path that aren't in U0 must transition to U0.

The mechanism for changing a power state varies with the state, who initiated the change, and whether the change applies to an entire link or a function in a device. Hubs implement host-programmable inactivity timers for each downstream-facing port for use in determining when to enter U1 and U2. Isochronous Timestamp packets don't prevent a device from entering a low-power state. To exit a low-power state, a link uses a hardware handshake implemented via low-frequency periodic signaling (LFPS).

U1

A host, hub, or device can request a transition to U1. The host can send a hub-specific Set Port Feature (PORT_LINK_STATE) request for a downstream-facing port on a hub. The hub then uses hardware-generated link commands to implement the state change on the link. When a hub's downstream-facing port is in U0 and an inactivity timer detects no bus activity on the port for the timer's specified period, the hub uses link commands to request to transition the link to U1. A device can use a device-specific policy in deciding when to request U1 entry via link commands. In all cases, the link partner can refuse to change to the requested state for example, if the port will soon have traffic to send or doesn't support U1.

When a host or device has a packet ready to transmit, a hardware handshake initiates exit from U1 to U0.

U2

When a link is in U1, if the downstream port supports U2 and the link partners' U2 inactivity timers time out, the link silently transitions to U2. When a host or device has a packet ready to transmit, a hardware handshake initiates exit from U2 to U0.

U3

Unlike USB 2.0, SuperSpeed doesn't support global suspends, where the host places the entire bus in the Suspend state by ceasing to send timing markers. SuperSpeed supports only selective suspend and function suspend.

In a selective suspend, a device enters the Suspend state on detecting that the device's link is in U3. Set Port Feature (PORT_LINK_STATE, U3) requests a hub to place a downstream-facing port and its link in U3. The hub uses hardware-generated link commands to implement the state change on the link. The downstream device enters the Suspend state on detecting that the link is in U3.

To suspend the entire bus, the host must request each downstream port on the bus to enter U3. When all of a hub's downstream ports are in U3, a host places the hub's upstream link in U3. Only a host can request to place a link in U3, and hubs must accept requests to place an enabled downstream port in U3.

To wake a device, the host sends a Set Port Feature (PORT_LINK_STATE, U0) request to the downstream-facing hub port that is the device's link partner. The hub uses hardware-generated link commands to transition the link to U0. On detecting that the link is in U0, the downstream device exits the Suspend state. A device can initiate exit from U3 via low frequency periodic signaling as described below under Function Suspend.

Function Suspend

For finer power control, a USB 3.0 host can place an individual function in the function suspend state while allowing other functions in the device (if any) to continue to communicate on the bus. To suspend a function, the host issues a Set Port Feature(FUNCTION_SUSPEND) request to an interface. In the high byte of wIndex, bit 0 requests the suspend state or normal operation, and bit 1 enables or disables function remote wakeup.

To resume communications with a suspended function, a host issues a Set Port Feature(FUNCTION_SUSPEND) request for normal operation. Note that exiting function suspend uses Set Port Feature rather than Clear Port Feature. If the device's link isn't in U0, the downstream-facing hub port that is the device's link partner uses low frequency periodic signaling to initiate the transition to U0. The hub then resumes communicating with the function.

A function with remote wakeup enabled can request to wake by sending a DEV_NOTIFICATION Transaction Packet with a Function Wake notification. If the device's link isn't in U0, before sending the notification, the device uses low frequency periodic signaling to transition the link to U0. The signaling propagates upstream from the device until reaching a hub that isn't in U3 and then propagates back downstream to the device requesting the wakeup.

If the host places a device in the Suspend state when one or more functions are suspended, the functions remain suspended when the device wakes. The host or device must then initiate exiting function suspend for the individual function(s). Both composite and non-composite devices can use function suspend.

Informing the Host of Delays

Hubs help manage bus traffic by informing the host of delays due to a device's being in a low-power state. On receiving a header packet addressed to a port in a low-power state, the hub sends a deferred header packet to the host, which halts communication attempts with the device. When the target port has transitioned to U0, the hub sends the header packet to the device with the Deferred bit set in the Link Control Word. To inform the host that the device is ready to communicate, the device sends an ERDY Transaction Packet.

Latency Tolerance Messages

USB 3.0 hosts can save additional power by obtaining information about the maximum delay each device can tolerate between sending an ERDY Transaction Packet and receiving a response from the host. The host can use more aggressive power management with devices that can handle long delays. The protocols for obtaining this information include the Set Feature(LTM_ENABLE) and Set SEL requests and DEV_NOTIFICATION Transaction Packets with Latency Tolerance Message Device Notifications. The SuperSpeed USB device capability descriptor indicates whether a device supports Latency Tolerance Message notifications.

Using PING

If a host initiates an isochronous transaction with a device in a low-power state, the device might be unable to transition to U0 in time to send or receive data in the scheduled service interval. To prevent this problem, the host uses PING and PING_RESPONSE Transaction Packets. Before beginning the isochronous transfer, the host sends a PING Transaction Packet, which causes all links between the device and host to transition to U0. The device returns a PING_RESPONSE Transaction Packet when the device is ready to transfer data. The host must send the PING far enough in advance of a scheduled transfer to enable the transfer to take place on time.

This use of PING is unrelated to the high-speed PING protocol described in Chapter 2.

Power Management under Windows

Recent PCs manage power according to the *Advanced Configuration and Power Interface Specification* (ACPI). A system that implements ACPI power management enables the operating system to conserve power by shutting down components, including suspending the USB bus, when the computer is idle.

PCs support these low-power, or sleeping, states:

In the S1 state, the display is off and drives are powered down. USB buses are suspended, but VBUS remains powered.

In the S3 state, the PCI bus's main power supply is off and memory isn't accessed, but system memory continues to be refreshed. USB buses are suspended. In older systems, USB's VBUS is not powered in the S3 state. In newer systems, VBUS is powered by the PCI bus's auxiliary supply (Vaux).

In the S4 state, the system context is saved to disk and the system, including the USB bus, is powered off.

You can view and change a system's power-management options in Control Panel > Power Options. Under Windows Vista, you can specify when the system enters S3, called sleep (Figure 16-4). The Advanced Settings tab includes options to enable or disable selective suspend for USB devices under USB settings and to select hibernation (S4) under Battery > Critical battery action.

Under Windows XP, the Power Schemes tab specifies when the system goes into standby and hibernation. Standby is either S1 or S3. On a system that has no USB devices that can wake the system, standby is S3. On a Windows XP system that has a USB keyboard, mouse, or another USB device that can wake the

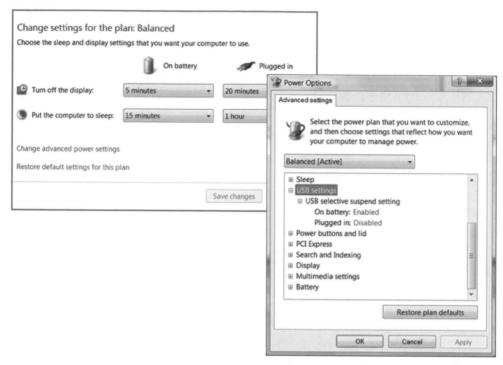

Figure 16-4. Windows Vista enables users to specify power-saving options that determine when USB devices enter the Suspend state.

system, the standby state is S1 due to problems in using S3 with some BIOSes and device hardware. The problems include loss of VBUS in the S3 state, false device removal and arrival notifications on resuming, resetting of devices during suspend and resume, and failure to resume fully.

For devices that have problems resuming from S3, a possible fix is to force the host controller to reset on resuming by adding a ForceHCResetOnResume value to the host controller's registry key. This approach is imperfect because some devices require a host-controller reset while others require no reset. To avoid problems, device designers should take care that their products behave properly whether the host controller resets or not.

To enable or disable remote wakeup capability for a specific device that supports remote wakeup, in Windows' Device Manager, select the device, right-click, select Properties > Power Management, and check or uncheck *Allow this device to bring the computer out of standby.*

17

Testing and Debugging

Besides the chip-specific development boards and debugging software described in Chapter 6, a variety of other hardware and software tools can help with testing and debugging USB devices and their host software. This chapter introduces tools available from the USB-IF and other sources. I also explain what's involved in passing tests for the Certified USB logo and Windows logo.

Tools

Without a doubt the most useful tool for USB device developers is a protocol analyzer, which enables monitoring USB traffic and other bus events. The analyzer collects data on the bus and decodes and displays the requested data. You can watch what happened during enumeration, detect and examine protocol and signaling errors, view data transferred during control, interrupt, bulk, and isochronous transfers, and focus on specific aspects of a communication.

A hardware analyzer is a combination of hardware and software, while a software analyzer consists only of software that runs on the device's host computer. The capabilities of the two types overlap, but each can also record and display information that isn't available to the other type.

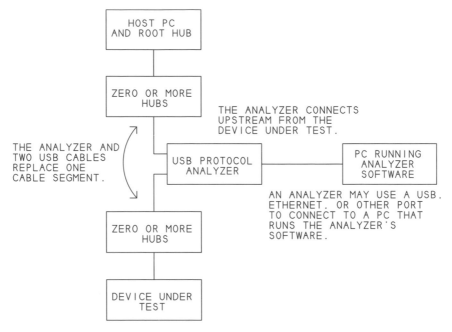

Figure 17-1. A hardware protocol analyzer monitors traffic between a device under test and the device's host. An interface to a PC (or logic analyzer) enables viewing the captured data.

Another useful tool is a traffic generator, which emulates a host or device and offers precise control over what goes out on the bus.

Hardware Protocol Analyzers

A hardware protocol analyzer is a piece of equipment that captures the signals in a cable segment without affecting the traffic in the segment. The analyzer connects in a cable segment upstream from the device under test (Figure 17-1). To enable viewing the captured traffic, the analyzer connects to a PC or logic analyzer. A connection to a PC may use USB or another port type such as Ethernet. Instead of a PC interface, some protocol analyzers connect to logic analyzers from Agilent or Tektronix.

With a hardware analyzer, you can see the data in the cable down to the individual bytes that make up each packet. There's no question about what the host or device did or didn't send. For example, if the host sends an IN token packet, you can see whether the device returned data or a NAK. You can view the packets in every stage of a control request. Time stamps enable you to see how often the host accesses an endpoint.

Analyzers are available from a variety of vendors and in a range of prices, including models that support SuperSpeed. If you develop only low- and full-speed devices, an analyzer that supports only these speeds can save on cost.

In this chapter, I use the Ellisys USB Explorer 200 USB 2.0 analyzer to illustrate the kinds of things you can do with an analyzer. Vendors update and improve their products, and new products become available, so check for the latest information when you're ready to buy.

The Hardware

The Explorer 200 requires two USB host controllers. One communicates with the analyzer and the other controls the bus being monitored. Both host controllers can be in the same PC, but when analyzing high-bandwidth traffic, using two PCs can prevent overflow errors.

One USB cable connects the Explorer to the PC running the Explorer's Visual USB Analysis software. The PC detects the Explorer as a USB device that uses a vendor-specific driver provided by Ellisys.

Two additional USB cables connect the analyzer in a cable segment upstream from the device being tested. One cable connects the analyzer to the device being tested or a hub upstream from the device. The other cable connects the analyzer to the host's root hub or another hub upstream from the analyzer. The combined length of the two cables should total 3 m or less. The cables must be short because the host and device should detect no difference in the bus traffic when the analyzer is present. The cables and the analyzer's electronics together emulate an ordinary cable segment of 5 m or less.

The Software

The Ellisys Visual USB Analysis Software enables you to start and stop data logging and to save, view, and print the results. Figure 17-2 shows data captured by an analyzer. You can specify the amount, type, and format of data the displayed. For less detail, you can elect to hide individual packets, repeated NAKs, and other information. You can specify criteria to display such as specific devices, endpoints, speeds, status codes, and control requests.

A Details pane provides more information about a request, transaction, packet, or other item in a row in the application's main window (Figure 17-3). A Data pane displays the individual bytes in hexadecimal and ASCII. You can also

411

Item	Device	Endpoint	Status	Speed	Comment	Time
Enter text here	Ent...	Enter ...	Ent...	Ente...	Enter text here	Enter text here
▪▪ Reset (4.0 s)						0.000 000 000
Suspended (159.2 ms)						3.954 854 458
Reset (11.0 ms)						4.114 037 395
⊟ GetDescriptor (Device)	0 (1)	0	OK	FS	8 bytes (12 01 00 02 00 00 00 08)	4.189 013 687
⊟ SETUP transaction	0 (1)	0	ACK	FS	8 bytes (80 06 00 01 00 00 40 00)	4.189 013 687
→ SETUP packet	0	0		FS		4.189 013 687
→ DATA0 packet				FS	8 bytes (80 06 00 01 00 00 40 00)	4.189 016 750
← ACK packet			ACK	FS		4.189 025 333
⊟ IN transaction	0 (1)	0	ACK	FS	8 bytes (12 01 00 02 00 00 00 08)	4.190 013 520
→ IN packet	0	0		FS		4.190 013 520
← DATA1 packet				FS	8 bytes (12 01 00 02 00 00 00 08)	4.190 016 625
→ ACK packet			ACK	FS		4.190 025 479
⊟ OUT transaction	0 (1)	0	ACK	FS	No data	4.192 013 250
→ OUT packet	0	0		FS		4.192 013 250
→ DATA1 packet				FS	No data	4.192 016 312
← ACK packet			ACK	FS		4.192 019 583
Reset (11.0 ms)						4.198 025 750
⊟ SetAddress (1)	0 (1)	0	OK	FS	No data	4.264 005 604
⊟ SETUP transaction	0 (1)	0	ACK	FS	8 bytes (00 05 01 00 00 00 00 00)	4.264 005 604
→ SETUP packet	0	0		FS		4.264 005 604
→ DATA0 packet				FS	8 bytes (00 05 01 00 00 00 00 00)	4.264 008 666
← ACK packet			ACK	FS		4.264 017 270
⊟ IN transaction	0 (1)	0	ACK	FS	No data	4.265 005 375
→ IN packet	0	0		FS		4.265 005 375
← DATA1 packet				FS	No data	4.265 008 458

Figure 17-2. Ellisys' USB Explorer 200 protocol analyzer includes Visual USB application software for viewing captured data. This example shows transactions and other events that occurred when a device was attached

search for specific items, including events, token-packet types, traffic to and from a specific device or endpoint, and data.

Additional software modules add support for triggering on events, decoding class-specific information, and exporting captured data in text, XML, and other formats.

Software Protocol Analyzers

A software-only protocol analyzer runs on the host computer of the device being tested. You can view traffic to and from any device that connects to any of the computer's host controllers.

A software analyzer can display driver information that a hardware analyzer can't access. As Chapter 8 explained, Windows drivers communicate with USB devices using I/O Request Packets (IRPs) that contain USB Request Blocks (URBs). A software analyzer can show the IRPs and URBs that a driver has submitted and the responses received from a device.

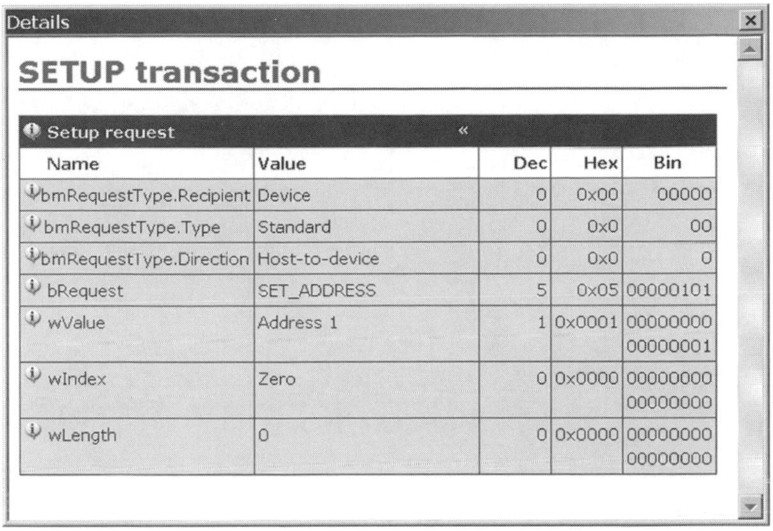

SETUP transaction

Setup request «				
Name	Value	Dec	Hex	Bin
bmRequestType.Recipient	Device	0	0x00	00000
bmRequestType.Type	Standard	0	0x0	00
bmRequestType.Direction	Host-to-device	0	0x0	0
bRequest	SET_ADDRESS	5	0x05	00000101
wValue	Address 1	1	0x0001	00000000 00000001
wIndex	Zero	0	0x0000	00000000 00000000
wLength	0	0	0x0000	00000000 00000000

Figure 17-3. The Details pane in Ellisys' Visual USB software has more information about a request, transaction, packet, or other event.

Software analyzers don't show anything that the host-controller or hub hardware handles on its own. For example, the analyzer won't show how many times an endpoint NAKed a transaction before returning an ACK or the precise time a transaction occurred on the bus.

Some software analyzers use a filter driver that loads when the operating system loads the driver for the device being monitored. Because the filter driver doesn't load until the host has enumerated the device, the analyzer can't show the enumeration requests and other events that occur at device attachment.

Sourcequest, Inc.'s SourceUSB is a software analyzer that records USB I/O requests and other events, including enumeration requests. You can view the requests along with additional information about the system's host controllers, the devices on the host controllers' buses, and the drivers assigned to each host controller and device. Figure 17-4 shows logged requests and additional information about the request in the selected row.

The SourceUSB application can also display a tree of all of the system's host controllers and their attached devices and provide information about the drivers assigned to each host controller and device. As with a hardware analyzer, you have much flexibility in selecting what information you want to log and view.

Another software-only analyzer is the SnoopyPro project, free with source code from *www.sourceforge.net*.

413

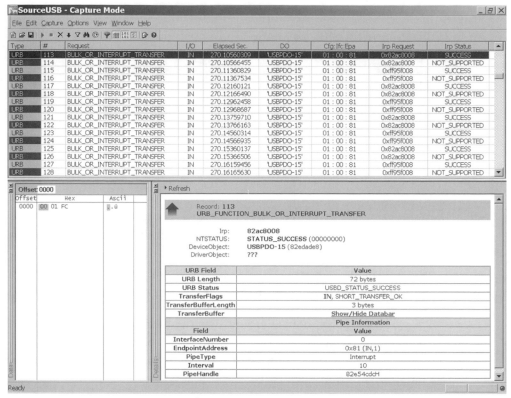

Figure 17-4. SourceUSB's application shows USB I/O requests at a host computer. These requests are for mouse communications.

Traffic Generators

Sometimes it's useful to be able to control bus traffic and signaling beyond what you can do from host software and device firmware. Some protocol analyzers can also function as traffic generators that emulate a host or device and give you precise control over the traffic that the emulated host or device places on the bus. In addition to generating valid traffic, a traffic generator can introduce errors such as bit-stuff and CRC errors. RPM Systems' Root 2 USB Test Host emulates a USB host and enables you to specify traffic to generate on the bus, control the bus voltage, and measure bus current.

The USB-IF provides a free *USB 2.0 Single Step Transaction Debugger* tool that enables initiating individual transactions with a high-speed device, including sending standard control requests.

Testing

The USB-IF and Microsoft offer testing opportunities for developers of USB devices and host software. Passing the tests can earn a product the right to display a Certified USB logo and one or more Microsoft Windows logos, or both types. A logo can give users confidence that a device will work as advertised. A driver that passes Microsoft's tests can receive a digital signature that enables the driver to install without security warnings.

Compliance

The USB-IF's compliance program provides tests for peripherals, hubs, host systems, On-The-Go devices, silicon building blocks, cable assemblies, and connectors. On passing the tests, the USB-IF asserts that the product has "reasonable measures of acceptability" and adds the product to its Integrators List of compliant devices. On receiving a signed license agreement and fee payment, the USB-IF authorizes the product to display a Certified USB logo. Even if you don't submit your device to formal compliance testing, you can use the tests to verify your device's performance.

To pass compliance testing, a device must meet the requirements specified in the appropriate checklists and pass tests of the device's responses to standard control requests, operation under different host-controller types and with other devices on the bus, and electrical performance. The USB 2.0 tests other than high-speed electrical tests are described in *Universal Serial Bus Implementers Forum Full and Low Speed Electrical and Interoperability Compliance Test Procedure*. The specifications, procedures, and tools for high-speed electrical tests are in additional documents and files on the USB-IF's website. Also check the web site for news on USB 3.0 compliance tests.

You can submit a device for compliance testing at a compliance workshop sponsored by the USB-IF or at an independent lab authorized by the USB-IF. To save time and expense, perform the tests as fully as possible on your own before submitting a product for compliance testing

Checklists

The compliance checklists contain a series of questions about a product's specifications and behavior. There are checklists for peripherals, hubs, hub and peripheral silicon, and host systems. The Peripheral checklist covers mechanical design, device states and signals, operating voltages, and power consumption.

Accompanying each question is a reference to a section in the USB specification with more information.

Device Framework

The Device Framework tests verify that a device responds correctly to standard control requests. The USB Command Verifier (USBCV) software utility performs the tests. The *USB Command Verifier Compliance Test Specification* describes the tests. The USBCV software and test-specification document are available from the USB-IF's website.

The USBCV software requires a PC with a USB 2.0 host controller. In addition, any low- or full-speed devices being tested must connect to the host via an external USB 2.0 hub. When you run USBCV, the software replaces the host-controller's driver with its own test-stack driver. On exiting USBCV, the software restores the original driver.

The USB-IF recommends running the software only on hosts that are using Microsoft's USB drivers. You can run the tests while using a USB mouse and keyboard, or you can use a PS/2 mouse and keyboard if the system supports them. Before running USBCV, create a Windows restore point so you can return to your previous system configuration if something goes wrong with the stack switch.

The software has test suites for Chapter 9, Current Measurement, HID, Hub, and OTG.

In the Chapter 9 tests, the host issues the standard control requests defined in Chapter 9 of the USB 2.0 specification and performs additional checks on the information returned by a device (Figure 17-5). For example, on retrieving a device descriptor, the software checks to see that the bMaxPacketSize0 value is valid for the device's speed and that the bDeviceClass value is either a value for a standard class or FFh (vendor-defined). The software requests the device descriptor when the device is in the default, address, and configured states, at both full and high speeds if the device supports both, and in every supported configuration.

The Chapter 9 tests also include these:

- Enumerate the device multiple times with different addresses.
- Verify that all bulk and interrupt endpoints can be halted and unhalted with Set Feature and Clear Feature requests.

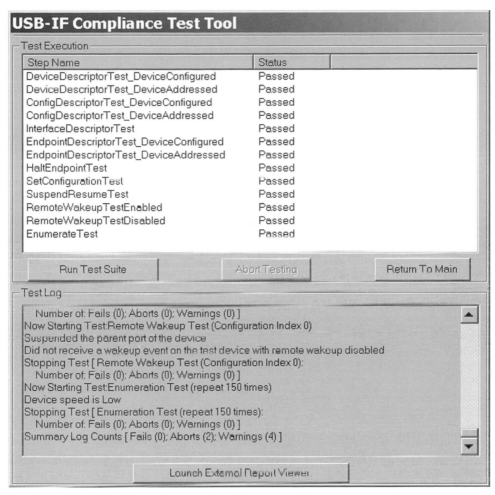

Figure 17-5. USBCV's Chapter 9 tests check the device's responses to the control requests defined in Chapter 9 of the USB specification.

- Ensure that the device returns STALL in response to receiving a request for an unsupported descriptor type.
- Ensure that the device returns STALL in response to receiving a Set Feature request for an unsupported feature.
- Suspend and resume the device.
- If the device supports remote wakeup, suspend the device and request the user to perform an action to wake the device.

The Current Measurement test suite pauses with the device in the unconfigured and configured states to enable measuring the bus current. In the unconfigured state, the device should draw no more than 100 mA. When configured, the device should draw no more than the amount specified in the bMaxPower field of the configuration descriptor for the currently active configuration.

Additional test suites provide tests for hubs, HID-class devices, and devices that return On-The-Go descriptors.

The software has two modes. Compliance Test mode runs an entire test suite. Debug mode enables selecting and running a single test within a suite and offers more control, such as selecting a configuration to use when running a test.

Interoperability Tests

The interoperability tests emulate a user's experience by testing a product with different host controllers and with a variety of other USB devices in use. The device must be tested under both EHCI/UHCI and EHCI/OHCI hosts and under hubs that do and don't support high speed. To enable testing both implementations of the S3 Sleep state, the device must be tested under a host that maintains VBUS and a host that removes VBUS on entering the S3 state. Devices are tested under these conditions:

- The bus is carrying control, bulk, interrupt, and isochronous transfers.
- There are five external hubs between the device and host.
- The device is 30 m from the host (28 m for low-speed devices).
- The bus is carrying full- and high-speed traffic.

For performing the tests, the test specification defines a Gold Tree configuration that contains a variety of hubs and other devices on the bus with the device under test. The test specification revision 1.3 lists these devices in the Gold Tree:

- Video camera: high speed, uses isochronous transfers, high power, bus powered.
- Mass storage device: high speed, uses bulk transfers, self powered.
- Flash media drive: high speed, uses bulk transfers, bus powered.
- Keyboard: low speed HID.
- Mouse: low speed HID.

- Seven hubs, consisting of five hubs that support all three bus speeds including one hub with multiple transaction translators and two hubs that support low and full speeds only.

The devices attach to the host in the configuration shown in Figure 17-6. Test labs can provide Gold Tree configurations.

On attachment, the host must enumerate and install the driver for the device (with user assistance to identify the driver's location if appropriate). The device must operate properly while the other devices in the Gold Tree are also operating. In addition, the device must continue to operate properly after each of these actions:

- Detach the device and reattach it to the same port.
- Detach the device and attach it to a different port.
- Do a warm boot. (Start > Shutdown > Restart.)
- Do a cold boot. (Start > Shutdown > Shutdown. Turn on the PC.)
- When the device is active, place the system in the S1 Sleep state and resume.
- When the device is idle, place the system in the S1 Sleep state and resume.
- When the device is active, place the system in the S3 Sleep state and resume.

A high-speed device must also be fully functional at full speed unless the USB-IF grants a waiver. The test specification has more details about the tests.

Waivers

A device can earn a USB Logo without passing every test. At its discretion, the USB-IF may grant a waiver of a requirement. For example, before the specification increased the limit for all devices, the USB-IF granted waivers to devices that drew up to 2.5 mA in the Suspend state.

The Certified USB Logo

A device that passes compliance testing is eligible to display the Certified USB logo. The logo also indicates if a device supports SuperSpeed, high speed, Certified Wireless, and On-The-Go (Figure 17-7). To use the logo, you must sign the USB-IF Trademark License Agreement. If you're not a member of the USB-IF, you must pay a logo administration fee ($2000 at this writing). The logo is different from the USB icon described in Chapter 19.

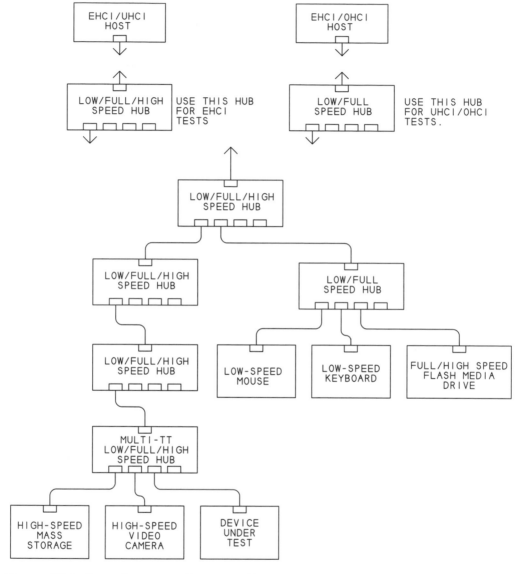

Figure 17-6. Compliance testing uses this Gold Tree configuration for testing how a device behaves in a system where other USB devices are in use.

TM & © 2000 USB-IF. All rights reserved.

TM & © 2000 USB-IF. All rights reserved.

TM & © 2000 USB-IF. All rights reserved.

TM & © 2000 USB-IF. All rights reserved.

TM & © 2008 USB-IF. All rights reserved.

© 2004 USB-IF. All rights reserved.

Figure 17-7. Devices that pass compliance testing can display a Certified USB logo. The logo indicates if the device supports high speed SuperSpeed, On-The-Go, or Wireless USB as appropriate. (Images courtesy of the USB Implementers Forum.)

Windows Logo

Microsoft licenses logos for display by qualifying products and their marketing materials. To earn the right to display a logo, the manufacturer must submit test logs that demonstrate that the product meets Microsoft's standards for compatibility, reliability, and security.

Benefits of a Windows logo include increased customer confidence in the product, the ability to distribute drivers via Windows Update, listing the product on Microsoft's Windows Marketplace, and inclusion in the *Windows Logo'd Products List* and *Windows Server Catalog*.

Tests

To qualify for a Windows logo, a USB device must pass a series of tests based on the USBCV tests from USB-IF. Other tests deal with device installation and for vendor-provided drivers, driver reliability. Devices such as printer, keyboard, and storage device have function-specific tests.

Each Windows family (such as Windows Vista, Windows XP, Windows Server 2008) has its own logo. Recent Windows editions support two logo versions. For example, under Windows Vista, products that meet baseline requirements can earn the *Works with Windows Vista* logo, while products that meet more rigorous requirements for ease of use, performance, and security can earn the *Certified for Windows Vista* logo.

Standard device functions each have a logo program with function-specific requirements. Devices that don't fit a category with a logo program can't display a Windows logo, but the manufacturer can submit the driver to Microsoft's Unclassified Signature program to obtain a digital signature. A submitted driver must pass tests on both 32-bit and 64-bit Windows editions.

The Windows Logo Kit (WLK) is a set of tools that developers can use to test devices and drivers on Windows. The kit is a free download from Microsoft.

Obtaining a license to display a Windows logo requires following these steps:

1. Download the WDK and WLK from Microsoft.

2. Obtain a code-signing ID and set up an organizational account with Microsoft's Windows Quality Online Services (Winqual) program. One form of code-signing ID is a Microsoft Authenticode Code Signing Digital ID. This ID is a digital certificate that a manufacturer can also use to sign driver files as described later in this chapter. A lower cost option is a VeriSign Organizational

Certificate, which enables opening a Winqual account but isn't valid for use with hardware products or for driver signing.

3. Use the Driver Test Manager (DTM) software in the WLK to perform the required tests and generate a submission package with test results. The product manufacturer must perform all tests either in house or by contracting with a test lab. You don't send the product to Microsoft.

4. When the product has passed the required tests, submit the package created by the DTM to Winqual. Winqual also requires a product name and a signed logo license agreement. On receiving approval, the product and its marketing materials are licensed to display the logo(s) applied for.

At this writing, the fee to set up a Winqual account is $250, and the fee to submit a product for logo licensing is $250. Each Windows family requires a separate submission fee. These fees are in addition to the fee to obtain a code-signing ID.

Digital Signatures

A digital signature for a driver enables Windows to verify that the driver files haven't been modified since the driver was signed and to identify the source, or publisher, of the driver. The digital signature is a data set contained in a catalog (*.cat*) file associated with the driver or embedded in the driver itself.

Microsoft or another certification authority (CA) issues a digital signature when a driver passes WHQL testing. For drivers that haven't passed WHQL testing, a vendor with an Authenticode Code Signing Digital ID can sign a driver using Microsoft's free SignTool utility.

A device's INF file can name a catalog file. Each INF file has its own catalog file, and one INF file can support multiple devices. Any change in an INF file, including adding a new Product ID or device release number, requires obtaining a new digital signature.

Recent Windows editions store information relating to digital signatures in two databases called *certificate stores*. The Trusted Publishers certificate store contains information about the Authenticode certificates of publishers whose drivers are trusted. Users with administrative access can add publishers to this store. The Trusted Root Certification Authorities certificate store contains information about CAs that have met Microsoft's requirements. Users with administrative access can add private CAs to this store.

Whether a driver installs on a system depends on the Windows edition, the system's security settings, whether the person installing the driver has administrative access, and whether the driver is signed. If the driver is signed, successful installation can depend on the source of the signature, whether the driver publisher's certificate is in the system's Trusted Publishers certificate store, and whether the CA that issued the publisher's certificate is in the Trusted Root Certification Authorities certificate store.

The 64-bit Windows editions require signed drivers. The 32-bit Windows editions will install unsigned drivers but may display warnings depending on system settings. Under Windows Vista, only users with administrative access can install unsigned drivers.

A driver signed by the Windows logo program installs without triggering security warnings. For other signed drivers, a dialog box with a security warning may appear if the driver publisher's certificate isn't in the computer's Trusted Publishers certificate store. In the dialog box, selecting the option to always trust software from the publisher adds that publisher to the system's Trusted Publishers certificate store.

18

Packets on the Bus

Understanding how data is encoded on the bus can help in understanding the capabilities and limits of devices. This chapter presents the essentials of the USB's encoding and data formats for USB 2.0 and SuperSpeed.

USB 2.0

The USB 2.0 specification defines bus states that correspond to signal voltages on the bus or conditions that the voltages signify. Different cable segments may be in different bus states. For example, in response to a request from the host, a hub might place one of its downstream ports in the Reset state while its other ports are in the Idle state. Low/full speed and high speed each have different defined bus states, though with many similarities.

Low Speed and Full Speed Bus States

Low and full speed support the same bus states, though some are defined differently depending on the speed of the cable segment. A low-speed segment is a segment between a low-speed device and its nearest hub. A full-speed segment is any other segment that carries data at low- or full-speed bit rates.

Differential 0 and Differential 1

When transferring data, the two states on the bus are Differential 0 and Differential 1. A Differential 0 exists when D+ is a logic low and D- is a logic high. A Differential 1 exists when D+ is a logic high and D- is a logic low. Chapter 19 has details about the voltages.

The Differential 0/1s don't translate directly into zero and one data states but instead indicate either a change in logic level, no change in logic level, or a bit stuff, as explained later in this chapter.

Single-ended 0

The Single-ended 0 (SE0) state occurs when both D+ and D- are logic low. The bus uses the SE0 state when entering the EOP, Disconnect, and Reset states.

Single-ended 1

The complement of SE0 is the Single-ended 1 (SE1). This state occurs when both D+ and D- are logic high. This is an invalid bus state and should never occur except as specified in the USB battery-charging specification.

Data J and Data K

In addition to the Differential 0 and Differential 1 states, which are defined by voltages on the lines, USB also defines two Data bus states, J and K. These are defined by whether the bus state is Differential 0 or Differential 1 and the speed of the cable segment:

Bus State	Data State	
	Low Speed	Full Speed
Differential 0	Data J	Data K
Differential 1	Data K	Data J

Defining the J and K states in this way makes it possible to use one terminology to describe an event or logic state even though the voltages on low- and full-speed lines differ. For example, a Start-of-Packet state exists when the bus changes from Idle to the K state. On a full-speed segment, the state occurs when D- becomes more positive than D+, while on a low-speed segment, the state occurs when D+ becomes more positive than D-.

Idle

In the Idle state, no drivers are active. On a full-speed segment, D+ is more positive than D-, while on a low-speed segment, D- is more positive than D+. Shortly after device attachment, a hub determines whether a device is low or full speed by checking the voltages on the Idle bus at the device's port.

Resume

When a device is in the Suspend state, a Data K state at the device's port signifies a resume from Suspend.

Start-of-Packet

The Start-of-Packet (SOP) bus state exists when the lines change from the Idle state to the K data state. Every transmitted low- or full-speed packet begins with an SOP.

End-of-Packet

The End-of-Packet (EOP) state exists when a receiver has been in the SE0 state for at least one bit time followed by a Data J state for at least one bit time. A receiver may optionally accept a shorter minimum time for the Data J state. At the driver, an SE0 is approximately two bit widths. Every transmitted low- or full-speed packet ends with an EOP.

Disconnect

A downstream port is in the Disconnect state when an SE0 has persisted for at least 2.5 μs.

Connect

A downstream port enters the Connect state when the bus has been in the Idle state for at least 2.5 μs and no more than 2.0 ms.

Reset

When an SE0 has lasted for 10 ms, the device must be in the Reset state. A device may enter the Reset state after an SE0 of at least 2.5 μs. A full-speed device that is capable of high-speed communications performs the high-speed handshake during the Reset state.

On exiting the Reset state, a device must be operating at its correct speed and must respond to communications directed to the default address (00h).

High Speed Bus States

Many of the high-speed bus states correspond to states for low and full speed, but a few are unique to high speed, and some low/full-speed states have no equivalents at high speed.

High-speed Differential 0 and Differential 1

The two bus states that exist when transferring high-speed data are High-speed Differential 0 and High-speed Differential 1. As with low and full speeds, a High-speed Differential 0 exists when D+ is a logic low and D- is a logic high, and a High-speed Differential 1 exists when D+ is a logic high and D- is a logic low. The voltage requirements differ at high speed, however, and high speed has additional requirements for AC differential levels.

High-speed Data J and Data K

The definitions for High-speed Data J and Data K states are identical to those for full-speed J and K.

Bus State	Data State (high speed)
Differential 0	High-speed Data K
Differential 1	High-speed Data J

Chirp J and Chirp K

The Chirp J and Chirp K bus states are present only during the high-speed detection handshake. The handshake occurs when a USB 2.0 hub has placed a downstream bus segment in the Reset state. In a Chirp J, D+ is more positive than D-, and in a Chirp K, D- is more positive than D+.

A high-speed device must use full speed on attaching to the bus. The high-speed detection handshake enables a high-speed device to tell a USB 2.0 hub that the device supports high speed and to transition to high-speed communications.

As Chapter 4 explained, shortly after detecting device attachment, a device's hub places a device's port and bus segment in the Reset state. When a high-speed-capable device detects the Reset, the device places its line in the

Chirp K state for 1–7 ms. A hub that communicates upstream at high speed detects the Chirp K and in response, sends an alternating sequence of Chirp K and Chirp J. The sequence continues until shortly before the Reset state ends. On detecting the Chirp K and Chirp J sequence, the device disconnects its full-speed pull-up, enables its high-speed terminations, and enters the Default state. A hub that communicates upstream at low/full speed ignores the device's Chirp K. The device doesn't see the answering sequence and knows that communications must take place at full speed.

High-speed Squelch

The High-speed Squelch state indicates an invalid signal. High-speed receivers must include circuits that detect the Squelch state, indicated by a differential bus voltage of 100 mV or less.

High-speed Idle

In the High-speed Idle state, no high-speed drivers are active and the low/full-speed drivers assert SE0. Both D+ and D- are between -10 and +10 mV.

Start of High-speed Packet

A Start-of-High-speed Packet (HSSOP) exists when a segment changes from the High-speed Idle state to the High-speed Data K state. Every high-speed packet begins with a Start of High-speed Packet.

End of High-speed Packet

An End of High-speed Packet (HSEOP) exists when the bus changes from the High-speed Data K or Data J state to the High-speed Idle state. Every high-speed packet ends with an End of High-speed Packet.

High-speed Disconnect

Removing a high-speed device from the bus also removes the high-speed line terminations at the device. Removing the terminations causes the differential voltage at the hub's port to double. A differential voltage of at least 625 mV on the data lines indicates the High-speed Disconnect state. A USB 2.0 hub contains circuits that detect this voltage.

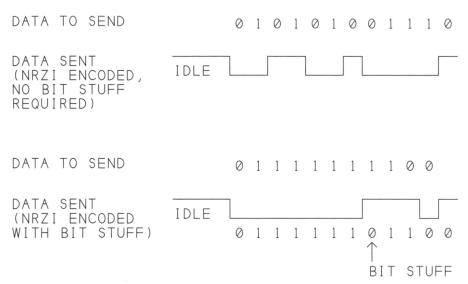

Figure 18-1. In NRZI encoding, a 0 causes a change and a 1 causes no change. Bit stuffing adds a 0 after six consecutive 1s.

Data Encoding

All data on a USB 2.0 bus is encoded using a format called *non-return to zero inverted* (NRZI) with bit stuffing. The encoding ensures that the receiver remains synchronized with the transmitter without the overhead of sending a separate clock signal or Start and Stop bits with each byte.

If you use an oscilloscope or logic analyzer to view USB data on the bus, you'll find that reading the bits isn't as easy as matching voltage levels to logic levels. Instead of defining logic zeroes and ones as voltages, NRZI encoding defines logic zero as a voltage change, and logic one as a voltage that remains the same. Figure 18-1 shows an example. Each logic zero results in a change from the previous state. Each logic one results in no change in the voltages. The bits transmit least-significant-bit first.

Fortunately, USB hardware performs the encoding and decoding automatically so device developers and programmers don't have to do it. The encoded data is harder to interpret on an oscilloscope or logic analyzer, but as Chapter 17 showed, a protocol analyzer will decode the data for you.

Staying Synchronized

Unlike other interfaces, USB requires no Start and Stop bits or clock line in the cable. Instead, USB 2.0 synchronizes the sender and receiver by using bit stuffing and SYNC fields. Each of these adds some overhead, but the amount is minimal, especially with large packets.

Bit Stuffing

The encoding uses bit stuffing because the receiver synchronizes on transitions. Data that is all zeroes has plenty of transitions. But for data that contains a long string of 1s, the lack of transitions could cause the receiver to get out of sync.

After six consecutive 1s, the transmitter stuffs, or inserts, a zero (represented by a transition). The bit stuffing ensures at least one transition for every seven bit widths. The receiver detects and discards any bit that follows six consecutive 1s. The overhead for bit-stuffing in random data is just 0.8%, or one stuff bit per 125 data bits.

SYNC Field

Because devices and the host don't share a clock, the receiver has no way of knowing exactly when a transmitter will send a transition that marks the beginning of a new packet. Thus, each packet begins with a SYNC field to enable the receiving device to align, or synchronize, its clock to the transmitted data. For low and full speeds, the SYNC pattern is eight bits: KJKJKJKK. The transition from Idle to the first K serves as a sort of Start bit that indicates the arrival of a new packet.

For high speed, the SYNC pattern is 32 bits: fifteen KJ repetitions, followed by KK. A high speed hub repeating a packet can drop up to four bits from the beginning of the sync field, so a SYNC field repeated by the fifth external hub in series can be as short as 12 bits.

The alternating Ks and Js provide transitions for synchronizing, and the final two Ks mark the end of the field. After receiving the SYNC pattern, the receiving device can accurately clock in the remaining bits in the packet. The price for synchronizing is adding 8 to 32 bit times to each packet. Large packets are thus much more efficient than smaller ones.

End of Packet

An EOP returns the bus to the Idle state in preparation for the next SYNC field. The EOP signal is different for low/full and high speed.

The low- or full-speed EOP is an SE0 that lasts for two bit widths.

At high speed, the signal is more complicated. High-speed receivers treat any bit-stuff error as an end of packet, so an HSEOP must cause a bit-stuff error.

For all high-speed packets except SOFs, the HSEOP is an encoded byte of 01111111 without bit stuffing. If the preceding bit was a J, the HSEOP is KKKKKKKK. The initial zero causes the first bit to be a change of state from J to K, and the following 1s mean that the rest of the bits don't change. If the preceding bit was a K, the HSEOP is JJJJJJJJ. The initial zero causes the first bit to be a change of state from K to J, and the following 1s mean that the rest of the bits don't change. In either case, the sequence of seven 1s causes a bit stuff error.

In high-speed SOFs, the HSEOP is 40 bits. This longer packet allows a hub time to detect the doubled differential voltage that indicates that a device has been removed from the bus. The encoded byte begins with a zero, followed by 39 ones, which results in an HSEOP consisting of 40 Js or 40 Ks. As with low and full speeds, this sequence results in a bit-stuff error that the receiver treats as an EOP.

Timing Accuracy

One tradeoff of increased speed is stricter timing requirements. High speed has the strictest timing, while low speed is the most tolerant. These are the tolerances for the clock at each speed:

Speed	Tolerance
Low	1.5%
Full	0.25%
High	0.05%

Devices typically derive their timing from a crystal. Many factors can affect a crystal's frequency, including initial accuracy, capacitive loading, aging of the crystal, supply voltage, and temperature. Because of its wider tolerance, low speed can use inexpensive ceramic resonators instead of quartz crystals

The signaling rate at a host or USB 2.0 hub must be within 0.05%, of the specified rate at all speeds. The frame intervals must be accurate as well, at 1 ms

±500 ns per frame or 125.0 ±62.5 µs per microframe. Each hub has its own timing source and synchronizes its transmissions to the host's SOF signals in each frame or microframe.

The USB specification also defines limits for data jitter, which is small variations in the timing of the individual bit transitions. Factors that affect data jitter are differences in the rise and fall times of the drivers, clock jitter, and random noise.

Packet Format

As Chapter 2 explained, all USB 2.0 data travels in packets, which contain information in defined fields. Table 18-1 lists the fields that USB 2.0 packets contain and their purposes.

SYNC

Each packet begins with an 8-bit SYNC field, as described earlier. The SYNC Field serves as the Start-of-Packet delimiter.

Packet Identifier

The packet identifier field (PID) is 8 bits. Bits 3..0 identify the packet type and bits 7..4 are the complement of these bits for use in error checking.

Chapter 2 introduced the PID codes for token, data, handshake and special packets. The lower two bits identify the PID type, and the upper two bits identify the specific PID.

Address

The address field is seven bits that identify the device the host is communicating with.

Endpoint

The endpoint field is four bits that identify an endpoint number within a device.

Frame Number

The frame-number field is eleven bits that identify the frame. The host sends this data in the SOF packet that begins each frame or microframe. After 7FFh, the number rolls over to zero. A full-speed host maintains an 11-bit counter

Table 18-1: USB 2.0 packets contain fields with defined contents.

Field Name	Size (bits)	Packet Types	Purpose
SYNC	8	all	Start of packet and synchronization
PID	8	all	Identify the packet type
Address	7	IN, OUT, Setup	Identify the function address
Endpoint	4	IN, OUT, Setup	Identify the endpoint
Frame Number	11	SOF	Identify the frame
Data	0 to 8192 (1024 bytes) for USB 2.0; 0 to 8184 (1023 bytes) for USB 1.x	Data0, Data1	Data
Token CRC	5	IN, OUT, Setup	Detect errors
Data CRC	16	Data0, Data1	Detect errors

that increments once per frame. A high-speed host maintains a 14-bit counter that increments once per microframe. Only bits 3–13 of the microframe counter transmit in the frame number field, so the frame number increments once per frame, with eight microframes in sequence having the same frame number.

Data

The Data field may range from zero to 1024 bytes, depending on the transfer type, the bus speed, and the amount of data in the transaction.

CRC

The CRC field is 5 bits for address and endpoint fields and 16 bits for data fields. The transmitting hardware normally inserts the CRC bits and the receiving hardware does the required error checking.

Inter-Packet Delay

USB 2.0 carries data from multiple sources, in both directions, on one pair of wires. Data can travel in just one direction at a time. To ensure that the previous transmitting device has had time to switch off its driver, the bus requires a brief delay between the end of one packet and the beginning of the next packet in a transaction. This delay is short, however, and devices must switch directions quickly.

The USB specification defines the delays differently for low/full and high speed. The delays are handled by hardware and require no support in code.

Test Modes

For use in compliance testing, the USB 2.0 specification adds five new test modes that all host controllers, hubs, and high-speed-capable devices must support.

An upstream-facing port enters a test mode in response to a Set Feature request with TEST_MODE in the wValue field. A downstream-facing port enters a test mode in response to the hub-class request Set Port Feature with PORT_TEST in the wValue field. In both cases, the wIndex field contains the port number and the test number. All downstream ports on a hub with a port to be tested must be in the suspended, disabled, or disconnected state.

An upstream-facing port exits the test mode when the device powers down and back up. A downstream-facing port exits the test mode when the hub is reset.

These are the five test modes:

Test_J

Value. 01h.

Action. The transceiver enters and remains in the High-speed Data J state.

Purpose. Test the high output drive level on D+.

Test_K

Value. 02h.

Action. The transceiver enters and remains in the High-speed Data K state.

Purpose. Test the high output drive level on D-.

Test_SE0_NAK

Value. 03h.

Action. The transceiver enters and remains in high-speed receive mode. Upstream-facing ports respond to IN token packets with NAK.

Purpose. Test output impedance, low-level output voltage, and loading characteristics. Test device squelch-level circuits. Provide a stimulus-response test for basic functional testing.

Test_Packet

Value. 04h.

Action. Repetitively transmit the test packet defined by the USB specification.

Purpose. Test rise and fall times, eye pattern, jitter, and other dynamic waveform specifications.

Test_Force_Enable

Value. 05h.

Action. Enable downstream-facing hub ports in high-speed mode. Packets arriving at the upstream-facing port are repeated at the port being tested. The disconnect-detect bit can be polled while varying the loading on the port.

Purpose. Measure the disconnect-detection threshold.

Other Values

Test-mode values 06h through 3Fh are reserved for future standard tests. Values C0–FFh are available for vendor-defined tests. All other values are reserved.

SuperSpeed

SuperSpeed's fast, dual-simplex interface and new power-management capabilities require different encoding, packet formats, and low-level protocols. A SuperSpeed transmitter scrambles and encodes data to be sent on the bus. A SuperSpeed receiver decodes and de-scrambles the received data.

Data Scrambling

Data scrambling eliminates repetitive patterns in the data. Doing so spreads the radiated EMI over a wider frequency spectrum and helps in meeting FCC requirements. To scramble data to be transmitted, a free-running linear feedback shift register implements a polynomial defined in the USB 3.0 specification. The transmitter XORs the output of the shift register with the data bits. Descrambling uses a complementary mechanism to recover the unscrambled data.

Encoding

SuperSpeed uses 8b/10b data encoding as specified in ANSI INCITS 230-1994. Other interfaces that use this encoding include PCI Express, Gigabit

Ethernet and IEEE-1394b. The encoding converts each byte value to a 10-bit Data Symbol for transmitting. The encoded data has no more than five ones or zeroes in series and contains equal numbers of ones and zeroes over time. As with USB 2.0 data, frequent transitions enable the receiver to synchronize with the transmitted data without requiring a separate clock line. The roughly equal numbers of transmitted ones and zeroes provide DC balance, which prevents errors that could occur due to a DC component in the signal. The encoding also enables error detecting by monitoring the number of received ones and zeroes over time.

Because the encoded data has more bits than the data being encoded, extra symbols are available to perform special functions. Data Symbols represent values from 00h to FFh and Special Symbols perform functions used in framing data and managing link-level communications.

The SuperSpeed signaling rate, or speed of the bits on the wires in each direction, is 5 Gbps. The USB 3.0 specification refers to the rate as 5 GT/s (GigaTransfers per second). The 8b/10b encoding increases the number of bits to be transmitted by 25%, so 5 Gbps on the bus translates to 4 Gbps, or 500 MB/s, of unencoded data. Framing, error detecting, and other protocols reduce the theoretical maximum data throughput to around 400 MB/s in each direction.

SuperSpeed links use low-frequency periodic signaling (LFPS) for exiting low-power states and performing Warm Resets. The signaling consists of bursts of a frequency for a specified time and repeat rate. The LFPS frequency is in the range 10–50 MHz, is easy to generate, and uses little power.

Link Layer

A SuperSpeed link is the physical and logical connection between two ports. The physical connection consists of a cable segment and the two ports, or link partners, the cable connects. The link partners manage the link by communicating via link commands and other signaling on the link when the wires aren't carrying other traffic. Each port provides state machines and buffers to manage the connection and data transfers with the link partner. State machines generate link commands to acknowledge received header packets, recover from errors, implement flow control, and manage power on the link. An upstream-facing port must detect when its link has been idle for 10 µs and send a special link command to indicate that the port is present. Link commands transmit when the link isn't carrying Transaction Packets. Downstream-facing ports detect device connection and removal and wakeup signaling. Link-layer protocols define how the link manages buffers, frames packets, and detects received packets. The link layer also handles training and synchronizing to establish connectivity between a device (which may be a hub) and its upstream link partner. To synchronize, a link partner transmits defined series of bytes called Ordered Sets, which the receiving link partner detects.

Reset

SuperSpeed defines two major categories of reset. A PowerOn Reset restores memory, registers, and other storage in the device to their default power-on states. An InBand Reset resets port settings and places the link in the U0 state while remaining powered. Two types of InBand Reset are the Warm Reset and Hot Reset. A Warm Reset uses low frequency periodic signaling and takes around 100 ms. A Hot Reset uses link-level training sequences of Ordered Sets, is much faster, and leaves more settings unchanged in the device.

The host requests an in InBand reset by issuing a hub-class Set Port Feature(Port_Reset) or SetPortFeature(BH_Port_Reset) request to the hub that is the target device's link partner. On receiving a request for a BH_Port_Reset, the hub issues a Warm Reset to the device. On receiving a request for a Port_Reset, if the link is in U3, the hub uses a Warm Reset, and if the link is in U0, the hub uses a Hot Reset. For other states, the USB 3.0 specification defines how a hub decides which reset to use.

19

The Electrical and Mechanical Interface

All of the protocols and program code in the world are no use if the signals don't make it down the wires in good shape. The electrical and mechanical interface play an important part in making USB a reliable way to transfer information.

If you're using USB-compliant cables and components, you don't need to know much about the electrical and mechanical interface. If you're designing printed-circuit boards with USB interfaces, you should understand the interfaces and how they affect your project's circuits.

This chapter presents the essentials about drivers and receivers and options for cables and connectors for USB 2.0 and USB 3.0. Those who want to go cable free will find a discussion of wireless options.

USB 2.0 Transceivers

The electrical signals on a USB 2.0 cable vary depending on the speed of the cable segment. Low-, full-, and high-speed signaling each use a different edge rate, which is a measure of the rise and fall times of the voltages on the lines and thus the amount of time required for an output to switch. The transceivers and supporting circuits that produce and detect the bus signals also vary depending on speed.

At any USB 2.0 speed, a transceiver must withstand the shorting of D+, D-, or both to GND, the other data line, or the cable shield at the connector. A requirement to withstand shorting to VBUS was reduced to a recommendation with the *5V Short Circuit Withstand Requirement Change* ECN to the USB 2.0 specification. Research showed that shorts to VBUS are extremely unlikely and that removing the requirement would allow reduced silicon area and power savings on chips.

Cable Segments

A cable segment connects a device (which may be a hub) to an upstream hub (which may be the root hub at the host). A segment's speed depends on the speed of the end device and the speeds supported by the host and upstream hubs. Figure 19-1 illustrates.

Low-speed segments exist only between low-speed devices and the hubs the devices' cables connect to. A low-speed segment carries only low-speed data and uses low-speed's edge rate and an inverted polarity compared to full speed.

A full-speed segment exists when the segment's downstream device communicates at full speed. When the downstream device is a hub, the segment may also carry data to and from low-speed devices that are downstream from the hub. In this situation, the low-speed data on the full-speed segment uses low-speed's bit rate but full speed's polarity and edge rate. The hub that connects to the low-speed device converts between low and full speed's polarity and edge rates. Full-speed segments never carry data at high speed. A high-speed-capable device that connects to a USB 1.x hub communicates at full speed.

High-speed segments exist when the host is USB 2.0 and all upstream hubs between the host and hub are USB 2.0. When the downstream device is a hub, the segment may also carry data to and from low- and full-speed devices that are downstream from the hub. All data in a high-speed segment travels at high speed, and the transaction translator in a downstream hub converts between low or full speed and high speed as needed.

On attachment, all USB 2.0 devices must communicate at low or full speed. When possible, a high-speed-capable device transitions from full to high speed shortly after the device is attached, during the high-speed detection handshake.

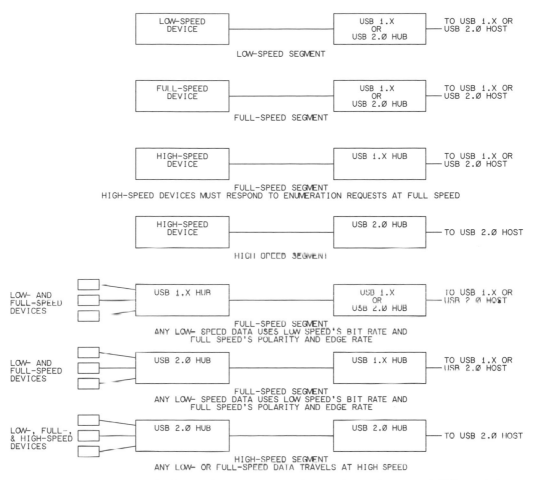

Figure 19-1. The speed of data in a segment depends on the capabilities of the device and its upstream hub.

Low- and Full-Speed Transceivers

Transceivers for low and full speeds can have a simpler design compared to transceivers for high speed.

Low- and Full-Speed Differences

Low-speed data differs electrically from full-speed data in three ways. The bit rate is slower, at 1.5 Mbps compared to 12 Mbps for full speed. The polarity of low-speed traffic is inverted compared to full speed. And low speed has a slower

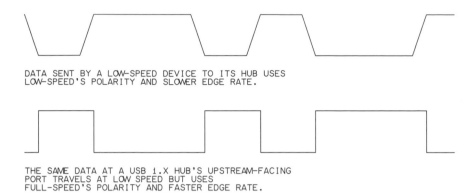

DATA SENT BY A LOW-SPEED DEVICE TO ITS HUB USES
LOW-SPEED'S POLARITY AND SLOWER EDGE RATE.

THE SAME DATA AT A USB 1.X HUB'S UPSTREAM-FACING
PORT TRAVELS AT LOW SPEED BUT USES
FULL-SPEED'S POLARITY AND FASTER EDGE RATE.

Figure 19-2. a USB 1.x hub converts between low- and full-speed's polarities and edge rates. (Not drawn to scale.)

edge rate compared to full speed. Figure 19-2 illustrates. The slower edge rate reduces reflected voltages on the line and makes it possible to use cables that have less shielding and are thus cheaper to make and physically more flexible.

The transceiver's hardware doesn't care about the signal polarity. The transceiver just retransmits the logic levels at its inputs. A driver that supports both speeds, such as a driver for a hub's downstream port, must switch between the two edge rates as needed.

The Circuits

Figure 19-3 shows port circuits and cable segments for low- and full-speed communications. Each transceiver contains a differential driver and receiver for sending and receiving data on the bus's twisted pair.

When transmitting data, the driver has two outputs that are 180 degrees out of phase: when one output is high, the other is low. A single driver can support both low and full speeds with an input that selects the edge rate.

The differential receiver detects the voltage difference between the lines. A differential receiver has two inputs and defines logic levels in terms of the voltage difference between the inputs. The output of the differential receiver is also specified as a logic-high or logic-low voltage referenced to ground.

Each port has two single-ended receivers that detect the voltages on D+ and D- with reference to signal ground. The logic states of the receivers' outputs indicate whether the bus is low or full speed or whether the bus is in the SE0 state.

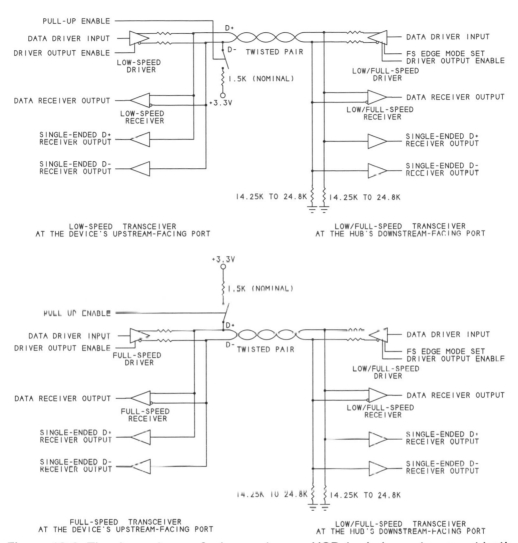

Figure 19-3. The downstream-facing ports on a USB 1.x hub must support both low and full speeds (except for ports with embedded or permanently attached devices). A device's upstream-facing port supports one speed. (Adapted from *Universal Serial Bus Specification Revision 2.0*.**)**

The drivers' output impedances plus a 36Ω series resistor at each driver's output act as source terminations that reduce reflected voltages when the outputs switch. The series resistors may be on-chip or external to the chip.

Pull-up and Pull-down Values

The pull-up resistor on D+ or D- at a device's upstream-facing port enables the hub to detect the device's speed. The hub's downstream-facing port has pull-down resistors on D+ and D-.

On devices with detachable cables, the pull-up resistors must connect to a positive voltage of 3.0–3.6V. Devices with captive cables can instead use an alternative means of termination, including connecting directly to VBUS. In selecting an alternatives means of termination, the designer must ensure that all signal levels meet the USB 2.0 requirements.

The USB 2.0 Engineering Change Notice *Pull-up/pull-down resistors* loosens the tolerances for pull-up and pull-down resistors that connect to a voltage source of 3.0–3.6V. The original values were 1.5k ±5% for the pull-ups and 15k ±5% for the pull-downs. The tolerances were loosened to make it easier to include the resistors on chip without requiring laser trimming of the values. Using the looser tolerances increases complexity at upstream-facing ports because the device must switch between two pull-up values depending on whether the bus is in the idle or active state. But overall, the new tolerances can reduce cost to device manufacturers. Devices that use the original 1.5k pull-ups don't have to switch values when switching between active and idle links.

High-speed Transceivers

A high-speed device must support control-transfer requests at full speed, so the device must contain transceivers to support both full and high speeds and logic to switch between them. A high-speed-capable device's upstream-facing transceivers aren't allowed to support low speed. In an external USB 2.0 hub, the downstream transceivers at ports with user-accessible connectors must support all three speeds.

Why 480 Megabits?

High speed's rate of 480 Mbps was chosen for several reasons. The frequency is slow enough to allow using the same cables and connectors as full speed. Components can use CMOS processes and don't require the advanced compensation used in high-speed digital signal processors. Tests of high-speed drivers showed

20–30% jitter at 480 Mbps. Because receivers can be designed to tolerate 40% jitter, this bit rate allows a good margin of error. And 480 is an even multiple of 12, so a single crystal can support both full and high speeds.

The use of separate drivers for high speed makes it easy to add high speed to an existing full-speed design. Current-mode drivers were chosen because they're fast.

The Circuits

Figure 19-4 shows upstream-facing transceiver circuits in a high-speed-capable device, and Figure 19-5 shows downstream-facing transceiver circuits in a USB 2.0 hub. The USB 2.0 specification requires downstream-facing transceivers, and thus all compliant hosts and hubs, to support all three speeds.

High speed requires its own drivers, so a high-speed device must contain two sets of drivers. For receiving, a transceiver may use a single receiver to handle all speeds or separate receivers for low/full speed and high speed.

When a high-speed driver transmits data, a current source drives one line with the other line at ground. The current source may be active all the time or only when transmitting. A current source that is active all the time is easier to design but consumes more power. USB 2.0 requires devices to meet the signal-amplitude and timing requirements beginning with the first symbol in a packet, and this requirement complicates the design of a current source that is active only when transmitting. If the driver keeps its current source active all the time, the driver can direct the current to ground when not transmitting on the bus.

In a high-speed-capable transceiver, the output impedance of the full-speed drivers has tighter tolerance compared to full-speed-only drivers ($45\Omega \pm 10\%$, compared to $36\Omega \pm 22\%$). The high-speed bus uses the full-speed drivers as electrical terminations and requires new values for impedance matching. Full-speed drivers that aren't part of a high-speed transceiver don't require a change in output impedance.

When the high-speed drivers are active, the full-speed drivers bring both data lines low (SE0 state). Each driver and its series resistor then function as a 45Ω termination to ground. Because each end of the cable segment has a driver, the line has a termination at both the source and the load. The double termination quiets the line more effectively than the source-only series terminations in full-speed segments. Using the full-speed drivers as terminations reduces the number of components.

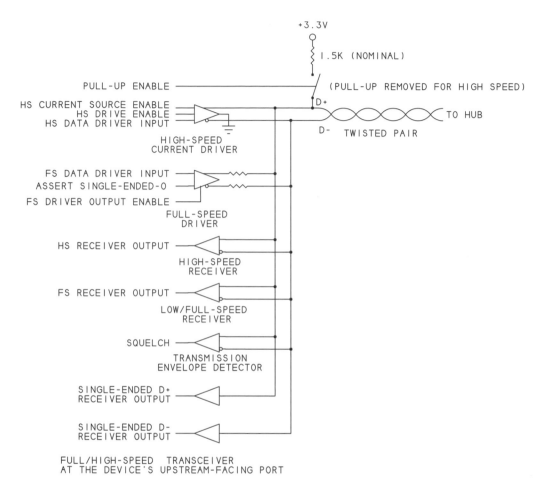

Figure 19-4. The upstream-facing port on a high-speed device must also support full-speed communications. (Adapted from *Universal Serial Bus Specification Revision 2.0*.)

The USB specification provides eye-pattern templates that show required high-speed transmitter outputs and receiver sensitivity. High-speed receivers must also meet new specifications that require the use of a differential time-domain reflectometer (TDR) to measure impedance characteristics.

All high-speed receivers must include a differential envelope detector to detect the Squelch (invalid signal) state indicated by a differential bus voltage of 100 mV or less. The downstream ports on all USB 2.0 hubs must also include a high-speed-disconnect detector that detects when a device has been removed from the bus.

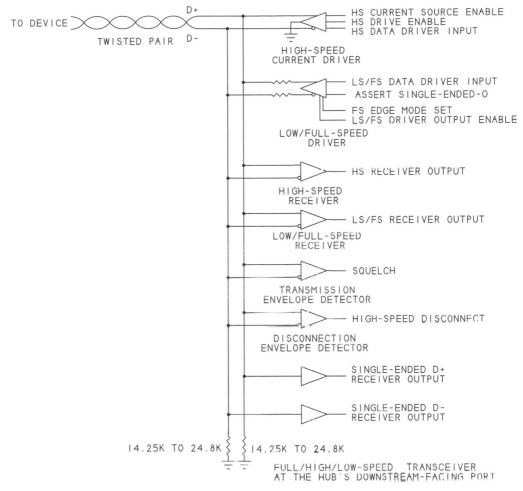

Figure 19-5. The downstream-facing ports on USB 2.0 hubs must support all three speeds (except ports with embedded or permanently attached devices). (Adapted from *Universal Serial Bus Specification Revision 2.0*.)

Other new responsibilities for high-speed-capable devices include managing the switch from full to high speed and handling new protocols for entering and exiting the Suspend and Reset states.

Switching to High Speed

In a low- or full-speed device, a pull-up on one of the signal lines indicates device speed. When a low- or full-speed device is attached or removed from the

447

bus, the voltage change due to the pull-up informs the hub of the change. High-speed-capable devices always attach at full speed, so hubs detect attachment of high-speed-capable devices in the same way.

As Chapter 18 explained, the switch to high speed occurs after the device has been detected during the Reset initiated by the hub's downstream port. A high-speed-capable device must support the high-speed handshake that informs the hub that the device is capable of high speed. When switching to high speed, the device removes its pull-up from the bus.

Detecting Removal of a High-speed Device

Because a device has no pull-up at high speed, the hub has to use a different method to detect device removal. Removing a device from the bus also removes the differential terminations, and the removal causes the differential voltage at the hub's port to double. On detecting the doubled voltage, the hub knows the device is no longer attached.

The hub detects the voltage by measuring the differential bus voltage during the extended End of High-speed Packet (HSEOP) in each high-speed Start-of-Frame Packet (HSSOP). A differential voltage of at least 625 mV indicates a disconnect.

Suspending and Resuming at High Speed

As Chapter 16 explained, USB 2.0 devices must enter the low-power Suspend state when the bus has been in the Idle state for at least 3 ms and no more than 10 ms. When the bus has been idle for 3 ms, a high-speed device switches to full speed. The device then checks the state of the full-speed bus to determine whether the host is requesting a Suspend or Reset. If the bus state is SE0, the host is requesting a Reset, and the device prepares for the high-speed-detect handshake. If the bus state is Idle, the device enters the Suspend state. On exiting the Suspend state, the device resumes at high speed.

Signal Voltages

Chapter 18 introduced USB's bus states. The voltages that define the states vary depending on the speed of the cable segment. The difference in the specified voltages at the transmitter and receiver mean that a signal can have some noise or attenuation and the receiver will still see the correct logic level.

Table 19-1: High speed has different driver and receiver specifications compared to low and full speed.

Parameter	Low/Full Speed (V)	High Speed (V)
V$_{OUT}$ low minimum	0	-0.010
V$_{OUT}$ low maximum	0.3	0.010
V$_{OUT}$ high minimum	2.8	0.360
V$_{OUT}$ high maximum	3.6	0.440
V$_{IN}$ low maximum	0.8	Limits are defined by the eye-pattern templates in the USB specification
V$_{IN}$ high minimum	2.0	

Low and Full Speeds

Table 19-1 shows the driver output voltages for low/full and high speeds. At low and full speeds, a Differential 1 exists at the driver when the D+ output is at least 2.8V and the D- output is no greater than 0.3V, with both referenced to the driver's signal ground. A Differential 0 exists at the driver when D- is at least 2.8V and D+ is no greater than 0.3V referenced to the driver's signal ground.

At a low- or full-speed receiver, a Differential 1 exists when D+ is at least 2V referenced to the receiver's signal ground, and the difference between D+ and D- is greater than 200 mV. A Differential 0 exists when D- is at least 2V referenced to the receiver's signal ground, and the difference between D- and D+ is greater than 200 mV. However, a receiver may optionally have less stringent definitions that require only a differential voltage greater than 200 mV, ignoring the requirement for one line to be at least 2V.

High Speed

At high speed, a Differential 1 exists at the driver when both the D+ output is at least 0.36V and the D- output is no greater than 0.01V referenced to the driver's signal ground. A Differential 0 exists at the driver when D- is at least 0.36V and D+ is no greater than 0.01V referenced to the driver's signal ground.

At a high-speed receiver, the input must meet the requirements shown in the eye-pattern templates in the USB 2.0 specification. The eye patterns specify maximum and minimum voltages, rise and fall times, maximum jitter in a transmitted signal, and the maximum jitter a receiver must tolerate. The specification explains how to make the measurements.

Table 19-2: The requirements for cables and related components differ for full/high-speed cables and cables that attach to low-speed devices.

Specification	Low Speed	Full/High Speed
Maximum length (typical) (m)	3	5
Inner shield and drain wire required?	yes (new in USB 2.0)	yes
Braided outer shield required?	no, but recommended	yes
Twisted pair required?	no, but recommended	yes
Common-mode impedance (Ω)	not specified	30 ±30%
Differential Characteristic impedance (Ω)	not specified	90
Cable skew (picoseconds)	< 100	
Wire gauge (AWG)	28 or larger diameter	
DC resistance, plug shell to plug shell (Ω)	0.6	
Cable delay	18 ns (one way)	5.2 ns/m
pull-up location at the device	D-	D+
Detachable cable OK?	no	yes
Captive cable OK?	yes	

USB 2.0 Cables

The USB specifications include cable and connector requirements that help ensure that signals will make it to their destinations without errors due to noise. The cable specifications also limit noise that radiates from the cable.

Conductors

USB 2.0 cables provide conductors for power, ground, and USB 2.0 communications. The cables contain wires for VBUS, ground, the D+ and D- signal wires, and a drain wire that connects to the cable shield (Table 19-3). Chapter 16 detailed the voltage and current limits for VBUS. The signal wires carry the data. Unlike RS-232, which has a TX line to carry data in one direction and an RX line for the other direction, USB 2.0's pair of wires carries a single differential signal, and data travels in one direction at a time.

Cables for low-speed segments have different requirements than cables for full- or high-speed segments (Table 19-2). A low-speed segment is a cable segment between a low-speed device and its hub. Any additional upstream segments between hubs are considered full- or high-speed segments. A low-speed cable must have the same inner shield and drain wire required for full speed. The

Table 19-3: A USB 2.0 cable has four wires plus a drain wire.

Wire	Name	Use	Color
1	VBUS	+5V	Red
2	GND	Ground reference	White
3	D+	Signal pair positive	Green
4	D-	Signal pair negative	Black
Shell	Shield	Drain wire	–

USB 2.0 specification also recommends, but doesn't require, a braided outer shield and a twisted pair for data, as on full- and high-speed cables. The USB 1.x specification required no shielding for low-speed cables.

Full- and high-speed segments can use the same cables. In a full/high speed cable, the signal wires must have a differential characteristic impedance of 90Ω. This value is a measure of the input impedance of an infinite, open line and determines the initial current on the lines when the outputs switch. The characteristic impedance for a low-speed cable isn't defined because the slower edge rates mean that the initial current doesn't affect the logic states at the receiver.

The USB 2.0 specification lists requirements for the cable's conductors, shielding, and insulation. These are the major requirements for full/high-speed cables:

Signal wires: twisted pair, 28 AWG or larger diameter.

Power and ground: non-twisted, 28 AWG or larger diameter.

Drain wire: stranded, tinned copper wire, 28 AWG or larger diameter.

Inner shield: aluminum metallized polyester

Outer shield: braided, tinned copper or equivalent braided material

The specification also lists requirements for the cable's durability and performance.

A low-speed device can use a full-speed cable if the cable meets all of the low-speed cable requirements including a maximum length of 3 m and not using a standard USB connector type at the device.

Connectors

USB 2.0 allows these options for the USB receptacle on a device: Standard B (also called Std B, Series B, or just "B"), Mini B, and Micro B. Figure 19-6

Figure 19-6. Approved cable plugs include (from left) Standard-A for hosts and Standard-B, Mini-B, and Micro-B for devices.

shows cable plugs that mate with these receptacles. Another option for devices is a captive cable, which uses a vendor-specific connector or is permanently attached to the device.

USB 2.0 hosts use the Standard A (also called Std A, Series A or "A") receptacle. USB On-The-Go products use Micro-AB receptacles, which can accept a cable with a Micro-A or Micro-B plug. Chapter 20 has more about On-The-Go connectors.

The USB 2.0 specification defines the Standard series connectors. ECNs define the Mini and Micro series connectors.

Mini and Micro plugs have an additional ID pin. On-The-Go devices use the ID pin to identify a device's default mode (host or function). Table 19-4 shows the pinout for the connectors.

All of the connectors are keyed so you can't insert a plug the wrong way. The connections for D+ and D- are recessed so the power lines connect first on attachment. The USB icon can identify a USB plug or receptacle (Figure 19-7). A "+" indicates support for high speed. A receptacle should mount so the USB icon on the top of the plug is visible to users inserting a plug.

Most devices have a single type-B connector. However, devices with multiple connectors are allowed. For example, a printer might have a port on the back to connect to a conventional host and a second port on the front to allow quick printing directly from a camera or portable computer. The USB-IF's *Embedded*

Figure 19-7. The USB icon identifies a USB plug or receptacle. A "+" indicates support for high speed.

Table 19-4: The Mini-B and Micro-B receptacles have an additional pin for OTG products.

Pin	Standard A, Standard B	Mini B, Micro B
1	VBUS	VBUS
2	D-	D-
3	D+	D+
4	GND	Open or >= 1MΩ
5	Not present	GND
Shell	Shield	Shield

Hosts and/or Multiple Receptacles document specifies that a device with multiple type-B connectors is allowed if all ports support the same speeds, if each connector has a device controller that operates independently from other device controllers in the device, and if all ports can enumerate at the same time.

Detachable and Captive Cables

USB 2.0 defines cables as being either detachable or captive. From the names, you might think that a detachable cable is one you can remove while a captive cable is permanently attached to its device. In fact, a captive cable can be removable as long as its downstream connector is *not* one of the standard USB connector types.

A detachable USB 2.0 cable must be full/high speed, with a Standard-A plug for the upstream connection and a Standard-B, Mini-B, or Micro-B plug for the downstream connection. A captive cable may be low or full/high speed. The upstream end has a Standard-A plug. For the downstream connection, a captive cable can be permanently attached or removable with a non-standard connector type. The non-standard connection doesn't have to be hot pluggable, but the Standard-A connection must be hot pluggable. Requiring low-speed cables to be captive eliminates the possibility of trying to use a low-speed cable in a full- or high-speed segment.

USB On-The-Go products have other cable options as described in Chapter 20.

Cable Length

USB 1.0 specified maximum lengths for cable segments. A full-speed segment could be up to 5 m and a low-speed segment could be up to 3 m. USB 1.1 and later dropped the length limits in favor of a discussion of characteristics that limit a cable's ability to meet timing and voltage specifications. On full- and high-speed cables, the limits are due to signal attenuation, cable propagation delay (the amount of time it takes for a signal to travel from driver to receiver), and voltage drops on the VBUS and GND wires. On low-speed cables, the length is limited by the rise and fall times of the signals, the capacitive load presented by the segment, and voltage drops on the VBUS and GND wires.

USB 1.0's limits of 3 m and 5 m are still good guidelines for cables with Standard-B and Mini-B plugs. Compliant cables of these lengths are readily available. Cables with Micro-B plugs have the special requirements of a a shorter maximum transmission delay (10 ns) and a resulting shorter maximum length of 2 m.

The USB specifications prohibit extension cables that extend a segment by adding a second cable in series. An extension cable for the upstream side of a cable would have a Standard-A plug on one end and a Standard-A receptacle on the other, while an extension cable for the downstream side would have a B plug and receptacle. Prohibiting extension cables eliminates the temptation to stretch a segment beyond the interface's electrical limits. Extension cables are available, but just because you can buy one doesn't mean that it's a good idea or that the cable will work. Instead, to extend the distance between a host and device, use hubs.

An exception is an active extension cable that contains a hub, a downstream port, and a cable. This type of cable works fine because it contains the required hub. Depending on the attached device, the hub may need its own power supply.

An option for long distances is to use an adapter as a bridge that converts between USB and Ethernet, RS-485, or another interface suitable for longer distances. The remote device supports the long-distance interface rather than USB.

Another approach enables accessing USB devices via a local Ethernet network. Two products that use this method are the AnywhereUSB hub from Digi International and the USB Server from Keyspan. The AnyWhereUSB hub contains one or more host controllers that communicate with the host PC over an Ethernet connection using the Internet Protocol (IP). The hub can attach to any Ethernet port in the PC's local network. The host drivers for the USB devices are on the PC. PC applications can access many USB devices that connect to the AnywhereUSB hub and use bulk and interrupt transfers. The interface has increased latency due to the added protocol layer. The USB Server works in a similar way.

Software-only products for accessing USB devices over a network are USB over Network from Fabula Tech and USB Redirector from Incentives Pro. To use these products to access a device attached to another computer in a network, you must install software on the PC the device attaches to and the PC(s) that will access the device.

Bus Length

A bus can have up to 5 external hubs in a tier. Thus, using 5 m cables, a device can be up to 30 m from its host. If the device is low speed, the limit is 28 m because the cable the connects to the low-speed device can be no more than 3 m. The limit on the number of hubs is due to the electrical properties of the hubs and cables and the resulting delays in propagating signals along the cable and through a hub.

Inter-Chip Connections

USB was developed as an interface to connect computers and peripherals via cables. But USB has also found uses in products that contain a host and an embedded or removable peripheral. In these products, communications between the host and peripheral don't require standard USB cables or connectors and can use lower supply voltages.

Two USB-IF standards for this type of interface are the *Inter-Chip USB Supplement* for low and full speeds and the *High-Speed Inter-Chip USB Electrical Specification* for high speed.

For both interface types, all of the following are true:

- The distance between the host and peripheral is 10 cm or less.
- The host doesn't allow peripheral attachment or removal while the inter-chip supply voltage is present.
- The interface can use a vendor-specific cable or on-board connection (circuit-board traces).

An interface that complies with the Inter-Chip USB Supplement must meet these requirements:

- The host always supports full speed and supports low speed if the host communicates with a low-speed peripheral. The peripheral may support low or full speed.
- The interface supports one or more of six defined supply-voltage classes with nominal voltages in the range 1–3V.

The low/full speed interface draws no bus current when idle. To save additional power, hardware can switch out the bus pull-up and pull-down resistors during traffic signaling.

The High-Speed Inter-Chip USB Electrical Specification defines an interface that uses a high-speed inter-chip (HSIC) synchronous serial interface. The interface uses 240-MHz double data rate (DDR) signaling, which transfers data on both the rising and falling clock edges. A 240-Mhz clock thus supports a 480-Mbps bit rate.

An interface that complies with the High-Speed Inter-Chip USB Electrical Specification must meet these requirements:

- The host and peripheral support high speed.
- The interface uses 1.2V LVCMOS voltages.

The HSIC interface consumes power only when a transfer is in progress.

USB 3.0

To support SuperSpeed, USB 3.0 adds transmitters and receivers and modifies the cables and connectors to carry the SuperSpeed signals.

Transmitters and Receivers

For SuperSpeed, each direction has a dedicated pair of wires with a differential transmitter at one end and a differential receiver at the opposite end. The hardware interface is based on the PCI Express (PCIe) Gen 2 interface used in expansion buses in PCs. In a PC, the bus uses multiple lanes to transfer multiple bits in the same direction at once. SuperSpeed uses a single lane with one signal pair for each direction.

A SuperSpeed transmitter must contain a circuit that detects an attached receiver's load of $18-30\Omega$. An RC charging circuit can perform this function. Because the SuperSpeed wires carry data at a single speed, an upstream hub that detects a SuperSpeed device knows the device's speed.

Cables

USB 3.0 cables can carry both USB 2.0 and SuperSpeed traffic. The cables have additional wires and connector contacts to support SuperSpeed.

Compatibility

USB 3.0 cables and connectors are backwards compatible with USB 2.0. Plugs on USB 2.0 cables fit USB 3.0 receptacles. A USB 2.0 cable attached to a USB 3.0 host or hub can carry low-, full-, and high-speed data.

A USB 3.0 Standard-A plug fits a USB 2.0 Standard-A receptacle. Thus you can use a USB 3.0 cable to attach a USB 3.0 device to a USB 2.0 host or hub and communicate at a USB 2.0 speed. Attaching a USB 2.0 device to a USB 3.0 host or hub requires a USB 2.0 cable. USB 3.0 Standard-B and USB 3.0 Micro-B plugs don't fit USB 2.0 receptacles.

To use SuperSpeed, all cables and receptacles in the links between the device and host must be USB 3.0.

Conductors

A USB 3.0 cable has ten wires (Table 19-5), which include USB 2.0's power, ground, and unshielded pair plus two shielded pairs with drain wires for Super-Speed. The SuperSpeed interface is dual simplex: each direction has its own pair of wires, each pair has its own ground, or drain, wire, and data can travel in both directions at once. (Full duplex is also bidirectional but uses a single, common ground wire.) The SuperSpeed wires can be shielded twisted pairs or twinaxial cable (twinax). Twinax is similar to coax but has two inner conductors

Table 19-5: A USB 3.0 cable has additional wires to support SuperSpeed

Wire	Name at Connector	Use	Color
1	PWR	VBUS power	Red
2	UTP_D-	Unshielded differential pair, negative (USB 2.0)	White
3	UTP_D+	Unshielded twisted pair, positive (USB 2.0)	Green
4	GND_PWRrt	Ground for power return	Black
5	SDP1-	Shielded differential pair,1, negative (SuperSpeed)	Blue
6	SDP1+	Shielded differential pair 1, positive (SuperSpeed)	Yellow
7	SDP1_Drain	Drain wire for SDP1.	–
8	SDP2-	Shielded differential pair 2, negative (SuperSpeed)	Purple
9	SDP2+	Shielded differential pair 2, positive (SuperSpeed)	Orange
10	SDP2_Drain	Drain wire for SDP2. Connects to pin 7 on the connectors.	–
Braid	Shield	External braid terminated onto metal shell of plug	–

instead of one. The characteristic impedance of shielded twisted pairs should be $90\,\Omega$.

USB 3.0 doesn't specify wire gauges but provides electrical data for typical values (26–34 AWG) and recommends using the smallest-diameter gauges that meet the electrical requirements of the cable assembly. Cable flexibility, which generally decreases with the AWG number, may also be a consideration. The cable's outer diameter must be in the range 3–6 mm.

Connectors

USB 3.0 connectors have five additional contacts for the two SuperSpeed signal pairs and the two drain wires, which terminate at the same pin. Figure 19-8 shows the connectors.

Table 19-6 shows which plugs can attach to different receptacle types. A USB 3.0 device can have a USB 3.0 Standard-B or USB 3.0 Micro-B receptacle, a captive cable with a USB 3.0 Standard-A plug, or the USB 3.0 Powered-B connector described below. A USB 3.0 host has a USB 3.0 Standard-A receptacle.

Except for the Mini-B, all USB 2.0 plugs can mate with a USB 3.0 receptacle of the same series. A USB 2.0 Standard-A plug fits a USB 3.0 Standard-A receptacle, a USB 2.0 Standard-B plug fits a USB 3.0 Standard-B receptacle, and a

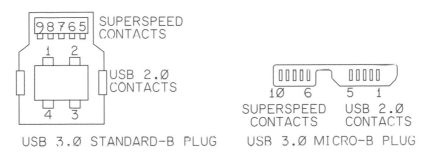

Figure 19-8. USB 3.0 connectors have additional contacts for the SuperSpeed wires. (Not drawn to scale.)

Table 19-6: USB 3.0 connectors are backwards compatible with USB 2.0 connectors.

Unit	Connector	Mates with
USB 2.0 host	USB 2.0 Standard-A receptacle	USB 2.0 Standard-A plug
USB 3.0 host	USB 3.0 Standard-A receptacle	USB 3.0 Standard-A plug
USB 2.0 device	USB 2.0 Standard-B receptacle	USB 2.0 Standard-B plug
	USB 2.0 Mini-B receptacle	USB 2.0 Mini-B plug
	USB 2.0 Micro-B receptacle	USB 2.0 Micro-B plug
	Captive cable with USB 2.0 Standard-A plug	USB 2.0 Standard-A receptacle USB 3.0 Standard-A receptacle
USB 3.0 device	USB 3.0 Standard-B receptacle	USB 2.0 Standard-B plug
	USB 3.0 Powered-B receptacle	USB 3.0 Standard-B plug USB 3.0 Powered-B plug
	USB 3.0 Micro-B receptacle	USB 2.0 Micro-B plug USB 3.0 Micro-B plug
	Captive cable with USB 3.0 Standard-A plug	USB 2.0 Standard-A receptacle USB 3.0 Standard-A receptacle

Figure 19-9. The plugs on compliant USB 3.0 cables should display the USB 3.0 icon. (Image courtesy of the USB Implementers Forum.)

USB 2.0 Micro-B plug fits a USB 3.0 Micro-B receptacle. There is no USB 3.0 Mini-B receptacle. Of course, cables with USB 2.0 plugs can't carry SuperSpeed traffic.

The USB 3.0 Standard-A plug and receptacle have the same form factors as the USB 2.0 Standard-A plug and receptacle. Thus a USB 3.0 Standard-A plug will mate with a USB 2.0 Standard-A receptacle. To support SuperSpeed, USB 3.0 Standard-A connectors use a 2-tier contact system with five additional contacts that lie behind the four USB 2.0 contacts on the plug.

Compliant USB 3.0 cables should display the USB 3.0 icon (Figure 19-9). The USB 3.0 specification recommends using Pantone 300 blue for the internal plastic housing on Standard-A connectors. The connector's outer shell can be any color.

Powered-B Connector

Under USB 2.0, Wireless USB adapters that connect to USB devices must provide their own power. USB 3.0's Powered-B connectors enable these and similar adapters to draw power from a device even when the device isn't configured or the link is in the Suspend state. The device must have a Powered-B receptacle, which has two extra contacts that can provide 5V at up to 1A to a connected adapter or other device. The adapter to be powered must have a permanently attached cable with a Powered-B plug. If the device instead uses a wired connection to a host or hub, the Powered-B contacts are unused. The Powered-B plug also fits a USB 3.0 Standard-B receptacle, so an adapter that supports self power can attach to devices that don't use the Powered-B contacts.

Table 19-7: USB 3.0 defines a host-to-host cable for SuperSpeed traffic.

USB 3.0 Standard-A Pin	Signal	USB 3.0 Standard-A Pin
1–3	no connect	1–3
4	GND	4
5	SDP1-	8
6	SDP1+	9
7	SDP1_Drain and SDP2_Drain	7
8	SDP2-	5
9	SDP2+	6

Cable Length

USB 3.0 doesn't specify a maximum cable length. For VBUS and GND, the specification provides a table that suggests maximum lengths for different AWG values to meet voltage-drop limits. A 3-m cable requires 22 AWG or larger diameter PWR and GND wires. For the signal wires, the specification defines limits for differential insertion loss, which is a measure of how much a signal degrades as it passes through a cable assembly. To comply with these limits, the signal wires in a 3-m cable must use 26 AWG or larger diameter wires.

Bus Length

Like USB 2.0, USB 3.0 allows five external hubs in a tier. A typical USB 3.0 cable is 3 m, so a typical maximum SuperSpeed bus length is 18 m. USB 2.0 devices can continue to use 5 m USB 2.0 cables with USB 3.0 hosts and hubs.

Host-to-Host Cables

USB 2.0 forbids cables that connect two hosts except for bridge cables that contain device controllers with a shared buffer. USB 3.0 defines a USB 3.0 Standard-A to USB 3.0 Standard-A cable for debugging and other specialized host-to-host applications with driver support. The cable is a crossover cable for the SuperSpeed lines (Table 19-7). VBUS, D-, and D+ have no connection.

Ensuring Signal Quality

The USB specifications for drivers, receivers, and cable design ensure that virtually all data transfers occur without errors. Requirements that help to ensure signal quality include the use of balanced lines and shielded cables, twisted pairs (required for full/high-speed), and slower edge rates for low-speed drivers.

Sources of Noise

Noise can enter a wire in many ways, including by conductive, common-impedance, magnetic, capacitive, and electromagnetic coupling. If a noise voltage is large enough and is present when the receiver is reading a transmitted bit, the noise can cause the receiver to misread the transmitted logic level. Very large noise voltages can damage components.

Conductive and common-impedance coupling require ohmic contact between the signal wire and the wire that is the source of the noise. Conductive coupling occurs when a wire brings noise from another source into a circuit. For example, a noisy power-supply line can carry noise into the circuit the supply powers. Common-impedance coupling occurs when two circuits share a wire, such as a ground return.

The other types of noise coupling result from interactions between the electric and magnetic fields of the wires themselves and signals that couple into the wires from outside sources, including other wires in the interface. Capacitive and inductive coupling can cause crosstalk, where signals on one wire enter another wire. Capacitive coupling, also called electric coupling, occurs when two wires carry charges at different potentials, resulting in an electric field between the wires. The strength of the field and the resulting capacitive coupling varies with the distance between the wires. Inductive, or magnetic, coupling occurs because current in a wire causes the wire to emanate a magnetic field. When the magnetic fields of two wires overlap, the energy in each wire's field induces a current in the other wire. When wires are greater than 1/6 wavelength apart, the capacitive and inductive coupling are considered together as electromagnetic coupling. An example of electromagnetic coupling is when a wire acts as a receiving antenna for radio waves.

Balanced Lines

One way USB eliminates noise is with the balanced lines that carry the differential signals. On balanced lines, noise that couples into the interface is likely to couple equally into both signal wires. At a differential receiver, which detects only the difference between the two wires' voltages, any noise that is common to both wires cancels out.

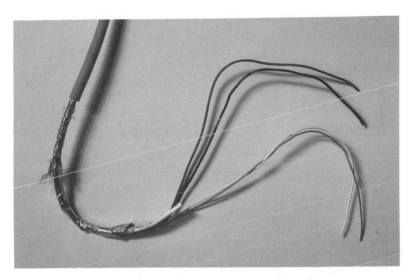

Figure 19-10. A full/high-speed USB cable contains a twisted pair for data, VBUS and GND wires, and aluminum metallized polyester and braided copper shields.

In contrast, in the unbalanced, single-ended lines that RS-232 and other interfaces use, the receiver detects the difference between a signal wire and a ground line shared by other circuits. The ground line is likely to be carrying noise from a number of sources, and the receiver sees this noise when it detects the difference between the signal voltage and ground.

Twisted Pairs

In a full/high-speed USB cable, the signal wires must be a twisted pair. Twisted pairs are also recommended for low-speed cables. A twisted pair is two insulated conductors that spiral around each other with a twist every few inches (Figure 19-10). The twisting reduces noise by reducing the amount of noise in the wires and by canceling noise that enters the wires. Twisting is most effective at eliminating low-frequency, magnetically coupled signals such as 60-Hz power-line noise.

Twisting reduces noise by minimizing the area between the conductors. The magnetic field that emanates from a circuit is proportional to the area between the conductors. Twisting the conductors around each other reduces the total area between them. The tighter the twists, the smaller the area. Reducing the area shrinks the magnetic field emanating from the wires and thus reduces the amount of noise coupling into the field.

A twisted pair tends to cancel any noise that enters the wires because the conductors swap physical positions with each twist. Any noise that magnetically couples into the wires reverses polarity with each twist. The result is that the noise present in one twist is cancelled by a nearly equal, opposite noise signal in the next twist. Of course, the twists aren't perfectly uniform and the canceling isn't perfect, but noise is much reduced.

Shielding

Metal shielding prevents noise from entering or emanating from a cable. Shielding is most effective at blocking noise due to capacitive, electromagnetic, and high-frequency magnetic coupling. USB 2.0 requires both low-speed and full/high-speed cables to be shielded, though the requirements differ.

In a full/high-speed cable, an aluminum metallized polyester shield surrounds the four conductors. Around this shield is an outer shield of braided, tinned copper wire. Between the shields and contacting both is a copper drain wire. The outside layer is a polyvinyl chloride jacket. The shield terminates at the connector plug.

A low-speed cable has the same requirements except that the braided outer shield is recommended but not required. USB 1.x required no shielding for low-speed cables on the premise that the slower rise and fall times made shielding unnecessary. The shielding requirement was added in USB 2.0 not because the USB interface is noisy in itself, but because the cables are likely to attach to computers that are noisy internally. Shielding helps keep the cable from radiating this noise and thus helps with passing FCC tests. The downside is that USB 2.0 low-speed cables are more expensive to make and physically less flexible.

USB 2.0 uses unshielded twisted pairs, but USB 3.0 requires shielding around each SuperSpeed signal pair and its drain wire. USB 3.0 cables must also have metal braid surrounding all of the wires and terminating at the metal shell.

Edge Rates

Because of low speed's slower data rate, drivers can use slower edge rates that reduce reflected voltages seen by receivers and noise that emanates from the cable.

When a digital output switches, a mismatch between the line's characteristic impedance and the load presented by the receiver can cause reflected voltages that affect the voltage at the receiver. If the reflections are large enough and last long enough, the receiver may misread a transmitted bit.

In low-speed cables, the slower edge rate ensures that any reflections have died out by the time the output has finished switching. The slow edge rate also means that the signals contain less high-frequency energy and thus the noise emanated by the cables is less.

Isolated Interfaces

Galvanic isolation can be useful in preventing electrical noise and power surges from coupling into a circuit. Circuits that are galvanically isolated from each other have no ohmic connection. Typical methods of isolation include using a transformer to transfer power by magnetic coupling and optoisolators to transfer digital signals by optical coupling.

USB devices shouldn't require isolation in conventional environments such as offices and classrooms. For industrial environments or other locations where devices might benefit from isolation, USB's timing requirements and USB 2.0's use of a single pair of wires for both directions make it difficult to isolate a device from its host. One solution is to isolate the non-USB components the device controller connects to. For example, in a motor controller with a USB interface, the motor and control circuits can be isolated from the USB controller and bus.

Another option is to use an isolated hub. B & B Electronics and Sealevel Systems offer hubs with isolated low/full-speed downstream ports.

Going Wireless

Replacing a USB cable with a wireless connection isn't a simple task. USB transactions involve communicating in both directions with tight timing requirements. For example, when a USB 2.0 host sends a token and data packet in the Data stage of an interrupt OUT transaction, the device must respond quickly with ACK or another code in the handshake packet.

But the idea of a wireless connection for USB devices is so compelling that multiple technologies have become available to incorporate USB in wireless applications. In many implementations, the wireless links use wired devices that serve as wireless bridges, or adapters. The bridge uses USB to communicate with the host and a wireless interface to communicate with the peripheral. The peripheral contains a wireless bridge to convert between the wireless interface and the peripheral's circuits.

Certified Wireless USB

The USB-IF's *Wireless Universal Serial Bus Specification* defines Certified Wireless USB. Revision 1.0 was released in 2005.

Certified Wireless USB supports speeds of up to 480 Mbps at 3 m and 100 Mbps at 10 m. The interface supports power-saving modes and uses encryption for security. The technology is ultrawideband (UWB) radio, which transmits in short bursts at very low power over a wide frequency spectrum. The UWB technology is defined in the ISO/IEC 26907/8 specifications, which evolved from specifications developed by the nonprofit WiMedia Alliance.

A USB host can have a built-in Wireless USB interface or a wired connection to a USB device that functions as a host wire adapter (HWA) that communicates via Wireless USB. In a similar way, a USB device can have a built-in Wireless USB interface or a wired connection to a device wire adapter (DWA) that communicates via Wireless USB.

Products with Certified Wireless USB interfaces have been slow to reach the market. Development kits have been expensive, making the interface impractical for many developers. However, notebook PCs with built-in Wireless USB interfaces are available, and in time development tools will likely become more affordable.

Cypress WirelessUSB

For low-speed devices, including HIDs, Cypress Semiconductor offers the WirelessUSB technology. The obvious market is wireless keyboards, mice, and game controllers. With a wireless range of up to 50 m, the technology is also useful for building and home automation and industrial control. The wireless interface uses radio-frequency (RF) transmissions at 2.4 GHz in the unlicensed Industrial, Scientific, and Medical (ISM) band.

A WirelessUSB system consists of a WirelessUSB bridge and one or more WirelessUSB devices (Figure 19-11). The bridge translates between USB and the wireless protocol and medium. The WirelessUSB device carries out the device's function (mouse, keyboard, game controller) and communicates with the bridge.

The bridge contains a USB-capable microcontroller and a WirelessUSB transceiver chip and antenna. The WirelessUSB device contains a Cypress PsOC or

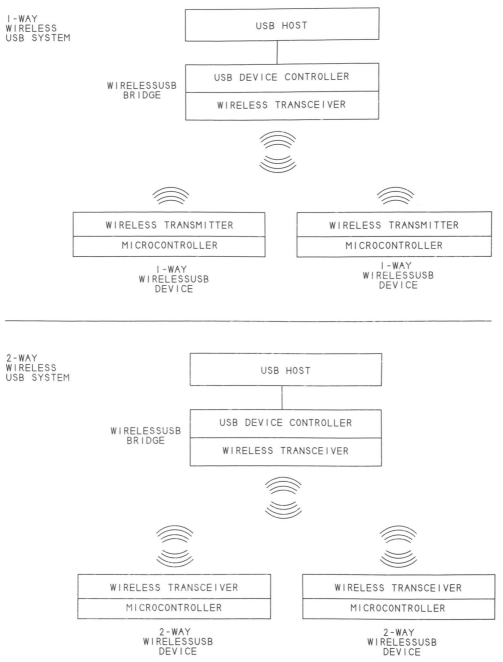

Figure 19-11. WirelessUSB provides a way to design low-speed devices that use a wireless interface.

another microcontroller and a WirelessUSB transmitter or transceiver chip and antenna. A device with a transceiver is 2-way: the device can communicate in both directions. A device with just a transmitter is 1-way: the device can send data to the host but can't receive data or status information. In both the bridge and device, the transmitter and transceiver chips use the SPI synchronous serial interface to communicate with their microcontrollers.

In a 2-way system, when a device has data to send to the host, the device's microcontroller writes the data to the transceiver chip, which encodes the data and sends it through the air to the bridge's transceiver. On receiving the data, the bridge returns an acknowledgement to the device, decodes the data, and sends the data to the host in conventional USB interrupt or control transfers. On failing to receive an acknowledgement from the bridge, the device resends the data.

When the host has data to send to the device, the host writes the data to the bridge's USB controller, which returns ACK (if not busy and the data is accepted) and passes the data to the bridge's transceiver. The transceiver encodes the data and sends it through the air to the WirelessUSB device. The device returns an acknowledgement to the bridge. On receiving a NAK or no reply, the bridge resends the data.

In a 1-way system, a device sends data to the host in much the same way as in a 2-way system except the device receives no acknowledgement from the host. To help ensure that the bridge and host receive all transmitted data, the device sends its data multiple times. Sequence numbers enable the bridge to identify previously received data.

With both systems, the host thinks it's communicating with an ordinary HID and has no knowledge of the wireless link.

A WirelessUSB link can have a data throughput of up to 62.5 kbps, but low-speed throughput is limited by the USB bandwidth available for low-speed control and interrupt transfers. A device and its bridge must use the same frequency/code pair. A single WirelessUSB bridge can use multiple frequency/code pairs to communicate with multiple devices. For faster performance, the microcontroller can use burst reads to read multiple registers in the WirelessUSB chip in sequence.

Other Options

Other ways to use USB in wireless devices include various wireless bridges and a wireless networking option.

ZigBee is an inexpensive, low-power, RF interface suitable for building and industrial automation and other applications that transmit at up to 250 kbps and over distances of up to 500 m. DLP Design's DLP-RF1 USB/RF OEM Transceiver Module provides a way to monitor and control a Zigbee interface from a USB port. The module's USB controller is FTDI's FT245BM. One or more DLP-RF2 RF OEM Transceiver Modules can communicate with the DLP-RF1.

The IrDA bridge class described in Chapter 7 defines a way for a USB device to use bulk transfers to communicate over an infrared link.

Another option is a vendor-specific wireless bridge that uses infrared, RF, or other wireless modules designed for use in robotics and other low- to moderate-speed applications. The bridge functions as a wired USB device that also supports a wireless interface. A remote device that supports the wireless interface carries out the peripheral's function. Firmware passes received wireless data to the host and passes received USB data to the device.

To use an existing USB device wirelessly, you may be able to use one of the USB/Ethernet products described earlier in this chapter along with a wireless network interface between the host PC and the hub/server.

20

Hosts for Embedded Systems

A USB host in a desktop system has many responsibilities, including supporting multiple bus speeds, managing communications with multiple devices, and providing power to every device connected to the root hub. PCs and other desktop computers have the resources to implement a full USB host. But many smaller systems can also benefit by functioning as hosts. A camera can connect to a USB printer. A data-acquisition device can store its data in a USB drive. A PDA can interface to a USB keyboard and mouse.

For many of these smaller, embedded systems, a conventional USB host is impractical and unnecessary. These systems typically communicate with just one or a few devices with defined requirements for bus power and might not need to support hubs.

A solution is to implement a limited capability host. For some applications, the best approach is a dual-role device that can switch functions between host and device as needed. Other applications require only host capability or require simultaneous host and device functions. USB supports all of these options.

USB On-The-Go

The On-The-Go (OTG) Supplement to the USB 2.0 specification defines a way for a USB device to function as a limited-capability host and as a peripheral (though not both at the same time). Version 1.0 of the OTG supplement was released in 2001. Version 1.3 was released in 2006.

When functioning as a host, the OTG device can communicate with the devices in its targeted peripheral list. Targeted peripherals can be any combination of other OTG devices and peripheral-only devices.

Capabilities and Limits

Table 20-1 compares the requirements of an OTG device functioning as a host and a conventional (not OTG) host. An OTG host doesn't have to support external hubs, multiple devices attached at the same time, or high and low speeds.

Because OTG communications often involve battery-powered devices, conserving power is important. For this reason, an OTG device that is providing VBUS is allowed to turn off VBUS when the bus is idle.

Communications occur in sessions. A session begins when VBUS is above the session-valid threshold voltage and ends when VBUS falls below this voltage. The Session Request Protocol (SRP) enables a device to request a session even if VBUS isn't present.

The OTG Connector

An OTG device must have one and only one Micro-AB receptacle, which can accept either a Micro-A plug or a Micro-B plug. For SuperSpeed devices, the USB 3.0 specification defines a USB 3.0 Micro-AB receptacle and USB 3.0 Micro-A plug. The Micro-A plugs are approved for use only with OTG devices. There is no approved Micro-A receptacle. The original OTG supplement specified a Mini-AB receptacle, but the USB-IF deprecated this option in 2007 and requires new designs to use the Micro-AB. For existing OTG devices with Mini-AB receptacles, substitute *Mini-* for *Micro-* in the connector discussions in this chapter.

The A-Device and B-Device

Every OTG connection is between an A-device and a B-device. The A-device is defined by the type of plug inserted in the USB receptacle. The A-device is

Table 20-1: Compared to a non-OTG host, an OTG device functioning as a host doesn't have to supply as much power and can use a single connector for host and peripheral functions.

Capability or Feature	USB 2.0 Conventional Host	USB 2.0 OTG Device Functioning as a Host
Communicate at high speed	yes	optional
Communicate at full speed	yes	yes
Communicate at low speed	yes	optional (not allowed in device mode)
Support external hubs	yes	optional
Provide targeted peripheral list	no	yes
Function as a peripheral	no	yes (when not functioning as a host)
Support Session Request Protocol	optional	yes
Support Host Negotiation Protocol	no	yes
Minimum available bus current per port	500 mA (100 mA if battery-powered)	8 mA
OK to turn off VBUS when unneeded?	no	yes
Connector	1 or more Standard A	1 Micro AB

either a host with a Standard-A plug inserted or an OTG device with a micro-A plug inserted. The device at the other end of the cable is the B-device. Initially, the A-device functions as the host, and the B-device functions as the peripheral. As described below, two connected OTG devices can use a protocol to swap functions when needed. The A-device always provides the VBUS voltage and current even when functioning as a peripheral.

Requirements for an OTG Device

A USB 2.0 OTG device must provide all of the following:

- The ability to function as a full-speed peripheral. Support for high speed is optional. The peripheral function must not use low speed.

- The ability to function as a host that can communicate with one or more full-speed devices. Support for low speed, high speed, and hubs is optional.

- Support for the Host Negotiation Protocol, which enables two OTG devices to swap roles. (The host becomes the peripheral and the peripheral becomes the host.)

473

- The ability to initiate and respond to the Session Request Protocol, which enables a device to request communications with the host even if VBUS isn't present.
- Support for remote wakeup.
- One and only one Micro-AB receptacle, which can accept either a Micro-A plug or a Micro-B plug.
- A targeted peripheral list that names the devices the host can communicate with.
- When functioning as the A-device, the ability to provide at least 8 mA of bus current or the amount required by the targeted peripherals, whichever is greater.
- A display or other way to communicate messages to users.

OTG adds complexity by requiring hosts to support the Host Negotiation Protocol and Session Request Protocol and requiring the ability to function as a peripheral. On the other hand, OTG reduces complexity and expense by using a single receptacle and by not requiring the host to supply large bus currents or support external hubs or all bus speeds.

The following paragraphs describe the requirements for OTG devices in more detail.

Full-speed Device Capability

Any device that implements OTG's limited-capability host must also be able to function as a USB peripheral. OTG host-only products aren't allowed. When functioning as a peripheral, an OTG device may support high speed and must not communicate at low speed.

Full-speed Host Capability

An OTG device functioning as a host must be able to communicate with one or more devices. The host must support full speed and may support low speed and/or high speed. The host doesn't have to support communications via hubs.

The Host Negotiation Protocol

The Host Negotiation Protocol (HNP) enables a B-device to request to function as a host. When connecting two OTG devices to each other, users don't have to worry about which end of the cable goes where. When necessary, the devices use HNP to swap roles.

When two OTG devices connect to each other, the A-device enumerates the B-device in the same way that a standard USB host enumerates its devices. During enumeration, the A-device retrieves the B-device's OTG descriptor, which indicates whether the B-device supports HNP. If the B-device supports HNP, the A-device can send a Set Feature request with a request code of hnp_enable. The request informs the B-device that it can use HNP to request to function as the host when the bus is suspended.

At any time after enumerating, if the A-device has no communications for the B-device, the A-device suspends the bus. A B-device that supports HNP may then request to communicate. The B-device can use HNP in response to user input such as pressing a button, or firmware can initiate HNP without user intervention.

An OTG A-device must support HNP. An OTG B-device must support HNP if the device's targeted peripheral list includes any OTG device. This requirement ensures that an OTG B-device can request to access the peripheral function of a supported OTG device. If the targeted peripheral list includes no OTG devices, the OTG B-device isn't required to support HNP because the peripherals will never use it.

Standard hubs don't recognize HNP signaling. If a hub is between the B-device and the A-device, the A-device must not send the hnp_enable request and the B-device can't use HNP.

When idle or functioning as a host, an OTG device should switch in its pull-down resistors on D+ and D-. When functioning as a peripheral, an OTG device should switch out its pull-down resistor on D+ only.

Requesting to Operate as a Host

This is the protocol the B-device uses to request to operate as the host:

1. The A-device suspends the bus.

2. If the devices were communicating at full speed, the B-device removes itself from the bus by switching out its pull-up resistor on D+. If the devices were communicating at high speed, the B-device switches in its pull-up on D+ for 1–147 ms, then switches the pull-up out. The bus is in the SE0 state.

3. The A-device detects the SE0 and connects to the bus as a device by switching in its pull-up resistor on D+. The bus is in the J state.

4. The B-device detects the J state and resets the bus.

5. The B-device enumerates the A-device and can then perform other communications with the device.

Returning to Operation as a Peripheral

When finished communicating, the B-device returns to its role as a peripheral using the following protocol:

1. The B-device stops all bus activity and may switch in its pull-up resistor.

2. The A-device detects a lack of activity for at least 3 ms and switches out its pull-up resistor or removes VBUS to end the session.

3. If VBUS is present and the B-device didn't switch in its pull-up in Step 1, the B-device switches in its pull-up to connect as a peripheral. The bus is in the J state.

4. If VBUS is present, the A-device resets the bus. The A-device can then enumerate and communicate with the B-device, suspend the bus, or end the session by removing VBUS.

The Session Request Protocol

If the A-device has turned off the VBUS voltage, a B-device can use the Session Request Protocol (SRP) to request the host to restore VBUS and begin a new session. The two SRP methods are data-line pulsing and VBUS pulsing. The B-device must try data-line pulsing first, followed by VBUS pulsing. An A-device that supports SRP must respond to one of the methods.

An A-device must respond to SRP if the device ever turns off VBUS while a micro-A plug is inserted. A B-device must support initiating SRP if the device wants to request communications with an OTG device when VBUS is off. A B-device whose targeted peripheral list has no devices that support SRP will have no need to initiate SRP.

In data-line pulsing, the device switches in its pull-up (on D+ or D-, depending on device speed) for 5–10 ms. In VBUS pulsing, the device must drive the VBUS line long enough for the host to detect the VBUS voltage but not long enough to damage a non-OTG host that isn't designed to withstand a voltage applied to VBUS. Because VBUS capacitance is much higher on a non-OTG host, the voltage rises more slowly. Within 5 seconds of detecting data-line pulsing or VBUS pulsing, the A-device must turn on VBUS and reset the bus.

Standard hubs don't recognize SRP signaling, so if there is a hub between the B-device and the A-device, the B-device can't use SRP. Non-OTG USB peripherals also have the option to support SRP.

Support for Remote Wakeup

When VBUS is present and the bus is suspended, an OTG device can use remote wakeup to request communications from an OTG device or other USB host.

Cables and Connectors

A device with a Micro-AB receptacle is an OTG device. Every OTG device must have one and only one Micro-AB receptacle, and any device with a Micro-AB connector must function as a OTG device. The Micro-AB receptacle can accept either a Micro-A plug or a Micro-B plug.

Figure 20-1 shows the cabling options. Two OTG devices connect to each other via a cable with a Micro-A plug on one end and a Micro-B plug on the other end. It doesn't matter which device has which plug.

A host or upstream hub connects to an OTG device via a Standard-A to Micro-B cable. A peripheral with a Micro-B receptacle connects to an OTG device with a Micro-A-to-Micro-B cable. A peripheral with a permanently attached cable with a Micro-A plug attaches directly to the OTG device.

A peripheral with a Standard-B or Mini-B plug or a captive cable with a Standard-A plug must use an adapter to connect to an OTG device. The adapter has a Micro-A plug and a Standard-A receptacle. The Micro-A plug attaches to the OTG device. The Standard-A receptacle accepts a Standard-A plug from a cable that attaches to the peripheral with a Standard-B or Mini-B plug or a captive cable. This adapter is the only approved adapter for standard USB cables.

Micro-A, Micro-B, and Micro-AB connectors have an ID pin that enables an OTG device to determine whether a Micro-A or Micro-B plug is attached. In a Micro-A plug, the ID pin is grounded. In a Micro-B plug, the ID pin is open or connected to ground via a resistance greater than 1MΩ. (The *MicroUSB Micro-B ID Pin Resistance* ECN raised this value from its original 100kΩ.) An OTG device typically has a pull-up resistor on the ID pin. If the pin is a logic low, the attached plug is a Micro-A. If the pin is a logic high, the attached plug is a Micro-B.

The USB 3.0 specification defines a USB 3.0 Micro-AB receptacle and USB 3.0 Micro-A plug that include contacts for SuperSpeed traffic.

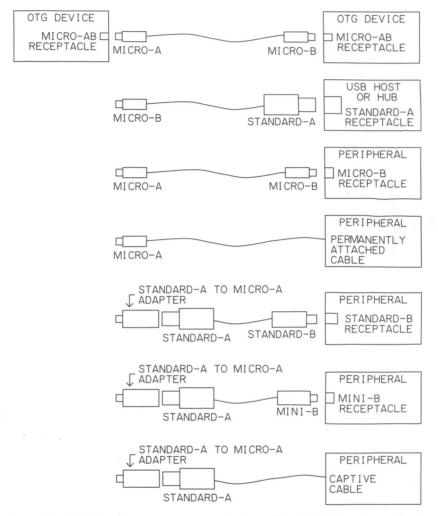

Figure 20-1. An OTG device can communicate with a USB host or a device on the OTG device's target peripheral list.

Bus Current

The ability to draw up to 500 mA per port from the bus is a convenience for users and a cost saver for device manufacturers. But providing this much current, or even the 100 mA that USB 2.0 battery-powered hosts must provide, can be a burden for some hosts. Some peripherals, including battery-powered ones, may not need bus power at all.

For these reasons, OTG devices have more flexible requirements for providing bus current. A USB 2.0 OTG device must provide the greater of 8 mA of bus current or the maximum amount the devices on the targeted peripheral list require, up to 500 mA.

To conserve power, an A-device can leave VBUS unpowered until the device detects SRP signaling or launches an application that uses USB. For faster response when a device is attached, an A-device can have an option to power the bus on detecting device attachment.

User Messages

Every OTG device must have a display or another means to display error messages to users. To pass compliance tests, an OTG device should support these messages:

Device not connected/responding. A device isn't working as expected.

Attached device not supported. A device isn't on the targeted peripheral list or a B-device is drawing more current than the A-device supports.

Unsupported hub topology. The device doesn't support hubs, the bus has more hub tiers than the A-device supports, or the bus is using another unsupported hub topology.

A very basic messaging system is a series of LEDs with each labeled with an error message.

The Targeted Peripheral List

Every OTG device must have a targeted peripheral list that names the devices the manufacturer has successfully tested with the OTG device. For each peripheral, the list should name the manufacturer and model number and describe the device. The list should not claim to support an entire class or other devices similar to those on the list. The OTG supplement doesn't say where the list must appear.

The OTG Descriptor

During enumeration, a device that supports HNP or SRP must include an OTG descriptor (Table 20-2) in the descriptors returned in response to a Get Descriptor request for the Configuration descriptor. The bmAttributes field tells whether the device supports HNP and SRP. A device that supports HNP must support SRP. The A-device doesn't need to know in advance if a device

Table 20-2: The OTG Descriptor indicates whether a device supports HNP and SRP.

Offset	Field	Size	Description
0	bLength	1	Descriptor length (3)
1	bDescriptorType	1	OTG (9)
2	bmAttributes	1	D2–D7: reserved, D1: 1 = HNP supported, 0 = HNP not supported D0: 1 = SNP supported, 0 = SNP not supported

supports SRP, but this information is included in the descriptor for use in compliance testing.

Feature Codes for HNP

The OTG supplement defines three codes for use in Set Feature requests.

A code of b_hnp_enable (03h) informs the B-Device that it can use HNP. The A-device sends this request if all of the following are true: the A-device supports HNP, the A-device will respond to HNP when the bus is suspended, and the B-device connects directly to the A-device with no hubs in between.

A code of a_hnp_support (04h) informs the B-device that the A-device supports HNP and the B-device is directly connected (no hubs). The A-device can send this request before configuring the B-device. The A-device can then enable HNP at a later time when the A-device is finished using the bus.

A code of a_alt_hnp_support (05h) notifies the B-device that the currently connected port does not support HNP, but that the A-device has an alternate port that does support HNP.

Other Host Options

Some embedded hosts don't need to function as a device at all, or they need to support host and device functions at the same time. For these applications, the USB-IF document *Requirements and Recommendations for USB Products with Embedded Hosts and/or Multiple Receptacles* offers guidance.

The document specifies logo requirements and presents additional recommendations for products that contain embedded host ports. Like OTG hosts, these hosts have limited resources and generally don't run general-purpose, user-installed software. The hosts may provide one or more device ports that function simultaneously with the host port.

Requirements

Table 20-3 compares embedded hosts and conventional hosts. Requirements for embedded hosts are similar to those for the host function of OTG devices.

Like an OTG device, an embedded host must provide a targeted peripheral list. Two versions of the list provide information for compliance testing and for users. For compliance testing, the list includes Vendor ID and Product ID numbers for the peripherals. For users, the list includes manufacturer names and model numbers. The list may name specific peripherals or a class of products such as mass storage along with specific tested devices in the class. The lists should indicate the supported speeds of the targeted peripherals.

The targeted peripherals determine the amount of bus power the host must provide and the supported bus speeds and transfer types. For each port, a host with specific targeted peripherals must supply the greater of 8 mA of bus current or the maximum amount the devices on the targeted peripheral list require, up to 500 mA. A host that supports a class must supply 500 mA per port. A host can support any single speed or multiple speeds but must support the speeds required by the devices in the targeted peripheral list. The host must support bulk, interrupt, and isochronous transfers as needed according to the requirements of the targeted peripherals.

Support for SRP and hubs is optional. A host that supports hubs can support a single hub only or the full tiered star topology of a conventional bus.

On attachment of a peripheral or hub, the host must indicate whether it supports the peripheral or hub configuration.

As on a conventional host, all ports on an embedded host should support the same speeds and devices. To inform users that a host port has limited capabilities, a graphical indicator at the connector is recommended. For example, a port that supports only printers might display a printer icon.

Device Ports

An embedded system with a host function can also support one or more peripheral functions with type-B connectors. Unlike OTG devices, the system can perform its host and peripheral functions at the same time. A data logger might have a Standard-A port that connects to a printer for printing logged data and a type-B port that connects to a conventional host for uploading data. The host

Table 20-3: Unlike an OTG device, a device that functions as an embedded host can also function as a peripheral at the same time.

Capability or Feature	USB 2.0 Conventional Host	USB 2.0 Embedded Host
Communicate at high speed	yes	As needed to support targeted peripherals
Communicate at full speed	yes	
Communicate at low speed	yes	
Support external hubs	yes	optional
Provide targeted peripheral list	no	yes
Function as a peripheral	no	optional, can be simultaneous with host function
Support Session Request Protocol	optional	optional
Minimum available bus current per port	500 mA (100 mA if battery-powered)	8 mA
Connector	1 or more Standard A	1 or more Standard A

and device ports don't have to support the same speeds, but all device ports should support the same speeds.

A non-OTG product that needs to function both as a device and as a host but not at the same time can use a vendor-specific connector. For operation as a device, the user attaches a cable that has a mating vendor-specific connector and a Standard-A plug. For operation as a host, the user attaches an adapter that has a mating vendor-specific connector and a Standard-A receptacle.

Designers of products that have both Standard-A and type-B receptacles should use product design, labeling, and product literature to communicate the product's function to users and make it clear that the product isn't a hub.

Controller Chips

Several manufacturers offer controller chips designed for use in OTG devices and embedded hosts. To function as a peripheral, the controller must support functions similar to those in the controllers described in Chapter 6. As with other device controllers, some OTG and embedded-host controllers contain a CPU while others must interface to an external CPU.

To function as an OTG host, the controller, possibly with the help of external circuits, must have the ability to send SOF packets, schedule and initiate Setup,

IN, and OUT transactions, provide VBUS, manage power, reset the bus, switch the pull-up and pull-down resistors as needed when changing roles, and detect the state of the ID pin. Some chips have internal charge pumps for supplying and controlling VBUS from a 3V supply. A controller may also provide timers, status signals, or other hardware support for SRP and HNP signaling.

Microcontrollers

Sources for microcontrollers with OTG and embedded-host capability include Cypress Semiconductor, Atmel, Microchip Technology, and NXP Semiconductors.

Cypress Semiconductor

As the name suggests, Cypress Semiconductor's CY7C67200 EZ-OTG controller is designed for use in OTG devices. The chip contains a 16-bit CPU and can function in two modes. In stand-alone mode, the controller is the device's main CPU. The CPU can read firmware from an I^{2}C EEPROM. In coprocessor mode, the controller interfaces to an external CPU that manages USB communications and other tasks. The CPU can communicate via either a parallel Host Peripheral Interface at up to 16 MB/s, a high-speed asynchronous serial interface at up to 2 Megabaud, or a Serial Peripheral Interface (SPI) at up to 2 Mbps.

The EZ-OTG has two USB ports and two serial interface engines that support low and full speeds. One port can function as an OTG device, a non-OTG embedded host, or a peripheral-only device port. The other port can function as a non-OTG host or peripheral-only device port.

The controller contains a ROM BIOS that executes an Idle task consisting of an endless loop that waits for an interrupt, executes the tasks in the Idle chain, and repeats. Firmware can add tasks to the Idle chain or replace the entire Idle task with device-specific programming.

Firmware development can use the free GNU Toolset, which includes a C compiler, assembler, make utility, linker, debugger and other utilities. Cypress provides Frameworks C code for performing USB-related tasks and accessing other components in the controller.

A tutorial and many examples are in the free e-book, *USB Multi-Role Device Design By Example*, by John Hyde, available from *www.usb-by-example.com*.

A related chip, the CY7C67300 EZ-HOST, adds an interface to external memory, two ports for each of the two SIEs, memory expansion capabilities, and more I/O features.

Atmel

Atmel's AVR series of microcontrollers includes the AT90USB1287, which has an OTG port that supports full and low speeds. The 8-bit chip has 128K of flash memory, 4K of EEPROM, and 8K of RAM. The 48 I/O bits support functions such as timer/counters, PWM channels, an ADC, USART, SPI, and analog comparator. A JTAG interface supports debugging.

Atmel provides an AT90USBxxx USB software library in C with support for OTG functions. The AT90USB647 is similar but has less memory.

Microchip Technology

Microchip Technology offers 16-bit and 32-bit microcontrollers with OTG and embedded-host capability. Chips in the 16-bit PIC24FJ256GB110 family contain a module that can function as a full-speed peripheral or a low/full-speed OTG or embedded host. The chips have flash memory for program storage and support a variety of I/O functions in addition to USB. The 16-bit architecture builds on the 8-bit architecture of the PIC18F4550. Microchip's USB Framework supports the PIC24F chips.

Chips in the 32-bit PIC32MX family offer similar capabilities with faster performance. Microchip provides a separate USB device and host stack for these chips.

NXP Semiconductors

NXP Semiconductors offers a variety of ARM-based microcontrollers with OTG and embedded-host capability. One example is the LPC3180, which contains a 32-bit ARM926EJ-S processor. The full-speed USB port requires an interface to an external transceiver with an I²C interface such as the ST-NXP Wireless ISP1301.

Interface Chips

Sources for OTG interface chips include ST-NXP Wireless and Oxford Semiconductor. Also see the Cypress CY7C67200 EZ-OTG described above.

ST-NXP Wireless

ST-NXP Wireless' ISP1362 is an interface-only chip for OTG devices. The chip contains an ISP1181B device controller and a host controller. Both controllers can communicate at full and low speeds. (The OTG device must use full speed when functioning as a peripheral.)

The controller interfaces to an external CPU using a 16-bit interface that can transfer data at up to 10 MB/s. The external CPU communicates with the controller by accessing its registers and buffer memory. The registers are compatible with the registers defined in the OHCI host-controller specification.

A descriptor defines a format for exchanging information with the host controller's driver. The descriptor consists of a header that contains information such as the endpoint number, transaction type (Setup, IN, OUT), bus speed, toggle-bit value, and a completion code, followed by data.

The chip contains two USB ports. One port can function as the OTG port in an OTG device or as a host or device port for a non-OTG host or device. The second port can function only as a host port and isn't recommended for use in OTG devices.

ST-NXP Wireless provides host, peripheral, and OTG drivers for PCI platforms running Linux, Windows CE, DOS, and the FlexiUSB real-time operating system and for Intel PXA250/Arm architecture platforms running Linux or Windows CE.

The ISP1761 is an OTG controller that supports high speed and can use a 16- or 32-bit CPU interface.

Oxford Semiconductor

Oxford Semiconductor's OXU210HP is a physically small, low-power interface chip especially suited for compact and inexpensive dual-role products.

The controller supports low, full, and high speeds and interfaces to an external CPU using a 16- or 32-bit data bus. Two USB ports can operate as one host and one OTG device, one host and one peripheral, or two hosts. Hardware or software can handle HNP. The chip supports multiple power-saving modes and a selectable clock frequency.

Driver options include host and peripheral drivers for Windows CE and Linux and USBLink drivers for real-time OSes.

The chip is one in a series of OTG-capable chips from Oxford Semiconductor.

I hope you've found this book useful. For more about USB developing, including device and host example code and links to product information, tutorials, articles, news, and updates, please visit my website at *www.Lvr.com.*

Jan

Index

Numerics

A

Index

Index

U

Index